FLORIDA & THE SOUTH'S
BEST TRIPS

28 AMAZING ROAD TRIPS

Adam Karlin,
Kate Armstrong, Ashley Harrell,
Kevin Raub, Regis St Louis

SYMBOLS IN THIS BOOK

✓ Top Tips

📖 History & Culture

📷 Essential Photo

🔗 Link Your Trips

👫 Family

🏃 Walking Tour

📱 Tips from Locals

🍷 Food & Drink

🍴 Eating

🚗 Trip Detour

🌳 Outdoors

🛏 Sleeping

📞 Telephone Number

@ Internet Access

📖 English-Language Menu

🕐 Opening Hours

📶 Wi-Fi Access

👪 Family-Friendly

🅿 Parking

🍃 Vegetarian Selection

🐾 Pet-Friendly

🚭 Nonsmoking

🏊 Swimming Pool

❄ Air-Conditioning

MAP LEGEND

Routes
- ▬ Trip Route
- ▬ Trip Detour
- ▬ Linked Trip
- ▬ Walk Route
- ▬ Tollway
- Freeway
- Primary
- Secondary
- Tertiary
- Lane
- Unsealed Road
- Plaza/Mall
- Steps
-)=(Tunnel
- Pedestrian Overpass
- Walk Track/Path

Boundaries
- ─── International
- ─── State/Province
- ┬── Cliff

Hydrography
- River/Creek
- Intermittent River
- Swamp/Mangrove
- Canal
- Water
- Dry/Salt/Intermittent Lake
- Glacier

Route Markers
- 〔97〕 US National Hwy
- 〔5〕 US Interstate Hwy
- 〔44〕 State Hwy

Trips
- 1 Trip Numbers
- 9 Trip Stop
- 🚶 Walking tour
- 🚗 Trip Detour

Population
- ✪ Capital (National)
- ◉ Capital (State/Province)
- ● City/Large Town
- ● Town/Village

Areas
- Beach
- Cemetery (Christian)
- Cemetery (Other)
- Park
- Forest
- Reservation
- Urban Area
- Sportsground

Transport
- ✈ Airport
- Ⓑ BART station
- Ⓣ Boston T station
- ⊕ Cable Car/Funicular
- Ⓜ Metro/Muni station
- Ⓟ Parking
- Ⓢ Subway station
- ⊕ Train/Railway
- ⊕ Tram
- Ⓤ Underground station

Note: Not all symbols displayed above appear on the maps in this book

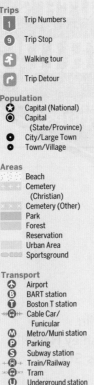

CONTENTS

Tennessee & Kentucky p265

The Carolinas p87

Mississippi, Louisiana & Arkansas p195

Georgia & Alabama p141

Florida p33

Contents cont.

ROAD TRIP ESSENTIALS

Classic Trips

Look out for the Classic Trips stamp on our favorite routes in this book.

5

WELCOME TO
FLORIDA &
THE SOUTH

Life is rich – make that indulgent – in the Southern states. Food, music, culture, history: all of it is robust, spiced to the hilt and alive.

The 28 road trips in this book will introduce you to that way-out crab shack, the sweltering juke joint and the lonely trail. We'll show you upscale kitchens and that romantic jazz club of your dreams, and we'll tell you the best (not necessarily the quickest) way to get there.

From the mighty Mississippi River to the Florida Keys, from a Blues Highway to the Nashville honky-tonks, from the Smoky Mountains and the Appalachian Trail to the vibrant, thrumming cities of Atlanta and Miami, you'll find your rhythm. And if you've only got time for one trip, make it one of our nine Classic Trips, which take you to the very best of Florida & the South. Turn the page for more.

Dry Tortugas National Park Fort Jefferson
PHIL SUNKEL / SHUTTERSTOCK ©

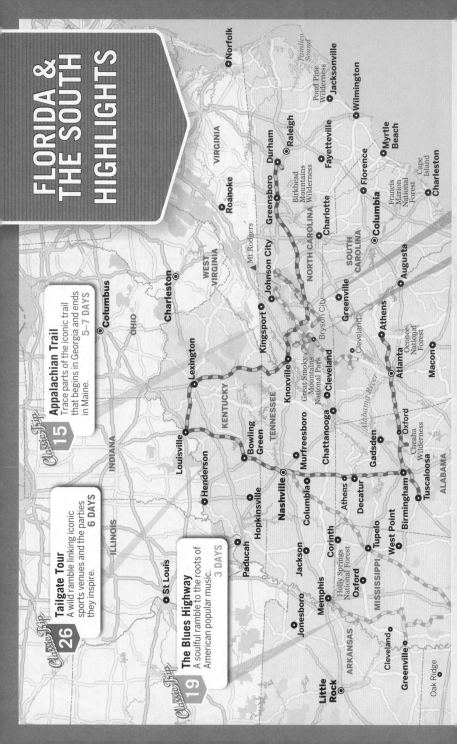

FLORIDA & THE SOUTH HIGHLIGHTS

Classic Trip 15
Appalachian Trail
Trace parts of the iconic trail that begins in Georgia and ends in Maine.   5–7 DAYS

Classic Trip 26
Tailgate Tour
A wild ramble linking iconic sports venues and the parties they inspire.   6 DAYS

Classic Trip 19
The Blues Highway
A soulful ramble to the roots of American popular music.   3 DAYS

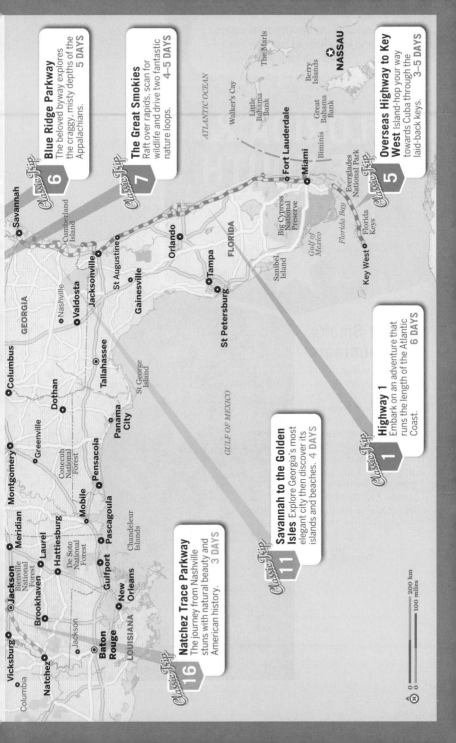

Classic Trip 6

Blue Ridge Parkway
The beloved byway explores the craggy, misty depths of the Appalachians. 5 DAYS

Classic Trip 7

The Great Smokies
Raft over rapids, scan for wildlife and drive two fantastic nature loops. 4–5 DAYS

Classic Trip 5

Overseas Highway to Key West Island-hop your way towards Cuba through the laid-back keys. 3–5 DAYS

Classic Trip 1

Highway 1
Embark on an adventure that runs the length of the Atlantic Coast. 6 DAYS

Classic Trip 11

Savannah to the Golden Isles Explore Georgia's most elegant city then discover its islands and beaches. 4 DAYS

Classic Trip 16

Natchez Trace Parkway
The journey from Nashville stuns with natural beauty and American history. 3 DAYS

NASSAU

The Marls

Berry Islands

Walker's Cay

Little Bahama Bank

Biminis

Great Bahama Bank

ATLANTIC OCEAN

Cumberland Island

Savannah

Columbus

GEORGIA

Nashville

Valdosta

Jacksonville

St Augustine

Gainesville

Orlando

FLORIDA

Tampa

St Petersburg

Tallahassee

St George Island

Dothan

Greenville

Panama City

Pensacola

Conecuh National Forest

Montgomery

Meridian

Laurel

Hattiesburg

De Soto National Forest

Mobile

Pascagoula

Gulfport

Chandeleur Islands

New Orleans

Baton Rouge

LOUISIANA

Jackson

Brookhaven

Bienville National Forest

Vicksburg

Natchez

Columbia

Big Cypress National Preserve

Fort Lauderdale

Miami

Everglades National Park

Sanibel Island

Gulf of Mexico

Florida Bay

Florida Keys

Key West

GULF OF MEXICO

0 200 km
0 100 miles

N

Florida & the South's best sights and experiences, and the road trips that will take you there.

FLORIDA & THE SOUTH
HIGHLIGHTS

Great Smoky Mountains

For one-of-a-kind thrills with cinematic backdrops, grab the wheel tight for **Trip 7: The Great Smokies**. Here, the Appalachian Trail climbs to mysterious, fog-wrapped peaks. Class III rapids crash through a narrow gorge. Black bears prowl like they own the place. And the tail of a dragon lures a few brave souls on a drive they'll never forget.

Trips

Great Smoky Mountains Fall landscape

Mississippi River *American Queen* steam boat

French Quarter

Wrought-iron balconies, ivy creeping over brick, Creole cottages and Caribbean architecture: the French Quarter of New Orleans reveals itself on **Trip 17: Southern Gothic Literary Tour**. Wander through lanes named for French royalty, seeking antique shops, art galleries, historic buildings, literary landmarks and quite possibly the oldest bar in the country.

Trips 17 21

Walt Disney World® Resort

Maybe you'll immediately don some mouse ears and give yourself over entirely. Or, it could take a minute. Either way, it's hard not to fall under Disney's spell, especially if you're traveling with children on **Trip 4: Doing Disney & More**. The Magic Kingdom is the heart of this sprawling resort that includes four theme parks and a host of activities 'imagineered' for optimal glee.

Trip 4

Antebellum Architecture

Most of the South's elaborate mansions were torched during the war, which is why the Georgian- and Federalist-style homes of Charleston on **Trip 10: Lowcountry & Southern Coast**, the Gothic Revival buildings of Savannah on **Trip 11: Savannah to the Golden Isles** and the spared mansions of Natchez and the River Road on **Trip 28: Big Muddy** are so compelling.

Trips 10 11 16 17 18 28

New Orleans French Quarter architecture

BEST ROADS FOR DRIVING

Highway 1 Roll down Florida's east coast.
Trip 1

Tail of the Dragon Swerve breathtaking hairpin turns. **Trip** 7

Overseas Highway Island-hop in your car.
Trip 5

Natchez Trace Parkway Where history and natural beauty collide. **Trip** 16

Arkansas State Highway 23 A simply stunning mountain drive. **Trip** 22

Mississippi River

The USA's most important river – historically and economically – bends through the South, uniting and defining it, blending cultures, sharing stories and mixing music. On **Trip 28: Big Muddy** you'll get an up-close view of this tempestuous beast. From Memphis to Natchez to New Orleans, you'll witness its natural beauty, grasp its immense power and consider its fragility.

Trips 16 18 19 28

13

Sanibel Island Search for seashells on the white-sand beach

Beaches

Nicknamed the Sunshine State, Florida could just as easily be called the Shoreline State. Thanks to its unique geography, you're never more than 60 miles from the beach. And those sandy stretches of coastline on **Trip 1: Highway 1** are as varied as they are plentiful, offering white-sand beaches bordered by emerald water, party towns where it's always spring break, peaceful barrier islands and cosmopolitan city beaches.

Trips 1 3 5 8 11

BEST OUTDOORS

Great Smoky Mountains National Park Bald summits, lonely trails and waterfalls. **Trips** 7 15

Natural Bridge State Park Home of the Red River Gorge, a rock-climbing mecca. **Trip** 24

Buffalo River Paddle a pristine, wild and scenic river. **Trip** 22

Everglades National Park Mangroves, manatees and gators. **Trip** 2

Gulf Islands National Seashore White sands and emerald waters. **Trips** 3 21

4E 77
ELVIS AARON PRESLEY

Elvis Presley was born in Tupelo, Mississippi
on January 8, 1935, the son of Vernon and
Gladys Presley. He moved to Memphis in 1948.
Soon after signing a contract with Sun Records
in 1954 he achieved tremendous popularity. His
musical and acting career in records, movies,
television, and concerts made him one of the
most successful and outstanding entertainers
in the world. He died on August 16, 1977 and is
buried here at his Memphis home, Graceland.

Graceland Entrance to the grand home of Elvis Presley

Appalachian Trail Misty forest track

Graceland

Graceland is no mere tourist attraction. It's a pilgrimage site for Elvis likers and lovers, glimpsed on **Trip 23: Elvis Presley Memorial Highway**. We are talking about a mansion, bought by Elvis in 1956 for $100,000, done up in the King's signature no-holds-barred, bling-blang aesthetic. Here's a jungle room, there's a carpeted ceiling, over here is a racquet ball court, and a private jet called Lisa Marie.

Trip

Appalachian Trail

Take the opportunity to trek along the same trail across three states within a single road trip. On **Trip 15: Appalachian Trail** you'll follow it through a stunning river gorge, wander up a series of bald mountains with layered Blue Ridge Mountain vistas, and rejoice in the silence and majesty only the wilderness can bring.

Trip

Southern BBQ

Dry rub in Memphis, Lexington or Eastern in North Carolina, and open pit whole hog in Georgia: you should be able to follow your nose to the nearest smoker wherever you land. But on **Trip 13: Hogs & Heifers: a Georgia BBQ Odyssey**, you'll travel from mountains to cities in search of the holy grail of succulent and spicy Georgia BBQ.

Trip

17

Civil War Monuments

Visit a battlefield and you'll learn they have a certain gravity. They are gifted with the power to silence even the busiest mind. Whether you're a history nut, a warrior or a pacifist, when you wrap your mind around the Battle of Shiloh on **Trip 27: Memphis to Nashville**, or Vicksburg on **Trip 28: Big Muddy**, there really is nothing left to say.

Trips 27 28

The Everglades

Take a walk on the wild side in the weird and wonderful Everglades. Encompassing more than 1.5 million acres, this national park is a unique ecosystem of wet prairie and home to hundreds of species of bird, fish, reptile and mammal. On **Trip 2: The Everglades** you can kayak alongside graceful manatees, spot nesting ibis, herons and ahingas, or hike among enigmatic alligators lolling near the water's edge.

Trip 2

(left) **The Everglades** View from the observation tower;
(below) **Atlanta** Martin Luther King Jr Birthplace

Civil Rights Sites

The roads around and between Atlanta, Montgomery, Selma, Birmingham and Memphis are graced with the memories of America's most fearless and loving citizens and stained with their blood. On **Trip 14: Civil Rights Tour** you'll visit the stages where the great drama unfolded, where so many confronted their fear and gave of themselves to challenge and change a nation for the better.

Trip 14

BEST LIVE MUSIC

Red's A real-deal Clarksdale juke joint. **Trips** 18 19 28

Station Inn A classic bluegrass honky-tonk. **Trips** 16 27

Chickie Wah Wah A wonderful jazz club in the Quarter. **Trip** 28

Rum Boogie Beale St blues courtesy of a tight house band. **Trips** 19 23

Bluebird Cafe Where singer-songwriters reign supreme. **Trips** 16 27

19

IF YOU LIKE...

KENNAN HARVEY / GETTY IMAGES ©

Appalachian Trail Hiking the iconic track

Music

We'll take you to the ragged, downbeat juke joints of Mississippi, then upriver to smoky Beale St nightclubs. You'll hear country stars of tomorrow wail in Nashville honky-tonks, and jazz men bring down the house in the Crescent City. Night music abounds.

19 **The Blues Highway** Get to the roots of American popular music on this iconic romp through the Mississippi Delta.

27 **Memphis to Nashville** Think: soul music museums, Beale St clubs, the Country Music Hall of Fame and hell-raising honky-tonks.

28 **Big Muddy** Listen to the soundtrack of the mighty Mississippi from Memphis to the Delta and down to New Orleans.

Beaches

Explore dollops of white sand off the Overseas Hwy, or take Hwy 1 to South Beach in Florida, get rugged and windswept on the sensational Outer Banks of North Carolina, then discover the most incredible driftwood beach you can imagine in Georgia.

1 **Highway 1** Hit all of Florida's east-coast hot spots and finish it off in South Beach.

5 **Overseas Highway to Key West** Roll along above azure waters and enjoy frequent layovers on powdery stretches of sand.

8 **North Carolina's Outer Banks** Dunes and lighthouses hug the highway in the Outer Banks, a stretch of barrier islands sheltering North Carolina's mainland.

11 **Savannah to the Golden Isles** Vast estuaries, old-world architecture and miles-long stretches of pristine sand.

Adventure

The whole point of a road trip is to get out of the car and onto the trail, or into the river, to cultivate that raw blast of nature love. And we've offered ample opportunity to indulge your wild side.

2 **The Everglades** Paddle through mangroves and alongside manatees, spot nesting ibis and herons, and hike among enigmatic gators guarding the water's edge.

7 **The Great Smokies** Ramble through one of America's favorite national parks, hike, camp, mountain bike and star gaze.

15 **Appalachian Trail** Hike through a river gorge, beneath towering waterfalls, to the top of bald summits with a view.

22 **Back Roads Arkansas** Shove off into the wild Buffalo River then hike to a precipice and absorb the silence.

The River Road Antebellum plantation home Oak Alley, Vacherie

History

Tangled up in so much history, the South is knotted with tension and wise with soul. Far from avoiding its past, the South confronts it. Is even proud of it (for better and worse). From Native Americans to American explorers, from Civil War to Civil Rights, here lie stories.

14 Civil Rights Tour
An iconic journey through the battlegrounds of the American Civil Rights movement.

16 Natchez Trace Parkway From indigenous medicine men to early American explorers to Civil War battlefields, and a town saved by Southern hospitality.

18 Historical Mississippi Mississippi is heavy with history, deep with regret and as soulful as any state in the union.

Architecture

Modernists beware, this part of the country is better known for its old-world grace. Savannah, Charleston, Natchez and the French Quarter in New Orleans lure legions by maintaining and restoring their relics with aplomb and charm.

10 Lowcountry & Southern Coast Stroll past stunning Georgian- and Federalist-style homes in downtown Charleston.

11 Savannah to the Golden Isles One of the most beautiful cities in America, Savannah has an abundance of period row houses surrounding shady old town squares.

28 Big Muddy From the antebellum homes and plantations of Natchez and the River Road to the, yes, Spanish accents of the French Quarter.

Southern Cuisine

Let's get something straight. You ain't here for the health food. But if you like fried chicken and shrimp, crawfish boils, po'boys and barbecue then you will be in your own high-calorie, deep-fried, open-pit wonderland. So you may as well add a bourbon chaser.

10 Lowcountry & Southern Coast Savor shrimp and grits, Frogmore stew and other seafood dishes, which often have a West African spin.

13 Hogs & Heifers: a Georgia BBQ Odyssey Sample pulled and chopped pork, ribs and more as you roll from big-city to small-town Georgia.

20 Cajun Country Spicy jambalaya, rich gumbo and étoufée swimming in buttered-up deliciousness await hungry travelers in Cajun Country.

21

NEED TO KNOW

CELL PHONES

Mobile phone network coverage is solid, so your Google Maps app will work except in the Ozarks and Blue Ridge Mountains. Hands-free driving only, or you'll be cited and fined.

INTERNET ACCESS

Wi-fi is available in the vast majority of hotels and most cafes. Midrange and top-end hotels always have at least one terminal available for guests.

FUEL

Gas stations are everywhere, except in national parks and some mountain areas. Expect to pay $3.50 to $4 per gallon.

RENTAL CARS

Budget (www.budget.com)
Dollar (www.dollar.com)
Enterprise (www.enterprise.com)
Hertz (www.hertz.com)

IMPORTANT NUMBERS

AAA (☏1-800-222-4357)
Emergencies (☏911)
Freeway Aid (☏511)

Climate

Nashville
GO Apr–Jun, Sep–Nov

Memphis
GO Apr–Jun, Sep–Nov

Atlanta
GO Apr–Jun

New Orleans
GO Apr–Jun

Miami
GO Mar–May

Tropical climate, rain year round
Tropical climate, wet & dry seasons
Warm to hot summers, mild winters
Mild to hot summers, cold winters

When to Go

High Season (Mar–Aug)

» South Florida beaches peak with spring break.

» Panhandle and northern beaches peak in summer.

» Orlando theme parks are busiest in summer.

» Summer wet season is hot and humid (May to September).

Shoulder (Feb & Sep)

» In South Florida, February has ideal dry weather, but no spring-break craziness.

» With school back in September, northern beaches and theme parks are less crowded; still hot.

» Prices drop from peak by 20% to 30%.

Low Season (Oct–Dec)

» Beach towns quiet until winter snowbirds arrive.

» Hotel prices can drop from peak by 50%.

» November–April dry season is best time to hike and camp.

» Holidays spike with peak rates.

Your Daily Budget

Budget: Less than $140
» Dorm beds/camping: $30–50

» Supermarket self-catering per day: $20

» Bicycle hire per day: $24–35

Midrange: $140–250
» Hotels: $100–200

» In-room meals and dining out: $50

» Rental car per day: $40–70

Top End: More than $250
» High-season beach hotel/resort: $250–400

» Gourmet dinner (for two): $150–300

Eating

Roadside & big-city diners Cheap and greasy.

Casual cafes & gastropubs More creative and flavorful.

Vegetarians Self-catering will be vital in more remote areas.

Price ranges refer to the cost of a main dish:

$	less than $15
$$	$15–$25
$$$	more than $25

Sleeping

B&Bs Quaint and romantic; available in every coastal, historic and mountain town. Generally affordable.

Hotels Range from adequate roadside corporate numbers to boutique and inspiring sleeps.

Camping Popular option for road-trippers. Bare-bones sites without plug-in options are best for car campers.

Price ranges refer to the cost of a double room with private bathroom:

$	less than $120
$$	$120–$200
$$$	more than $200

Arriving in Florida & the South

Miami International Airport

Taxi Flat rate for the 40-minute drive to South Beach ($35).

Bus The Miami Beach Airport Express (bus 150) costs $2.65 and stops all along Miami Beach, from 41st to the southern tip.

Shuttle SuperShuttle runs a shared-van service, costing about $22 to South Beach.

Hartsfield–Jackson Atlanta International Airport

Rental Car A courtesy monorail connects to a single rental car complex where all companies are located.

MARTA (Metropolitain Atlanta Rapid Transit Authority) Costs $2.50. Runs every 15 to 20 minutes from 6am to 11pm.

Shuttle $16.50 to $20.50 to Downtown, Midtown and Buckhead.

Taxi $30 to $40 to Downtown, Midtown and Buckhead.

Charlotte Douglas International Airport

Rental Car Rental counters are on Lower Baggage Claim level.

Bus Look for green Sprinter bus (Rte 5) to Charlotte

Transportation Center in Uptown, every 20 to 30 minutes.

Taxi $25 to city center, minimum $14 for drop-offs within 3 miles of airport.

Money

ATMs are widely available.

Tipping

Tipping is standard: restaurants 15% to 25%; taxis 10% to 15%; bars $1 per drink.

Useful Websites

Lonely Planet (lonelyplanet.com/florida) Pre-trip planning and traveler advice.

Scout Mob (www.scoutmob.com) What's hot in Atlanta.

Mississippi Blues Trail (www.msbluestrail.org) Maps, towns, markers and historical info for the official Blues Trail.

Kentucky Bourbon Trail (www.kybourbontrail.com) The official website for all things bourbon.

Opening Hours

Bars 5pm to midnight Sunday to Thursday, to 2am or 3am Friday and Saturday

Restaurants breakfast 7am to 10:30am, lunch 11:30am to 2:30pm, dinner 5pm to 11pm

Shops 10am to 6pm Monday to Thursday, to 7pm Friday and Saturday, 11am to 5pm Sunday

For more, see Road Trip Essentials (p328).

CITY GUIDE

MIAMI

From the copious murals of artsy Wynwood to the vibrant Cuban community in Little Havana, Miami delivers exactly the cornucopia of experiences you would expect from a major metropolis. Just across the causeway, dazzling Miami Beach beckons with lush, sandy beaches, glamorous nightlife and streets lined with art-deco gems.

Miami Beach Art-deco district

Getting Around

Get around downtown Miami with the free Metromover – equal parts bus, monorail and train – or rely on cabs. Car is best for the sprawling suburbs. Once you get to Miami Beach, walk or rollerblade like everybody else. Bike share options now exist in Miami proper and Miami Beach.

Parking

Metered street parking is available in South Beach, but municipal parking garages are usually the easiest and cheapest option; look for giant blue 'P' signs. Downtown, street parking is scarce but not unheard of; most attractions offer garage parking.

Where to Eat

The best new spots for dining are in Wynwood, Midtown and the Design District; Coral Gables is also an established foodie hot spot. You can find inexpensive Cuban food all around town, but most notably around Calle Ocho in Little Havana.

Where to Stay

Miami Beach is packed with options along Collins Ave and Ocean Dr, most in renovated deco properties. Downtown has high-end chains, the most sumptuous on Brickell Key.

Useful Websites

Visit Florida (www.visitflorida.com) Official state tourism website.

Florida State Parks (www.floridastateparks.org) Links to state parks.

Lonely Planet (www.lonelyplanet.com/florida) Planning and fellow-traveler advice.

Trips Through Miami 🔢

Miami & the Keys

For more, check out our city and country guides. www.lonelyplanet.com

PESKYMONKEY / GETTY IMAGES ©

TOP EXPERIENCES

➡ Walk the Deco District

There's something to be said for the sheer joy of exploring South Beach on foot. OK, it's hot, but walk during the early evening and you'll see one of urban America's great vistas: a marvelous interplay of tangerine sunset, shady palms, deco architecture and the glow of early 20th-century neon.

➡ Soak up the Spectacle

A string of eccentrics didn't just make Miami home; they forged the city. Palatial skylines, visible from neighborhoods such as Brickell, or literal palaces, like the Vizcaya, speak to a desire to chase dreams and build monuments to them, no matter the cost.

➡ A Latin-Caribbean Capital

Miami is an American city in the truest sense of 'Americas'. The town's collision of Cubans, Haitians, Colombians, Nicaraguans and North Americans (to name a few) yields a distinct flavor, which can be soaked up at cultural events like Viernes Culturales, or along almost any given city street in Little Haiti, Little Havana or Hialeah.

➡ Art Attack

The wall murals and dedicated graffiti of Wynwood are hard to miss, and as public art goes, it's been a game changer for this neighborhood. Swing by in the evening, snap a photo, and go bar-hopping with the hip kids.

CITY GUIDE

New Orleans Wrought-iron balconies in the French Quarter

NEW ORLEANS

New Orleans is American, but also identifiably elsewhere – Caribbean, African, French, Spanish and, occasionally, another galaxy. The faded beauty, prioritization of food, drink and music over deadlines, elegant architecture and gorgeous entropy, and a population that includes artists, poets and eccentrics, all combine into one sultry breath of travel romance.

Getting Around

Outside of the French Quarter you need a car or bicycle to properly explore New Orleans in a timely manner. Streetcars ($1.25/3/9 per trip/one-day/three-day pass) are romantic but slow. Buses ($1.25) are faster, but require route map memorization. Taxis cost around $3.50 from flag drop plus $2 per mile.

Parking

Street parking is prevalent outside of the French Quarter and Central Business District. If you end up using a hotel lot or public garage, bank on at least $30 a day for the privilege.

Where to Eat

Some of the best restaurants in the city are in the Garden District and Uptown; many are located on or near Magazine St, the city's top shopping strip. The French Quarter has both good restaurants and tourist traps. Newer restaurants pop up everywhere, but especially within the CBD.

Where to Stay

Lovely hotels with modern amenities ensconced in historic buildings pepper the French Quarter. Head to the Central Business District and Warehouse District for big box hotels, and the Garden District and Faubourg Marigny for cute B&Bs.

Useful Websites

New Orleans Online (www.neworleansonline.com) Database of all things New Orleans.

Gambit (www.bestofneworleans.com) Weekly newspaper with culture coverage and listings.

Trips Through New Orleans 17 21 28

Atlanta Cityscape by night

ATLANTA

With a young population, a thrumming economy, a dab of Hollywood glitz, plenty of hipster panache and some damn fine places to eat, sip and sleep, Atlanta has never been more inviting. Although it can sprawl, there's solid mass transit and enough green to make it utterly liveable.

Getting Around

Atlanta is bigger than it looks but the MARTA system – part subway, part bus line, single trip $2.50 – has decent coverage, and once you're Midtown or downtown, you can walk. If you want to get to Decatur or the Eastside, though, it does make sense to drive.

Parking

Parking lots in Decatur are easy to find. You can park on the street or at meters in Little Five Points and the Virginia Highlands, but in Midtown and downtown you'll need to find a lot or a garage ($15 to $20 per day).

Where to Eat

Locavore restaurants and greasy-spoon diners can be found across the city. The Westside beckons with new farm-to-table options, while Eastside Atlanta boasts newer, edgier spots. Decatur is practically a foodie city within a city.

Where to Stay

Boutique hotels sprinkle Midtown, making it the clear choice for centrality and variety; the corporate towers downtown aren't bad. Buckhead is rather isolated, but the rooms are plush. Virginia Highlands has a tried-and-true neighborhood feel.

Useful Websites

Atlanta (www.atlanta.net) Atlanta's Convention & Visitor's Bureau portal.

Atlanta Magazine (www. atlantamagazine.com) A glossy monthly, and an authority on the restaurant scene.

Scoutmob (www.scoutmob. com) A terrific resource on what's new and hot in the city.

Trips Through Atlanta

12 13 14

27

FLORIDA
& THE SOUTH
BY REGION

Let the humid breeze dampen your hair as you explore winding roads. You'll roll from moon-lashed marshlands to the flint-and-granite spine of the Appalachians, and cross a quilt of farmlands and exuberant cities.

Tennessee & Kentucky (p265)

Some of America's most beautiful vistas can be discovered in the mountains and hill country of these states, which span the upcountry South.

Get an enjoyable bourbon buzz going on Trip 25

Follow the course of North America's greatest river on Trip 28

Mississippi, Louisiana & Arkansas (p195)

The landscape's surreal, people are friendly, and New Orleans is nonstop fun. Keep your eyes, and more importantly, ears attuned in this cradle of great American music.

Hear the blues in a sweaty shack on Trip 19

Dance a Cajun two-step with cold beer in hand on Trip 20

The Carolinas (p87)

Dynamic cities and gorgeous scenery can be found in North and South Carolina, bracketed by golden Atlantic beaches and a rugged wall of forested mountains.

Traverse the rocky spine of the South while driving the Blue Ridge on Trip 6

Soak up sweaty, sultry Charleston on Trip 10

Georgia & Alabama (p141)

Delicious food, kicking music, mountain hikes, historical alleyways and complex history characterize the trips to be had in this corner of the Deep South.

Eat barbecue until you groan on Trip 13

Trace the arc of justice won – and still fought for – on Trip 14

Florida (p33)

In the Sunshine State you can discover almost anything: magic kingdoms and modern art museums; dinosaur descendants and Disney princesses; Spanish fortresses and scrubby pine forests. Just don't expect elevation or altitude.

Enjoy alligator sightings as you embark across the Everglades on Trip 2

Drive from the mainland to Key West on Trip 5

FLORIDA
& THE SOUTH
Classic Trips

JUPITERIMAGES / GETTY IMAGES ©

5

What Is a Classic Trip?

All the trips in this book show you the best of Florida and the South, but we've chosen nine as our all-time favorites. These are our Classic Trips – the ones that lead you to the best of the iconic sights, the top activities and the unique Florida and Southern experiences. Look out for Classic Trips throughout the book.

Above: Aerial view of the Florida Keys
Left: Lifeguard tower at Miami Beach

31

Florida

Vacationers have flocked to Florida since the late 1800s, when Henry Flagler built his famous railroad down the coast. The state's status as vacation paradise was cemented when Walt Disney snapped up a sizable chunk of it in the 1960s to build his new theme park.

There's no denying the state's appeal, and its incessant sunshine and natural beauty make it particularly well suited for road-tripping. The narrow peninsula packs in the hedonistic pleasures, from white-sand beaches to fantasy-fueled amusement parks – with historical monuments, natural wonders and roadside attractions sprinwkled liberally along the way.

Florida

ALABAMA

Mobile

Pensacola

Destin

Panama City

St Joseph Bay

Apalachicola

Tallahassee

Perry

Apalachee Bay

Gulf of Mexico

0   200 km
0   100 miles

GEORGIA

Valdosta
White Springs
Fernandina Beach
Jacksonville
St Augustine
Gainesville
FLORIDA
Daytona Beach
Ocala
New Smyrna Beach
omosasso Springs
Canaveral National Seashore
Titusville
pring Hill
Orlando
Cape Canaveral
earwater
Tampa 4
ATLANTIC OCEAN
St Petersburg
95
Bradenton
Vero Beach
Sarasota
Venice
Lake Okeechobee
1
Fort Myers
Clewiston
Palm Beach
Sanibel Island
Naples
75
Fort Lauderdale
Everglades City
41
2
Hollywood
Homestead
Miami
Dry Tortugas National Park
Biscayne National Park
Flamingo
Key Largo
Key West
5
Marathon
1

✓ DON'T MISS

Fort George Island

Peek into Old Florida at this Cultural State Park, one of several historical stop-offs on Trip 1

Flamingo

It's a bit of a trek, but rowing in solitude among mangroves and manatees makes it totally worthwhile. Learn more on Trip 2

Mennello Museum

This tiny Orlando museum showcases the work of Earl Cunningham and other primitive and folk artists. Check it out on Trip 4

Indian Key

To see this abandoned island settlement in all its decaying glory, you have to work for it: it's only accessible by boat on Trip 5

African Queen

More than just a roadside relic, the famous steamboat chugs along while passengers re-create scenes from the movie on Trip 5

The Everglades Kayaking among mangroves

1

Highway 1

Glittering Miami provides a spectacular grand finale to this epic coastal road trip featuring miles and miles of beaches interspersed with fascinating historical sights.

TRIP HIGHLIGHTS

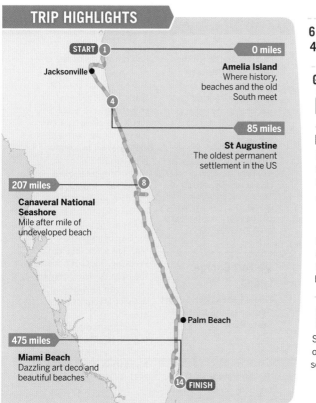

START 1 — **0 miles**

Jacksonville

Amelia Island
Where history, beaches and the old South meet

4

85 miles

St Augustine
The oldest permanent settlement in the US

207 miles

8

Canaveral National Seashore
Mile after mile of undeveloped beach

● Palm Beach

475 miles

Miami Beach
Dazzling art deco and beautiful beaches

14 **FINISH**

6 DAYS
475 MILES / 764KM

GREAT FOR...

BEST TIME TO GO

November to April, when it's warm but not too hot.

 ESSENTIAL PHOTO

Rows of colorful art-deco hotels along Ocean Ave at Miami Beach.

 BEST FOR HISTORY

St Augustine is the oldest permanent settlement in the US.

Miami Beach Art-deco architecture

37

Classic Trip

1 Highway 1

Drive the length of Florida all the way down the coast and you'll get a sampling of everything we love about the Sunshine State. You'll find the oldest permanent settlement in the United States, family-friendly attractions, the Latin flavor of Miami and – oh, yeah – miles and miles of beaches right beside you, inviting you to stop as often as you want.

TRIP HIGHLIGHT

1 Amelia Island

Start your drive just 13 miles south of the Georgia border on Amelia Island, a glorious barrier island with the moss-draped charm of the Deep South. Vacationers have been flocking here since the 1890s, when Henry Flagler's railroad converted the area into a playground for the rich. The legacy of that golden era remains visible today in Amelia's central town of Fernandina Beach, with 50 blocks of historic buildings, Victorian B&Bs and restaurants housed in converted fishing cottages. The best introduction to the town is a half-hour horse-drawn carriage tour with the **Old Towne Carriage Company** (☏904-277-1555; www.ameliacarriagetours.com; 115 Beech St, Fernandina Beach; half-hour adult/child $15/7).

🍴 🛏 p46

The Drive » Meander down Hwy 1A for about half an hour, passing both Big and Little Talbot Island State Parks. After you enter Fort George Island, take the right fork in the road to get to the Ribault Club.

2 Fort George Island

History runs deep at **Fort George Island Cultural State Park** (☏904-251-2320; www.floridastateparks.org/fortgeorgeisland; 11241 Fort George Rd; ☉8am-sunset; P). Enormous shell middens date the island's habitation by Native Americans to more than 5000 years ago. In 1736 British general James Oglethorpe erected a fort in the area, though it's long since vanished and its exact location is uncertain. In the 1920s flappers flocked to the ritzy **Ribault Club** (☏904-251-2802; www.nps.gov/timu; 11241 Fort George Rd; ☉9am-5pm Wed-Sun) for Gatsby-esque bashes with lawn bowling and yachting. Today it houses the island's visitor center, which can provide you with a CD tour of the area.

Perhaps most fascinating – certainly most sobering – is **Kingsley Plantation** (☏904-251-3537; www.nps.gov/timu;

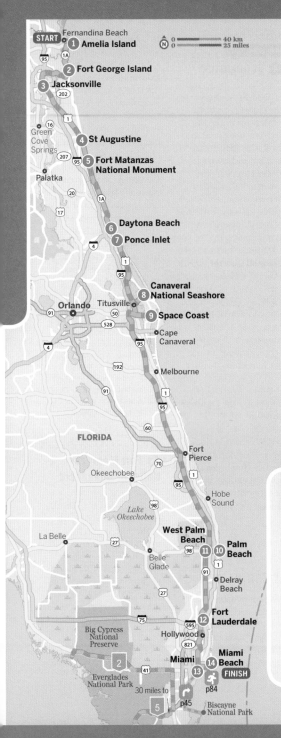

Map legend/labels:

START — Fernandina Beach
1 Amelia Island
2 Fort George Island
3 Jacksonville
Green Cove Springs
4 St Augustine
5 Fort Matanzas National Monument
Palatka
6 Daytona Beach
7 Ponce Inlet
8 Canaveral National Seashore
Orlando — Titusville
9 Space Coast
Cape Canaveral
Melbourne
FLORIDA
Fort Pierce
Okeechobee
Lake Okeechobee
Hobe Sound
La Belle
West Palm Beach
Belle Glade
11 10 Palm Beach
Delray Beach
Big Cypress National Preserve
12 Fort Lauderdale
Hollywood
2 Everglades National Park
Miami
14 Miami Beach
13 FINISH
30 miles to
5 p45 — Biscayne National Park
p84

0 40 km
0 25 miles

11676 Palmetto Ave; ⊙9am-5pm; P), Florida's oldest plantation house, built in 1798. Because of its remote location, it's not a grand Southern mansion, but it does provide a fairly unflinching look at slavery through exhibits and the remains of 23 slave cabins.

The Drive » Follow Hwy 105 inland 15 miles to I-95, then shoot straight south into downtown Jacksonville, a distance of about 24 miles.

3 Jacksonville

With its high-rises, free-ways and chain hotels, Jacksonville is a bit of a departure from our coast-al theme, but it offers lots of dining options, and its restored historic districts are worth a wander. Check out the Five Points and San Marco neighbor-hoods; both are charm-ing, walkable areas lined

LINK YOUR TRIP

5 Overseas Highway to Key West

Continuing on down Hwy 1 is a natural; the trip begins 1½ hours south of Miami.

2 The Everglades

Drive one hour southwest to pick up this trip, or go straight west and pick it up at Shark Valley.

FLORIDA 1 HIGHWAY 1

with bistros, boutiques and bars.

It's also a good chance to work in a little culture at the **Cummer Museum of Art** (www.cummer.org; 829 Riverside Ave; adult/student $10/6; ⊙10am-9pm Tue, to 4pm Wed-Sat, noon-4pm Sun), which has a genuinely excellent collection of American and European paintings, Asian decorative art and antiquities; or the **Museum of Modern Art Jacksonville** (MOCA; ☑904-366-6911; www.mocajacksonville. org; 333 N Laura St; adult/child $8/2.50; ⊙11am-5pm Tue-Sat, to 9pm Thu, noon-5pm Sun), which houses contemporary paintings, sculptures, prints, photography and film.

✕ p46

The Drive » Take Hwy 1 southwest for an hour straight into St Augustine, where it becomes Ponce de Leon Blvd.

TOP TIP:
THE ROAD LESS TAKEN

Despite its National Scenic Byway designation, oceanfront Hwy A1A often lacks ocean views, with wind-blocking vegetation growing on both sides of the road. Unless you're just moseying up or down the coast, Hwy 1 or I-95 are often better choices for driving long-distance.

TRIP HIGHLIGHT

④ St Augustine

Founded by the Spanish in 1565, St Augustine is the oldest permanent settlement in the US. Tourists flock here to stroll the ancient streets, and horse-drawn carriages clip-clop past townsfolk dressed in period costume. It's definitely touristy, with tons of museums, tours and attractions vying for your attention. Start with the **Colonial Quarter** (☑904-342-2857; www.colonialquarter. com; 33 St George St; adult/child $13/7; ⊙10am-5pm), a re-creation of 18th-century St Augustine complete with craftspeople demonstrating blacksmithing, leather working and other trades.

While you're here, don't miss the **Lightner Museum** (☑904-824-2874; www.lightnermuseum.org; 75 King St; adult/child $10/5; ⊙9am-5pm) located in the former Hotel Alcazar. We love the endless displays of everything from Gilded Age furnishings

to collections of marbles and cigar-box labels.

Stop by the **Visitor Information Center** (☑904-825-1000; www. floridashistoriccoast.com; 10 W Castillo Dr; ⊙8:30am-5:30pm) to find out about your other options, including ghost tours, the Pirate and Treasure Museum, Castillo de San Marcos National Monument, and the Fountain of Youth, a goofy tourist attraction disguised as an archaeological park that is purportedly the very spot where Ponce de Leon landed.

✕ 🛏 p46

The Drive » Take the Bridge of Lions toward the beach then follow Hwy 1A south for 13 miles to Fort Matanzas. To catch the 35-person ferry, go through the visitor center and out to the pier. The ride lasts about five minutes and launches hourly from 9:30am to 4:30pm, weather permitting.

---

⑤ Fort Matanzas National Monument

By now you've seen firsthand that the Florida coast isn't all about fun in the sun; it also has a rich history that goes back hundreds of years. History buffs will enjoy a visit to this tiny Spanish **fort** (☑904-471-0116; www. nps.gov/foma; 8635 Hwy A1A, Rattlesnake Island; ⊙9am-5:30pm; P) built in 1742. Its purpose? To guard Matanzas Inlet – a waterway leading straight up to St Augustine – from British invasion.

On the lovely (and free) boat ride over, park rangers narrate the fort's history and explain the gruesome origins of the name. ('Matanzas' means 'slaughters' in Spanish; let's just say things went badly for a couple hundred French Huguenot soldiers back in 1565.)

The Drive » Hopping over to I-95 will only shave a little bit off the hour-long trip; you might as well enjoy putting along Hwy 1A to Daytona Beach, 40 miles south.

- - - - - - - - - - - - - - - - - -

6 Daytona Beach

With typical Floridian hype, Daytona Beach bills itself as 'The World's Most Famous Beach.' But its fame is less about quality – the beach is actually mediocre – than the size of the parties this expansive beach has witnessed during spring break, Speedweeks and motorcycle events when half a million bikers roar into town. One Daytona title no one disputes is 'Birthplace of NASCAR,' which started here in 1947. Its origins go back as far as 1902 to drag races held on the beach's hard-packed sands.

NASCAR is the main event here. Catch a race at the **Daytona International Speedway** (📞800-748-7467; www. daytonainternationalspeedway. com; 1801 W International Speedway Blvd; tours from

$18; ⊙tours 9:30am-3:30pm). When there's no race, you can wander the massive stands for free or take a tram tour of the track and pit area. Race-car fanatics can indulge in the **Richard Petty Driving Experience** (📞800-237-3889; www.drivepetty.com; from $109; ⊙dates vary) and feel the thrill of riding shotgun or even taking the wheel themselves.

✕ ⎸ p46

The Drive » Take South Atlantic Ave 10 miles south along the coast to get to Ponce Inlet.

- - - - - - - - - - - - - - - - - -

7 Ponce Inlet

What's a beach road trip without a good lighthouse? About 6 miles south of Daytona Beach is the **Ponce de Leon Inlet Lighthouse & Museum** (📞386-761-1821; www.ponceinlet.org; 4931 S Peninsula Dr; adult/child $7/2; ⊙10am-6pm Sep-May, to 9pm Jun-Aug; 🅿 ♿). Stop by for a photo op with the handsome red-brick tower built in 1887, then climb the 203 steps to the top for great views of the surrounding beaches. A handful of historic buildings comprise the museum portion of your tour, including the light-keeper's house and the Lens House, where they show off a collection of Fresnel Lenses.

The Drive » Backtrack up Atlantic, then cut over to Hwy 1/FL 5 and head south for 20

minutes. Pre-planning pays here, because your route depends on where you're heading. One road goes 6 miles south from New Smyrna Beach, and another 6 miles north from the wildlife refuge. Both dead-end, leaving 16 miles of beach between them.

- - - - - - - - - - - - - - - - - -

TRIP HIGHLIGHT

8 Canaveral National Seashore

These 24 miles of pristine, windswept beaches comprise the longest stretch of undeveloped beach on Florida's east coast. On the north end is family-friendly Apollo Beach, which shines in a class of its own with gentle surf and miles of solitude. On the south end, Playalinda Beach is surfer central.

Just west of (and including) the beach, the 140,000-acre **Merritt Island National Wildlife Refuge** (📞321-861-5601; www.fws.gov/merrittisland; Black Point Wildlife Dr, off FL 406; vehicle $10; ⊙dawn-dusk) is an unspoiled oasis for birds and wildlife. It's one of the country's best birding spots, especially from October to May (early morning and after 4pm), and more endangered and threatened species of wildlife inhabit the swamps, marshes and hardwood hammocks here than at any other site in the continental US.

Stop by the visitor center for more information; an easy quarter-mile boardwalk will

Classic Trip

MICHAELWARRENPIX / GETTY IMAGES ©

DENNIS K. JOHNSON / GETTY IMAGES ©

WHY THIS IS A CLASSIC TRIP
MARIELLA KRAUSE, WRITER

Who doesn't love cruising down the coast? This trip is a natural for shoreline, seafood and sunshine – but it doesn't rely solely on beach culture. It's a remarkably well-rounded drive that culminates in the world-class city of Miami, with diversions along the way that include worthwhile art exhibits, peaceful nature preserves and some of the United State's oldest historical sites.

Top: Canaveral National Seashore
Left: Rocket Garden, Kennedy Space Center
Right: The historic Spanish settlement of St Augustine

SAMOT / SHUTTERSTOCK ©

whet your appetite for everything the refuge has to offer. Other highlights include the Manatee Observation Deck, the 7-mile Black Point Wildlife Drive, and a variety of hiking trails.

The Drive » Although Kennedy Space Center is just south of the Merritt Island Refuge, you have to go back into Titusville, travel south 5 miles on Hwy 1/FL 5, then take the Nasa Causeway back over to get there.

9 Space Coast

The Space Coast's main claim to fame (other than being the setting for the iconic 1960s TV series *I Dream of Jeannie*) is being the real-life home to the **Kennedy Space Center** (☎866-737-5235; www.kennedyspacecenter.com; NASA Pkwy, Merritt Island; adult/child 3-11yr $50/40; ☉9am-6pm) and its massive visitor complex. Once a working space-flight facility, Kennedy Space Center is shifting from a living museum to a historical one since the end of NASA's space shuttle program in 2011.

✕ p47

The Drive » Hop back onto the freeway (I-95) for the 2½-hour drive south to Palm Beach.

10 Palm Beach

History and nature give way to money and culture as you reach the southern part of the coast, and

Palm Beach looks every inch the playground for the rich and famous that it is. But fear not: the 99% can stroll along the beach – kept pleasantly seaweed-free by the town – ogle the massive gated compounds on A1A or window-shop in uber-ritzy Worth Ave, all for free.

The best reason to stop here is **Flagler Museum** (561-655-2833; www.flaglermuseum.us; 1 Whitehall Way; adult/child $18/10; 10am-5pm Tue-Sat, noon-5pm Sun), housed in the spectacular, beaux-art-styled Whitehall Mansion built by Henry Flagler in 1902. You won't get many details about the railroad mogul himself, but you will get a peek into his opulent lifestyle, including his own personal train car.

The Drive » When you're ready to be back among the commoners, head back inland. West Palm Beach is just a causeway away.

⑪ West Palm Beach

While Palm Beach has the money, West Palm Beach has the largest art museum in Florida, the **Norton Museum of Art** (561-832-5196; www.norton. org; 1451 S Olive Ave; adult/ child $12/5; noon-5pm Tue-Sun). The Nessel Wing features a colorful crowd-pleaser: a ceiling made from nearly 700 pieces of handblown glass by Dale Chihuly. Across the street, the **Ann Norton Sculpture Garden** (561-832-5328; www.ansg.org; 253 Barcelona Rd; adult/child $15/7; 10am-4pm Wed-Sun) is a real West Palm gem.

Come evening, if you're not sure what you're in the mood for, head to **CityPlace** (561-366-1000; www.cityplace.com; 700 S Rosemary Ave; 10am-10pm Mon-Sat, noon-6pm Sun), a massive outdoor shopping and entertainment center. There you'll find a slew of stores, about a dozen restaurants, a 20-screen movie theater and the Harriet Himmel Theater – not to mention free concerts in the outdoor plaza.

✕ 🛏 p47

The Drive » Fort Lauderdale is a straight shot down I-95, 45 miles south of Palm Beach. Taking Hwy 1A will add more than half an hour to your trip.

⑫ Fort Lauderdale

Fort Lauderdale Beach isn't the spring-break destination it once was, although you can still find outposts of beach-bummin' bars and motels in between the swanky boutique hotels and multi-million-dollar yachts. Few visitors venture far inland except maybe to dine and shop along Las Olas Blvd; most spend the bulk of their time on the coast, frolicking at water's edge. The promenade – a wide, brick, palm-tree-dotted pathway swooping along the beach – is a magnet for runners, in-line skaters, walkers and cyclists. The white-sand beach, meanwhile, is one of the nation's cleanest and best.

The best way to see Fort Lauderdale is from the water. Hop on board the **Carrie B** (954-642-1601; www.carriebcruises.com; 440 N New River Dr E; tours adult/child $24/13; tours 11am, 1pm & 3pm, closed Tue & Wed May-Sep) for a 1½-hour riverboat tour that lets you get a glimpse of the ginormous mansions along the Intracoastal and New River. Or, for the best unofficial tour of the city, hop on the **Water Taxi** (954-467-6677; www.watertaxi.com; day pass adult/child $26/12), whose drivers

3, 2, 1...BLASTOFF!

Along the Space Coast, even phone calls get a countdown, thanks to the local area code: 321. It's no coincidence; in 1999 residents led by Robert Osband petitioned to get the digits in honor of the rocket launches that took place at Cape Canaveral.

offer lively narration of the passing scenery.

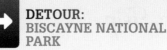 p47

The Drive » Things are heating up. Miami is just half an hour south of Fort Lauderdale down I-95.

----

13 Miami

Miami moves to a different rhythm from anywhere else in the USA, with pastel-hued, subtropical beauty and Latin sexiness at every turn. Just west of downtown on Calle Ocho (8th St), you'll find Little Havana, the most prominent community of Cuban Americans in the US. One of the best times to come is the last Friday of the month during **Viernes Culturales** (Cultural Fridays; www.viernesculturales. org; ⊘7-11pm last Fri of month), a street fair showcasing Latino artists and musicians. Or catch the vibe at **Máximo Gómez Park** (cnr SW 8th St & SW 15th Ave; ⊘9am-6pm), where old-timers gather to play dominoes to the strains of Latin music.

Wynwood and the Design District are Miami's official arts neighborhoods; don't miss the amazing collection of murals at **Wynwood Walls** (www.thewynwood walls.com; NW 2nd Ave, btwn 25th & 26th Sts), surrounded by blocks and blocks of even more murals that form sort of a drive-though art gallery.

p47

The Drive » We've saved the best for last. Cross over the Julia Tuttle Causeway or the MacArthur Causeway to find yourself in art-deco-laden Miami Beach.

TRIP HIGHLIGHT

14 Miami Beach

Miami Beach dazzles at every turn. It has some of the best beaches in the country, with white sand and warm, blue-green water, and it's world-famous for its people-watching. Then there's the deco. Miami Beach has the largest concentration of deco anywhere in the world, with approximately 1200 buildings lining the streets around Ocean Dr and Collins Ave. Arrange a tour at the **Art Deco Welcome Center** (✆305-672-2014; www.mdpl.org; 1001 Ocean Dr, South Beach; ⊘9:30am-5pm Fri-Wed, to 7pm Thu) or pick up a walking-tour map in the gift shop.

Running alongside the beach, Ocean Ave is lined with cafes that spill out onto the sidewalk; stroll along until you find one that suits your cravings. Another highly strollable area is Lincoln Road Mall, a pedestrian promenade that's lined with stores, restaurants and bars.

Get a taste of all Miami Beach has to offer on our walking tour, p84.

p47

DETOUR:
BISCAYNE NATIONAL PARK

Start: 14 Miami Beach
About an hour's drive south of Miami Beach, **Biscayne National Park** (✆305-230-1144, boat tours 786-335-3644; www.nps.gov/bisc; 9700 SW 328th St; boat tours adult/child $35/25; ⊘7am-5:30pm) is a protected marine sanctuary harboring amazing tropical coral reef systems, most within sight of Miami's skyline. It's only accessible by water: you can take a glass-bottomed-boat tour, snorkel or scuba dive, or rent a canoe or kayak to lose yourself in this 300-sq-mile system of islands, underwater shipwrecks and mangrove forests.

FLORIDA **1** HIGHWAY 1

Eating & Sleeping

FLORIDA | HIGHWAY 1

Amelia Island ❶

✖ Café Karibo & Karibrew   Fusion $$
(☎904-277-5269; www.cafekaribo.com; 27
N 3rd St, Fernandina Beach; mains $8-26;
🕑11am-3pm Mon, to 9pm Tue-Sat, 10:30am-
3pm Sun; 🛜) This funky side-street favorite
serves a large and eclectic menu of sandwiches,
soups, salads and healthy treats in a sprawling
two-story space with a shady patio hung with
twinkling Christmas lights. Down a Sloppy
Skip's Stout at the adjacent Karibrew brewpub.

🛏 Elizabeth Pointe Lodge   B&B $$$
(☎904-277-4851; www.elizabethpointelodge.com;
98 S Fletcher Ave, Fernandina Beach; r/ste from
$299/380; P🛜) Atmosphere oozes from this
eccentric yet stylish 1890s Nantucket-shingle-
style maritime inn, perched on the ocean 2 miles
from downtown. Porches offer the best seats on
the island for sunrise. Elegant rooms have plush
beds and oversized tubs.

Jacksonville ❸

✖ Black Sheep
Restaurant   Modern American $$
(☎904-380-3091; www.blacksheep5points.
com; 1534 Oak St; lunch/dinner mains from $9/14;
🕑10:30am-10pm Mon-Thu, to 11pm Fri & Sat,
9:30am-3pm Sun; 🛗) Good, local ingredients,
delicious food, a rooftop bar and a craft cocktail
menu. Try miso-glazed duck confit, citrus-
marinated tofu, pastrami sandwiches or crispy
skinned fish cooked in brown butter, or cardamom
pancakes and salmon bagels for Sunday brunch.

✖ Bistro Aix   French, Mediterranean $$$
(☎904-398-1949; www.bistrox.com; 1440 San
Marco Blvd; mains $14-37; 🕑11am-10pm Mon-
Thu, to 11pm Fri, 5-11pm Sat, 5-9pm Sun) Dine with
fashionable foodies on fusion Mediterranean
dishes bursting with global flavors, from wine-
braised chicken to duck cassoulet. More than
250 wines by the bottle, and 50 by the glass.
Reservations recommended.

St Augustine ❹

✖ Spanish Bakery & Cafe   Bakery $
(☎904-342-7859; www.spanishbakerycafe.com;
42½ St George St; mains $4-6.50; 🕑10am-5pm
Sun-Thu, to 8pm Fri & Sat) This diminutive stucco
bakeshop serves empanadas, sausage rolls and
other conquistador-era favorites. Sells out quick.

✖ Floridian   Modern American $$
(☎904-829-0655; www.thefloridianstaug.com;
39 Cordova St; mains $14-25; 🕑11am-3pm Wed-
Mon, 5-9pm Mon-Thu, to 10pm Fri & Sat) Oozing
hipster-locavore earnestness, this farm-to-table
restaurant serves whimsical neo-Southern
creations. Service and vibe may be too cool for
school, but it's hard to fault the food: fried green
tomato bruschetta and seafood zucchini linguine
pair perfectly. No reservations means long waits.

🛏 Casa Monica   Historic Hotel $$$
(☎904-827-1888; www.casamonica.com; 95
Cordova St; r $200-280, ste from $440; P🛜🏊)
Built in 1888, this is *the* luxe hotel in town, with
turrets and fountains adding to the Spanish-
Moorish castle atmosphere. Rooms are richly
appointed, with wrought-iron triple-sheeted
beds and Bose sound systems. Some suites have
Jacuzzis, and the location can't be beaten.

Daytona Beach ❻

✖ Dancing Avocado Kitchen   Cafe $
(☎386-947-2022; www.dancingavocadokitchen.
com; 110 S Beach St; mains $8-14; 🕑8am-4pm
Tue-Sat; 🌿🛗) Delicious gluten-free and mostly
vegetarian-friendly items feature at this colorful
kitchen, but you'll still find a spicy jerk chicken
wrap and obligatory mahi sandwich basket.

🛏 Tropical Manor   Resort $
(☎386-252-4920; www.tropicalmanor.com; 2237
S Atlantic Ave, Daytona Beach Shores; r $88-135;
P🛜🏊🛗) This immaculate, family-friendly
beachfront property is like a playful pastel vision
of Candy Land. A variety of configurations from
motel rooms to suites and cottages are available.

Space Coast ❾

✗ Fat Snook — Seafood $$$

(☎321-784-1190; www.thefatsnook.com; 2464 S
Atlantic Ave; mains $22-33; ⊙5:30-10pm) Hidden
inside an uninspired building, tiny Fat Snook
stands out as an oasis of fine cooking. Gourmet
seafood is expertly prepared with unexpected
herbs and spices influenced by Caribbean
flavors. Reservations strongly recommended.

West Palm Beach ⓫

✗ Rhythm Cafe — Fusion $$$

(☎561-833-3406; www.rhythmcafe.cc; 3800 S
Dixie Hwy; mains $21-30; ⊙5:30-10pm Tue-Sat,
to 9pm Sun & Mon) There's no lack of flair at
this colorful, upbeat bistro set in a converted
drugstore in West Palm's antiques district.
The equally vibrant menu ranges from goat's
cheese pie to 'the best tuna tartare ever' to a
pomegranate-infused catch of the day.

⊨ Hotel Biba — Motel $

(☎561-832-0094; www.hotelbiba.com; 320
Belvedere Rd; r $149-179; ✳🛜🏊) This place
lacks a bit of color but is one of the better
budget options around. It's clean and well
located a block from the Intracoastal, perched
on the edge of the El Cid district.

Fort Lauderdale ⓬

✗ BREW Urban Cafe Next Door — Cafe $

(☎954-357-3934; www.facebook.com/
brewnextdoor; 537 NW 1st Ave; ⊙7am-7pm; 🛜)
Despite its unwieldy name, Brew is the coolest
thing going in Fort Lauderdale: a kick-ass cafe
located in a weird, semi-abandoned studio space
filled with bookshelves. Worth it for the coffee.

✗ Le Tub — American $$

(☎954-921-9425; www.theletub.com; 1100 N
Ocean Dr; mains $9-20; ⊙11am-1am Mon-Fri,
noon-2am Sat & Sun) Decorated exclusively with
flotsam collected along Hollywood Beach, this
quirky burger joint is routinely named 'Best in
America.' Everything is prepared from scratch and
in a small kitchen so expect a wait. It's worth it.

⊨ Riverside Hotel — Hotel $$

(☎954-467-0671; www.riversidehotel.com;
620 E Las Olas Blvd; r/ste from $219/479;
🅿✳🛜🏊🐾) This well-located Fort

Lauderdale landmark (c 1936) with plush floral
carpet and an air of grandeur has two room
types: larger, executive rooms in the newer
12-story tower, and those in the historic 1936
building. Classic rooms overlooking Las Olas are
the pick. Valet parking is a hefty $27 per night.

Miami ⓭

⊨ Biltmore Hotel — Historic Hotel $$$

(☎855-311-6903; www.biltmorehotel.com;
1200 Anastasia Ave; r/ste from $409/560;
🅿✳🛜🏊🐾) Though the Biltmore's standard
rooms can be small, a stay here is a chance to
sleep in the lap of US luxury. Explore palatial
grounds, read a book in the opulent lobby, sun
underneath enormous columns and take a dip in
the largest hotel pool in continental USA.

Miami Beach ⓮

✗ 11th St Diner — Diner $

(☎305-534-6373; www.eleventhstreetdiner.com;
1065 Washington Ave; mains $10-20; ⊙7am-
midnight Sun-Wed, 24hr Thu-Sat) You've seen the
art-deco landmarks, now eat in one: a Pullman-
car diner trucked down from Wilkes-Barre, PA.
Classics include oven-roasted turkey, baby back
ribs and mac 'n' cheese – plus breakfast all hours.

✗ Pubbelly — Fusion $$

(☎305-532-7555; www.pubbellyboys.com/
miami/pubbelly; 1418 20th St; sharing plates
$11-24, mains $19-30; ⊙6pm-midnight Tue-Thu
& Sun, to 1am Fri & Sat; 🍸) Delicious Pubbelly
skews between Asian, North American and Latin
American, gleaning the best from all cuisines.
Hand-crafted cocktails go down a treat.

⊨ Clay Hotel — Hotel $$

(☎305-250-0759; www.clayhotel.com; 1438
Washington Ave; r $140-250; ✳🛜) Packaged in a
100-year-old Spanish-style villa, the Clay has clean
and comfortable rooms in a medina-like maze of
adjacent buildings. If you're on a budget but don't
want a dorm/hostel atmosphere, head here.

⊨ Pelican Hotel — Boutique Hotel $$$

(☎305-673-3373; www.pelicanhotel.com; 826
Ocean Dr; r $260-420; ✳🛜) A mad experiment
of 29 themed rooms that come off like a fantasy-
suite hotel dipped in hip. From the cowboy-
hipster chic to jungly electric tiger stripes, all
the rooms are completely different, and include
quality sound systems and high-end fixtures.

The Everglades

Wade into the Everglades' vast 'river of grass,' where alligators float through mangrove swamps, birds soar across flooded horizons and endangered manatees perform elegant underwater ballet in the bays.

2

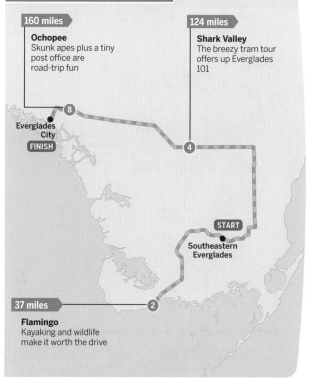

TRIP HIGHLIGHTS

160 miles

Ochopee
Skunk apes plus a tiny post office are road-trip fun

124 miles

Shark Valley
The breezy tram tour offers up Everglades 101

8
Everglades City
FINISH

4

START
Southeastern Everglades

2

37 miles

Flamingo
Kayaking and wildlife make it worth the drive

2–3 DAYS
170 MILES / 274KM

GREAT FOR...

BEST TIME TO GO
December to April is best for both weather and wildlife.

ESSENTIAL PHOTO
Alligators lounging in the sun at Shark Valley.

BEST FOR FAMILIES
Milkshakes and a petting zoo at Robert Is Here.

Big Cypress Preserve Alligators glide through the waters

2 The Everglades

The enticing Everglades are what make South Florida truly unique. This ecological wonderland is the USA's largest subtropical wilderness, flush with endangered and rare species, including its star attraction, the alligator (and lots of them). It's not just a wetland, swamp, prairie or grassland – it's all of the above, twisted into a series of soft horizons, long vistas and sunsets that stretch across your entire field of vision.

① Southeastern Everglades

Begin your Everglades adventure at **Ernest Coe Visitor Center** (☏305-242-7700; www.nps.gov/ever; 40001 State Rd 9336; ◷9am-5pm mid-Apr–mid-Dec, from 8am mid-Dec–mid-Apr), with excellent, museum-quality exhibits and tons of information on park activities. Check ahead for a schedule of ranger-led programs, most of which start 4 miles down at **Royal Palm Visitor Center** (☏305-242-7700; www.nps.gov/ever; State Rd 9336;

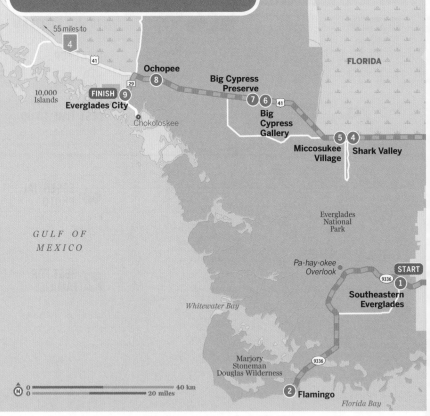

⊘9am-4:15pm). You'll also find the short **Anhinga Trail** (⊘24hr) here, offering astounding wildlife-watching opportunities.

Heading further into the park, several trails and scenic viewpoints give you a closer look at the park, including **Pa-hay-okee Overlook**, a raised platform that peeks over one of the prettiest bends in the river of grass, and the challenging **Christian Point Trail**, which runs through mangrove forest, prairie and hardwood hammock to the edge of Florida Bay.

The Drive » Continue southwest on SR 9336, which takes you past long fields of marsh prairie, white, skeletal forests of bald cypress and dark clumps of mahogany hammock. The Flamingo Visitor Center is 34 miles south of Royal Palm.

- - - - - - - - - - - - - - - -

TRIP HIGHLIGHT

② Flamingo

You've come this far, and for your efforts you're rewarded with the opportunity to canoe into the bracken heart of the swamp. Hit the **Flamingo Visitor Center** (☏239-695-2945; www.nps.gov/ever; State Rd 9336; ⊘8am-4:30pm mid-Nov–mid-Apr) for a map of local canoe trails, such as **Nine Mile Pond**, a 5.5-mile loop that leads you into Florida Bay. You can rent canoes and kayaks at **Flamingo Marina** (☏239-

695-3101; ⊘store 7am-5:30pm Mon-Fri, from 6am Sat & Sun), and be transported to various trailheads for an additional fee. While you're at the marina, it's worth sticking around to see if any manatees show up. This is also a great spot to see the rare American crocodile.

🛏 p55

The Drive » Head back the way you came in; it's the only way out. Six miles past Ernest Coe Visitor Center, go north on Tower Rd. You'll pass Robert Is Here and then Homestead is just a few miles further up.

- - - - - - - - - - - - - - - -

③ Homestead/ Florida City

Every good road trip needs a kooky tourist attraction, and thus Homestead – in addition

HURRICANE IRMA

Research for this trip was conducted before the devastating category 4 hurricane Irma hit Florida in September 2017. Those planning to travel to the Everglades region please see p338 for more details.

§ **LINK YOUR TRIP**

1 **Highway 1**
After driving down the Florida coast, start this Everglades trip just one hour southwest of Miami.

4 **Doing Disney & More**
Drive 1½ hours north to Sanibel Island to pick up the end of this trip, then drive it in reverse order.

to being a good base of operations for the southeastern portion of the Everglades – humbly offers up the **Coral Castle** (🕿305-248-6345; www.coral castle.com; 28655 S Dixie Hwy; adult/senior/child $18/15/8; ⊙8am-6pm Sun-Thu, to 8pm Fri & Sat), which isn't a castle at all but a monument to both unrequited love and all that is weird and wacky about southern Florida.

In the early 20th century, a Latvian man who had been left at the altar channeled his grief into building a sculpture garden out of more than 1000 tons of coral rock. That he did it by himself, in the dead of night (when it was cooler), using no heavy machinery imbues the place with a sense of mystery. At the very least, it's an impressive feat of engineering.

✕ ⛏ p55

The Drive » Head 20 miles north on FL 997/177th Ave until you hit the Tamiami Trail, aka Hwy 41. Shark Valley is 18 miles west. Look for alligators (unless you're driving) in the canal that runs alongside the road.

- - - - - - - - - - - - - - - - -

TRIP HIGHLIGHT

❹ Shark Valley

Alligators, alligators and more alligators! If that's what you've come to find, you won't be disappointed at **Shark Valley** (🕿305-221-8776; www.nps.gov/ever/ planyourvisit/svdirections .htm; 36000 SW 8th St, N 25°45.27.60', W 80°46.01.01';

car/cyclist/pedestrian $25/8/8; ⊙9am-5pm; P ♿). Kick back and enjoy the view during an excellent two-hour **tram tour** (🕿305-221-8455; www. sharkvalleytramtours.com; adult/child under 12yr/senior $25/19/12.75; ⊙ departures 9:30am, 11am, 2pm, 4pm May-Dec, hourly on the hour 9am-4pm Jan-Apr) that follows a 15-mile asphalt trail where you'll see copious amounts of alligators in the winter months.

Not only do you get to experience the park from the shady comfort of a breezy tram, but the tour is narrated by knowledgeable park rangers who give a fascinating overview of the Everglades and its inhabitants. Halfway along the trail the tour stops long enough to let you climb a 50ft-high observation tower, an out-of-place concrete structure that offers a dramatic panorama of the park.

The Drive » Exiting the park, turn left onto the Tamiami Trail, then immediately turn back off again. The Miccosukee Village is just past the park entrance.

- - - - - - - - - - - - - - - - -

❺ Miccosukee Village

Not so much a quaint little Native American village as a handful of commercial ventures, Miccosukee Village nonetheless offers insight into Native American life in the Everglades.

The centerpiece is the **Miccosukee Indian Museum** (🕿305-552-8365; www.miccosukee.com; Mile 70, Hwy 41; adult/child/5yr & under $12/6/free; ⊙9am-5pm; P ♿), just half a mile down the road from Shark Valley. Informative and entertaining, the open-air museum showcases the culture of the Miccosukee via guided tours of traditional homes, a crafts gift

Everglades swamplands Bald cypress trees reflected in still waters

store, dance and music performances, and live alligator shows in which a tribal member wrestles with a gator, while sharing enlightening facts about these prehistoric creatures. Afterwards, visitors are invited to have their picture taken while holding a wee gator.

Across the road, catch an **airboat ride** that includes a stop at a Miccosukee camp that's more than 100 years old.

The Drive » Continuing west on the Tamiami Trail, you'll pass trees, trees and more trees. After about 20 minutes you'll see Big Cypress Gallery on your left.

6 Big Cypress Gallery

If you're torn as to the relative beauty of the Everglades, stop by the

Big Cypress Gallery
(☎239-695-2428; www.clyde butcher.com; 52388 Tamiami Trail; ⊙10am-5pm; ℗), featuring the stunning black-and-white photography of Clyde Butcher. The photographer has been capturing the essence of the Everglades for over 40 years, and there's something about seeing his large-scale prints – some of which

are taller than you are – that will make you see the Everglades in a whole new way.

The Drive » The Oasis Visitor Center is on the right, less than a mile west of Big Cypress Gallery.

❼ Big Cypress Preserve

North of the Tamiami Trail you'll find this enormous undeveloped preserve that's integral to the Everglades' ecosystem. Encompassing 1139 sq miles, the preserve is indeed big, so where to start? Orient yourself at the **Oasis Visitor Center** (☎239-695-1201; www.nps. gov/bicy; 52105 Tamiami Trail E; ☯9am-4:30pm; ♿). In addition to trail maps you'll find great exhibits for the kids and an outdoor, water-filled ditch popular with alligators.

Further down the Tamiami Trail, but still part of the preserve, you'll find the **Kirby Storter Boardwalk**, a short elevated stroll through a mature cypress dome replete with orchids, bromeliads and the possibility of wildlife that makes you glad it's elevated.

The Drive » Keep going: your next stop is 16 miles west of the Oasis Visitor Center (and 8 miles past Kirby Storter Boardwalk).

TRIP HIGHLIGHT

❽ Ochopee

In tiny Ochopee, you'll find the **Skunk Ape Research Headquarters** (☎239-695-2275; www.skunkape.info; 40904 Tamiami Trail E; adult/child $12/6; ☯9am-5pm; **P**), a tongue-in-cheek endeavor dedicated to finding the southeastern USA's version of Bigfoot. The gift shop stocks all your skunk-ape necessities, and there's even a reptile and bird zoo in back run by a true Florida eccentric, the sort of guy who wraps albino pythons around his neck for fun. While you're there, look into **Everglades Adventure Tours** (EAT; ☎800-504-6554; www. evergladesadventuretours.com; 40904 Tamiami Trail E; 2hr canoe/pole-boat tour per person $89/109), offering some of the best private tours of the Everglades we've found, led by some genuinely funny guys with great local knowledge.

Ochopee is also home to the **Smallest Post Office in the United States**, a comically tiny edifice with very limited hours (you try sitting in there for more than a few hours a day). It's a fun photo op, and a great place to mail a postcard.

🍴 p55

The Drive » Just over 4 miles west of the post office, turn left onto CR 29 and go 3 more miles to reach the not-so-booming town of Everglades City.

❾ Everglades City

One of the best ways to experience the serenity of the Everglades is by paddling the network of waterways that skirt the northwest portion of the park. Somehow desolate yet lush, tropical and foreboding, the **10,000 Islands** consist of many (but not really 10,000) tiny islands and a mangrove swamp that hugs the southwesternmost border of Florida.

Most islands are fringed by narrow beaches with sugar-white sand, but note that the water is brackish, and very shallow most of the time. It's not Tahiti, but it's fascinating. **The Wilderness Waterway**, a 99-mile path between Everglades City and Flamingo, is the longest canoe trail in the area. Look for canoe rentals and guided boat trips at the **Gulf Coast Visitor Center** (☎239-695-2591; www.ever gladesnationalparkboattours gulfcoast.com; 815 Oyster Bar Lane, off Hwy 29; canoe/single kayak/tandem kayak per day $38/45/55; ☯9am-4:30pm mid-Apr–mid-Nov, from 8am mid-Nov–mid-Apr; ♿).

🍴 🛏 p55

Eating & Sleeping

Flamingo ❷

🛏 Flamingo Campground   Campground $

(📞877-444-6777; www.nps.gov/ever/planyourvisit/flamcamp.htm; per campsite with/without hookups $30/20) There are more than 200 camping sites at the Flamingo Visitor Center, some of which have electrical hookups. Escape the RVs by booking a walk-in site. Reserve well ahead (via www.reserveamerica.com) for one of the nine waterfront sites.

Homestead/Florida City ❸

🍴 Robert Is Here   Market $

(📞305-246-1592; www.robertishere.com; 19200 SW 344th St, Homestead; juices $7-9; ⊙8am-7pm) More than a farmers' stand, Robert's is an institution. This is Old Florida at its kitsch best, in love with the Glades and the agriculture that surrounds it. You'll find loads of exotic, Florida-grown fruits not seen elsewhere – including black sapote, carambola (star fruit), dragon fruit, sapodilla, guanabana (soursop), tamarind, sugar apples, longans and passion fruit. The juices are fantastic.

🍴 Rosita's   Mexican $

(📞305-246-3114; www.rositasrestaurantfl.com; 199 W Palm Dr, Florida City; mains $8-12; ⊙8:30am-9pm) There's a working-class Mexican crowd here, testament to the sheer awesomeness of the tacos and burritos. Everyone is friendly, and the mariachi music adds a festive vibe to the place.

🛏 Everglades International Hostel   Hostel $

(📞305-248-1122; www.evergladeshostel.com; 20 SW 2nd Ave, Florida City; camping per person $18, dm $30, d $61-75, ste $125-225; P ❄ 🛜 ⛲) Located in a cluttered, comfy 1930s boarding house, this friendly hostel has good-value dorms, private rooms and 'semi-privates' (you have an enclosed room within the dorms and share a bathroom with dorm residents). The creatively configured backyard is the best feature.

Ochopee ❽

🍴 Joanie's Blue Crab Café   American $$

(📞239-695-2682; www.joaniesbluecrabcafe.com; 39395 Tamiami Trail E; mains $12-17; ⊙11am-5pm Thu-Tue, closed seasonally, call ahead; 🚗) This quintessential shack, east of Ochopee, with open rafters, shellacked picnic tables and alligator kitsch, serves filling food of the fried variety on paper plates. Crab cakes are the thing to order. There's live music on Saturdays and Sundays from 12:30pm and a rockabilly-loving jukebox at other times.

Everglades City ❾

🍴 Oyster House   Seafood $$

(📞239-695-2073; www.oysterhouserestaurant.com; 901 Copeland Ave; mains lunch $12-18, dinner $19-30; ⊙11am-9pm Sun-Thu, to 10pm Fri & Sat; 🚗 ♿) Besides serving the Everglades staples of excellent seafood (oysters, crab, grouper, cobia, lobster), this buzzing, family-run spot serves up alligator dishes (tacos, jambalaya, fried platters) and simpler baskets (burgers, fried seafood), plus not-to-be-missed desserts. The cabin-like interior is decorated with vintage knickknacks and taxidermy.

🛏 Everglades City Motel   Motel $$

(📞239-695-4224; www.evergladescitymotel.com; 310 Collier Ave; r $150-250; P ❄ 🛜 ♿) With large renovated rooms that have all the mod cons (flat-screen TVs, fridges, coffeemakers) and friendly staff that can hook you up with boat tours, this motel is good value for those spending time near the 10,000 Islands.

🛏 Ivey House Bed & Breakfast   B&B $$

(📞877-567-0679; www.iveyhouse.com; 107 Camellia St; inn $100-180, lodge $90-100, cottage $180-230; P ❄ 🛜 ♿) This friendly, family-run tropical inn offers a variety of well-appointed accommodations: bright spacious inn rooms overlooking a pretty courtyard, cheaper lodge rooms (with shared bathrooms) and a freestanding two-bedroom cottage with a kitchen and screened-in porch. The pool (covered in winter) is a great year-round option for a swim.

North Florida Backwaters & Byways

3

Emerald Coast, Redneck Riviera...call it what you will, but Florida's beaches along the Gulf Coast are dazzling, and inland you'll find interesting towns that give you a warm Southern welcome.

TRIP HIGHLIGHTS

240 miles

Wakulla Springs
Unspoiled nature where Tarzan once played

START
Pensacola
2

Tallahassee
5

FINISH
10

Gulf Islands National Seashore
White-sand beaches stretch on and on

9 miles

Weeki Wachee
Campy fun at a classic Florida roadside attraction

510 miles

5–7 DAYS
510 MILES / 820KM

GREAT FOR...

BEST TIME TO GO
April to November has consistently great weather.

📷 ESSENTIAL PHOTO
A real, live mermaid performing in an underwater grotto at Weeki Wachee Springs.

✓ BEST FOR NATURE
Birds, lush foliage and crystal-clear springs at Wakulla Springs State Park.

Crystal River Florida manatees

North Florida Backwaters & Byways

3

Kick off your trip with spectacular white-sand beaches along the Gulf Coast, then meander back roads and byways to discover northern Florida's hidden treasures. Along the way you'll find crystal-clear springs that you can enjoy from an inner tube or glass-bottomed boat, come face-to-face with a Florida manatee, and end your trip with a classic roadside attraction starring the mermaids of Weeki Wachee.

① Pensacola

Visitors come here from all over the South for an all-American blue-collar vacation experience: snow-white beaches, jam-packed seafood restaurants, and bars where beer flows like water. Despite its beachy casualness, Pensacola has a more serious side, too, reflecting the town's 300-year history. Get a taste at downtown's **Historic Pensacola Village** (☎850-595-5985; www.historicpensacola.org; Tarragona & Church St; adult/

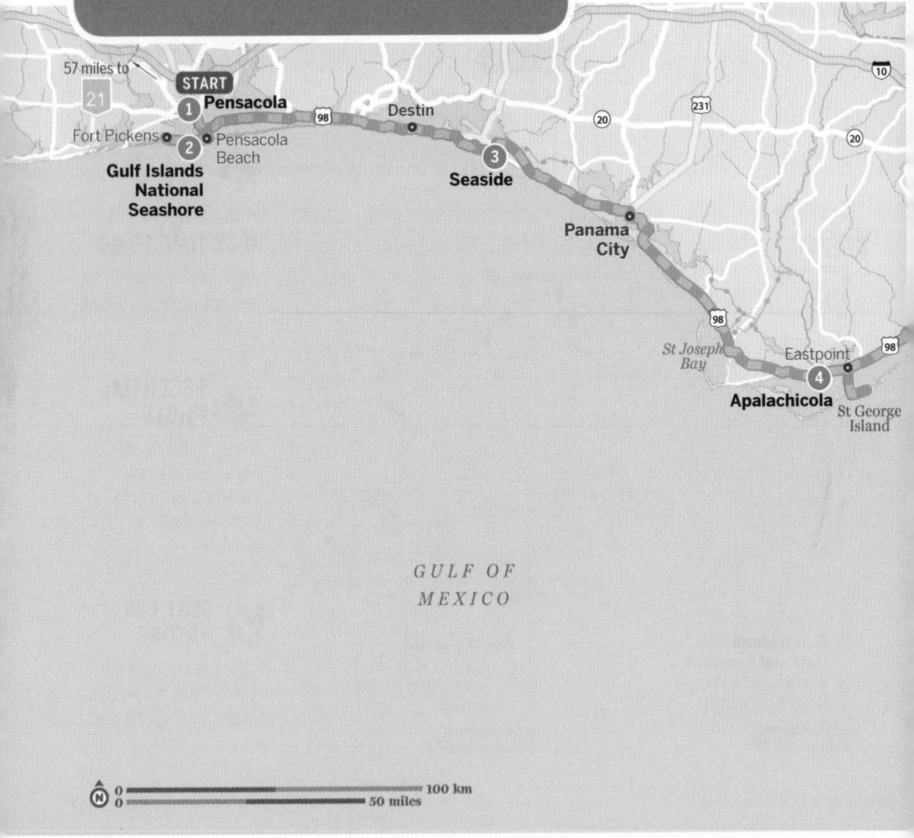

---

57 miles to

21

START

① **Pensacola**

Fort Pickens ○

② ○ Pensacola Beach

98 Destin ○

Gulf Islands National Seashore

③

Seaside

Panama City ○

10

231

20

20

98

St Joseph Bay

98

Eastpoint

④

Apalachicola

St George Island

GULF OF MEXICO

0 — 100 km
0 — 50 miles
Ⓝ

child $8/4; ⊙10am-4pm Tue-Sat; [P] [♿], a well-preserved collection of 19th-century buildings. A military town at heart, Pensacola is also where you'll find the Pensacola Naval Air Station, home to both the elite Blue Angels squadron (www.blueangels.navy.mil) and a don't-miss collection of jaw-dropping military aircraft at the **National Museum of Naval Aviation** (📞800-327-5002; www.navalaviationmuseum.org; 1750 Radford Blvd; ⊙9am-5pm; [♿]).

🍴 🛏 p63

The Drive » Take Hwy 98 south across two causeways to get to Pensacola Beach; head west to get to Gulf Islands National Seashore and Fort Pickens. It's a distance of 18 miles from downtown Pensacola to Fort Pickens.

TRIP HIGHLIGHT

❷ Gulf Islands National Seashore

You'll get your first taste of the area's lovely white sands at Pensacola Beach and the neighboring

LINK YOUR TRIP

21 Gulf Coast
Start with the Gulf Coast trip, then continue on 57 miles to pick this one up in Pensacola.

4 Doing Disney & More
Just one hour south of Weeki Wachee, you can join up with the Disney trip in Tampa.

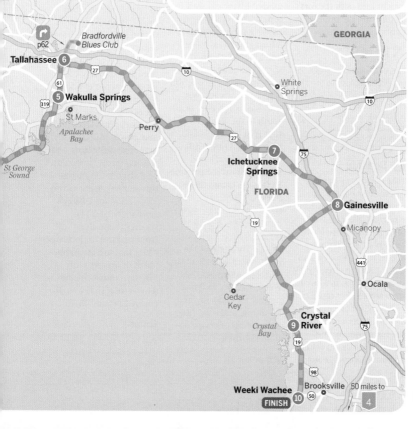

Gulf Islands National Seashore (☎850-934-2600; www.nps.gov/guis; vehicle $15; ☼sunrise-sunset; ♿), part of a 150-mile stretch of undeveloped beach on Santa Rosa Island. At the western end of the island, poke around **Fort Pickens** (☎850-934-2600; www.nps.gov/guis/learn/historyculture/fort-pickens; 1400 Fort Pickens Rd; 7-day pass pedestrian & cyclist/car $7/15; ☼sunrise-sunset; Ⓟ♿), a crumbling wreck of a 19th-century fort that sits practically right on the beach – a great compromise for history buffs and beach lovers traveling together. A small museum gives you insight into both the fort's history and the impressive natural surroundings.

✖ 🛏 p63

The Drive ⟫ Follow FL 399 to Hwy 98, traveling through Fort Walton Beach and past several oceanfront state parks. Detour on Hwy 30A to reach Seaside, about 1½ hours away.

- - - - - - - - - - - - - - - - - -

❸ Seaside

Take a breather in picturesque Seaside, a tiny pastel town that may feel strangely like a movie set. That's because it was; remember *The Truman Show*? It was about an unwitting star in a reality TV show who lived in a small, surreally perfect town.

A handful of eateries and art galleries surround the town square, and right across the street is an absolutely gorgeous

beach. A group of vintage silver Airstream trailers form a food court in the center of town, selling everything from fresh-juice smoothies to grilled kabobs for picnicking at the beach.

The Drive ⟫ Continue southeast along the coast for about 100 miles, passing through the carnival-esque beach town of Panama City, and the quiet little waterfront town of Mexico Beach.

- - - - - - - - - - - - - - - - - -

❹ Apalachicola

Apalachicola harbors several historic 19th- and 20th-century buildings, all stationed along a self-guided historical walking tour with stops that include Southern mansions, a former general store and an old-fashioned ships' chandlery.

From Apalachicola, you can cross the causeway into Eastpoint, then head south to the sliver of land that is St George Island, where you'll find 9 miles of glorious beach and sand dunes at the pristine **St George Island State Park** (☎850-927-2111; www.floridastateparks.org/stgeorge island; 1900 E Gulf Beach Dr; vehicle $6; ☼8am-dusk; Ⓟ♿). Throughout the park, boardwalks lead to shell-sprinkled beaches, where shallow waters are perfect for canoeing and kayaking, and a 2.5-mile nature trail offers exceptional birding.

🛏 p63

The Drive ⟫ Head northeast on Hwy 98. After skirting Tates Hell State Forest and crossing Ochlockonee Bay, go north on Spring Creek Hwy (365) then east on Hwy 267 to reach the entrance to Wakulla Springs. The whole drive takes about an hour and a half.

- - - - - - - - - - - - - - - - - -

TRIP HIGHLIGHT

❺ Wakulla Springs

There's something slightly magical about **Wakulla Springs State Park** (☎850-561-7276; www.floridastateparks.org/wakullasprings; 465 Wakulla Park Dr; vehicle/pedestrian $6/2; ☼8am-sunset; Ⓟ♿); perhaps that's why Walt Disney was once rumored to be considering it for the location of his new theme park. Take a boat tour of the wildlife-filled Wakulla River, which was used as a movie set for several Tarzan movies, as well as *The Creature from the Black Lagoon*. Here, mossy cypress trees and mangroves mingle with manatees, alligators and wading birds. (It wouldn't be a stretch to imagine this serene outing as the inspiration for Disney's Jungle Cruise.) The springs themselves flow from massive underwater caves that are an archaeologist's dream, with fossilized bones including a mastodon that was discovered around 1850.

🛏 p63

The Drive ⟫ Tallahassee is just half an hour north up Hwy 61.

AURORA PHOTOS / ALAMY STOCK PHOTO ©

Weeki Wachee Springs Underwater mermaid performance

6 Tallahassee

Closer to Atlanta than it is to Miami, Florida's capital is far more Southern than most of the state it administrates. Downtown, the 1845 **Tallahassee Historic Capitol** (☎850-487-1902; www.flhistoriccapitol.gov; 400 S Monroe St; ⏰9am-4:30pm Mon-Fri, from 10am Sat, from noon Sun) is fetchingly draped by candy-striped awnings and topped by a glass dome. Dig deeper into Florida history at **Mission San Luis** (☎850-245-6406; www.missionsanluis.org; 2100 W Tennessee St; adult/child $5/2; ⏰10am-4pm Tue-Sun; P ♿), the 60-acre site of a 17th-century Spanish and Apalachee mission that's been wonderfully reconstructed, especially the soaring Council House. Tours provide visitors with a fascinating taste of life as it was 300 years ago.

🛏 p63

The Drive » Make your way southeast for 110 miles along Hwy 27 (FL 20), a sleepy, two-lane highway that heads through the town of Perry – and not a whole lot else.

7 Ichetucknee Springs

After journeying through the land of white-sand beaches, get your freshwater fix at **Ichetucknee Springs State Park** (☎386-497-4690; www.floridastateparks.org/ichetuckneesprings; 12087 SW US 27, Fort White; car/person $6/5; ⏰8am-sunset; P). The main reason to visit? Relaxing in a giant inner tube and floating through gin-clear waters on the lazy, spring-fed Ichetucknee River.

The park doesn't rent tubes, but local farmers do, for about $5; find

61

DETOUR: BRADFORDVILLE BLUES CLUB

Start: 6 Tallahassee

After dark, follow rural back roads north of I-10 to **Bradfordville Blues Club** (📞850-906-0766; www. bradfordvilleblues.com; 7152 Moses Lane, off Bradfordville Rd; tickets $15-35; ⏰10pm Fri & Sat). Down the end of a dirt road lit by tiki torches, you'll find a bonfire raging under the live oaks at this hidden-away juke joint that hosts excellent national blues acts.

them along the highway on your way in. Admission is limited; arrive early as capacity is often reached by mid-morning. From May to September the park offers a shuttle service to take you from the south entrance to the launch points, allowing you to float back down to your car.

The Drive » After drying off, keep following Hwy 27 (FL 20) southeast 40 miles to Gainesville.

- - - - - - - - - - - - - - - - - -

8 Gainesville

Gainesville is an energetic, upbeat city, routinely ranked among the country's best places to live and play. It's also home to the nation's second-largest university, the sprawling University of Florida. A student vibe infuses the entire city, with loads of economical eats, cool bars, and indie and punk rock clubs.

While you're there, stop in at the excellent **Florida Museum of Natural History** (📞352-846-2000; www.flmnh.ufl.edu; 3215 Hull Rd; ⏰10am-5pm Mon-Sat,

1-5pm Sun; P ♿), if for no other reason than the Butterfly Rainforest. As you stroll among waterfalls and tropical foliage, hundreds of butterflies flutter freely in the soaring, screened vivarium.

🍴 🏠 p63

The Drive » Time to reverse our trajectory and head back to the Gulf Coast. Crystal River is about an hour and a half southwest of Gainesville.

- - - - - - - - - - - - - - - - - -

9 Crystal River

Between December and March, **Crystal River National Wildlife Refuge** (📞352-563-2088; www.fws. gov/crystalriver; 1502 SE Kings Bay Dr; ⏰8am-5:30pm Mon-Fri) offers your best bet for seeing endangered manatees in the wild. It's an unforgettable thrill to take a glass-bottomed-boat cruise, paddle a kayak or go snorkeling while encountering 'sea cows' in their natural habitat. Consider access via the **Three Sisters Springs** (📞352-586-1170; www.threesisterssspringsvisitor.

org; 123 NW US 19; adult/child $15/7.50; ⏰8am-5pm) trail.

For a more casual manatee experience, venture further south to **Homosassa Springs Wildlife State Park** (📞352-628-5343; www.floridastateparks. org/homosassasprings; 4150 S Suncoast Blvd; adult/child 6-12yr $13/5; ⏰9am-5:30pm), an old-school outdoor Florida animal encounter. It features a wealth of Florida's headliner species, but the highlight is an underwater observatory where you can go eyeball to eyeball with lettuce-nibbling manatees and enormous schools of fish. Time your visit for the manatee program (11:30am, 1:30pm and 3:30pm).

The Drive » Your final stop is a straight shot south down Hwy 19. It's 28 miles from Crystal River, 20 miles from Homosassa Springs.

- - - - - - - - - - - - - - - - - -

TRIP HIGHLIGHT

10 Weeki Wachee

Since 1947, tourists have been lured north down the coast by the kitschy siren song of **Weeki Wachee Springs** (📞352-592-5656; www.weekiwachee.com; 6131 Commercial Way, Spring Hill; adult/child 6-12yr $13/8; ⏰9am-5:30pm), one of Florida's original roadside attractions. Guests flock here to watch glamorous mermaids perform in their underwater grotto. There's also a wilderness river cruise, and swimming and waterslides at adjoining Buccaneer Bay water park.

Eating & Sleeping

Pensacola ❶

✗ Dharma Blue — International $$

(📞850-433-1275; www.dharmablue.com; 300 S Alcaniz St; mains $15-30; ⏱10am-2pm & 5-9:30pm Sat & Sun, 5-9:30pm Mon-Fri; 🚻) The eclectic menu of this compact local favorite ranges from semolina-dusted calamari and grilled duck to mouthwatering sushi. A casual, welcoming vibe extends from the charming, chandelier-adorned interior to the sunny patio.

🛏 Pensacola Victorian B&B — B&B $$

(📞850-434-2818; www.pensacolavictorian. com; 203 W Gregory St; r $95-150; 🅿🛜) This stately 1892 Queen Anne building offers four lovingly maintained guest rooms. The standout is Suzanne's Room, with its hardwood floors, blue toile prints and claw-foot tub. It's about a mile north of downtown Pensacola.

Gulf Islands National Seashore ❷

✗ Native Café — Breakfast $

(www.thenativecafe.com; 45a Via de Luna Dr; mains $5-13; ⏱7:30am-3pm; 🛜🚻) This funky breakfast and lunch spot is a welcome addition to the fried-fish stretch. Try a shrimp po' boy, grilled chicken sandwich, fish tacos, rice and beans or seafood gumbo – or, for a cheap morning jump-start, eggs Benedict or pancakes.

🛏 Paradise Inn — Motel $$

(📞850-932-2319; www.paradiseinn-pb.com; 21 Via de Luna Dr; r $99-140; 🅿❄🛜🐾) Across from the beach, this sherbet-colored motel is a cheery place thanks to its popular bar and grill (ask for a quiet room near the parking lot). Compact quarters are spick and span with tiled floors and brightly painted walls.

Apalachicola ❹

🛏 Coombs House Inn — B&B $$

(📞850-653-9199; www.coombshouseinn.com; 80 6th St; r $99-159; 🛜) This stunning yellow Victorian inn was built in 1905 and features black-cypress wall paneling, fireplaces, a carved oak staircase, leaded glass windows and beadboard ceilings. Settle into one of the fabulous rooms and join in for nightly wine socials in the dining room. A lavish breakfast is served each morning.

Wakulla Springs ❺

🛏 The Lodge at Wakulla Springs — Lodge $$

(📞850-421-2000; www.wakullaspringslodge. com; 550 Wakulla Park Dr; r from $130; 🅿) Time has stood still at this faded 1937 lodge, a charming Spanish-style building with an enormous faux-stone fireplace in the lobby. Its 27 basic, scruffy rooms have original marble floors, walk-in wardrobes and no TVs. The lodge's grandiose **Ball Room Restaurant** is a favorite with Tallahassee locals – try the fried chicken and the famous bean soup.

Tallahassee ❻

🛏 Hotel Duval — Hotel $$$

(📞850-224-6000; www.hotelduval.com; 415 N Monroe St; r $184-309; 🅿🛜) Sleek and modern, this centrally located 117-room hotel has all the mod cons, and a hip interior that's more stylish than pretentious – rare with spots that are so overtly design-conscious. The rooftop bar and lounge is open until 2am most nights.

Gainesville ❽

✗ Satchel's Pizza — Pizza $

(📞352-335-7272; www.satchelspizza.com; 1800 NE 23rd Ave; menu items $3-15; ⏱11am-10pm Tue-Sat; 🅿) Satchel's makes a strong claim to the best pizza on Florida's east coast, a reputation buttressed by enormous crowds of happy patrons. Grab a seat at a mosaic courtyard table or in the back of a gutted 1965 Ford Falcon. Most nights there's live music in the Back 40 Bar, with its head-scratchingly eccentric collection of trash and treasure.

🛏 Camellia Rose — B&B $$

(📞352-395-7673; www.camelliaroseinn.com; 205 SE 7th St; r $145-225; 🅿🛜) Modern upgrades (Jacuzzi tubs) integrate seamlessly with antique furniture in this fabulously restored 1903 Victorian building with a wide front porch.

Doing Disney & More

Whether you are a kid, have a kid, or ever were a kid, you'll love this adventure-filled trip that absolutely refuses to let you be bored.

4

TRIP HIGHLIGHTS

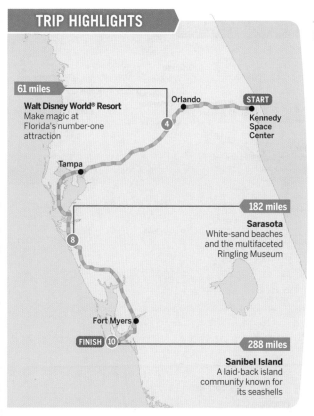

61 miles

Walt Disney World® Resort
Make magic at Florida's number-one attraction

182 miles

Sarasota
White-sand beaches and the multifaceted Ringling Museum

288 miles

Sanibel Island
A laid-back island community known for its seashells

6–10 DAYS
288 MILES /
464KM

GREAT FOR...

BEST TIME TO GO
April to May to avoid peak crowds.

 ESSENTIAL PHOTO
You hugging Mickey Mouse at Walt Disney World® Resort.

 BEST FOR LOW-KEY FUN
Searching for seashells on Sanibel Island.

Walt Disney World® Resort Fireworks over Cinderella Castle in the Magic Kingdom® Park

4 Doing Disney & More

Let your inner child loose at Mickey's Magic Kingdom, but don't stop there; you'll find plenty more to entertain you in dizzying Orlando. On the east coast, NASA's Kennedy Space Center is a major attraction based on real-world wonder. And on the west coast there are spectacular white-sand beaches and tons of attractions that are family friendly without being too kid-centric.

❶ Kennedy Space Center

Kick off your trip on Florida's Space Coast, where NASA was founded in the 1950s. Here you'll find the Kennedy Space Center (p43), from which the first moon landing was launched. Although NASA's space-shuttle program has ended for the time being, it's still a mind-blowing attraction. Devote most of your day to the science exhibits and historical museum, IMAX theaters, shuttle-launch simulator and Rocket

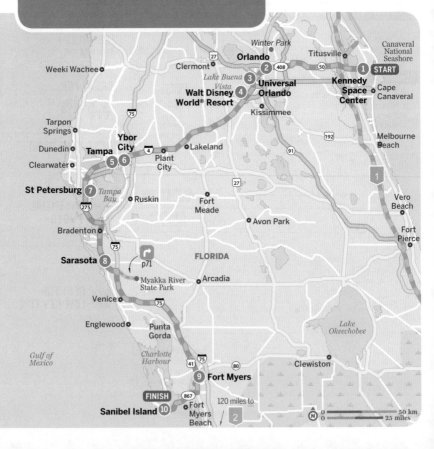

Garden, featuring replicas of classic rockets towering over the complex.

But first take a hop-on, hop-off bus tour of working NASA facilities, which depart every 15 minutes from 10am to 2:45pm. And don't be surprised if your bus driver points out alligators hanging out by the roadside or bald eagles nesting in nearby trees. That's because NASA is surrounded by Merritt Island National Wildlife Refuge (p41). Want to log some beach time before heading inland? **Canaveral National Seashore** (☎386-428-3384; www.nps.gov/cana; car/bike $10/1; ⏰6am-8pm) protects the longest stretch of undeveloped dunes on Florida's east coast.

The Drive » Make the short hop over to Orlando and its cornucopia of theme parks and attractions, just 52 miles inland.

LINK YOUR TRIP

1 **Highway 1**
The first half of the Highway 1 trip is the very best way to get to the first stop on this trip.

2 **The Everglades**
From I-75 it's only about an hour south to pick up the end of this trip and drive it in reverse order.

② Orlando

While it's quite easy to get caught up in the isolated worlds of Disney or Universal Orlando – squeezing in one more ride, one more parade, one more show – Orlando has so much more. Take the time to explore its lovely neighborhoods, rich performing-arts scene and several fantastic gardens, parks and museums. Picturesque **Loch Haven Park**, with 45 acres of parks, huge shade trees and three lakes, is home to several museums that are worth a visit: **Orlando Museum of Art** (☎407-896-4231; www.omart.org; 2416 N Mills Ave; adult/child $15/5; ⏰10am-4pm Tue-Fri, from noon Sat & Sun; 👪); **Mennello Museum of American Art** (☎407-246-4278; www.mennellomuseum.org; 900 E Princeton St; adult/child 6-18yr $5/1; ⏰10:30am-4:30pm Tue-Sat, from noon Sun); and **Orlando Science Center** (☎407-514-2000; www.osc.org; 777 E Princeton St; adult/child $20/14; ⏰10am-5pm Thu-Tue; 👪).

Just north in **Winter Park**, a sweet one-hour **Scenic Boat Tour** (☎407-644-4056; www.scenicboattours.com; 312 E Morse Blvd; adult/child $14/7; ⏰hourly 10am-4pm; 👪) floats through 12 miles of tropical canals and lakes while the enthusiastic tour guide talks about the mansions, Rollins College and other sites along the way. After your tour, wan-der Winter Park's trendy **Park Ave**, where you'll have a slew of restaurants and bars to choose from.

✕ 🍽 p73

The Drive » Universal Orlando is 10 miles southwest of Downtown Orlando via I-4. Bring quarters; it's a toll road.

③ Universal Orlando

Just a bit smarter, funnier and faster than dear old Disney, **Universal Orlando Resort** (☎407-363-8000; www.universalorlando.com; 1000 Universal Studios Plaza; single park adult 1/2 days $105/185, child $100/175, both parks adult/child $155/150; ⏰daily, hours vary) gets your adrenaline pumping with revved-up rides and entertaining shows. The megaplex features two theme parks, a water park, three hotels and **Universal City-Walk**, an entertainment district that connects the two parks.

The first of the two parks, **Universal Studios**, has a Hollywood backlot feel and simulation-heavy rides dedicated to television and the silver screen, from *The Simpsons* and *Shrek* to *Revenge of the Mummy* and *Twister*.

If you have to choose between the two parks, there's lots to love within the themed 'worlds' that comprise **Islands of Adventure**. You might find yourself riding high on Marvel Super Hero Island, delighting at the whimsy of Seuss Landing,

or exploring the ersatz-mystical Lost Continent. But the most magical of all is the **Wizarding World of Harry Potter**, where you can immerse yourself in Hogwarts and Hogsmeade, both brought to life in exquisite, rib-tickling detail.

The Drive » Are we there yet? Are we there yet? Are we there yet? OK fine. We're going there now. The exit for Disney World is another 10 minutes southwest of Universal Orlando. You can't miss it; there's more than a sign or two.

- - - - - - - - - - - - - -

TRIP HIGHLIGHT

④ Walt Disney World® Resort

Covering 40 sq miles, **Walt Disney World® Resort** (📞407-939-5277; www.disneyworld.disney. go.com; Lake Buena Vista,

outside Orlando; daily rates vary, see website for packages & tickets up to 10 days; 🚻) is the largest theme park resort in the world. It includes four separate theme parks, two water parks, hotels, restaurants and two shopping and night-life districts – proving that it's not such a small world, after all. But it's not about size. The park's appeal is in the fact that

Universal Orlando Resort Dudley Do-Right's Ripsaw Falls® ride, Islands of Adventure theme park

few visitors can inoculate themselves against Disney's highly infectious enthusiasm and warm-hearted nostalgia.

The centerpiece of it all is the **Magic Kingdom** (1180 Seven Seas Dr; $100-119, prices vary daily; ⊙9am-11pm, hours vary), land of the iconic Cinderella Castle and rides such as Space Mountain, the Haunted Mansion and Pirates of the Caribbean. This is where the fireworks and nighttime light parade illuminate Main Street, USA, and as far as Disney mythology goes, it doesn't get better.

But what about those other parks? Park Hopper Passes let you experience them all. **Epcot** (200 Epcot Center Dr; $100-119, prices vary daily; ⊙11am-9pm, hours vary) is a more low-key experience with rides, interactive exhibits and the World Showcase, an interesting toe-dip into the cultures of 11 countries.

Disney's Hollywood Studios (351 S Studio Dr; $100-119, prices vary daily; ⊙9am-10pm, hours vary) doesn't bring the magic but it does have the two most exciting rides: the unpredictable elevator in the Twilight Zone

LOCAL KNOWLEDGE: YOUR DAY AT DISNEY

Disney expectations run high, but long waits, and getting jostled and tugged through crowds and lines, can leave the kids, and you, exhausted. Here are some simple tips:

Download the 'My Disney Experience' app Make reservations, reserve FastPass+ attractions, view listings and programs plus your own schedule.

Take advantage of 'My Disney Experience' Reserve your three FastPass+ attractions per day (www.disneyworld.disney.go.com) in advance.

Stock up on snacks Snack packets and bananas will save the irritation of waiting in line for sub-par, overpriced food. Buy a sandwich early to picnic at your leisure.

Arrive at the park at least 30 minutes before gates open Don't window-shop or dawdle – march to the rides and then kick back for the afternoon.

Tower of Terror and the Aerosmith-themed Rock 'n' Roller Coaster.

Finally, **Disney's Animal Kingdom** (2101 Osceola Pkwy; $100-119, prices vary daily; ⊙9am-7pm, hours vary) is a sometimes surreal blend of rides, African safari, shows and dinosaurs. It's best at animal encounters and shows, with the 110-acre Kilimanjaro Safaris as its centerpiece.

✕ ⌖ p73

The Drive » From Walt Disney World® Resort, it's an easy one-hour drive southwest down I-4 to get to Tampa.

- - - - - - - - - - - - - - -

⑤ Tampa

Sprawling and business-like, Tampa is actually much more fun and intriguing than it first

appears. So many new museums, parks and restaurants have popped up recently that the city is dangerously close to becoming stylish. It's also a great family destination, with enough entertainment to last a week.

Florida Aquarium (☎813-273-4000; www.flaquarium.org; 701 Channelside Dr; adult/child $25/20; ⊙9:30am-5pm; 🚻) is one of the state's best, with all kinds of activities and programs, and **Lowry Park Zoo** (☎813-935-8552; www.lowryparkzoo.com; 1101 W Sligh Ave; adult/child $33/25; ⊙9:30am-5pm; P 🚻) gets you as close to the animals as possible. You can fulfill your adrenaline craving with epic rides woven through an African-theme wildlife

park at **Busch Gardens** (☎888-800-5447; www.buschgardenstampabay.com; 10165 McKinley Dr; 3yr & up $95; ⊙10am-6pm, hours vary), and across the street is **Adventure Island** (☎888-800-5447; www.adventure-island.com; 10001 McKinley Dr; adult/child 3-9yr $55/50, parking $15; ⊙ hours vary), a massive water park with slides and rides galore.

⌖ p73

The Drive » Your next stop is actually within Tampa, but it has such a distinct flavor we decided to make it its own separate destination. Ybor City is a short car or trolley ride northeast of downtown.

- - - - - - - - - - - - - - -

⑥ Ybor City

Historic buildings with wrought-iron balconies, cigar factories lining brick-lined streets, an early 1900s ambience with a distinctly Latin flavor...what is this place? Welcome to Ybor City, a historic neighborhood established by Don Vicente Martinez Ybor, a cigar factory owner who drew hundreds of immigrant workers to the area.

The main drag is 7th Ave (La Septima), and the **visitor center** (☎813-241-8838; www.ybor.org; 1600 E 8th Ave; ⊙10am-5pm Mon-Sat, noon-5pm Sun) provides an excellent introduction, with walking-tour maps, a small museum and other info. Just a few blocks away, the **Ybor City Museum State Park** (☎813-247-6323; www.ybor

museum.org; 1818 E 9th Ave; adult/child $4/free; ☺9am-5pm Wed-Sun) chronicles the history of cigar-making in interesting if text-heavy exhibits, but the real draw is the excellent historical walking tour.

For true local flavor, don't miss the Columbia Restaurant (p73). Built in 1905, it's Florida's oldest, and its 15 dining rooms sprawl over an entire city block, each decorated in a traditional Spanish style. Reserve ahead to be seated for one of the exuberant, twice-nightly flamenco shows.

✗ p73

The Drive » Across a causeway and out toward the beaches is Tampa's artier and more youthful sibling, St Petersburg. It's about a half-hour drive southwest of downtown Tampa.

➐ St Petersburg

Breezy and strollable, downtown St Pete's sits right on the waterfront of Tampa Bay, which is lined with spiffy new museums, galleries, restaurants and bars. But the headline attraction here is the **Salvador Dalí Museum** (☎727-823-3767; www.thedali.org; 1 Dali Blvd; adult/child 6-12yr $24/10, after 5pm Thu $10; ☺10am-5:30pm Fri-Wed, to 8pm Thu) and its dazzling home on the water.

The eccentric Spanish artist painted melting clocks, grew an exaggerated handlebar mustache

to look like King Philip, and once filled a Rolls-Royce with cauliflower. The largest collection of his work outside of Spain doesn't have *the* melting clocks, but it does have *some* melting clocks, as well as *Dreams of Dalí*, an immersive 360-degree virtual reality experience of the eponymous painting.

With a collection as broad as the Dalí's is deep, the **St Petersburg Museum of Fine Arts** (☎727-896-2667; www.mfastpete.org; 255 Beach Dr NE; adult/child 7-18yr $17/10; ☺10am-5pm Mon-Sat, to 8pm Thu, noon-5pm Sun) is also worth a stop. The collection traverses world antiquities and follows art's progression through

nearly every era. Several large galleries showcase special exhibitions.

✗ p73

The Drive » Heading south on I-275 over the soaring Sunshine Skyway Bridge spanning Tampa Bay, you might feel like you're in a car commercial; several have been filmed here. Sarasota is 45 minutes south of St Petersburg.

TRIP HIGHLIGHT

➑ Sarasota

One of Sarasota's loveliest features is its luscious, white-sand beaches. **Lido Beach** is closest and has free parking, but 5 miles away **Siesta Key** has sand like confectioners' sugar and is one of Florida's best.

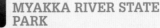

DETOUR: MYAKKA RIVER STATE PARK

Start: ➑ Sarasota

About a half-hour from downtown Sarasota, the 39,000-acre **Myakka River State Park** (☎941-361-6511; www.floridastateparks.org/park/Myakka-River; 13208 State Rd 72; car/bike $6/2; ☺8am-sunset) is a wildlife preserve starring Florida's oldest resident – the 200-million-year-old American alligator. Between 500 and 1000 alligators make their home in Myakka's slow-moving river and its shallow, lily-filled lakes, and you can get up close and personal with these toothsome beasts with an airboat or tram tour (adult/child $15/7.50) or by renting a canoe or kayak (first/additional hours $20/5). Check the website for seasonal schedules.

The extensive park's hammocks, marshes, pine flatwoods and prairies are home to a great variety of wildlife, and 38 miles of trails crisscross the terrain. Don't miss the easy, dramatic Canopy Trail. The park's seven paved miles and various dirt roads make for excellent cycling, and bird-watchers can spot great egrets, flocks of white pelicans and blue herons.

The best reason to visit Sarasota is the wonderful, whimsical **Ringling Museum Complex** (☎941-359-5700; www.ringling.org; 5401 Bay Shore Rd; adult/child 6-17yr $25/5; ⊙10am-5pm Fri-Wed, to 8pm Thu; 🚻), a 66-acre complex where one admission gets you into three museums. To begin with, you can tour John and his wife Mabel's Venetian Gothic mansion called **Ca d'Zan**, an over-the-top palace on the water. Also on the grounds is the **John & Mabel Museum of Art**, an excellent art museum that includes a re-created room from the Astor mansion. But the real standout here is the one-of-a-kind **Museum of the Circus**. It has costumes, props, posters, antique circus wagons and an extensive miniature model, that let you relive the excitement of the big-top era.

To find out what else Sarasota has to offer, stop by the **visitor information center** (☎941-706-1253; www.visitsarasota.org; 1710 Main St; ⊙10am-5pm Mon-Sat; 🛜).

✕ 🛏 p73

The Drive » Head inland a few miles to catch I-75, then go 52 miles south to pick up Hwy 41/ Tamiami Trail to the town of Fort Myers. The whole trip takes just over an hour.

- - - - - - - - - - - - - - - -

⑨ Fort Myers

Workaday, sprawling Fort Myers is overshadowed by the region's pretty beaches and sophisti-

cated, upscale towns. However, a facelift has spruced up the historic riverfront district (along 1st St between Broadway and Lee St) into an attractive, brick-lined collection of restaurants and bars.

Just a sleepy resort town in 1885, Fort Myers was pretty enough to entice Thomas Edison to build his winter home here. A few decades after Edison moved in, his good friend Henry Ford bought the property next door and now you can see how the early innovators lived at the **Edison & Ford Winter Estates** (☎239-334-7419; www.edisonfordwinterestates.org; 2350 McGregor Blvd; adult/child $20/12, guided tours adult $30, child $18-25; ⊙9am-5:30pm). In addition to Edison's winter home, you'll see his laboratory, gardens and a museum dedicated to his work, as well as the estate Henry Ford bought next door and the largest banyan tree in the continental US. Guided tours leave every hour on the hour, from 10am until 4pm.

The Drive » With all you've seen and done on this trip, it might be time to downshift a little bit. Luckily, Fort Myers is just a short drive from Sanibel and Captiva Islands, southwest 23 miles down Hwy 867 and over a 2-mile causeway with a $6 toll.

- - - - - - - - - - - - - - - -

TRIP HIGHLIGHT

⑩ Sanibel Island

Ahhhhh, it's island time. Upscale but unpreten-

tious, these two slivers of barrier island have a carefully managed shoreline that feels remarkably lush and undeveloped. Bikes are the preferred mode of travel, and the most challenging activity you'll engage in will be searching for shells – something Sanibel is particularly known for.

In addition to its fabulous beaches, Sanibel's 6300-acre **JN 'Ding' Darling National Wildlife Refuge** (☎239-472-1100; www.fws.gov/dingdarling; 1 Wildlife Dr; car/cyclist/pedestrian $5/1/1; ⊙7am-sunset) is a splendid refuge, home to an abundance of seabirds and wildlife. It has an excellent nature center, a 5-mile Wildlife Drive, narrated tram tours and easy kayaking in Tarpon Bay.

If an afternoon thunderstorm should break, it's the perfect opportunity to visit the **Bailey-Matthews Shell Museum** (☎239-395-2233; www.shellmuseum.org; 3075 Sanibel-Captiva Rd; adult/child 5-12yr/child 12-17yr $15/7/9; ⊙10am-5pm). Like a mermaid's jewelry box, it is dedicated to shells, yet it's much more than a covetous display of treasures. It's a crisply presented natural history of the sea and its shelled creatures – nearly a must after a day spent combing the beaches.

✕ p73

Eating & Sleeping

Orlando ②

✖ Ravenous Pig   American $$$

(📞407-628-2333; www.theravenouspig.com;
565 W Fairbanks; mains $14-32; ⏱11:30am-3pm
& 5-10pm Mon-Sat, 10:30am-3pm & 5-9pm Sun)
This chef-owned hipster spot is the cornerstone of
Orlando's restaurant trend for locally sourced food.
The shrimp and grits is a must; $15. Don't miss.

🛏 Barefoot Suites   Motel $

(📞407-589-2127; 2754 Florida Plaza Blvd,
Kissimmee; ste from $129; P ❄ 🤶 🏊 🚹) Bright
and spacious one- and two-bedroom suites in a
yellow six-story building. Low-key, friendly and
close to Disney, with kitchens and washer/dryers.

🛏 Courtyard at Lake Lucerne   B&B $

(📞407-648-5188; www.orlandohistoricinn.com;
211 N Lucerne Circle E, Downtown; r incl breakfast
from $140; P ❄ 🤶 🚹) A lovely option with
spacious rooms. Enchanting gardens, a genteel
breakfast and complimentary cocktails help
forgive a location under two highway overpasses.

Walt Disney World® Resort ④

✖ California Grill   American $$$

(📞407-939-3463; www.disneyworld.disney.
go.com; 4600 World Dr, Disney's Contemporary
Resort; mains $36-51; ⏱5-10pm; 🚹) A beloved
rooftop classic with magnificent views of Magic
Kingdom fireworks, offering everything from
sushi to triple-cheese flatbread. Reserve ahead.

🛏 Disney's Wilderness
Lodge   Resort $$$

(📞407-939-5277, 407-824-3200; www.
disneyworld.disney.go.com; 901 Timberline Dr;
r from $359; P ❄ 🤶 🏊 🚹) The handsome
lobby's low-lit tepee chandeliers, totem pole and
dramatic 80ft fireplace echo national-park lodges
of America's Old West, with wooded surrounds
and a hidden lagoonside location.

Tampa ⑤

🛏 Tahitian Inn   Hotel $$

(📞813-877-6721; www.tahitianinn.com; 601
S Dale Mabry Hwy, South Tampa; r from $155;
P ❄ @ 🤶 🏊 🚹 🐾) This family-owned, full-
service hotel offers fresh, boutique stylings on

the cheap. Nice pool, and the quaint cafe offers
outdoor seating by a waterfall and koi pond.

Ybor City ⑥

✖ Columbia Restaurant   Spanish $$$

(📞813-248-4961; www.columbiarestaurant.com;
2117 E 7th Ave; mains lunch $11-26, dinner $20-31;
⏱11am-10pm Mon-Thu, to 11pm Fri & Sat, noon-
9pm Sun) This Spanish Cuban restaurant is the
oldest in Florida, with 15 elegant dining rooms
and romantic, fountain-centered courtyards.
The owner is zealous about authentic cuisine.

St Petersburg ⑦

✖ Brick & Mortar   Modern American $$

(📞727-822-6540; www.facebook.com/
brickandmortarkitchen; 539 Central Ave; mains
$14-25; ⏱5pm-9pm Tue, to 10pm Wed & Thu;
4:30pm-11pm Fri & Sat) This New American
experiment dominates St Pete's restaurant scene.
Try divine house carpaccio with leek, goat's
cheese mousse, a touch of truffle oil and a single
ravioli stuffed with deliciously runny egg yolk.

Sarasota ⑧

✖ Jim's Small Batch Bakery   Bakery $

(📞941-922-2253; 2336 Gulf Gate Dr; items $1-10;
⏱8am-6pm Mon, to 4pm Tue-Thu, 9am-4pm Fri &
Sat) A delicious stop for breakfast and lunch. All-
butter croissants, candied bacon BLTs, creamy
quiches and cups of soup for $3.50.

🛏 Hotel Ranola   Boutique Hotel $$

(📞941-951-0111; www.hotelranola.com; 118
Indian Pl; r $109-179, ste $239-269; P ❄ 🤶)
The nine rooms feel like a designer's brownstone
apartment: free-spirited and effortlessly artful,
but with real working kitchens. It's urban funk,
walkable to downtown Sarasota.

Sanibel Island ⑩

✖ Island Cow   Southern US $$

(📞239-472-0606; www.sanibelislandcow.com;
2163 Periwinkle Way; mains $8-19; ⏱7am-10pm)
This colorful island cafe serves up breakfasts,
sandwiches, wraps and tropical cocktails. Live
music makes it an easy choice any time of day.

Overseas Highway to Key West

5

Redefining the road trip, the Overseas Hwy lets you drive straight out into the ocean toward Cuba, surrounded by water as you hop from island to island.

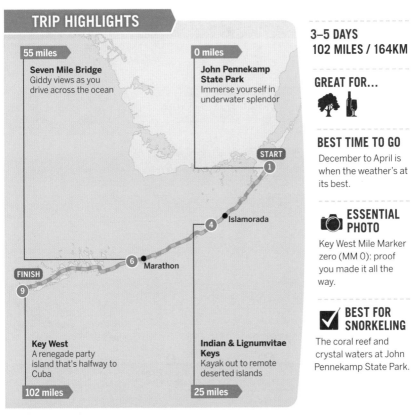

TRIP HIGHLIGHTS

55 miles
Seven Mile Bridge
Giddy views as you drive across the ocean

0 miles
John Pennekamp State Park
Immerse yourself in underwater splendor

START
1

4 Islamorada

6 Marathon

FINISH
9

Key West
A renegade party island that's halfway to Cuba
102 miles

Indian & Lignumvitae Keys
Kayak out to remote deserted islands
25 miles

3–5 DAYS
102 MILES / 164KM

GREAT FOR...

BEST TIME TO GO
December to April is when the weather's at its best.

ESSENTIAL PHOTO
Key West Mile Marker zero (MM 0): proof you made it all the way.

BEST FOR SNORKELING
The coral reef and crystal waters at John Pennekamp State Park.

Key Largo Boaters enjoy the clear, protected waters of Molasses Reef

Classic Trip

5 Overseas Highway to Key West

There's no better way — short of hopping on a plane — to enjoy such an utter feeling of escape from the mainland as driving through the Florida Keys. The motto here seems to be 'do whatever the hell you want.' Pull off the highway for biker bars, seafood grills and blissful beaches — wherever and whenever the crazy spirit of these islands moves you.

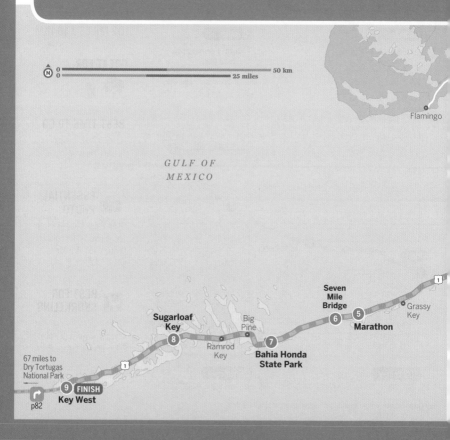

0 — 50 km
0 — 25 miles

GULF OF MEXICO

Flamingo

Seven Mile Bridge

6

Sugarloaf Key

8

Big Pine

5 Marathon

Grassy Key

1

Ramrod Key

7 Bahia Honda State Park

67 miles to Dry Tortugas National Park

1

9 FINISH Key West

p82

① John Pennekamp State Park

The Keys don't dillydally in delivering an oceanic treat. One of the first things you'll encounter on the Overseas Hwy is **John Pennekamp Coral Reef State Park** (☎305-451-6300; www.pennekamp park.com; Mile 102.6 ocean-side; car with 1/2 people $4.50/9, cyclist or pedestrian $2.50; ☻8am-sunset, aquarium to 5pm; **P** 👪), the USA's first underwater park.

HURRICANE IRMA

Research for this trip was conducted before the devastating category 4 hurricane Irma hit Florida in September 2017. Those planning to travel to the Florida Keys please see p338 for details.

It's a true jewel box beneath the sea, a vast living coral reef that's home to a panoply of sea life. You never know what you'll see underwater, except for one predictable favorite: the oft-photographed statue Christ of the Deep, a sunken 4000lb bronze statue.

Your options for exploring the reef include a popular 2½-hour glass-bottom boat tour on a 65ft catamaran from which you can ooh and aah at fili-greed flaps of soft coral, technicolor schools of fish, dangerous-looking barracudas and massive sea turtles.

You can also take a snorkeling or two-tank diving trip, or go DIY and rent a canoe ($20 per hour) or kayak ($12/30 per hour/half day) and journey through a 3-mile network of water trails. Call the park for reservations and departure times.

Everglades National Park

12 miles to ②

42 miles to ①

Key Largo

John Pennekamp State Park ① START

② **Key Largo**

Tavernier

Florida Bay

③ **Islamorada**

④

Indian & Lignumvitae Keys

LINK YOUR TRIP

1 Highway 1
Only a 60-mile stretch of Hwy 1 separates these two trips; combining them is a natural.

2 The Everglades
This trip is the other way out of the Keys, starting on the eastern edge of the Everglades less than an hour from Key Largo.

Classic Trip

The Drive » Your instructions for most of this trip will be the same: drive further southwest along the Overseas Hwy. This first leg is a short one; the park and the town of Key Largo are practically spooning.

- - - - - - - - - - - - - - - - - -

❷ Key Largo

Key Largo (both the name of the town and the island it's on) is slightly underwhelming at a glance, especially given the romantic notions that may have been placed in your head by hearing it mentioned in pop culture references ranging from Humphrey Bogart to the Beach Boys.

As you drive onto the islands, Key Largo resembles a long line of low-lying hammock and strip development. But that's from the highway. Head down a side road and duck into this warm little bar, or that converted Keys plantation house, and the island idiosyncrasies become more pronounced.

Speaking of pop culture, the actual **African Queen** (☏305-451-8080; www.africanqueenflkeys. com; 99701 Overseas Hwy, Key Largo Holiday Inn; canal cruise/dinner cruise $49/89) – a steamboat used in the 1951 movie starring Humphrey Bogart and

Katharine Hepburn – has been restored to her former, er, splendor, and you can relive the movie aboard the tiny vessel on a canal or dinner cruise. If you behave better than Hepburn's character, the captain might even let you take the helm for a bit.

✗ 🛏 p83

The Drive » Continue south to your next stop, Islamorada, which sounds like an island but is actually a string of several islands. It is here where the trees open up and you finally start to feel like you're in the islands.

- - - - - - - - - - - - - - - - - -

❸ Islamorada

When you reach Islamorada, you'll finally feel like you're in the islands. Here at last are unbroken horizons of sea and sky, one perfect shade of blue mirroring the other. Near mile marker 73.5, sandy **Anne's Beach** (Mile 73.5 oceanside; 👶) opens upon a sky-bright stretch of calm waters for splashing about beside a tunnel of hardwood hammock. Kids will love getting stuck in the tidal mudflats. Down the road, **Robbie's Marina** (☏305-664-8070; www.robbies.com; Mile 77.5 bayside; kayak & stand-up paddleboard rentals $45-80; ⏱9am-8pm; 👶) is a combo tourist shop, fishing marina and cruise-boat operator. From here you can kayak over to the virgin tropical rainforest of Lignumvitae Key, tour Indian

Key's historical ruins or go fishing on a party boat. Don't forget to look in on the fearsome tarpon fish before you leave.

✗ p83

The Drive » You can't drive to your next stop; like many of the Keys, these two can only be reached by boat. You can rent a canoe or kayak or catch a charter from Robbie's Marina.

- - - - - - - - - - - - - - - - - -

TRIP HIGHLIGHT

❹ Indian & Lignumvitae Keys

Take a boat tour or paddle out to either of these remote islands, both of which are on the National Register of Historic Places and offer a serene glimpse into what Florida was like before cars, condos and cheap souvenir T-shirts.

An island ghost town, **Indian Key** (☏305-664-2540; www.floridastateparks. org/indiankey; Mile 78.5 oceanside; $2.50; ⏱8am-sunset) contains the ruins of a 19th-century settlement. In the 1830s it was a thriving town, complete with a warehouse, docks, streets, hotel and about 40 to 50 permanent residents. However, the settlement was wiped out in a Native American attack during the Second Seminole War, and now all that remains are crumbling foundations. It's a serene if sometimes eerie experience, to walk among ruins and paddle around in utter isolation.

On the bay side, the isolated **Lignumvitae Key Botanical State Park** (☎305-664-2540; www.floridastateparks.org/lignumvitaekey; admission/tour $2.50/2; ⏱8am-5pm Thu-Mon, tours 10am & 2pm Fri-Sun Dec-Apr) has virgin tropical forests and the 1919-built Matheson House. Douse yourself in bug spray and consider long sleeves – mosquitoes have overtaken the island – to see some beautifully undeveloped island during weekend tours.

The Drive » From Robbie's Marina, settle in for a half-hour drive to Marathon, the halfway point between Key Largo and Key West.

- - - - - - - - - - - - - - - - - -

⑤ Marathon

Marathon sits right on the halfway point between Key Largo and Key West, and is a good place to stop on a road trip across the islands. It's perhaps the most 'developed' key outside Key West, in the sense that it has large shopping centers and a population of a few thousand.

Stop and stretch your legs at **Crane Point Museum** (☎305-743-9100; www.cranepoint.net; Mile 50.5 bayside; adult/child $15/10; ⏱9am-5pm Mon-Sat, from noon Sun; P 🚻 👶), a nature center with walking trails through a hardwood hammock and wildlife exhibits for kids, including marine

touch tanks. And if you're ready to hop in the ocean, **Sombrero Beach** (Sombrero Beach Rd, off Mile 50 oceanside; ⏱7:30am-dusk; P 🚻 👶) is a wonderful park with shady picnic areas, nicer-than-you'd-expect bathrooms and a playscape for the kiddos. It's one of the few white-sand, mangrove-free beaches in the Keys.

🍴 🛏 p83

The Drive » The almost aptly named Seven Mile Bridge starts just past Marathon and continues on for (shhh, don't tell) just under 7 miles.

- - - - - - - - - - - - - - - - - -

TRIP HIGHLIGHT

⑥ Seven Mile Bridge

Take a deep breath because next up on the horizon is the gasp-worthy Seven Mile Bridge. Florida is full of head-spinning cause-ways, but none longer than this beauty soaring over the Gulf of Mexico. Driving across it provides one of the most memorable stretches of road anywhere.

Parallel to the road is the **Old Seven Mile Bridge**, a hurricane-battered railway and auto causeway no longer in use. Below the old bridge, about 2 miles from the mainland, **Pigeon Key** (☎305-743-5999; www.pigeonkey.net; Mile 47 oceanside; adult/child $12/9; ⏱tours 10am, noon & 2pm) is a National Historic District. Hop on a ferry over to the island to amble around an early 20th-century railroad workers' village built by real-estate tycoon Henry Flagler, or come just for the snorkeling and sun-splashed beach.

The Drive » Just a couple of miles after the bridge touches down and you're back on land, you'll reach the entrance to Bahia Honda State Park on your left.

- - - - - - - - - - - - - - - - - -

⑦ Bahia Honda State Park

This park, with its long, white-sand (and seaweed-strewn) beach is the big attraction in these parts. As Keys beaches go, this

TOP TIP: MILE MARKERS

Many Keys' addresses are noted by their proximity to mile markers (indicated as MM), which start at MM 126 in Florida City and count down to MM 0 in Key West. They might indicate whether they're 'oceanside,' which is the south side of the highway, or 'bayside,' which is north.

Classic Trip

WHY THIS IS A CLASSIC TRIP
MARIELLA KRAUSE, WRITER

This is one of my favorite road trips of all time. Leaving the mainland gives you a unique sense of escape, and when you're out there surrounded by ocean, you can't help but feel like you've truly gotten away. It's only fitting that quirky Key West is the last stop – your reward for going all the way to the end.

Top: Rail bridge and beach, Bahia Honda State Park
Left: Perky's Bat Tower, Sugarloaf Key
Right: Happy hour by the wharf, Key West

one is probably the best natural stretch of sand in the island chain, but we wouldn't vote it best beach in the continental USA (although Condé Nast did...in 1992). As a tourist, the more novel experience is walking a stretch of the old Bahia Honda Rail Bridge, which offers nice views of the surrounding islands. Or check out the nature trails (ooh, butterflies!) and science center, where helpful park employees help you identify stone crabs, fireworms, horseshoe crabs and comb jellies.

The **park concession** (☎305-872-3210; www.bahiahondapark.com; Mile 37; car $4-8, cyclist & pedestrian $2.50; ⏰8am-sunset; 🚿) offers daily 1½-hour snorkeling trips at 9:30am and 1:30pm (adult/child $30/25). Reservations are a good idea in high season.

The Drive » Your next stop is another 17 miles along, and you'll need directions to find it. On Sugarloaf Key, turn right at the sign for the Sugarloaf airport, near mile marker 17, then take the right side of the fork in the road.

----

⑧ Sugarloaf Key

Ready for a little tidbit of randomness? Just off the highway (only about one minute out of your way) you'll find **Perky's Bat Tower**, a 1920s real-estate-developer's vision gone awry. To eliminate

Classic Trip

pesky mosquitoes from his planned vacation resort, Richter Perky imported a colony of bats (he'd heard they'd eat mosquitoes) and moved them into a custom-made 35ft tower that resembles an Aztec-inspired fire lookout. The bats promptly flew off, never to return, and the mosquitoes lived happily on. The tower is the only vestige of the development that would have been.

The Drive » Can you feel the excitement? You're only about half an hour away from the end of the road: Key West. Or is that the beginning of the road? Hwy 1 technically begins in Key West, counting up from mile marker zero. Once you hit town, drive all the way to the edge;

that's where the heart of Old Town is located.

TRIP HIGHLIGHT

❾ Key West

Key West has enjoyed a long and colorful history that includes pirates, sunken treasures, literary legends and lots of ghosts. A visit to the **Ernest Hemingway Home and Museum** (📞305-294-1136; www.hemingwayhome.com; 907 Whitehead St; adult/child $14/6; ⏱9am-5pm) is practically mandatory, him being the unofficial patron saint of Key West and all. Bearded docents lead tours every half-hour, during which they spin yarns of Papa, his wives and his famous six-toed cats.

Love a good ghost story? Key West is full of them. You might just find out your guesthouse is

haunted during the **Key West Ghost & Mysteries Tour** (📞786-530-3122; www.keywestghostandmysteries tour.com; tours depart from Duval & Caroline Sts; adult/child $18/10; ⏱tours 9pm), and you'll hear all about the creepy antics that got Robert the haunted doll confined to **East Martello** (📞305-296-3913; www.kwahs.org/museums/fort-east-martello/history; 3501 S Roosevelt Blvd; adult/child $10/5; ⏱9:30am-4:30pm).

The Keys are home to the only living coral barrier reef in the United States, which means snorkeling here is excellent. Warm, clear water and white sand make conditions ideal, and the fish are vibrant about a half-hour boat ride from the island.

At sunset, crowds fill **Mallory Square** (www.mallorysquare.com; 🚻) for the Sunset Celebration, a nightly festival where you'll see jugglers, fire-eaters and street performers of every stripe. And at the end of the day, bar aficionados flock to the **Green Parrot** (📞305-294-6133; www.green parrot.com; 601 Whitehead St; ⏱10am-4am), a fine purveyor of old-school Key West ambience. Purported to be the oldest bar on the island, it's also one of the best places in town to hear a live band.

🍴 🛏 p83

DETOUR: DRY TORTUGAS NATIONAL PARK

Start: ❾ Key West

Seventy miles beyond the end of the Overseas Hwy, **Dry Tortugas National Park** (📞305-242-7700; www.nps.gov/drto) is a 2¼-hour ferry ride or 40-minute seaplane flight out into the Gulf of Mexico. This small cluster of coral reefs, named 'The Turtles' by Spanish explorer Ponce de León, is a hot spot for diving, snorkeling, bird-watching, fishing and exploring Civil War–era **Fort Jefferson**, a striking hexagonal centerpiece of red brick rising up from the emerald waters. Getting here isn't easy, or cheap, but it's worth it for the middle-of-nowhere experience at America's most inaccessible national park.

Eating & Sleeping

Key Largo ❷

✕ Alabama Jack's   Bar $
(58000 Card Sound Rd; ⊘11am-7pm) Everyone raves about the conch fritters; and the fact that Jack's closes nightly due to onslaughts of mosquitoes means it's as authentically Florida as they come. Country bands take the stage on weekends from 2pm to 5pm. It's just before the tollbooth over the Card Sound Bridge.

✕ Mrs Mac's Kitchen   American $$
(☏305-451-3722; www.mrsmacskitchen.com; Mile 99.4 bayside; mains breakfast & lunch $9-16, dinner $16-30; ⊘7am-9:30pm Mon-Sat; P 🐾) At homey Mrs Mac's service is warm and personable, and the breakfasts are delicious. The menu packs in locals, visitors, their dogs and pretty much everyone else on the island.

🛏 Largo Resort   Hotel $$$
(☏305-451-0424; www.largoresort.com; Mile 102 bayside; r from $450; P ❄ 🛜 🏊) This secluded resort with private beach sits on three pristine acres. Sunny bungalows are beautifully appointed with king-sized beds, marble bathrooms with rain showers, and modern furnishings in a minimalist design, with greenery all around.

Islamorada ❸

✕ Island Grill   Seafood $$
(☏305-664-8400; www.keysislandgrill.com; 85501 Overseas Hwy; breakfast $5-10, mains $9-25; ⊘7am-10pm Sun-Thu, to 11pm Fri & Sat) The ramshackle waterfront building may not look like much, but you'll be surprised by how tasty the peel-and-eat shrimp and conch fritters are. Casual, contemporary Floribbean fare with breezy ocean views and lotsa live bands.

Marathon ❺

✕ Keys Fisheries   Seafood $$
(☏866-743-4353; www.keysfisheries.com; 3502 Louisa St; mains $12-27; ⊘11am-9pm; P 🐾) The lobster Reuben is the stuff of legend here. Sweet, chunky, creamy – so good you'll be daydreaming about it afterward. But all the seafood is excellent. Expect pleasant levels of seagull harassment as you dine on a working waterfront.

🛏 Lime Tree Bay Resort Motel Motel $$
(☏305-664-4740; www.limetreebayresort. com; Mile 68.5 bayside; r $180-360; ❄ 🛜 🏊) Hammocks and lawn chairs provide front-row seats for spectacular sunsets at this 2.5-acre waterfront hideaway. Rooms are comfortably set, the best with balconies overlooking the water. Extensive facilities include tennis courts, bikes, kayaks and stand-up paddleboards.

Key West ❽

✕ Camille's   Fusion $$
(☏305-296-4811; www.camilleskeywest.com; 1202 Simonton St; mains breakfast & lunch $6-15, dinner $18-28; ⊘8am-3pm & 6-10pm; 🌿) For more than two decades the homey facade of locals' favorite Camille's has concealed a sharp kitchen that makes a mean chicken-salad sandwich, stone crab claws with Dijon mayo and a macadamia-crusted yellowtail.

✕ Blue Heaven   American $$$
(☏305-296-8666; www.blueheavenkw.com; 729 Thomas St; mains breakfast & lunch $10-17, dinner $22-35; ⊘8am-10:30pm; 🌿) Dine in a ramshackle, tropical plant-filled garden where Hemingway once officiated boxing matches. This place gets packed with customers who wolf down delectable breakfasts (blueberry pancakes) and Keys cuisine with French touches (yellowtail snapper with citrus beurre blanc).

🛏 Mermaid & the Alligator   Guesthouse $$$
(☏305-294-1894; www.kwmermaid.com; 729 Truman Ave; r winter $330-380, summer $230-290; P ❄ 🛜) It takes a real gem to stand out amid Keys hotels, but this place, in a 1904 mansion, more than pulls it off. Nine rooms are individually designed with a great mix of modern comfort, Keys Colonial ambience and playfulness.

🛏 Cypress House   Hotel $$$
(☏305-294-5229; www.historickewyinns. com/the-inns/cypress-house/; 601 Caroline St; r $240-350; P ❄ 🛜 🏊) This plantation-like getaway has wraparound porches, leafy grounds, a secluded swimming pool and spacious, individually designed bedrooms with attractive modern furnishings in the heart of Old Town.

STRETCH YOUR LEGS
MIAMI BEACH

Start/Finish Ocean Dr

Distance 3 miles

Duration Three hours

Greater Miami sprawls, but compact Miami Beach packs in the sights, making it perfect for an afternoon of exploring on foot. Get a taste of its famous art-deco district, as well as its luscious, white-sand beaches.

Take this walk on Trip

1

Ocean Drive

Ocean Dr is the classic Miami strip, where neon-accented art-deco buildings line the way for an endless parade of cars, in-line skaters and pedestrians. Stop at the **Art Deco Museum** (www. mdpl.org/welcome-center/art-deco-museum; 1001 Ocean Dr; $5; ☉10am-5pm Tue-Sun, to 7pm Thu) for an overview of South Beach architectural style, from its tropical and nautical motifs to those eye-catching cantilevered eyebrows.

The Walk » Head north. To fully appreciate the architecture, stick to the park side of the street. At 13th St, note the Carlyle Hotel, where *The Birdcage* was filmed. Cross Lummus Park to get to the beach.

Lummus Park & South Beach

Take off your shoes and dig your toes into some of the most luscious sand you've ever felt, and stare out at (or run straight toward) the teal-green water that's shallow and warm enough to splash around in for hours. Run up and down if you must – cartwheels in the sand would not be inappropriate – but be sure to notice the six floridly colored lifeguard stands that stretch along this strip.

The Walk » Walk (or wade) up the beach and find the path that takes you to Lincoln Rd just past the Loews Hotel. (If you get to the Sagamore you've gone too far.) Walk two blocks west along Lincoln until you reach Washington Ave.

Lincoln Road Mall

Calling Lincoln Rd a mall is technically accurate, but misses the point. Yes, you can shop, and there are sidewalk cafes galore. But this outdoor pedestrian promenade between Alton Rd and Washington Ave is really about seeing and being seen; there are times when it feels less like a road and more like a runway.

The Walk » Head south down busy Collins Ave, another thoroughfare that's lined with deco treasures. At 13th St, hop over one block to Washington Ave.

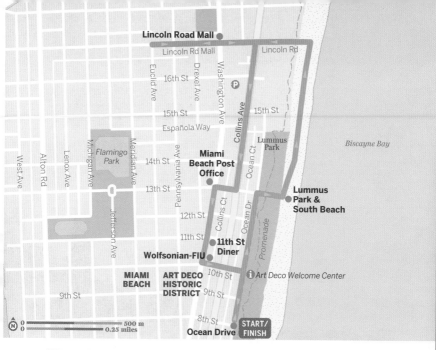

Miami Beach Post Office

Ahhh, Miami Beach. Even its municipal buildings are treasured works of art. A fine example of Streamline Moderne, the **Miami Beach Post Office** (1300 Washington Ave; ⊙8am-5pm Mon-Fri, 8:30am-2pm Sat) was built in 1937 as part of the Works Progress Administration (WPA). Duck inside to mail some postcards and check out the striking ceiling mural of a stylized night sky.

The Walk » Just two blocks down – and they're not very interesting blocks, so we're tempted to send you back over to Collins – is a vintage dining experience.

11th St Diner

Many art-deco buildings evoke modes of transportation, such as planes, trains or ships. Well, the shiny little 11th St Diner (p47) does more than evoke: it's actually housed in a classic Pullman train car. Pull over for refreshments; the inside is as cute as the outside.

The Walk » Now that you're refreshed, head just a few doors down; your next stop is in the same block.

Wolfsonian-FIU

A fascinating museum that's part of Florida International University, the **Wolfsonian-FIU** (☎305-531-1001; www.wolfsonian.org; 1001 Washington Ave; adult/child $10/5, 6-9pm Fri free; ⊙10am-6pm Mon, Tue, Thu & Sat, to 9pm Fri, noon-6pm Sun, closed Wed) showcases artifacts from the height of the Industrial Revolution from the late 19th to mid-20th century. The exhibits span transportation, urbanism, industrial design, advertising and political propaganda, and give some intriguing insight as to what was going on in the world while all that deco was being built.

The Walk » It's just two short blocks along 10th St to get back to Ocean Dr. Between 7th and 8th is a fetching strip of buildings including the Colony Hotel, which you'll recognize instantly if you've ever watched anything set in Miami Beach.

The Carolinas

Sparkling beaches, rugged mountains and have-another-biscuit hospitality. Yep, the Carolinas share more than just a name and a border.

For a drive on the wild side, North Carolina is the place to start. In the western mountains the Blue Ridge Parkway and Great Smokies serve up wildlife, white water and lofty peaks. In the east, windswept dunes and roaming mustangs keep the cruising wild in the Outer Banks.

South Carolina has its share of adventure, but the scenery and history slow the pace. Lowcountry roads meander past plantations and mossy live oaks while Upcountry byways take in battlefields and mountain foothills. And rocking chairs are everywhere – just waiting to ruin your itinerary.

Blue Ridge Parkway Riding on the Linn Cove Viaduct
MATT MUNRO / LONELY PLANET ©

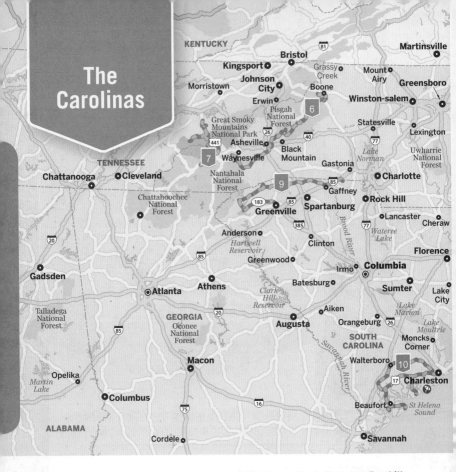

The Carolinas

DON'T MISS

Biltmore Legacy
For less of the formality and more of the family, visit the new Vanderbilt exhibit on Trip 6

Museum of the Cherokee Indian
Learn about three Cherokee chiefs who journeyed to England and met with King George III on Trip 7

Bodie Island Lighthouse
This 1872 lighthouse with an original Fresnel lens is open to visitors. Visit on Trip 8

Cowpens National Battlefield
Walk the battlefield to witness how terrain, planning and luck propelled Patriot forces to victory on Trip 9

King's Farm Market
You'll spend more time than planned at this roadside market where the conversation is easy and the baked goods delicious. Visit on Trip 10

Jockey's Ridge State Park Hang-gliding above the dunes

Classic Trip

Blue Ridge Parkway

6

This drive on the USA's favorite byway curves through the leafy Appalachians, where it swoops up the East Coast's highest peak and stops by the nation's largest mansion.

TRIP HIGHLIGHTS

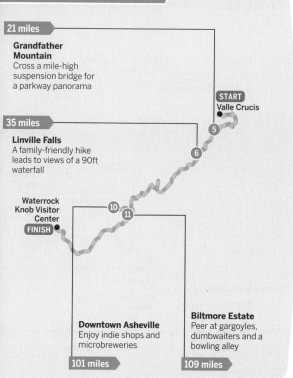

21 miles

Grandfather Mountain
Cross a mile-high suspension bridge for a parkway panorama

35 miles

Linville Falls
A family-friendly hike leads to views of a 90ft waterfall

Waterrock Knob Visitor Center
FINISH

START
Valle Crucis

Downtown Asheville
Enjoy indie shops and microbreweries
101 miles

Biltmore Estate
Peer at gargoyles, dumbwaiters and a bowling alley
109 miles

**5 DAYS
210 MILES / 338KM**

GREAT FOR...

BEST TIME TO GO
May to October for leafy trees and open attractions.

ESSENTIAL PHOTO
The mile-high suspension bridge at Grandfather Mountain.

BEST FOR FAMILIES
Enjoy a steam-train ride, gem mining, easy hiking and old-fashioned candy.

Grandfather Mountain The famed 228ft-long suspension bridge

Classic Trip

6 Blue Ridge Parkway

The Blue Ridge Parkway stretches 469 miles, from Shenandoah National Park in Virginia to Great Smoky Mountains National Park in North Carolina. In the Tar Heel State, the road carves a sinuous path through a rugged landscape of craggy peaks, crashing waterfalls, thick forests and charming mountain towns. Three things you'll see? Whitetail deer, local microbrews and signs for Grandfather Mountain. And one piece of advice: at breakfast, never say no to a biscuit.

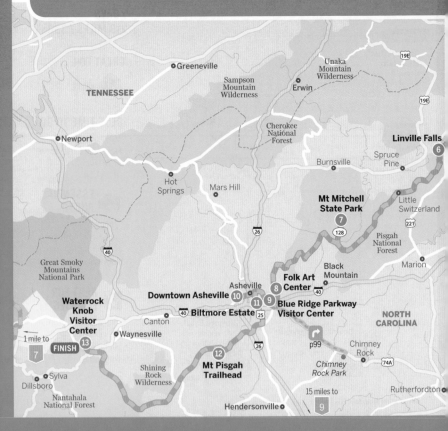

1 Valle Crucis

How do you start a road trip through the mountains? With a good night's sleep and all the right gear. You'll find both in Valle Crucis, a bucolic village west of Boone. After slumbering beneath sumptuous linens at the Mast Farm Inn (p100), a 200-year-old farmhouse, ease into the day sipping coffee from a rocking chair on the inn's front porch.

Down the road is the **Original Mast General Store** (☎828-963-6511; www. mastgeneralstore.com; Hwy 194; ⏰10am-6pm Mon-Sat, noon-6pm Sun; 🚻) and its **Annex** (⏰7am-6:30pm Mon-Sat, noon-6pm Sun). The first of several Mast general stores across the region, the original sells many of the same products that it did when it opened in 1883. Today you'll find bacon and hard candy as well as hiking shoes and French country hand towels. The Annex building, just south on Hwy 194, sells outdoor apparel and hiking gear.

🛏 p100

The Drive » Drive south on Hwy 194, also known as Broadstone Rd, through 3 miles of rural splendor. At Hwy 105 turn left.

---

2 Boone

If you're traveling with kids or wannabe prospectors, stop at **Foggy Mountain Gem Mine** (☎828-963-4367; www.foggymountaingems. com; 4416 Hwy 105 S; buckets $30-325; ⏰10am-5pm; 🚻) to pan for semiprecious stones, which are sold by the bucketload. There are several gem-mining spots near the parkway, but Foggy Mountain, a smaller company, is operated by graduate gemologists who may take their craft a bit more seriously. After sifting your rocks in a miner's flume line, the gemologists will cut and mount your favorite finds in any number of settings.

In downtown Boone, home of Appalachian State, you'll find shopping and dining on **King St**. Keep an eye out for the bronze statue of local bluegrass legend Doc Watson. He's strumming a Gallagher guitar like nobody's business at the corner of King and Depot Sts.

🍴 p100

The Drive » From King St, turn on to Hwy 321 just past the Dan'l Boone Inn restaurant. Drive 4 miles then turn right at the theme park.

Valle Crucis
START 1
Boone
2
105 421
Moses H Cone
Memorial Park
4 321
105 5 3 Blowing Rock
Grandfather Mountain
321
Lake James
Morganton

N 0 ____ 20 km
0 ____ 10 miles

LINK YOUR TRIP

7 The Great Smokies
Continue past the last parkway milepost, Mile 469, to the entrance to the national park.

9 Greenville & Cherokee Foothills Scenic Highway
Drive south on Hwy 25 from Asheville to South Carolina and SC 11.

Classic Trip

❸ Blowing Rock

The parkway runs just above the village of Blowing Rock, which sits at an elevation of 4000ft. On a cloudy morning, drive south on Hwy 321 to the top of the mountain to check out the cloud-capped views of surrounding peaks. The eastern continental divide runs through the bar at the Green Park Inn (p100), a white-clapboard grand hotel that opened in 1891. They say author Margaret Mitchell worked on *Gone with the Wind* while staying here.

A rite of passage for every North Carolina child is the **Tweetsie Railroad** (☎800-526-5740; www.tweetsie.com; 300 Tweetsie Railroad Lane; adult $45, child 3-12yr $30; ⏰9am-6pm daily Jun–mid-Aug, Fri-Sun mid-Apr–May, mid-Aug–Oct; ♿), a theme park where Appalachian culture meets the Wild West. The highlight? A 1917 coal-fired steam locomotive that chugs past marauding Indians and heroic cowboys. Midway rides, fudge shops and family-friendly shows round out the fun.

🍴🛏 p100

The Drive » The entrance to the Blue Ridge Parkway is in Blowing Rock, 2.3 miles south of the Tweetsie Railroad. Once on the parkway, drive south 2 miles.

❹ Moses H Cone Memorial Park

Hikers and equestrians share 25 miles of carriage roads on the former **estate** (Mile 294) of Moses H Cone, a wealthy philanthropist and conservationist who made his fortune in denim. His mansion and grounds were given to the national park service in the 1950s. His Colonial Revival mansion, completed in 1901, now houses the **Parkway Craft Center** (☎828-295-7938; www.southernhighlandguild.org; Mile 294; ⏰9am-5pm mid-Mar–Nov). The shop sells high-end crafts made by members of the Southern Highland Craft Guild. Free tours of the 2nd floor of

---

BLUE RIDGE PARKWAY TRIP PLANNER

Construction of the parkway began in 1935, during the Great Depression, after the government harnessed the strength of thousands of out-of-work young men in the Civilian Conservation Corps. The parkway wasn't fully linked together until 1987, when the Lynn Cove Viaduct opened.

» The maximum speed limit is 45mph.

» Long stretches of the road close in winter and may not reopen until March. Many visitor centers and campgrounds are closed until May. Check the park service website (www.nps.gov/blri) for the latest information about road closures and the opening dates for facilities.

» The North Carolina section of the parkway begins at Mile 216.9, between the Blue Ridge Mountain Center in Virginia and Cumberland Knob in North Carolina.

» There are 26 tunnels on the parkway in North Carolina (and just one in Virginia). Watch for signs to turn on your headlights.

» For more trip-planning tools, check the websites for the Blue Ridge Parkway Association (www.blueridgeparkway.org) and the Blue Ridge National Heritage Area (www.blueridgeheritage.com).

the mansion, Flat Top Manor, are offered on Saturdays and Sundays June through mid-October at 10am, 11am, 2pm and 3pm. Tours fill up. To reserve a spot call ☎828-295-3782 on the Friday before your visit.

The Drive ›› Head south on the parkway, passing split rail fences, stone walls, streams and meadows. Just south of Mile 304 the parkway curves across the Linn Cove Viaduct, the last section of the parkway to be completed, in 1987, because of the terrain's fragility. Exit on to Hwy 221 at Mile 305 and drive 1 mile south.

- - - - - - - - - - - - - - - - - -

TRIP HIGHLIGHT

❺ Grandfather Mountain

Don't let a fear of heights keep you from driving up to the famed swinging bridge near the peaks of **Grandfather Mountain** (☎828-733-4337; www.grandfather.com; Blue Ridge Pkwy Mile 305, Linville; adult $20, child 4-12yr $9; ⊙8am-7pm Jun-Aug, closes earlier fall, winter & spring). Yes, the 228ft-long bridge is 1 mile above sea level and yes, you can hear its steel girders 'sing' on gusty days, but the ground is just 80ft below the span. Nothing to sneeze at, for sure, but it's not the Grand Canyon, and the views of nearby mountains are superb. The small nature museum spotlights local flora and fauna as well as regional explorer Daniel Boone.

Behind the museum, black bears, deer and otters roam a small animal habitat. Grandfather Mountain is a Unesco Biosphere Reserve.

Park attractions have been privately managed by the Morton family since the 1950s. The North Carolina State Park System purchased the mountain's backcountry lands in 2008, and Grandfather Mountain State Park (www.ncparks.gov) was established the following year. State park trails can be accessed from the parkway for free, or from parking lots inside the attraction with paid admission. The strenuous but varied Grandfather Trail runs 2.4 miles from the suspension bridge parking lot along the mountain's crest, ending atop Calloway Peak; the trail includes cables and ladders.

The Drive ›› Follow the parkway south and turn left just south of Mile 316 to reach Linville Falls.

- - - - - - - - - - - - - - - - - -

TRIP HIGHLIGHT

❻ Linville Falls

Have time for just one hike? Then hop out of your car for the moderate 1.6-mile Erwin's View Trail (round-trip) at popular Linville Falls. Here, the Linville River sweeps over two separate falls before crashing 2000ft through a rocky gorge. The trail crosses

the river then follows it downstream. At half a mile, a spur trail leads to a view of the Upper Falls. The 90ft Lower Falls are visible from the Chimney View and Gorge View overlooks just ahead. At the latter you'll also see the imposing Linville Gorge. Ponder the scope of it all at the trail's last stop, the Erwin's View Overlook.

The Drive ›› Drive south on the parkway and turn right, south of Mile 355, on to NC 128. Follow NC 128 into the park.

- - - - - - - - - - - - - - - - - -

❼ Mt Mitchell State Park

Be warned. A trip to **Mt Mitchell** (☎828-675-4611; www.ncparks.gov; 2388 State Hwy 128; ⊙7am-10pm May-Aug, closes earlier rest of year) might lead to a fight. Will you drive to the top of the highest mountain east of the Mississippi, or will you hike there? Make your decision at the park office (open 8am to 5pm daily April to October; closed weekends November to March), which sits beside a 2-mile trail to the 6684ft summit.

At the top you'll see the grave of the mountain's namesake, Dr Elisha Mitchell. A dedicated professor from the University of North Carolina, he died after a fall while trying to verify the height of the mountain in 1857. A circular ramp beside the grave

Classic Trip

ALEX GRICHENKO / GETTY IMAGES ©

MARY TERRIBERRY / SHUTTERSTOCK ©

WHY THIS IS A CLASSIC TRIP
KEVIN RAUB, WRITER

As a card-carrying member of the road-trip fan club, I rank the iconic Blue Ridge Parkway right up there with the best of the great American four-wheeled journeys. In the fall, the parkway comes alive in a kaleidoscopic barrage of intense color, turning one of the country's most fabled roads into a fantastical passageway of deep ruby red and burnt-orange foliage.

Top: View across Lake Lure
Left: Linville Lower Falls
Right: Bluegrass musicians, Asheville

leads to panoramic views of the surrounding Black Mountains and beyond.

The Drive ❯❯ Return to the parkway and drive south to Mile 382. During the last two weeks of June look for blooming rhododendrons.

----

❽ Folk Art Center

As you enter the lobby at the **Folk Art Center** (📞828-298-7928; www.south ernhighlandguild.org; Mile 382; 🕙9am-6pm Apr-Dec, to 5pm Jan-Mar), look up. A row of handcrafted Appalachian chairs hangs from the walls above. They're an impressive calling card for the gallery here, which is dedicated to Southern artisanship. The chairs are part of the Southern Highland Craft Guild's permanent collection, which holds more than 2400 traditional and modern crafts. Items from the collection – pottery, baskets, quilts, woodcarvings – are displayed on the 2nd floor. The Allanstand Craft Shop on the 1st floor sells a range of fine traditional crafts.

The Drive ❯❯ Turn right on to the parkway and drive south. After crossing the Swannanoa River and I-40, continue to Mile 384.

----

❾ Blue Ridge Parkway Visitor Center

Sit back and let the scenery come to you at this helpful **visitor center**

Classic Trip

(☎828-298-5330; www.nps.
gov/blri; Mile 384; ⊙9am-
5pm), where a big-screen
film, *Blue Ridge Parkway
– America's Favorite
Journey*, captures the
beauty and wonder of the
drive. A park service rep-
resentative can provide
details about trails along
the parkway at the front
desk. For a list of regional sites and activities,
slide the digital monitor
across the interactive
I-Wall map at the back of
the main hall. The adja-
cent regional information
desk has brochures and
coupons for Asheville
area attractions.

The Drive ›› Drive north,
backtracking over the interstate
and river, and exit at Tunnel Rd,
which is Hwy 70. Drive west to
Hwy 240 west and follow it to
the exits for downtown Asheville.

TRIP HIGHLIGHT

⑩ Downtown Asheville

Hippies. Hipsters. Hikers.
And a few high-falutin'
preppies. This 4H Club
gives Asheville its funky
charm. Just look around.
Intellectual lefties gather
at **Malaprop's Bookstore
& Cafe** (☎828-254-6734;
www.malaprops.com; 55
Haywood St; ⊙9am-9pm Mon-
Sat, to 7pm Sun; 🛜), where
the shelves stretch from
banned books to South-
ern cooking. And the
hipsters? They're nibbling

silky truffles at **Chocolate
Fetish** (www.chocolatefetish.
com; 36 Haywood St; truffles
$2.25; ⊙11am-7pm Mon-Thu,
to 9pm Fri & Sat, noon-6pm
Sun) or sipping home-
grown ale at microbrew-
eries like the convivial
– and hoppy – **Wicked
Weed** (www.wickedweedbrew-
ing.com; 91 Biltmore Ave; pints
$4.50-6.40; ⊙11:30am-11pm
Mon & Tue, to midnight Wed &
Thu, to 1am Fri & Sat, noon-11pm
Sun; 🛜). At the engaging
Thomas Wolfe Memorial
(www.wolfememorial.com; 52
N Market St; museum free,
house tour adult $5, child 7-17yr
$2; ⊙9am-5pm Tue-Sat), the
city celebrates its most fa-
mous angsty son, Thomas
Wolfe, who penned the
Asheville-inspired novel
Look Homeward, Angel.

Hikers can shop for
new boots at the impres-
sive **Tops for Shoes**
(www.topsforshoes.com; 27 N
Lexington Ave; ⊙10am-6pm
Mon-Sat, 1-5pm Sun) and outdoor gear at **Mast General
Store** (www.mastgeneralstore.
com; 15 Biltmore Ave; ⊙10am-
6pm Mon-Thu, to 9pm Fri &
Sat, noon-6pm Sun). And the
preppies? They're working
inside the downtown
banks and law firms – and
checking out the same
places as everybody else.

The finishing touch?
The sidewalk busker
fiddling a high-lonesome
mountain tune. It'll put a
spring in your step while
maybe just breaking your
heart.

✕ 🛏 p100

BLUEGRASS & MOUNTAIN MUSIC

For locally grown fiddle-and-banjo music, grab your
dance partner and head deep into the hills of the High
Country. Regional shows and music jams are listed
on the Blue Ridge Music Trails (www.blueridgemusic.
org) and the Blue Ridge National Heritage Area (www.
blueridgeheritage.com) websites.

Here are three to get you started:

Mountain Home Music Concert Series (www.
mountainhomemusic.com) Spring through fall,
enjoy shows by Appalachian musicians in Boone on
scheduled Saturday nights.

Isis Music Hall (www.isisasheville.com) Local
bluegrass greats are known to pop into the Tuesday-
night sessions, an Asheville tradition.

Historic Orchard at Altapass (www.altapass
orchard.org) On weekends May through October,
settle in for an afternoon of music at Little
Switzerland, at Mile 328.

The Drive >> Follow Asheland Ave, which becomes McDowell St, south. After crossing the Swannanoa River, the entrance to the Biltmore Estate is on the right.

- - - - - - - - - - - - - - - -

TRIP HIGHLIGHT

⑪ Biltmore Estate

The destination that put Asheville on the map is the 175,000-sq-ft **Biltmore Estate** (☎ 800-411-3812; www.biltmore.com; 1 Approach Rd; adult $65, child 10-16yr $32.50; ⊙ house 9am-4:30pm, with seasonal variations). The French château–style megamansion, built by shipping and railroad heir George Vanderbilt II, was completed in 1895 after six years of work by hundreds of artists, craftspeople and educated professionals. The Vanderbilt-Cecil family still owns the estate. The entrance fee is steep, so arrive early to get your money's worth, and note that tours of the house are self-guided. The $11.75 audio tour is worth purchasing for the extra details. For an additional $20 you can take a general guided tour or join a specialized behind-the-scenes guided tour focusing on architecture, the family or the servants. Children aged 10 to 16 are free June through August with an adult paid admission.

In addition to the mansion there are gardens, trails, lakes, restaurants, two top-end hotels and a winery, with complimentary wine tasting. At the estate's Antler Hill Village, romantics shouldn't miss the new **Fashionable Romance: 60 Years of Vanderbilt Family Wedding Fashion** exhibit in the Biltmore Legacy building.

The Drive >> After exiting the grounds, turn right on to Hwy 25 and continue to the parkway, not quite 3.5 miles, and drive south.

- - - - - - - - - - - - - - - -

⑫ Mt Pisgah Trailhead

For a short hike to a panoramic view, pull into the parking lot beside the Mt Pisgah Trailhead just beyond Mile 407. From here, a 1.6-mile trail (one-way) leads to the mountain's 5721ft summit, which is topped by a lofty TV tower. The trail is steep and rocky in its final stretch, but you'll be rewarded with views of the French Broad River Valley

DETOUR: CHIMNEY ROCK PARK

Start: ⑩ **Downtown Asheville**

The American flag flaps in the breeze atop this popular park's namesake 315ft granite monolith. The top can be reached by elevator or by stairs – lots and lots of stairs. Once on top, look east for amazing views of Lake Lure. Another draw is the hike around the cliffs to 404ft Hickory Nut Falls. Scenes from the *Last of the Mohicans* were filmed at the **park** (www.chimneyrockpark.com; Hwy 64/74A; adult $15, child 5-15yr $7; ⊙ 8:30am-6pm mid-Mar–Nov, 10am-4:30pm Fri-Tue Dec–mid-Mar). There's a small exhibit about the movie inside the Sky Lounge. From Asheville, follow Hwy 74A east for 20 scenic, but very curvy, miles.

and Cold Mountain, the latter made famous by Charles Frazier's novel of the same name. One mile south is a campground, a general store, a restaurant and an inn.

The Drive >> The drive south passes the Graveyard Fields Overlook, which has short trails to scenic waterfalls. The 6047ft Richland-Balsam Overlook at Mile 431.4 is the highest point on the parkway. From here, continue south another 20 miles.

- - - - - - - - - - - - - - - -

⑬ Waterrock Knob Visitor Center

This trip ends at the Waterrock Knob Visitor Center (Mile 451.2), which sits at an elevation of nearly 6000ft. With a four-state view, this scenic spot is a great place to see where you've been and to assess what's ahead. Helpful signage attaches a name to the mountains on the distant horizons.

Eating & Sleeping

Valle Crucis ❶

🛏 Mast Farm Inn   B&B $$

(📞828-963-5857; www.themastfarminn.com;
2543 Broadstone Rd; r/cottage from $109/205;
🅿 ❄ 📶) In the beautiful hamlet of Valle
Crucis, this restored farmhouse defines rustic
chic with worn hardwood floors, claw-foot tubs
and handmade toffees on your bedside table.
Nine cabins and cottages also available. Settle
into the 1806 Loom House log cabin, fire up the
wood-burning fireplace and never leave.
Rates include an evening happy hour with local
cheeses and sweets.

Boone ❷

🍴 Dan'l Boone Inn   Southern US $$

(📞828-264-8657; www.danlbooneinn.com;
130 Hardin St; breakfast adult $11, child $6-8,
dinner adult $18, child $7-11; ⏲11:30am-8:30pm
Mon-Thu, to 9pm Fri & Sat, to 8:30pm Sun Jun-
Oct, hours vary rest of year; 📶👶) Quantity is
the name of the game at this restaurant, and
the family-style meals are a Boone (sorry) for
hungry hikers. Open since 1959. Cash or
check only.

🍴 Melanie's Food Fantasy   Cafe $$

(www.melaniesfoodfantasy.com; 664 W King St;
breakfast $6-10, lunch & dinner $9-14; ⏲8am-
2pm Mon-Wed, 8am-2pm & 5-9pm Thu-Fri,
8am-2:30pm & 5-9pm Sat, 8:30am-2:30pm
Sun; 🖊) On cutesy King St hippie types gobble
up serious breakfast dishes (scrambles, eggs
Benedict, omelets, waffles, pancakes) with a
side of home fries at this farm-to-fork favorite,
always with a vegetarian option (tempeh,
soysage etc). Later in the day, excellent creative
Southern fare (chipotle-honey salmon and grits,
blackened pimento-cheese burger) is on the
menu.

Blowing Rock ❸

🍴 Bistro Roca   Modern American $$

(📞828-295-4008; www.bistroroca.com; 143
Wonderland Trail; lunch $9-16, dinner $9-34;
⏲11am-3pm & 5-10pm Wed-Mon; 📶) This
cozy, lodge-like bistro, tucked just off Main
St, occupies a Prohibition-era building and
does upscale New American fare (lobster or
pork-belly mac 'n' cheese, kicked-up habanero
burgers, wood-fired pizzas, mountain-trout
banh-mi sandwiches) with an emphasis on local
everything. Order anything with the duck bacon
and you're all set.

🛏 Cliff Dwellers Inn   Motel $$

(📞828-414-9596; www.cliffdwellers.com; 116
Lakeview Tce; r/apt from $99/149; 🅿 ❄ 📶👶)
From its perch above town, this well-named
motel lures guests with good service,
reasonable prices, stylish rooms and balconies
with sweeping views.

🛏 Green Park Inn   Historic Hotel $$

(📞828-414-9230; www.greenparkinn.com; 9239
Valley Blvd; r $89-299; 🅿 ❄ 📶👶) The eastern
continental divide runs through the bar at this
white-clapboard grand hotel that opened in
1891. They say author Margaret Mitchell worked
on *Gone with the Wind* while staying here.

Asheville ❿

🍴 12 Bones   Barbecue $

(www.12bones.com; 5 Foundy St; dishes $5.50-
22; ⏲11am-4pm Mon-Fri) How good is this
BBQ? Well, former president Obama and wife
Michelle stopped by a few years ago for a meal.
The slow-cooked meats are smoky tender, and
the sides, from the jalapeño-cheese grits to the
smoked-potato salad, will bring you to the brink
of the wild heart of life.

✖ Sunny Point Cafe   Cafe $

(www.sunnypointcafe.com; 626 Haywood
Rd; breakfast $3.50-11, mains $6.50-14.50;
⊙8am-2:30pm Sun-Mon, to 9:30pm Tue-Sat)
In the morning, solos, couples and ladies-who-
breakfast fill this bright West Asheville spot
that's loved for its hearty, homemade fare. The
insanely good and towering huevos rancheros,
with feta cheese and chorizo sausage, should
come with an instruction manual! The cafe and
its alt-hippie waitstaff embraces the organic and
fresh, and even has its own garden. The biscuits
are divine.

✖ Admiral   Modern American $$

(☎828-252-2541; www.theadmiralnc.com; 400
Haywood Rd; small plates $12-17, large plates $17-
34; ⊙5-10pm; 🛜) This concrete bunker beside
a car junkyard looks divey on the outside. But
inside? That's where the magic happens. This
low-key West Asheville spot is one of the state's
finest New American restaurants, serving wildly
creative dishes – saffron tagliatelle with lima
beans, zucchini and basil pesto – that taste
divine.

✖ Tupelo Honey   Southern US $$

(☎828-255-4863; www.tupelohoneycafe.
com; 12 College St; brunch $6-17, lunch & dinner
$9.50-30; ⊙11am-9pm Mon-Fri, 9am-9pm Sat
& Sun) This Asheville-based chain is a long-time
favorite known for New Southern fare such as
shrimp and grits with goat's cheese. Tupelo-
born Elvis would have surely loved the fried-
chicken BLT with apple-cider bacon! Brunches
are superb, but no matter the meal, say yes to
the biscuit. And add a drop of honey.

🛏 Sweet Peas Hostel   Hostel $

(☎828-285-8488; www.sweetpeashostel.com;
23 Rankin Ave; dm/pod $32/40, r with/without
bath $105/75; ✳ @ 🛜) This spick-and-
span hostel gleams with IKEA-like style, with
shipshape steel bunk beds and blond-wood

sleeping 'pods.' The loft-like space is very open
and can be noisy (the downstairs Lexington Ave
Brewery adds to the ruckus but hey, there's a
discount) – what you lose in privacy and quiet,
you gain in style, cleanliness, sociability and an
unbeatable downtown location.

🛏 Campfire Lodgings   Campground $$

(☎828-658-8012; www.campfirelodgings.com;
116 Appalachian Village Rd; tent sites $35-40,
RV sites $50-70, yurts $115-135, cabins $160;
Ⓟ ✳ 🛜) All yurts should have flat-screen
TVs, don't you think? Sleep like the world's
most stylish Mongolian nomad in one of these
furnished multiroom tents, on the side of a
wooded hill. Cabins and tent sites are also
available. RV sites have stunning valley views
and wi-fi access.

🛏 Aloft Asheville   Hotel $$$

(☎828-232-2838; www.aloftasheville.
com; 51 Biltmore Ave; r from $250-450;
Ⓟ ✳ @ 🛜 ☒ 🐾) With a giant chalkboard in
the lobby, groovy young staff, and an outdoor
clothing store on the 1st floor, this place looks
like the seventh circle of hipster. The only thing
missing is a wool-cap-wearing bearded guy
drinking a hoppy microbrew – oh, wait, over
there. We jest. Once settled, you'll find the staff
knowledgeable and the rooms colorful and
spacious.

🛏 Omni Grove Park Inn   Historic Hotel $$$

(☎828-252-2711; www.omnihotels.com; 290
Macon Ave; r $149-419; Ⓟ ✳ @ 🛜 ☒ 🐾) This
titanic arts-and-crafts-style historic stone lodge
beckons a bygone era of Americana mountain
glamor and, with its hale-and-hearty look, sets
a tone for adventure. Did you notice the lobby
fireplaces? Of course you did: the 36ft-wide
behemoths can accommodate a standing grown
man inside their hearths and there is an elevator
ascending to the chimney within each!

Classic Trip

The Great Smokies

Alas, Hobbiton and Narnia don't exist. But if you crave a land of wonders, take this drive through the Smokies, home to technicolor greenery, strutting wildlife, whispering waterfalls and the irrepressible Dollywood.

7

TRIP HIGHLIGHTS

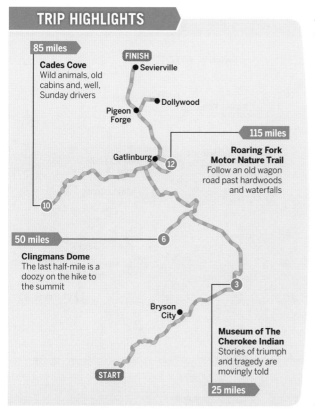

85 miles

Cades Cove
Wild animals, old cabins and, well, Sunday drivers

FINISH
● Sevierville

● Dollywood
Pigeon Forge

115 miles

Roaring Fork Motor Nature Trail
Follow an old wagon road past hardwoods and waterfalls

Gatlinburg ● 12

10

50 miles ———— 6

Clingmans Dome
The last half-mile is a doozy on the hike to the summit

3

Bryson City ●

Museum of The Cherokee Indian
Stories of triumph and tragedy are movingly told

START

25 miles

4–5 DAYS
160 MILES / 257KM

GREAT FOR...

BEST TIME TO GO
April to June for greenery and water-falls, and September and October for colorful leaves.

ESSENTIAL PHOTO
Leave your car to photograph tree-covered mountains from the Newfound Gap Overlook.

 BEST FOR OUTDOORS
Bike the Cades Cove loop on an official 'no-car' morning.

Great Smoky Mountains National Park An elk roams in the mist

Classic Trip

7 The Great Smokies

While the beauty of the Great Smokies can be seen from your car, the exhilarating, crash-bang, breathe-it-in wonder of the place can't be fully appreciated until you leave your vehicle. Hold tight as you bounce over Nantahala rapids. Give a nod to foraging black bears as you bicycle Cades Cove. And press your nose against windows in downtown Gatlinburg, where ogling short stacks is the best way to choose the right pancake place.

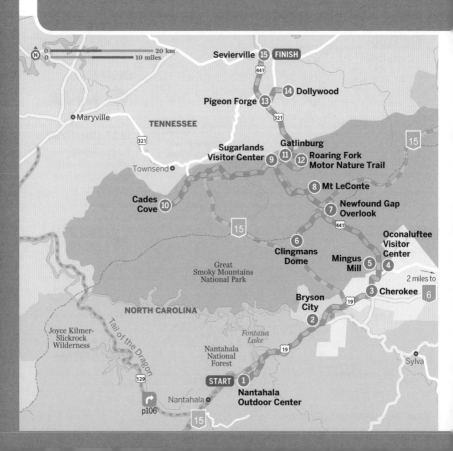

1 Nantahala Outdoor Center

Splash, bang, wheeeeee... there's no easing into this trip, which starts in the mountain-fed rivers and rugged valleys of western North Carolina, a region famed for its fantastic kayaking and white-water rafting.

The **Nantahala Outdoor Center** (NOC; ☏828-785-5082, 828-785-4850; www.noc.com; 13077 Hwy 19 W; ducky rental per day $35, guided trips $50-200; ⊙8am-8pm Jun-Jul, earlier Aug-May) launches trips on the class II and III rapids of the Nantahala River from its sprawling outpost near Bryson City. Ride a group raft or a two-person ducky through the wide, brown river gorge. The company also offers white-water trips on six other Appalachian rivers. Experienced

LINK YOUR TRIP

15 Appalachian Trail

The AT crosses Hwy 441 at Newfound Gap Overlook.

6 Blue Ridge Parkway

From Oconaluftee Visitor Center, drive south on Hwy 411 to the entrance of the parkway.

paddlers can brave the 9-mile trip down the roiling class IV-V Cheoah ($169 to $189), launching from nearby Robbinsville.

At the Adventure Center, which is part of the NOC campus, sign up to zip line or to climb an alpine tower. Also on-site is an outdoor store, a year-round restaurant and lodging, which includes campsites, cabins, a hostel and an inn. The Appalachian Trail crosses the property, and the Great Smoky Mountain Railroad stops here.

The Drive ≫ Follow Hwy 19 north about 12.5 miles on a twisty, wooded path that winds past rafting companies and oh-so-many signs for boiled peanuts. Take exit 67 into downtown Bryson City.

2 Bryson City

This friendly mountain town is a great base camp for exploring the North Carolina side of the Smokies. The marquee attraction is the historic **Great Smoky Mountains Railroad** (☏800-872-4681; www.gsmr. com; 226 Everett St; Nantahala Gorge trip adult from $55, child 2-12yr from $31), which departs from downtown and plows through the dramatic Nantahala Gorge and across the Fontana Trestle. The former Murphy Branch Line, built in the late 1800s, brought unheard-of luxuries such as books,

factory-spun cloth and oil lamps. Themed trips on the red-and-yellow trains include a Great Pumpkin–themed trip in the fall and the Christmas-time Polar Express, which stops at the North Pole to pick up Santa.

✖ 🛏 p112

The Drive ≫ Continue 10 miles north on Hwy 19.

TRIP HIGHLIGHT

3 Cherokee

The Cherokee people have lived in this area since the last ice age, though many died on the Trail of Tears. The descendants of those who escaped or returned are known as the Eastern Band of the Cherokee. Make time for the **Museum of the Cherokee Indian** (☏828-497-3481; www. cherokeemuseum.org; 589 Tsali Blvd/Hwy 441, at Drama Rd; adult $11, child 6-12yr $7; ⊙9am-5pm daily, to 7pm Mon-Sat Jun-Aug). The earth-colored halls trace the history of the tribe, with artifacts such as pots, deerskins, woven skirts and an animated exhibit on Cherokee myths. The tribe's modern story is particularly compelling, with a detailed look at the tragedy and injustice of the Trail of Tears. This mass exodus occurred in the 1830s, when President Andrew Jackson ordered more than 16,000 Native Americans

removed from their southeastern homelands and resettled in what's now Oklahoma. The museum also spotlights a fascinating moment in Colonial-era history: the 1760s journey of three Cherokees to England, where they met with King George III.

The Drive » Drive 3 miles north on Hwy 441, passing the Blue Ridge Parkway.

---

④ Oconaluftee Visitor Center

If they're offering samples of regional preserves at the **Oconaluftee Visitor Center** (☏828-497-1904; www.nps.gov/grsm; 1194 Newfound Gap Rd, North Cherokee; ☺8am-7:30pm Jun-Aug, hours vary Sep-May), say yes. But pull out your money because you'll want to take a jar home. Here you'll also find interactive exhibits about the park's history and ecosystems. Helpful guides ($1) about specific attractions are also available. For this trip, the *Day Hikes* pamphlet and the guides to Cades Cove and the Roaring Fork Motor Nature Trail are helpful supplements.

Behind the visitor center, the pet-friendly Oconaluftee River Trail follows the river for 1.5 miles to the boundary of the Cherokee reservation. Pick up a free backcountry camping permit if you plan to go off-trail. The adjacent **Mountain Farm Museum** (www.nps.gov/grsm; ☺9am-5pm daily mid-Mar–mid-Nov, plus Thanksgiving weekend) is a 19th-century farmstead assembled from buildings from various locations around the park. The worn, wooden structures, including a barn, a blacksmith shop and a smokehouse, give a glimpse into the hardscrabble existence of Appalachian settlers.

The Drive » Drive half a mile north on Hwy 441. The parking lot is on the left.

---

⑤ Mingus Mill

Interested in old buildings and 1800s commerce? Then take the short walk to **Mingus Mill** (Mingus Creek Trail, Cherokee; ☺9am-5pm daily mid-Mar–mid-Nov, plus Thanksgiving weekend). This 1886 gristmill was the largest in the Smokies. If the miller is there, he can explain how the mill grinds corn into cornmeal. Outside, the 200ft-long wooden millrace directs water to the building. There's no waterwheel here because the mill used a cast-iron turbine.

The Drive » Return to Hwy 441 and turn left, continuing toward Gatlinburg. Turn left and drive 7 miles on Clingmans Dome Rd.

TRIP HIGHLIGHT

⑥ Clingmans Dome

At 6643ft, Clingmans Dome is the third-highest mountain east of the Mississippi. You can drive almost all the way to the top, but the final climb to the summit's Jetsons-like observation tower requires a half-mile walk

---

↱ DETOUR: TAIL OF THE DRAGON

Start: ① Nantahala Outdoor Center

A dragon lurks in the rugged foothills of the southwestern Smokies. This particular monster is an infamous drive that twists through Deals Gap beside the national park. According to legend, the 11-mile route, known as the Tail of the Dragon, has 318 curves. From the Nantahala Outdoor Center, drive south on Hwy 19/74 to Hwy 129. Follow Hwy 129 north. The dragon starts at the North Carolina and Tennessee state line. Godspeed and drive slowly. And may you tame the dragon like a Targaryen.

GREAT SMOKY MOUNTAINS NATIONAL PARK TRIP PLANNER

Established in 1934, **Great Smoky Mountains National Park** (www.nps.gov/grsm) attracts more than nine million travelers per year, making it the most-visited national park in America.

Newfoundland Gap Rd/Hwy 441 is the only thoroughfare crossing the entire 521,000-acre park, traversing 33 miles of deep oak and pine forest, and wildflower meadows. The park sits in two states: North Carolina and Tennessee. The Oconaluftee Visitor Center welcomes visitors arriving on Hwy 441 in North Carolina; Sugarlands Visitor Center is the Tennessee counterpart.

Orientation & Fees

Great Smoky charges no admission fee, nor will it ever; this proviso was written into the park's original charter as a stipulation for a $5 million Rockefeller family grant. Stop by a visitor center to pick up a park map and the free *Smokies Guide* newspaper. The park is open all year although some facilities are only open seasonally, and roads may close due to bad weather. Leashed pets are allowed in campgrounds and on roadsides, but not on trails, with the exception of the Gatlinburg and Oconaluftee River trails.

Camping

The park currently operates seven developed campgrounds. None have showers or hookups. **Reservations** (📞877-444-6777; www.recreation.gov) are required at Cataloochee Campground, and they may be made at Elkmont, Smokemont, Cosby and Cades Cove. Big Creek and Deep Creek are first-come, first-served.

Traffic

If you're visiting on a summer weekend, particularly on the Tennessee side, accept that there is going to be a lot of traffic. Take a break by following trails into the wilderness.

---

on a paved trail. It's a very steep ascent, but there are resting spots along the way. The trail crosses the 2174-mile Appalachian Trail, which reaches its highest point on the dome.

From the tower, on a clear day, enjoy a 360-degree view that sweeps in five states. Spruce- and pine-covered mountaintops sprawl for miles. The **visitor station** (📞865-436-1200; Clingmans Dome Rd; ⊙10am-6pm Apr-Oct, 9:30am-5pm Nov) beside the parking lot has a bookstore and a shop.

The weather here is cooler than at lower elevations, and rain can arrive quickly. Consider wearing layers and bringing a rain poncho. And in case you're wondering, a dome is a rounded mountain.

The Drive ≫ Follow Clingmans Dome Rd back to Hwy 441. Cross Hwy 441 and pull into the overlook parking area.

---

7 Newfound Gap Overlook

There's a lot going at the intersection of US 441 and Clingmans Dome Rd. Here, the **Rockefeller Monument** pays tribute to a $5 million donation from the Rockefeller Foundation that helped to complete land purchases needed to create the park. President Franklin D Roosevelt formally dedicated Great Smoky Mountains National Park in this spot in 1940. The overlook sits at the border of North Carolina and Tennessee, within the 5046ft Newfound Gap. Enjoy expansive mountain views from the parking area or hop on the **Appalachian Trail** (see p183) for a stroll.

Classic Trip

WHY THIS IS A CLASSIC TRIP
AMY C BALFOUR, WRITER

As a kid, I loved reading adventure novels set in imaginary kingdoms, those otherworldly places filled with misty mountains, abandoned fortresses and a giant or two. The Great Smokies feel like one of those kingdoms, especially in spring when the forest is a luminous green, the animals are waking up and the trails meander into drifting fog.

Above left: Sunset over Newfound Gap
Above right: Observation tower, Clingmans Dome

The Drive ≫ From here, follow Hwy 441 north into Tennessee for about 5 miles to the parking lot.

- - - - - - - - - - - - - - - - - -

8 Mt LeConte

Climbing 6593ft Mt LeConte is probably the park's most popular challenge, sure to give serious hamstring burn. The **Alum Cave Trail**, one of five routes to the peak, starts from the Alum

SEAN PAVONE / GETTY IMAGES ©

DIGIDREAMGRAFIX / GETTY IMAGES ©

Cave parking area on the main road. Follow a creek, pass under a stone arch and wind your way steadily upward past thickets of rhododendron, myrtle and mountain laurel. It's a 5.5-mile hike to LeConte Lodge, where you can join the Rainbow Falls Trail to the summit.

🛏 p112

The Drive ›› Continue on Newfound Gap Rd. Turn left into the parking lot at Little River Rd.

9 Sugarlands Visitor Center

At the juncture of Little River and Newfound Gap Rds is the **Sugarlands Visitor Center** (☏865-436-1291; www.nps.gov/grsm; 107 Park Headquarters Rd; ⏰8am-7:30pm Jun-Aug, hours vary Sep-May), the park headquarters and main Tennessee entrance. Step inside for exhibits about plant and animal life (there's a stuffed wild boar only a mama boar could love), and a bookstore. Several ranger-led talks and tours meet at Sugarlands.

🛏 p112

The Drive ›› Turn on to Little River Rd for a gorgeous 25-mile drive beside lively flowing waterways. The road passes Elkmont Campground then becomes Laurel Creek Rd. Watch for cars stopping suddenly as drivers pull over to look at wildlife.

TRIP HIGHLIGHT

⑩ Cades Cove

This secluded valley contains the remnants of a 19th-century settlement. It's accessed by an 11-mile, one-way loop road that has numerous pull-offs. From these, you can poke around old churches and farmhouses or hike trails through postcard-perfect meadows filled with deer, wild turkeys and the occasional bear. For good wildlife viewing, come in the late afternoon when the animals romp with abandon.

The narrow loop road has a speed limit of 10mph and can get crowded (and maddeningly slow) in high season. For a more tranquil experience, ride your bike, or walk, on a Wednesday or Saturday morning from early May through late September – cars are banned from the road between 7am and 10am. Rent a bike at the Cades Cove Campground Store ($4 to $6 per hour).

Also recommended is the 5-mile round-trip hike to **Abrams Falls**. Trailhead parking is after the Elijah Oliver Place.

Stop by the **Cades Cove Visitor Center** (📞865-436-7318; Cades Cove Loop Rd; ⏱9am-7:30pm May-Jul, closes earlier rest of year) for ranger talks.

🛏 p112

The Drive ›› Return to the Sugarlands Vistor Center then turn left on to Hwy 441, which is called parkway between Gatlinburg and Sevierville. Drive 2 miles to Gatlinburg.

⑪ Gatlinburg

Driving out of the park on the Tennessee side is disconcerting. All at once you pop out of the tranquil green tunnel of trees and into a blinking, shrieking welter of cars, motels, pancake houses, minigolf courses and Ripley's Believe It or Not Museums. Welcome to Gatlinburg. It's Heidi meets Hillbilly in this vaguely Bavarian-themed tourist wonderland, catering to Smokies visitors since the 1930s. Most of the tourist attractions are within the compact, hilly little downtown.

Once it's repaired after fire damage, the **Gatlinburg Sky Lift** (📞865-436-4307; www.gatlinburgskylift.com; 765 Parkway; adult/child $16.50/13; ⏱9am-11pm Jun-Aug, varies rest of year), a repurposed ski-resort chairlift, will whisk you high over the Smokies.

You'll fill up your camera's memory card with panoramic snapshots.

🍴 🛏 p112

The Drive ›› From the parkway in downtown Gatlinburg, turn right on to Historic Nature Trail/Airport Rd at the Gatlinburg Convention Center. Follow it into the national park, continuing to the marked entrance for the one-way Roaring Fork Motor Nature Trail.

TRIP HIGHLIGHT

⑫ Roaring Fork Motor Nature Trail

Built on the foundations of a 150-year-old wagon road, the 6-mile Roaring Fork loop twists through strikingly lush forest. Sights include burbling cascades, abundant hardwoods, mossy boulders and old cabins once inhabited by farming families. The isolated community of Roaring Fork was settled in the mid-1800s, along a powerful mountain stream. The families that lived here were forced to move when the park was established about 100 years later.

For a waterfall hike, try the 2.6-mile round-trip walk to **Grotto Falls** from the Trillium Gap Trailhead. Further down the road, check out the Ephraim Bales cabin, once home to 11 people.

The *Roaring Fork Auto Tour Guide*, for sale for $1 in the Oconaluftee and Sugarlands visitor centers, provides details about plant life and buildings along the drive. No buses, trailer or RVs are permitted on the motor road.

The Drive » At the end of Roaring Fork Rd turn left on to E Parkway. Less than 1 mile ahead, turn right at Hwy 321S/Hwy 441. Drive 7 miles to Pigeon Forge.

- - - - - - - - - - - - - - - - - -

13 Pigeon Forge

The town of Pigeon Forge is an ode to that big-haired, big-busted angel of East Tennessee, Dolly Parton – who's known to be a pretty cool chick.

Born in a one-room shack in the nearby hamlet of Locust Ridge, Parton started performing on Knoxville radio at age 11 and moved to Nashville at 18 with all her worldly belongings in a cardboard suitcase. She's made millions singing about her Smoky Mountain roots and continues to be a huge presence in her hometown, donating money to local causes and riding a glittery float in the annual Dolly Parade.

Wacky museums and over-the-top dinner shows line the parkway, the main drag.

The Drive » Turn right on to the parkway and drive 2 miles southeast. Then turn left on to Dollywood Lane/Veterans Blvd and follow signs to Dollywood, about 2.5 miles away.

- - - - - - - - - - - - - - - - - -

14 Dollywood

Dolly Parton's theme park **Dollywood** ([📞]865-428-9488; www.dollywood.com; 2700 Dollywood Parks Blvd, Pigeon Forge; adult/child $67/54; ⊙Apr-Dec) is an enormous love letter to mountain culture. Families pour in to ride the country-themed thrill rides and see demonstrations of traditional Appalachian crafts. You can also tour the bald-eagle sanctuary or worship at the altar of Dolly in the Chasing Rainbows life-story museum. The adjacent Dollywood's Splash Country takes these themes and adds water.

The Drive » Return to the parkway and follow it north 4.5 miles into downtown Sevierville. Turn left on to Bruce St and drive one block to Court Ave.

- - - - - - - - - - - - - - - - - -

15 Sevierville

On the front lawn of the downtown courthouse (125 Court Ave) you might see a few happy folks getting their pictures taken in front of the statue of a young Dolly Parton. Wearing a ponytail, her guitar held loose, it captures something kind of nice. You know where's she's from, where her music is going to take her, and how it all ties in to this tough, but always beautiful, mountain country.

WATERFALLS OF THE SMOKIES

The Smokies are full of waterfalls, from icy trickles to roaring cascades. Here are a few of the best:

Grotto Falls You can walk behind these 25ft-high falls, off Trillium Gap Trail.

Laurel Falls This popular 80ft fall is located down an easy 2.6-mile paved trail.

Mingo Falls At 120ft, this is one of the highest waterfalls in the Appalachians.

Rainbow Falls On sunny days, the mist here produces a rainbow.

Eating & Sleeping

Bryson City ②

✖ Cork & Bean   Cafe $$

(☎828-488-1934; www.brysoncitycorkandbean.com; 16 Everett St; brunch $6.50-12.50, lunch $8-11.50, dinner $18-35.50; ⏱4:30-9pm Mon-Thu, 11am-9pm Fri, 9am-9pm Sat & Sun, hours vary outside summer; 🛜) Big windows frame the Cork & Bean, a chic restaurant-bar in downtown Bryson City. With its emphasis on locally grown and organic fare, you'll feel less guilty digging into the eatery's crepes and sandwiches after your local hike. Look for eggs Benedict and huevos rancheros on the weekend brunch menu, Andouille sausage, duck and wild-boar étoufée at dinner and local craft beers on tap.

🛏 Fryemont Inn   Inn $$

(☎828-488-2159; www.fryemontinn.com; 245 Fryemont St; lodge/ste/cabin incl breakfast & dinner from $165/$205/260; nonguest breakfast $10-12, dinner $20-31; ⏱restaurant 8am-10am & 6-8pm Sun-Tue, 6-9pm Fri & Sat mid-Apr–late Nov; 🅿 ♿) The view of Bryson City and the Smokies from the porch of the lofty Fryemont Inn is hard to beat. This historic family-owned mountain lodge feels like summer camp with its bark-covered main building and a common area flanked by a stone fireplace. No TVs or air-con in the lodge rooms. Wi-fi is available in the lobby, cottage and balcony suites. The room rate includes breakfast and dinner at the on-site restaurant, which is open to the public.

Mt LeConte ⑧

🛏 LeConte Lodge   Cabin $

(☎865-429-5704; www.lecontelodge.com; cabins per person incl breakfast & dinner adult/4-12yr $145/85; ⏱mid-Mar–mid-Nov) The park's only non-camping accommodation is LeConte Lodge, and the only way to get to the lodge's rustic, electricity-free cabins is via five uphill hiking trails varying in length from

5.5 (Alum Cave Trail) to 8 miles (Boulevard), it's so popular you need to reserve up to a year in advance.

Sugarlands Visitor Center ⑨

🛏 Elkmont
Campground   Campground $

(☎865-436-1271; www.recreation.gov; Little River Rd; tent/RV sites $17-23; ⏱early Mar-Nov; 🐾) The park's largest campground is on Little River Rd, 5 miles west of Sugarlands Visitor Center. Little River and Jakes Creek run through this wooded campground and the sound of rippling water adds tranquility. There are 200 tent and RV campsites and 20 walk-in sites. All are reservable beginning May 15. Like other campgrounds in the park, there are no showers, or electrical or water hookups. There are restrooms.

Cades Cove ⑩

🛏 Cades Cove
Campground   Campground $

(☎865-448-2472; www.recreation.gov; tent/RV sites $17/20) This woodsy campground with 159 sites is a great place to sleep if you want to get a jump on visiting Cades Cove. There's a camp store, drinking water and bathrooms, but no showers. There are 29 tent-only sites.

Gatlinburg ⑪

✖ Pancake Pantry   Breakfast $

(www.pancakepantry.com; 628 Parkway; breakfast $8-12, lunch $8-11; ⏱7am-3pm; 🐾) Gatlinburg has a thing for pancakes, and this is the place that started it all. The Pantry's secret is simple: real butter, honest-to-goodness fresh whipped cream and everything made from scratch. We recommend the Swedish pancakes, with lashings of lingonberry jam. At lunch there's gourmet sandwiches with funny names like The Polish Aristocrat, which can be ordered ahead for picnics by the waterfalls of Great Smoky.

✕ Smoky Mountain Brewery
American $$

(www.smoky-mtn-brewery.com; 1004 Parkway; mains $8.50-24; ⊙11:30am-11pm Sun-Thu, to midnight Fri & Sat; 🛜) American pub grub like quesadillas, chicken fingers, pizzas, burgers and pasta dishes are A-OK, but it's the microbrewed beer (nine on tap), multiple TV sets and raucous ski-lodge atmosphere that really packs in the crowds.

✕ Wild Boar Saloon & Howard's Steakhouse
Steak $$

(☎865-436-3600; www.facebook.com/TheWildBoarSaloon; 976 Parkway; mains $10-37; ⊙11am-11pm Apr-Jan, to 9pm winter; 🛜) Since 1946 this dark creekside saloon has been serving burgers, ribs and a tasty pulled-pork shoulder drenched in homemade sauce. But it's known for its steaks and Bloody Marys and for being the oldest joint in town. On an nice day, the creekside patio is a winner.

🛏 Bearskin Lodge
Lodge $$

(☎877-795-7546; www.thebearskinlodge.com; 840 River Rd; d $79-220; 🅿 ❄ 🛜 🌊) This shingled riverside lodge is blessed with timber accents and a bit more panache than other Gatlinburg comers. All of the 96 spacious rooms have flat-screen TVs and some come with gas fireplaces and private balconies jutting over the river.

🛏 Hampton Inn
Hotel $$

(☎865-436-4878; www.hamptoninn3.hilton.com; 967 Parkway; d $89-269; 🅿 @ 🛜 🌊) Yep, it's part of a chain, but the hotel sits in the thick-of-the-action on Parkway. Decor is modern, and furnishings include an easy chair and ottoman. Rooms with king beds have a fireplace. Ahhh.

8

North Carolina's Outer Banks

This slender chain of barrier islands wears its heart on its fragile sleeve. Windswept dunes. Bird-filled marshes. Solitary lighthouses. The scenery and landmarks are products of the unique, ever-shifting geography.

TRIP HIGHLIGHTS

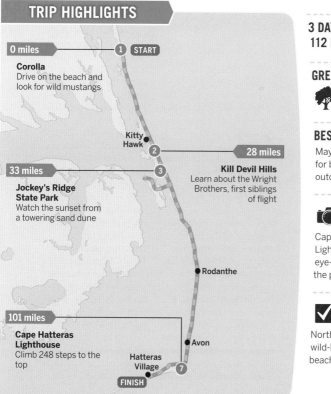

0 miles

1 START

Corolla
Drive on the beach and look for wild mustangs

Kitty Hawk

2

28 miles

3

Kill Devil Hills
Learn about the Wright Brothers, first siblings of flight

33 miles

Jockey's Ridge State Park
Watch the sunset from a towering sand dune

● Rodanthe

101 miles

Cape Hatteras Lighthouse
Climb 248 steps to the top

● Avon

Hatteras Village

7

FINISH

3 DAYS
112 MILES / 180KM

GREAT FOR...

BEST TIME TO GO

May through October for beach days and outdoor fun.

ESSENTIAL PHOTO

Cape Hatteras Lighthouse for an eye-catching link to the past.

☑ BEST FOR FAMILIES

North of Corolla, take a wild-horse tour on the beach.

Bodie Island The 1872-built lighthouse

North Carolina's Outer Banks

Wild mustangs kick off this trip, which starts in the untamed northern reaches of the Outer Banks. From here, the road flows south on a thread of barrier islands, the first line of defense against the roaring Atlantic. Nature is a big draw, with sand dunes, sea oats and coastal views as constant companions. The history impresses too, with lost colonists, flying machines, terrifying shipwrecks and a floating platoon of Doritos.

TRIP HIGHLIGHT

① Corolla

More than 100 wild horses, descendants of Colonial Spanish mustangs, graze among the sea oats north of Corolla. There's no paved road north of town, and the main highway is... the beach.

Check out a few exhibits about the horses at the **museum** (☎252-453-8002; www.corollawildhorses.com; 1129 Corolla Village Rd; ⊗10am-4pm Mon-Sat, to 2pm Sun) run by the Corolla Wild Horse Fund. The group also leads two-hour wild-horse tours (adult/child $45/20). Numerous commercial outfitters also offer tours, including **Corolla Outback Adventures**

(☎252-453-4484; www.corollaoutback.com; 1150 Ocean Trail; 2hr tours adult $50, child under 13yr $25) run by a knowledgeable long-time local, Jay Bender.

Historic Corolla Village is home to the **Currituck Beach Lighthouse** (www.currituckbeachlight.com; 1101 Corolla Village Rd; adult $10, child under 8yr free; ⊗9am-5pm late Mar-Nov), the northernmost of the Outer Banks' six lighthouses. The impressive all-brick sentinel has guided sailors since 1875. The grounds are free, but to appreciate the view, buy a ticket ($7) and climb 214 steps. Learn more about the surrounding marshes at the nearby **Outer Banks Center for Wildlife**

Education (www.ncwildlife.org/obx; 1160 Village Lane; ⊗9am-5pm Mon-Fri; 🚻).

The Drive ≫ Hwy 12 starts in Corolla. Follow it south past beach cottages, shopping centers and sand dunes. After Duck and Southern Shores, where there are great places to eat and overnight (p121), turn left on to Hwy 158 south. Hwy 158 is also called the Bypass or S Croatan Hwy.

TRIP HIGHLIGHT

② Kill Devil Hills

The hilltop monument at Mile 7.5 is a majestic calling card for the **Wright Brothers National Memorial** (☎252-473-2111; www.nps.gov/wrbr; 1000 North Croatan Hwy, Kitty Hawk; adult $7, child under 16yr free; ⊗9am-5pm) in Kill Devil Hills. It is is NOT, however, the site of the world's first airplane flight. Nope, the 12-second ride started at the bottom of the hill, and a 6-ton boulder marks the spot. Orville Wright was at the controls during the history-making flight on December 17, 1903. His brother Wilbur steadied the wings as the plane left the ground.

There's a life-size reproduction of the Wrights' flying machine in the visitor center plus numerous exhibits about the brothers, who funded their research with proceeds from their bicycle shop in Dayton, OH. Don't miss the ranger-led 'Flight Room Talk,' a 30-minute talk that describes the

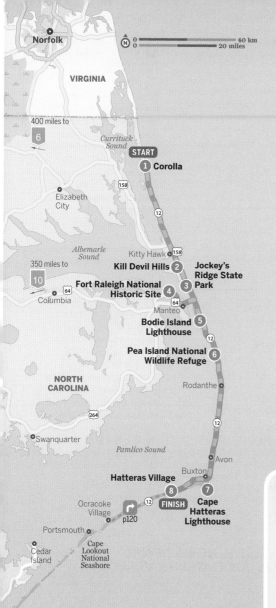

brothers' ingenuity and perseverance.

Behind the monument, look for a bronze-and-steel replica of the plane. Scramble across the wing – it's allowed! – to get a feel for its complexity.

✗ 🛏 p121

The Drive » Continue south on Hwy 158 to Mile 12.

- - - - - - - - - - - - - - - - - -

TRIP HIGHLIGHT

③ Jockey's Ridge State Park

Kick off your shoes for a leg-stretching climb up **Jockey's Ridge** (www.ncparks.gov/jockeys-ridge-state-park; 300 W Carolista Dr, Nags Head; ⊗8am-9pm May-Aug, varies rest of year), the largest sand dune on the East Coast. With a 360-degree view that sweeps in the Atlantic Ocean and Roanoke Sound, it's a gorgeous spot to watch the sunset. Impress your friends

LINK YOUR TRIP

 10 Lowcountry & Southern Coast

For a mood-drenched look into the past, drive west to I-95 south and Charleston.

 6 Blue Ridge Parkway

Leave the beaches for the mountains by taking Hwy 64 west to I-40 west.

with tales (and video) of your hang-gliding prowess by booking a lesson with **Kitty Hawk Kites** (📞252-441-6800; www. kittyhawk.com; 3933 S Croatan Hwy, Jockey's Ridge Crossing, Nags Head; bike rental per day $15, kayaks $39-59, stand-up paddleboards $59-69), which also has a satellite office inside the park.

The Drive » Follow Hwy 12 south through the town of Nags Head, where you can grab a bite (p121), to Hwy 64 west, which crosses the sound. On Roanoke Island, turn right to follow Hwy 64 through Manteo to Fort Raleigh Dr.

----

4 Fort Raleigh National Historic Site

Roanoke Island is the site of one of North America's most enduring mysteries. A group of 116 British colonists disappeared from their settlement here in the late 1580s. Were they killed by drought? Did they try to sail home? Or did they leave with a local Native American tribe, as suggested by the word 'Croatan' carved

into a tree? Learn more at the **visitor center** (www. nps.gov/fora; 1401 National Park Dr, Manteo; ⊙grounds dawn-dusk), which has exhibits and a short film.

In summer, sit outside for the *Lost Colony Outdoor Drama,* a popular musical about the colonists by Pulitzer Prize-winning North Carolina playwright Paul Green. The play celebrated its 75th anniversary in 2012.

Before the show, wander the 16th-century-style **Elizabethan Gardens** (📞252-473-3234; www. elizabethangardens.org; 1411 National Park Dr, Manteo; adult $9, child 6-17yr $6; ⊙9am-7pm Jun-Aug, shorter hours Sep-May) next door. Trails pass by flower gardens, the world's largest statue of Queen Elizabeth I and a live oak that was probably alive when the colonists arrived.

The Drive » Return to Hwy 12. Follow it south into Cape Hatteras National Seashore, a good option for camping (p121). From here it's 6 miles to Bodie Island Lighthouse Rd and almost 60 miles to Hatteras Village.

----

5 Bodie Island Lighthouse

Cape Hatteras National Seashore is a mesmerizing place. Its boundaries extend some 70 miles across the whisper-thin barrier islands of Bodie, Hatteras and Ocracoke.

Today you can survey the landscape from atop the 156ft **Bodie Island Lighthouse** (📞255-473-2111; www.nps.gov/caha; 8210 Bodie Island Lighthouse Rd, Nags Head; museum free, tours adult $8, child under 11yr $4; ⊙visitor center 9am-5pm, lighthouse to 4:30pm late Apr–early Oct; ♿), which opened to visitors for the first time in 2013. The 1872 lighthouse has its original Fresnal lens – a rarity. Entry is by guided tour. Tickets can be reserved by phone or purchased on a first-come, first-served basis. In the visitor center a small museum spotlights the lighthouse keepers who tended the light. The island and lighthouse are pronounced 'body.'

The Drive » Oregon Inlet rolls into view just south of the

✓ **TOP TIP: COASTAL NC NATIONAL WILDLIFE REFUGE GATEWAY VISITOR CENTER**

This comprehensive **visitor center** (📞252-473-1131; www.fws.gov/ncgatewayvc; 100 Conservation Way, Manteo; ⊙9am-4pm Mon-Sat, noon-4pm Sun), which opened in 2012 in Manteo, provides information about the region's 11 national wildlife refuges and their activities, from a Red Wolf Howling Safari at Alligator River to the Wings over Water Wildlife Festival in October. Multimedia exhibits examine the region's flora, fauna and history.

Roanoke Island Elizabethan Gardens, adjacent to Fort Raleigh National Historic Site

119

DETOUR: OCRACOKE

Start: ❽ **Hatteras Village**

Why take the free ferry from Hatteras to Ocracoke? To slow down and escape the modern grind. Gone are the ubiquitous beachwear shops and BrewThru convenience stores of the Carolina coast; instead, in their place, are handmade craft stores, organic coffee shops and hemp design boutiques. Here you can camp by the beach where the wild ponies run, enjoy a fish sandwich in a local pub, bike around the narrow streets of Ocracoke Village or visit the 1823 Ocracoke Lighthouse. For the ferry schedule, check www.ncdot.gov/ferry.

lighthouse. After the marina, Hwy 12 swoops on to Hatteras Island.

TRIP HIGHLIGHT

❼ Cape Hatteras Lighthouse

What happens when erosion and tidal movement have caused a 4800-ton, 1.25-million-brick lighthouse to end up within almost 100ft of the shorelines? You pick it up and move it, of course. That's what happened to the black-and-white-striped **Cape Hatteras Lighthouse** (✆252-475-9000; www.nps.gov/caha; 46368 Lighthouse Rd, Buxton; climbing tours adult $8, child under 12yr $4; ☺visitor center 9am-5pm, lighthouse to 4:30pm mid-Apr–early Oct) in 1999. After 60 years of erosion stabilization attempts, the National Park Service authorized this controversial project. Over 23 very slow days, the lighthouse was moved – safely – 2900ft from the shore, completely unscathed.

❻ Pea Island National Wildlife Refuge

More than 350 species of migrating birds have landed at this refuge on the northern end of Hatteras Island. To scan for birds, stroll the half-mile, fully accessible North Pond Trail or step inside the **visitor center** (✆252-987-2394; www.fws.gov/refuge/pea_island; Hwy 12, Rodanthe; ☺visitor center 9am-4pm, trails dawn-dusk) where there's a spotting scope. In summer, check the online calendar for turtle talks and canoe tours. A 90-minute bird walk is offered Friday mornings at 8am; call for additional dates.

The Drive ›› Continue south on Hwy 12 passing through the villages of Rodanthe, Waves and Salvo.

Today, as you walk up its 248 steps (equal to a 12-story building), imagine being the lighthouse keeper, carrying the 5-gallon, 40lb canister of oil on your back each day. Today, rangers don't advise the climb on an empty stomach. Guided full-moon climbs are offered in summer.

A two-story museum in the former double keepers' quarters provides an overview of the island's interesting history.

The Drive ›› Drive 12 miles south, passing through Frisco and into Hatteras Village. When you see the ferry landing, stay left for museum just ahead.

❽ Hatteras Village

More than 500 ships have met their maker in the battering waves off the coast of the Outer Banks. In Hatteras Village, the **Graveyard of the Atlantic Museum** (✆252-986-2995; www.graveyardoftheatlantic.com; 59200 Museum Dr; ☺10am-4pm) displays shipwreck artifacts dating back hundreds of years. One highlight is a WWII enigma machine recovered from a German submarine that sunk in 1942. In 2006 a container filled with thousands of Doritos bags washed ashore near Frisco. According to one local, casseroles topped with crumpled Doritos were quite popular at social gatherings in the months that followed.

✗ ⊨ p121

Eating & Sleeping

Duck & Southern Shores ❶

✗ John's Drive-In   Seafood, Ice Cream $

(www.johnsdrivein.com; 3716 N Virginia Dare Trail, Kitty Hawk; mains $2.25-9.50; ⊗11am-5pm Thu-Tue) A Kitty Hawk institution for perfectly fried baskets of mahi-mahi, to be eaten at outdoor picnic tables and washed down with one of hundreds of possible milkshake combinations. Some folks just come for the soft-serve. It closes down off season.

🛏 Sanderling Resort & Spa   Resort $$$

(✆252-261-4111; www.sanderling-resort.com; 1461 Duck Rd, Duck; r $160-599, ste $599-750; P ❄ 🛜 🏊) Newly remodeled rooms have given this posh place a stylish kick in the pants. Or should we say the Lululemons? Because yes, the resort does offer sunrise yoga on the beach. Decor is impeccably tasteful, and the attached balconies are an inviting place to enjoy the ocean sounds and breezes. The property includes several restaurants and bars, and a spa offering luxe massage. Daily resort fee is $30 from mid-May to October, $15 from November to mid-May.

Kill Devil Hills ❷

✗ Kill Devil Grill   Seafood, American $$

(✆252-449-8181; www.thekilldevilgrill.com; 2008 S Virginia Dare Trail; lunch $7-13, dinner $10-22; ⊗11:30am-9pm Tue-Thu, to 10pm Fri & Sat) Yowza, this place is good. It's also historic – the entrance is a 1939 diner that's listed in the national registry of historic places. Pub grub and seafood arrive with tasty flair, and portions are generous. Check out the specials, where the kitchen can really shine.

🛏 Shutters on the Banks   Hotel $$

(✆252-441-5581; www.shuttersonthebanks.com; 405 S Virginia Dare Trail; r $69-269; P ❄ 🛜 🏊) Centrally located in Kill Devil Hills, this welcoming 86-room beachfront hotel exudes a snappy, colorful style. The inviting rooms come with plantation windows and colorful art as well as flat-screen TV, refrigerator and microwave. Some rooms come with a full kitchen.

Nags Head ❸

✗ Tortugas' Lie   Seafood $$

(www.tortugaslie.com; 3014 S Virginia Dare Trail; lunch $5-20, dinner $8-23; ⊗11:30am-9pm Wed-Mon) The interior isn't dressed to impress – surfboards, license plates – but who cares? The reliably good seafood, burritos and burgers go down well with the beer. And kids will be perfectly fine. Guy Fieri stopped by in 2012 and scrawled his signature on the wall. Fills up by 6:30pm.

Cape Hatteras National Seashore ❹

🛏 Oregon Inlet Campground   Campground $

(✆252-441-6246; www.recreation.gov; 12001 NC Hwy 12, Nags Head; tent sites $28; ⊗mid-Apr–late Nov) Near Bodie Island Lighthouse, Oregon Inlet is the northernmost campground on Cape Hatteras National Seashore. Facilities include 120 sites and flush toilets and unheated showers.

Hatteras Village ❽

✗ Breakwater Restaurant   Seafood $$$

(✆252-986-2733; www.breakwaterhatteras.com; 57896 Hwy 12; mains $14-30; ⊗5-9pm Apr-Sep) This restaurant beside the sound has been serving food for nearly 30 years. Come here for steamed seafood, fresh fish and and big daddy crab cakes.

🛏 Breakwater Inn   Motel $

(✆252-986-2565; www.breakwaterhatteras.com; 57896 Hwy 12; r/ste from $179/213, motel from $117; P ❄ 🛜 🏊 🍽) The end of the road doesn't look so bad at this three-story shingled inn. Rooms come with kitchenette and a private deck with views of the sound. On a budget? Try one of the older 'Fisherman's Quarters' rooms, with microwave and refrigerator. The inn is near the Hatteras–Ocracoke ferry landing.

Greenville & Cherokee Foothills Scenic Highway

9

This trip begins with a Revolutionary battle on a mountaintop, rolls through woodland valleys steeped in legend and ends with dramatic cascades in the center of Greenville.

TRIP HIGHLIGHTS

81 miles

Caesars Head State Park
Watch migrating hawks soar on the thermal breezes

0 miles

Kings Mountain National Military Park
A Revolutionary War turning point

START
1

3

4

7

FINISH

Table Rock State Park
Hike to the top of a mountain famed for its granite face

93 miles

Greenville
The downtown waterfall is a stunning centerpiece

172 miles

2 DAYS
172 MILES / 277KM

GREAT FOR...

BEST TIME TO GO
April to November for leafy canopies and waterfall hikes; September to November for the Hawk Watch.

ESSENTIAL PHOTO
Table Rock Mountain with its massive granite face.

BEST FOR HISTORY
The battle at Kings Mountain was pivotal for the Patriots during the Revolutionary War.

Table Rock State Park Viewed from Caesars Head State Park

9 Greenville & Cherokee Foothills Scenic Highway

Cherokees once roamed the upcountry foothills, which they called the 'Great Blue Hills of God.' Geologically known as the Blue Ridge escarpment, it's the spot where the Blue Ridge Mountains drop dramatically to meet the Piedmont. Frontier patriots, secretive moonshiners and the mighty Duke Energy have all used the region's hills and streams to their advantage. The dynamic heart is Greenville, with its downtown waterfalls and lively city sidewalks.

TRIP HIGHLIGHT

❶ Kings Mountain National Military Park

As Major Patrick Ferguson learned on the summit of Kings Mountain, threatening American patriots is never a good idea. In the fall of 1780, General Lord Cornwallis ordered Ferguson to subdue the frontier militias of the western Carolinas. In a message to the patriots, who were known as the Overmountain Men, Ferguson proclaimed:

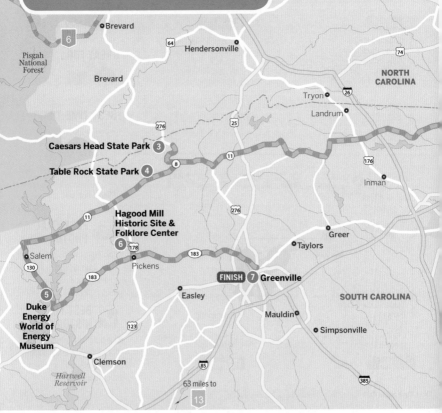

'If you do not desist your opposition to the British Arms, I shall march this army over the mountains, hang your leaders and lay waste your country with fire and sword.'

In response, 900 annoyed frontiersmen crossed the mountains, joined forces and surrounded Ferguson and his 1000-man army. Comfortable with close-range combat, the patriots used the mountain's thick trees as cover as they climbed the slopes. After a short period of intense fighting, Ferguson was dead, his troops decimated.

At **Kings Mountain National Military Park** (☎864-936-7921; www.nps.gov/kimo; Hwy 216; ⏱9am-5pm, to 6pm Sat & Sun Jun-Aug) a 1.5-mile paved interpretative trail explores the forested battlefield. At the visitor center, a 26-minute film describes the fight, which was a turning point in the Revolutionary War. A small museum spotlights the battle's major players.

The Drive » Take SC 216 to I-85 south. Follow it to exit 92 and SC 11 south, which is the Cherokee Foothills Scenic Hwy (if you get to the Giant Peach – aka the peach butt – you've gone too far). The profile of a Cherokee is emblazoned on markers along the byway. Drive 10 miles.

---

❷ Cowpens National Battlefield

On January 17, 1781, American commander Daniel Morgan executed a brilliant tactical maneuver – the double envelopment – against a larger, better-equipped British force during the Battle of Cowpens. His resounding success inspired Colonial forces and propelled them on their path to final victory at Yorktown. At **Cowpens National Battlefield** (☎864-461-2828; www.nps.gov/cowp; 4001 Chesnee Hwy, Gaffney; ⏱9am-5pm, auto loop closes 4:30pm), don't limit yourself to the auto

LINK YOUR TRIP

6 Blue Ridge Parkway

After ascending Table Rock, take Hwy 25 north for a posthike microbrew in Asheville.

13 Hogs & Heifers: a Georgia BBQ Odyssey

For some old-school BBQ, follow I-85 south toward Lexington.

loop, which skirts the central fighting area. Signs scattered across the actual battlefield mark the positions of the different companies and explain Morgan's tactics. Even if you're not fascinated by military history, the strange tranquility of the place makes it worthy of a stroll.

The Drive » From the park, continue south 50 miles on SC 11. The byway passes farms, fields, produce stands and Baptist churches before rolling into the woods. Follow Hwy 276 as it twists upward through the park.

TRIP HIGHLIGHT

❸ Caesars Head State Park

Sometimes you want to earn your stunning view – with a 10-mile hike or an all-day bike ride. Other times you just want to step out of your car, walk 30 steps and say 'Wow!' The overlook at **Caesars Head State Park** (☎864-836-6115; www.southcarolinaparks.com; 8155 Geer Hwy, Cleveland; trail access $2; ☻9am-9pm mid-Mar–early Nov, to 6pm rest of year, visitor center hours vary) falls cheerfully into the latter category. This lofty viewpoint atop the Blue Ridge Escarpment offers a sweeping panorama of regional mountains and foothills. From here, Table Rock Mountain juts into view almost dead ahead. During the fall **Hawk Watch** (Sep-Nov), migrating hawks catch thermals here – and impress visitors – as they travel south for winter. If you do want to exercise, try the 4.4-mile round-trip hike to a view of 420ft **Raven Cliff Falls**.

The Drive » Take Hwy 8 to SC 11 south then drive 4.6 miles.

TRIP HIGHLIGHT

❹ Table Rock State Park

Table Rock Mountain is the region's marquee natural attraction. A 3124ft-high mountain with a striking granite face, it's ready-made for photographs. According to Cherokee legend, the mountain served as a table for a giant chieftain, who ate there after a hunt. While dining, he used Stool Mountain as his seat.

The 7.2-mile round-trip hike to its summit at **Table Rock State Park** (☎864-878-9813; www.southcarolinaparks.com; 158 Ellison Lane, Pickens; Jun-Nov adult/child 6-15yr $5/3, Dec-May adult/child under 16yr $2/free; ☻7am-7pm Sun-Thu, to 9pm Fri & Sat, extended hours mid-May–early Nov) is a popular local challenge.

TABLE ROCK STATE PARK: CIVILIAN CONSERVATION CORPS

In 1933 President Franklin D Roosevelt established the Civilian Conservation Corps (CCC), a workforce of 250,000 young men. Its mission? To conserve and improve America's resources. Within 10 years Roosevelt's 'Tree Army' had laid 28,087 miles of trails and created or improved more than 800 state parks. The CCC built 16 state parks in South Carolina. Construction of Table Rock State Park began in 1935. CCC projects at Table Rock include the concession building, a lodge, most cabins, all trails and the 36-acre Pinnacle Lake.

Greenville Falls Park and Liberty Bridge

For a good view of the mountain, take a seat at the park **visitor center**, which is also an information center for the scenic highway.

Visitors can spend the night in one of 14 cabins constructed by the Civilian Conservation Corps. The second Saturday of the month, catch a bluegrass jam here as part of the annual Music on the Mountain Series. Need more options? There's camping, plus swimming and fishing in Pinnacle Lake.

p129

The Drive » Return to SC 11 south and drive 19 miles to SC 130. Turn left and continue south 10 miles, passing through Salem, where there's a great B&B (p129). SC 130 becomes Rochester Hwy.

----

5 Duke Energy World of Energy Museum

After all those trees and waterfalls, it just seems right to stop and stretch your legs at...a nuclear power plant. But hey, why not? The self-guided tour inside the **Duke Energy World of Energy Museum** (☎800-777-1004; www.duke-energy.com/world ofenergy; 7812 Rochester Hwy, Seneca; ⏰9am-5pm Mon-Fri) at the Oconee Nuclear Station provides a pretty darn interesting look at electricity and how it has been produced in the region, from the use of water power to coal to uranium. The nuclear plant went online in 1973, and today it can provide electricity for more than 1.7 million average-sized homes.

The Drive » Take SC 130 south to E Pickens Hwy/SC 183. Turn left and drive 14 miles. At Hwy 178, turn left and drive 3 miles. Turn left on to Hagood Mill Rd.

LOCAL KNOWLEDGE: GREENVILLE'S MICE ON MAIN

Inquisitive children and fun-loving adults (with good eyesight) will get a kick out of a downtown scavenger hunt in Greenville called Mice on Main. The treasures are nine bronze mice placed in different spots along Main St between the Hyatt Regency and the Westin Poinsett. The project, inspired by the childhood book *Goodnight Moon*, was the brainchild of a local high-school student, Jim Ryan, who wanted downtown to feel like a special place. As you find the mice, located on both sides of the street, you'll learn more about the city. Pick up a list of mouse-hunt clues at the visitor center (206 S Main St) or online (www.greenvillecvb.com).

6 Hagood Mill Historic Site & Folklore Center

You'll find more than a historic mill at this stream-side site (☎864-898-2936; www.co.pickens.sc.us; 138 Hagood Mill Rd, Pickens; ☺10am-4pm Wed-Sat) in Pickens County. Several hundred petroglyphs have been discovered in the upcountry, and in 2003 a collection of stick-figure carvings were found on a rock near the mill. The site's namesake attraction, the 1845 gristmill, has a 20ft wooden waterwheel. The mill was in continuous commercial operation until 1966. Today it's back in production on the third Saturday of every month, when

there's also live bluegrass music. Also on-site are two relocated log cabins, one dating from 1791, as well as an old moonshine still.

The Drive » Return to SC 183 and follow it east 20 miles into downtown Greenville.

TRIP HIGHLIGHT

7 Greenville

Greenville has one of America's most inviting downtowns. The Reedy River twists through the city center, and its dramatic falls tumble beneath Main St at **Falls Park** (www.fallspark.com). For a photo of the falls, stroll on to the graceful Liberty Bridge, a 345ft-long suspension bridge.

Main St itself rolls past a lively array of

boutiques, eateries and craft-beer pubs. Whimsical quotes from notables such as Oscar Wilde, Erma Bombeck and Will Rogers – called 'Thoughts on a Walk' – dot the sidewalk. In the evening, the trees are illuminated by twinkling white lights. Stop by the **visitor center** (☎864-233-0461; www.visitgreenvillesc.com; 206 S Main St; ☺8am-5pm Mon-Fri, 9am-5pm Sat, noon-4pm Sun) for a public-art map and clues for Mice on Main.

For exercise, try the **Swamp Rabbit Trail** (www.greenvillerec.com), a 17.5-mile path for hikers and cyclists on an old railway line that links downtown to Furman University. Pop into the regionally famed **Mast General Store** (www.mastgeneralstore.com; 111 N Main St; ☺10am-6pm Mon-Thu, 10am-9pm Fri & Sat, noon-6pm Sun) for outdoor gear and old-time candy then sample peach whiskey at **Dark Corner Distiwllery** (www.darkcornerdistillery.com; 241 N Main St; ☺11am-7pm Mon-Sat). The Dark Corner is the nickname given to the secretive upland corner of Greenville County, which was famed for its bootlegging and hardscrabble Scots-Irish residents.

✗ ⊨ p129

Eating & Sleeping

Table Rock State Park ④

⌂ Table Rock State Park
Campground & Cabins   Campground $

(☏864-878-9813; www.southcarolinaparks.
com; 158 Ellison Lane, Pickens; campsites
$16-21, cabins $52-181; ❄) The 14 CCC-built
cabins (one to three bedrooms) have air-con,
kitchenette and coffeemaker. Campers have a
choice of 93 campsites with water and hookups,
spread across two separate wooded camping
areas. There are also five walk-in sites ($9 to
$13). All sites can be reserved.

Salem ④

⌂ Sunrise Farm B&B   B&B $$

(☏864-944-0121; www.sunrisefarmbb.com;
325 Sunrise Dr; r $106-136, cottage $136-154;
P ❄ 🛜 🛗 🐾) Join Cisco the Bolivian llama
and sheep, pygmy goats, cats and a Lhasa Apso
on acres of pastoral lands.

Greenville ⑦

✕ Coffee Underground   Cafe $

(www.coffeeunderground.info; 1 E Coffee St;
pastries & desserts $2-5, sandwiches $8; ⊙7am-
10pm Mon-Thu, 7am-11:30pm Fri, 8am-11:30pm
Sat, 8am-10pm Sun; 🛜) Try the Marabella
chicken wrap and the Black Tiger milkshake
at this welcoming indie coffee shop. The
chocolate-chunk cookies are darn good too. It's
located at the bottom of the stairs at the corner
of Main and Coffee Sts.

✕ Lazy Goat   Mediterranean $$

(☏864-679-5299; www.thelazygoat.com; 170
River Pl; lunch $7-14, dinner small plates $7-13,

dinner mains $10-28; ⊙11am-9pm Mon-Thu,
to 10pm Fri & Sat) Nibble pimiento cheese and
ciabatta bread and sip wine beside the river at
this stylish spot, known for its Mediterranean
small plates.

✕ Lemongrass   Thai $$

(www.lemongrassthai.net; 106 N Main St; lunch
$10-13, dinner $12-22; ⊙11:30am-2:30pm
Mon-Fri, 5:30-10pm Mon-Thu, 5:30-10:30pm Fri
& Sat) Dine on delicious noodle dishes, curries
and Bangkok street dishes, with jazz playing in
the background, at this stylish Thai restaurant
tucked in a narrow space on Main St.

⌂ Pettigru Place   B&B $$

(☏864-242-4529; www.pettigruplace.com; 302
Pettrigru St; r $175-249; P ❄ 🛜) A six-room
downtown B&B with quaint themed rooms – we
dig the downstairs Africa room, with epic walk-
in shower; and the upstairs Green Rabbit room,
with great patio overlooking the charming front
gardens – and a good mix of modern (shared
Keurig coffeemaker, flat-screen TV) and retro
conveniences (shared 1929 GE fridge stocked
with sodas etc). Some have spa tub and/or
electric fireplace. The helpful host has Southern
hospitality down pat.

⌂ Westin
Poinsett   Hotel $$$

(☏864-421-9700; www.westinpoinsett
greenville.com; 120 S Main St; r $189-309;
P ❄ @ 🛜 🐾) This grand hotel, which
originally opened in 1925, is in the heart of
downtown, just steps from Reedy River Falls.
Past guests include Amelia Earhart, Cornelius
Vanderbilt and Bobby Kennedy. There's new
carpeting, sconces and wall vinyl throughout
the hotel, while rooms tilt toward the basic
(bathrooms are set for a remodel soon). Parking
is $7.50 per day; pets are $75 per stay.

Lowcountry & Southern Coast

Century-old churches. Timeless marshes. Ancient live oaks and Spanish moss. On this Lowcountry loop, the past rises up to say hello. Except on Parris Island, where it yells, 'Move it marine!'

10

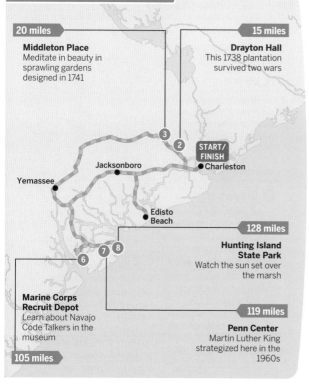

TRIP HIGHLIGHTS

20 miles

Middleton Place
Meditate in beauty in sprawling gardens designed in 1741

15 miles

Drayton Hall
This 1738 plantation survived two wars

Jacksonboro

START/ FINISH
Charleston

Yemassee

Edisto Beach

128 miles

Hunting Island State Park
Watch the sun set over the marsh

Marine Corps Recruit Depot
Learn about Navajo Code Talkers in the museum

105 miles

119 miles

Penn Center
Martin Luther King strategized here in the 1960s

3 DAYS
265 MILES / 426KM

GREAT FOR...

BEST TIME TO GO

From spring to fall for the Gullah Festival, fresh produce at roadside stands and sunny weather for outdoor adventures.

 ESSENTIAL PHOTO

Sunset over the marsh at Hunting Island State Park.

 BEST FOR CULTURE

From boot camp to bottle trees, you'll learn the traditions of unique coastal communities.

Charleston Gullah storyteller Carolyn Jabulile White

131

Lowcountry & Southern Coast

The Lowcountry welcomes travelers with a warm embrace – straight from the 1700s. This coastal region, which stretches from Charleston south to Georgia, is a tangle of islands, inlets and tidal marshes. This drive sweeps in plantation life, military history, Gullah culture and a landmark African American school, all set among a moody backdrop of coastal wilds.

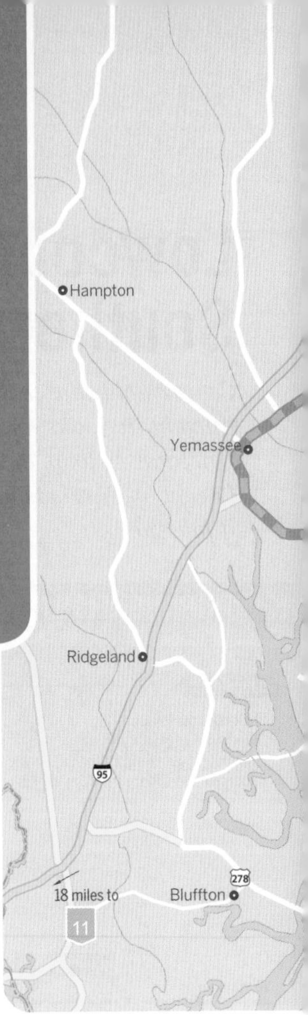

1 Charleston

Charleston is a city for savoring. Stroll past Rainbow Row, take a carriage ride, study the antebellum architecture and enjoy buttery shrimp and grits on a stylish verandah. Historically, the city is best known for its role in the start of the Civil War. The first shots of the conflict rang out on April 12, 1861, at **Fort Sumter** (www. nps.gov/fosu), a pentagon-shaped island in the harbor. **Boat tours** (🚤boat tour 843-722-2628, park 843-883-3123; www.fortsumtertours. com; 340 Concord St; adult $21, child 4-11yr $13) depart from Aquarium Wharf at the eastern end of Calhoun St and from Patriot's Point in Mt Pleasant. To explore

Charleston's historical district, see p138,

🍴 🛏 p137

The Drive » From the wharf, follow Calhoun St west through Charleston to Hwy 61, also known as Ashley River Rd. Follow it north for about 10 miles.

TRIP HIGHLIGHT

2 Drayton Hall

Three plantations – Drayton Hall, Magnolia Plantation and Middleton Place – border Ashley River Rd, their gardens, swamps and graveyards hidden behind a line of oaks and Spanish moss.

The first plantation on the drive is **Drayton Hall** (📞843-769-2600; www.dray tonhall.org; 3380 Ashley River Rd; adult/child $22/10, grounds only $12; 🕘9am-5pm Mon-Sat, 11am-5pm Sun, last tour 3:30pm), built in 1738 and unique for its Georgian-Palladian architecture. It was the only plantation along the Ashley River to survive the Revolutionary and Civil Wars. It also survived the great earthquake of 1886. The plantation is unique because it has been preserved,

Hampton

Yemassee

Ridgeland

95

18 miles to   Bluffton
11

278

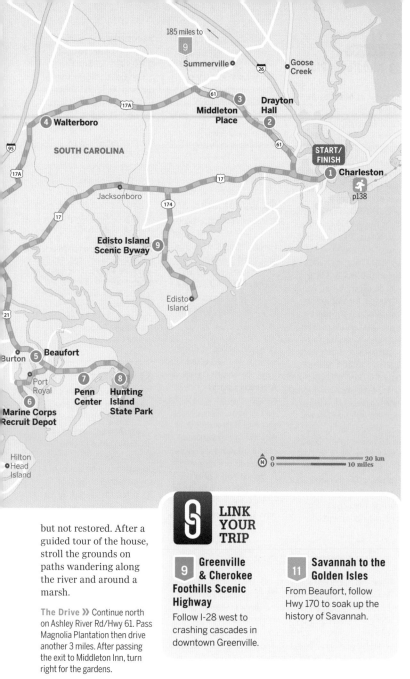

185 miles to
9

Summerville

Goose
Creek

26

61
3 Drayton
Hall
Middleton
Place
2
17A

4 Walterboro

61

START/
FINISH

95

SOUTH CAROLINA

17
1 Charleston

17A

Jacksonboro

p138

174

Edisto Island
9
Scenic Byway

Edisto
Island

21

Burton 5 Beaufort

Port
Royal
7
Penn
Center
8
Hunting
Island
State Park
6
Marine Corps
Recruit Depot

Hilton
Head
Island

N   0   20 km
    0   10 miles

but not restored. After a
guided tour of the house,
stroll the grounds on
paths wandering along
the river and around a
marsh.

The Drive ≫ Continue north
on Ashley River Rd/Hwy 61. Pass
Magnolia Plantation then drive
another 3 miles. After passing
the exit to Middleton Inn, turn
right for the gardens.

**LINK
YOUR
TRIP**

9 **Greenville
    & Cherokee
Foothills Scenic
Highway**
Follow I-28 west to
crashing cascades in
downtown Greenville.

11 **Savannah to the
     Golden Isles**
From Beaufort, follow
Hwy 170 to soak up the
history of Savannah.

❸ Middleton Place

Designed in 1741, the vast gardens at **Middleton Place** (📞843-556-6020; www.middletonplace.org; 4300 Ashley River Rd, Summerville; gardens adult $28, child 6-13yr $10, house-museum tour extra $15; ⊙9am-5pm) are the oldest in the US. One hundred slaves spent a decade terracing and digging the precise geometric canals. The property was the Middleton family seat from the 1700s through the Civil War.

The grounds are a mix of classic formal French gardens and romantic woodland settings. The garden wandering is superb – one lonely path leads to a band of stone cherubs blissfully rocking out. There are also flooded rice patties and fields of rare-breed farm animals. Union soldiers burned the main house in 1855, but a guest wing, built in 1755 and later restored, still stands today. It contains a museum with Middleton family furnishings and historic documents.

Bring a picnic lunch – this place is pretty perfect – or enjoy a traditional Lowcountry plantation lunch of she-crab soup and hoppin'john at the highly regarded **cafe**.

The Drive » Follow Hwy 61 north to its junction with Hwy 17A. Turn left. Take Hwy 17A south for 24 miles.

❹ Walterboro

The town of Walterboro calls itself the 'The Front Porch of the Lowcountry,' and a red rocking chair greets guests at the **welcome center** (📞843-538-4353; www.walterborosc.org; 1273 Sniders Hwy; ⊙9am-5pm Mon-Sat).

Downtown, shoppers can peruse a dozen antique stores before visiting the **South Carolina Artisans Center** (www.scartisanscenter.com; 318 Wichman St; ⊙9am-5pm Mon-Sat, 1-5pm Sun). Here, folk art, fine art and traditional crafts fill several rooms in a rambling house.

Boardwalks and trails wind through 842 acres of swampland at the new **Walterboro Wildlife**

Sanctuary (www.walterborosc.org). One path tracks the Savannah Stage Coach Rd, which dates to Colonial times. Entrances are off Jefferies Blvd at Beach Rd and Detreville St. The park's original name, the Great Swamp Sanctuary, was scrapped in 2013 because the town council thought the word 'swamp' had negative connotations, especially for urban visitors. We beg to differ.

The Drive » From Walterboro, continue south on Hwy 17A to Yemassee. For brochures and history, turn right at Hwy 17 and continue to the Low Country Visitor Center at Frampton Plantation. Otherwise, turn left on Hwy 17 and continue to Beaufort.

❺ Beaufort

The streets are lined with antebellum homes. Magnolias drip with Spanish moss. Boats shimmer on the river. Gobs of cafes and galleries crowd the downtown. The town is so darn charming that it's often the backdrop for Hollywood films set in the South, from the *Big Chill* to the *Prince of Tides* to *Forrest Gump*. Walk, eat, shop...or just nap on the porch at your B&B.

🍴 🛏 p137

The Drive » Take the Sea Island Pkwy over the river then turn right on to Hwy 21N, following it about 5.5 miles to Parris Island. Take the first exit toward Malecon Dr. Follow the signs to the museum.

BLUE BOTTLE TREES

That tree in the distance? The one with the branches sprouting empty blue bottles? Say hello to your first bottle tree, a tradition that traces back to 9th-century Congo. According to lore, haunts and evil spirits, being of a curious nature, crawl inside the bottles to see what they can find. They become trapped and then are destroyed by the morning sunlight. Stop and listen. On a windy night you might just hear them moan.

Drayton Hall A uniquely preserved plantation home

TRIP HIGHLIGHT

6 Marine Corps Recruit Depot

More than 17,000 men and women endure boot camp each year at the Parris Island recruiting depot (www.mcrdpi.marines.mil), which has trained marines since 1915. The experience was made notorious by Stanley Kubrick's *Full Metal Jacket*.

The Modern Marine Wing at the **Parris Island Museum** (www.parrisisland museum.com; 111 Panama St; ☺10am-4:30pm Mon-Wed & Sat & Sun, 8am-4:30pm Thu-Fri)

describes marine participation in recent wars. Check out the Navajo Code Talkers display – not one of their transmissions was ever compromised during WWII. Another exhibit spotlights famous former marines, including Gene Hackman, Shaggy and George Jones. Check the website for dates for the popular **Friday graduations**. You will be asked to show ID and maybe car registration before driving on to the grounds (foreign nationals must show a passport).

The Drive » Return to the Sea Island Pkwy and turn right. Drive almost 5 miles east to Dr Martin Luther King Jr Dr. Turn right.

TRIP HIGHLIGHT

7 Penn Center

East of Beaufort is a series of marshy, rural islands including St Helena Island, considered the heart of Gullah Country. The nonprofit **Penn Center** (☏843-838-2474; www.penncenter.com/museum; 16 Penn Center Circle W, St Helena Island; adult $7, child 6-16yr $3; ☺9am-4pm Tue-Sat) preserves and celebrates Sea Island culture. Here, the York W Bailey Museum traces the history of Penn School, established in

GULLAH CULTURE

African slaves were transported across the Atlantic from the Rice Coast (Sierra Leone, Senegal, the Gambia and Angola) to a landscape that was shockingly similar – swampy coastlines, tropical vegetation and hot, humid summers.

These new African Americans retained many of their homeland traditions, even after the fall of slavery and into the 20th century. The resulting Gullah (also known as Geechee in Georgia) culture has its own language, an English-based Creole with many African words and sentence structures, and many traditions, including fantastic storytelling, art, music and crafts. The Gullah culture is celebrated annually with the energetic **Gullah Festival** (www.theoriginalgullahfestival.org; ⊘late May) in Beaufort on the last weekend in May.

1862, which was one of the nation's first schools for freed slaves. Martin Luther King used the site in the 1960s as a retreat for strategic, nonviolent planning during the Civil Rights movement.

The Drive » Return to the Sea Island Pkwy. Follow it east over expansive marshes then cross the Harbor River Bridge.

- - - - - - - - - - - - - - - - -

TRIP HIGHLIGHT

⑧ Hunting Island State Park

With its tidal lagoons, maritime forest, bone-white beach, and 3000 acres of salt marsh, **Hunting Island State Park** (☏843-838-2011; www.southcarolinaparks.com/huntingisland; 2555 Sea Island Pkwy; adult $5, child 6-15yr $3; ⊘visitor center 9am-5pm Mon-Fri, 11am-5pm Sat & Sun, nature center 9am-5pm Tue-Sat, daily Jun-Aug) is a

nature lover's dream, though the park suffered extensive damage at the wrath of Hurricanes Matthew and Irma (see p338) – so call ahead to see if it's back up and running at full capacity before setting out. There are 8 miles of hiking and biking trails. On a rainy day, try climbing the 175 steps inside the light-house, with lofty views of the coast as your reward. At the nature center you can learn about local wildlife. The boardwalk behind the nature center is a great place to catch the sunset. The park was also the setting for the Vietnam War scenes in *Forrest Gump*, which were filmed in the marsh.

🛏 p137

The Drive » Backtrack north on Hwy 21 to its junction with Hwy 17 north. Drive almost 30 miles. Turn right on to Hwy 174.

⑨ Edisto Island Scenic Byway

With its old churches, grassy marshes and moss-draped oaks, the 17-mile Edisto Island Scenic Byway is a classic Low-country drive. It stretches along Hwy 174 from the Atlantic Intracoastal Waterway south to Edisto Beach State Park.

Swoop over the waterway then take the first right to the **Dawhoo Landing** parking area. A map here lists byway attractions. Turn around for a nice view of the graceful McKinley Washington, Jr Bridge. Continue south to King's Farm Market for local produce, baked goods, jams and Cheerwine.

For history, visit the sometimes-open **Edisto Island Museum** and the 1831 **Presbysterian Church**. Next up? The snakey **Edisto Island Ser-pentarium** (www.edistoserpentarium.com; 1374 Hwy 174; adult/child $15/11; ⊘10am-6pm Mon-Sat Jun–early Sep, hours vary Thu-Sat spring & fall) followed by the mystery tree – look right, into the marsh, to see its seasonal decorations. Last is **Edisto Beach State Park** (☏843-869-2156; www.southcarolinaparks.com; 8377 State Cabin Rd; adult $5, child 6-15yr $3; tent/RV sites from $20/44, cabins from $149; 🛜), with camping just steps from the shore. From here, return to Charleston.

🍴 p137

Eating & Sleeping

Charleston ❶

✖ Ordinary   Seafood $$$

(📞843-414-7060; www.eattheordinary.com;
544 King St; small plates $6-18, large $21-55;
🕐5-10:30pm Tue-Sun) Inside a cavernous
1927 bank building, this buzzy seafood hall
and oyster bar feels like the best party in town.
The menu is short, but the savory dishes are
prepared with finesse – from the oyster sliders
to the lobster rolls to the nightly fish dishes.

🛏 Ansonborough Inn   Hotel $$

(📞800-522-2073; www.ansonboroughinn.com;
21 Hasell St; r from $169-329; P ❄ @ 📶) Droll
neo-Victorian touches such as the closet-sized
British pub and the formal portraits of dogs add
a sense of fun to this intimate Historic District
hotel, which also manages to feel like an antique
sailing ship. Huge guest rooms mix old and
new, with worn leather couches, high ceilings
and flat-screen TVs. Complimentary wine and
cheese social, with great pimiento cheese, runs
from 5pm to 6pm and you can take it up to the
lovely flower-potted rooftop.

Beaufort ❺

✖ Lowcountry Produce   Southern US $

(www.lowcountryproduce.com; 302 Carteret St;
breakfast $9-15, sandwiches $10-18; 🕐8am-
3pm; 📶) A fantastic cafe and market for picnic
rations such as pies, housemade relishes,
local cheeses – all kinds of Lowcountry-spun
awesomeness (except that cream-cheese
lasagna, that ain't right!). Or eat in and indulge
in an Oooey Gooey, a grilled pimiento-cheese
sandwich with bacon and garlic-pepper jelly
(one hot mess!) or a tasty crab-cake sandwich
with Brussels-sprouts slaw. It's a madhouse
here on weekends for good reason.

✖ Sgt White's   Southern, Barbecue $

(1908 Boundary St; meat & 3 sides platter $9;
🕐11am-3pm Mon-Fri) A retired marine sergeant
serves up classic meat-and-three platters. At

the counter, order your juicy BBQ ribs or meat
dish, then choose three sides, which can include
collards, okra stew and cornbread.

🛏 Cuthbert House Inn   B&B $$$

(📞843-521-1315; www.cuthberthouseinn.com;
1203 Bay St; r $179-245; P ❄ 📶) The most
romantic of Beaufort's B&Bs, this sumptuously
grand white-columned mansion is straight out
of Gone with the Wind II. Antique furnishings are
found throughout, but monochromatic walls
add a fresh, modern feel. Some rooms have a
river view (three have fireplaces). On his march
through the South in 1865, General William T
Sherman slept at the house. You'll be smitten
from the parking lot – the front gardens are
gorgeous.

Hunting Island State Park ❽

🛏 Hunting Island State
Park Campground   Campground $

(📞office 843-838-2011, reservations 866-
345-7275; www.southcarolinaparks.com; 2555
Sea Island Pkwy; tent sites $18-20, RV sites
$18-45, cabins $249; 🕐6am-6pm, to 9pm early
Mar–early Nov) At one of South Carolina's most
visited parks, you can camp under pine trees
or palm trees. Several campsites are just steps
from the beach. All sites are available by walk-
up, but reservations are advisable in summer.
The campground was heavily damaged by
Hurricanes Matthew and Irma and was closed
through 2017. Call ahead for updates.

Edisto Island Scenic Byway ❾

✖ King's Farm Market   Market $

(www.kingsfarmmarket.com; 2559 Hwy 174;
🕐10am-5pm Mon-Sat, to 4pm Sun Feb-Dec)
It's not just about the fresh produce, the
macadamia-nut cookies, the key lime pie, the
blackberry cobbler, the jalapeño-pimento
cheese, or the sandwiches and casseroles. It's
also about the easygoing friendliness. C'mon
already, come in.

STRETCH YOUR LEGS
CHARLESTON

Start/Finish Husk

- -

Distance 1.8 miles

- -

Duration Three to four hours

Few cities evoke the same storied romanticism as Charleston. But the romance can overshadow the darker elements of the city's past. This stroll, which includes a slave mart, a dungeon and a city park, examines the city's compelling but contradictory history.

Take this walk on Trip

10

Husk

Every great walking tour begins with just the right lunch – always a sure thing at **Husk** (📞843-577-2500; www. huskrestaurant.com; 76 Queen St; brunch & lunch $10-17, dinner $29-34; ⊙11:30am-2:30pm Mon-Sat, 5:30-10pm Sun-Thu, 5:30-11pm Fri & Sat, brunch 10am-2:30pm Sun). The creation of acclaimed chef Sean Brock, Husk is one the South's most buzzed-about restaurants. Everything on the menu is grown or raised in the South and the menu changes daily. The setting, in a two-story mansion, is elegant but unfussy.

The Walk » Follow Queen St east to Meeting St. Turn right. Walk one block south to Chalmers St, the city's red-light district in the 1700s. Cross Church St. The museum is ahead on the left.

Old Slave Mart

Charleston was a major marketplace for the African slave trade. In 1856 the city banned the selling of slaves on the streets, which drove merchants indoors. The **Old Slave Mart Museum** (www.nps.gov/nr/travel/charleston/osm. htm; 6 Chalmers St; adult $8, child 5-17yr $5; ⊙9am-5pm Mon-Sat) sits inside one of the resulting auction houses. Text-heavy exhibits illuminate the slave experience and slave trading; the few artifacts, such as leg shackles, are especially chilling. For first-hand stories, listen to the oral recollections of former slave Elijah Green, born in 1853.

Save $2 with a combination ticket to the Old Exchange.

The Walk » Continue east on Chalmers St to State St and turn right. Walk south to Broad St. Turn left. The Old Exchange is one block ahead.

Old Exchange & Provost Dungeon

This 1771 Georgian-Palladian **custom house** (www.oldexchange.org; 122 E Bay St; adult $10, child 7-12yr $5; ⊙9am-5pm; ♿) is certainly impressive, but it's the brick dungeon underneath that wows the crowds. On the docent-led tour of this basement space, you'll learn about the

pirates imprisoned here in 1718, when it was part of a battery guard house. The British kept American patriots captive in the space during the Revolutionary War. After the war, several of them returned to the building to ratify the United States Constitution.

The Walk » Follow E Bay St south. As you climb on to the promenade, grab your camera for photos of Rainbow Row, a line-up of candy-colored townhouses.

The Battery & White Point Gardens

Soak in more history at the Battery, the southern tip of the Charleston peninsula which is buffered by a seawall. Fortifications and artillery were here during the Civil War. In the gardens, stroll past cannons and statues of military heroes, and ponder the risk-filled lives of the pirates who were hanged here. From the promenade, look for Fort Sumter. The island fortress was fired upon by Confederates on April 12, 1861 – the first shots of the Civil War.

The Walk » From the gardens, walk north on Meeting St.

Nathaniel Russell House

Built in 1808, the Federal-style **Nathaniel Russell House** (www.historiccharleston. org; 51 Meeting St; adult $12, child 6-16yr $5; ⏱10am-5pm Mon-Sat, 2-5pm Sun, last tour 4:30pm) is noted especially for its spectacular, self-supporting spiral staircase and its English garden. Russell, a merchant from Rhode Island, was known in Charleston as the King of the Yankees. The home underwent major renovations in 2013, which added exhibits and preserved architectural features.

The Walk » Continue north on Meeting St. Its junction with Broad St is known as the Four Corners of the Law, with a federal post office, a state courthouse, City Hall and a church each occupying one of the corners. Broad St here is known as Gallery Row. Follow Meeting St to Queen St for a cocktail at the speakeasy-style bar at Husk.

Georgia & Alabama

Georgia and Alabama are a microcosm of the South, on the one hand home to jet-set cities and urban glitterati, and on the other, a slow lifestyle steeped in tradition and history. In Georgia, Atlanta tempts visitors with slick design hotels, hipster bars, sensational restaurants and world-class cultural attractions. There's wine-drenched Dahlonega in the north; prim and proper Savannah, a gorgeous Southern belle with an edge, to the south; and tempting barbecue throughout. Alabama, steeped in palpable and captivating civil rights history, is also home to two iconic sports venues, and offers Birmingham, an endearing up-and-coming city, and a progressive example of the new South.

Birmingham The Old Mill along Shades Creek, Mountain Brook
ROBBIE BREWER / 500PX ©

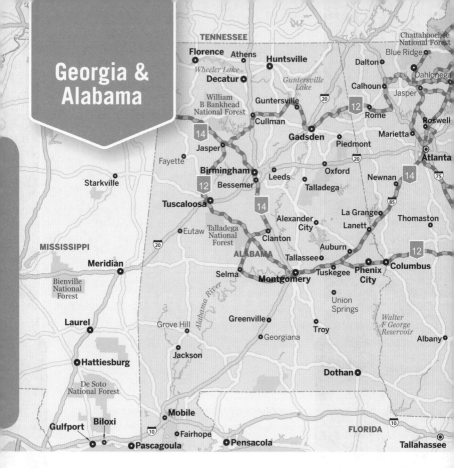

Georgia & Alabama

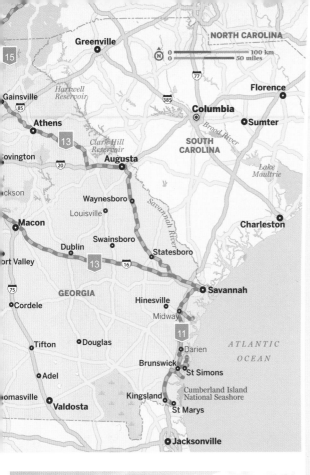

DON'T MISS

Savannah

Savannah has European elegance, a Southern spirit, shady squares, tasty cafes and a leafy, compact historical core that is as inviting as it is pedestrian-friendly. Experience it on Trips 11 13

Sweet Auburn

A historic corner of downtown Atlanta that gifted us Martin Luther King, a middle-class pastor's son who became the ultimate humanitarian and world leader. Explore it on Trip 14

Dahlonega

This charming former gold-mining town now draws visitors to its vineyards set amid stunning mountain vistas. White or red? Taste it all on Trip 12

Birmingham

Unlike Alabama's other cities and towns scarred by oppressive history, Birmingham deftly balances its progressive present with its dark past, by revealing itself completely. See it on Trip 14

CHADSOC / GETTY IMAGES ©

Dahlonega Vineyard-studded hills

Classic Trip

11

Savannah to the Golden Isles

Georgia's Golden Isles are a 100-mile stretch of maritime forests, wildlife-rich estuaries, scrubby dunes, wild beaches and coastal towns that evoke a bygone era. Georgia's best-kept secret is out.

TRIP HIGHLIGHTS

0 miles

Savannah
Antebellum architecture, leafy streets and squares

① START

● Sunbury Crab Company

147 miles

Jekyll Island
Turn-of-the-century lore, good cycling, stunning beaches

⑥

122 miles

Little St Simons Island
Empty beaches, raw nature, silence

● St Simons Island

⑧

● St Marys

FINISH

4 DAYS
165 MILES / 266KM

GREAT FOR...

BEST TIME TO GO

Coastal spring (March to May), when the weather warms but humidity remains human.

 ESSENTIAL PHOTO

Driftwood Beach: where full-grown oaks end up as driftwood, roots and all.

 BEST FOR OUTDOOR ACTIVITIES

Because who doesn't love days and days on the beach?

Jekyll Island Exposed oaks at Driftwood Beach

145

11 Savannah to the Golden Isles

Georgia has one of America's most diverse and interesting shorelines. Its barrier islands are (mostly) pristine jewels and it's home to one-third of the entire East Coast's salt marshes, and preserved 18th- and 19th-century Southern architecture. Plus it's just a damn fine place to get away from it all. And when you begin in artsy and elegant Savannah, this trip becomes even more breathtaking.

TRIP HIGHLIGHT

❶ Savannah

Like a Southern belle with a wild side, this grand historic town revolves around formal antebellum architecture and the revelry of local students from the **Savannah College of Art and Design (SCAD)**. With its gorgeous mansions and wonderfully beautiful squares, Savannah preserves its past with pride and grace, but has ample grit and soul.

Here, even an aimless wander is life-affirming. Make sure to visit **Forsyth Park**, from where you can follow our walking tour (p192), and the **Owens-Thomas House** (☎912-790-8800; www.telfair.org; 124 Abercorn St; adult/senior/child $20/18/15; ☺noon-5pm Sun & Mon, 10am-5pm Tue-Sat), a 19th-century villa that exemplifies English Regency–style architecture, known for its symmetry. Modernists will appreciate the striking, and ambitious, **SCAD Museum of Art** (www.scadmoa.org; 601 Turner Blvd; adult/child under 14yr $10/free; ☺10am-5pm Tue-Wed, to 8pm Thu, to 5pm Fri & Sat, noon-5pm Sun), while the **Jepson Center for the Arts** (JCA; ☎912-790-8800; www.telfair.org; 207 W York St; adult/child $20/15; ☺noon-5pm Sun & Mon, 10am-5pm Tue-Sat; ♿) makes for another interesting peek.

The shopping on Broughton St is underrated, and handbag obsessives should duck into **Satchel** (☎912-233-1008; www.shopsatchel.com; 4 E Liberty St; ☺10am-6pm Mon-Sat, 11am-3pm Sun), which is owned and operated by the designer herself.

For the best photo op in town, head to the Avenue of the Oaks at the **Wormsloe Plantation Historic Site** (see the boxed text, p170).

🍴 🛏 p154, p218

The Drive » The gateway to Brunswick and the Golden Isles is Hwy 17, which rolls south from Savannah on a scenic coastal tack through several tiny, picturesque Georgia towns. It's about 40 miles from Savannah to Midway Pass, then take a 15-minute detour east on Hwy 84 past Fort Morris until the road ends.

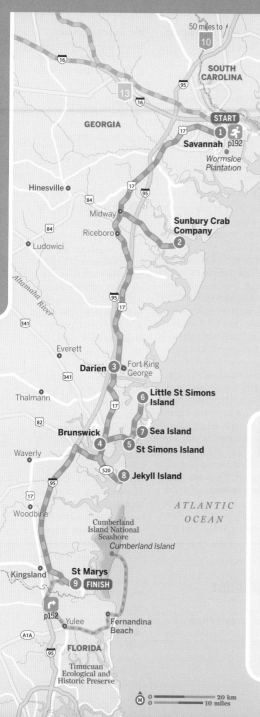

50 miles to 10

SOUTH CAROLINA

GEORGIA

START

1

Savannah p192

Wormsloe Plantation

Hinesville

Midway

Riceboro

Ludowici

Sunbury Crab Company

2

Everett

Darien 3 Fort King George

Thalmann

Brunswick

4

Little St Simons Island 6

Sea Island 7

St Simons Island 5

Jekyll Island 8

Waverly

Woodbine

ATLANTIC OCEAN

Cumberland Island National Seashore

Cumberland Island

Kingsland

St Marys

9 FINISH

p152

Yulee

Fernandina Beach

FLORIDA

Timucuan Ecological and Historic Preserve

0   20 km
0   10 miles

2 Sunbury Crab Company

Sunbury Crab Company
(☎912-884-8640; www.sunburycrabco.com; 541 Brigantine Dunmore Rd, Sunbury; mains $8-27; ☺5-10pm Wed-Fri, noon-10pm Sat, noon-8:30pm Sun) is one of those truly special finds that elude most travelers. Here you'll find a Key West–style tree house built with reclaimed wood from old barns and department stores. The menu is whatever is fresh that day: blue crab caught that morning by the son; shrimp caught by the neighbor; and oysters brought in by the uncle. All of it is steamed and chased by cold beer overlooking the gorgeous St Catherines Sound.

LINK YOUR TRIP

13 Hogs & Heifers: A Georgia BBQ Odyssey

Savannah includes a stop on this decadent, carnivorous jaunt into the pit-smoked soul of Georgia's spiciest, juiciest kitchens.

10 Lowcountry & Southern Coast

Hop across the border, from one historic town to another, where the food only gets better.

Classic Trip

The Drive » Head back to Hwy 17 and follow it south for another 40 miles into the small town of Darien.

----

③ Darien

Darien is a simple, relatively sprawling yet quiet town sheltered by trees and surrounded by marsh, with a middling historic core dotted with middle- and working-class homes, but there is one remarkable site. **Fort King George** (📞912-437-4770; www.gastateparks.com/FortKingGeorge; 302 McIntosh Road SE; adult/senior/child 6-18yr/child under 5yr $7.50/7/4.50/free; ⏰9am-5pm Tue-Sat, 2-5:30pm Sun; 🅿️ 👶) is a remarkably reconstructed version of Georgia's first fort, a British outpost dating to 1721. The fort overlooks a vast estuary, and is surrounded by mossy oaks. Expect to spot egrets and storks and to be serenaded by songbirds. It's a beautiful scene. There

are also two restaurants of note here.

The Drive » Thus far, Hwy 17 has often felt like it was hugging the interstate, nothing more than a glorified frontage road. For the next 17 miles south, however, the roads diverge, and Hwy 17 begins snaking through the estuary and courting the sea breeze.

----

④ Brunswick

The town of Brunswick is a vaguely historic town, worth a stroll for its antique shops and the potpourri of architectural styles along its main drag, Newcastle St, and throughout its Old Town National Register Historic District. Even better is the pleasant marina where egrets and pelicans soar and dive and weathered old shrimp boats bob on the canal. The land seems to be carved by rivers, canals and inlets on all sides. An interesting way to kill an afternoon is to hop aboard a genuine shrimp trawler. The **Lady Jane Shrimp Boat** (📞912-265-5711; www.shrimpcruise.com; 1200 Glynn Ave; adult/child under 6yr $40/35; 👶) takes

tourists out trawling for shrimp in St Simons Sound. Before you know it, the shrimp is peeled and served.

The Drive » Brunswick is separated from the Golden Isles by a causeway, which leads rather dramatically to the St Simons islands. Head east on the causeway for 5 miles to get to St Simons.

----

⑤ St Simons Island

Roughly the size of Manhattan, St Simons is the largest of the Golden Isles and the most developed, with a clutch of cute shops and cafes and an L-shaped pier that juts out over the sea. The pier is part of **Neptune Park** (📞912-279-2836; www.glynncounty.org; 550 Beachview Dr; ⏰ mini-golf 2:30-8pm Mon-Thu, to 9pm Fri & Sat, 1-8pm Sun; 👶), which unfurls with a lawn and two play areas all the way to the old **Lighthouse Museum** (📞912-638-4666; www.saintsimonslighthouse.org; 610 Beachview Dr; adult/child 5-11yr $10/5; ⏰10am-5pm Mon-Sat, 1:30-5pm Sun).

Activities on St Simons range from a satisfying two-hour kayak trip with **Ocean Motion** (📞912-638-5225; www.stsimonskayaking.com; 1300 Ocean Blvd; per person $49, bicycle rentals half/full day $15/19), through the island's marshes, or you could head over to **King & Prince Golf Course** (📞912-638-3631; www.kingandprince.com; 201 Arnold Rd; resort guest/nonguest per

> **TOP TIP:**
> **BRUNSWICK FIRST FRIDAYS**
>
> If you happen to be in Brunswick for **First Friday** (www.brunswickgeorgia.net; ⏰5-8pm), held the first Friday of the month, you'll enjoy perusing the local art and antique galleries, and enjoy wine and bites with the locals.

GEORGIA'S BEST BEACHES

Georgia's coastline is long and languid, with ample beaches fringing oak woodlands and rambling estuaries. Unfortunately, not all of said beaches are created equal. If you're craving that idyllic stretch of Georgian sand, one (or more) of these will do.

» **Cumberland Island** One of the two most pristine of Georgia's barrier islands, the beaches on the west coast are lovely, with views of the nearby estuary. You'll see ample birdlife, and, on its southern tip, south of the Dungeness Ruins, you can often find shark teeth in the sand. But the east coast is where you'll want to swim and camp. Find **Stafford Beach**, one long, unbroken strip of sand accessible by pedal and boot, road and trail.

» **Little St Simons Island** This private, 10,000-acre island includes an unbroken and pristine **7-mile-long beach**, which unfurls along its east coast.

» **Jekyll Island** For a comfortable stretch of sand, where you can lay out and enjoy a day at the beach, find **Borden Lane** on the east coast and follow it to pay dirt. For something otherworldly fantastic, it's all about **Driftwood Beach** at dawn.

» **St Simons Island** With the village occupying the south end of the island, and the Hampton-like estates walling off access to the beaches in the north, you'll head to Massengale Park where you'll have access to the wide and inviting **East Beach**.

person $75/115; ⊘8am-5pm) at Hampton Club, one of Georgia's finest. **East Beach**, the island's best, can be accessed at **Massengale Park**, where there is ample parking. Here, white sand rolls south for more than a mile to a point backed by scrubby dunes.

While the coast is obviously lovely, inland residential neighborhoods draped in regal, mossy oaks are likewise magical. Wandering the quiet clean streets beneath those mighty trees can be positively Savannah-like.

✕ ⊨ p154

The Drive 》 The soothing drive to the end of the island passes stables and seaside estates while heading north along Frederica Rd, Lawrence Rd and Hampton Point Dr. That last road is where you'll find the marina with transportation to the island next door, if you have a reservation, of course.

TRIP HIGHLIGHT

❻ Little St Simons Island

This unhurried, 10,000-acre island is an unspoiled jewel. Four successive stages of vegetation (dune meadow, wax myrtle and sweet grass, pine forest and climax maritime forest) make it a haven for kayaking, interpretive nature tours and birding, all of which are led by naturalists who are intimately knowledgeable about the local ecosystem. It's a miraculous getaway – full of European fallow deer, sea turtles and gators – that is preciously undeveloped.

But access is an issue, as the only way to enjoy it is by booking with the all-inclusive Lodge on Little St Simons Island (p154), or by joining one of its day trips, which includes passage to the island, an island tour, a gourmet Lowcountry lunch, and an afternoon to explore its 7 miles of pristine beach. Trips depart from St Simons Island at 10:30am and return at 4:30pm. You probably won't want to leave, but you have to. Book at least a month in advance for day trips.

⊨ p154

The Drive 》 Once you're back on St Simons Island, head for the traffic circle on Frederica Rd where you'll find the well-signed turn to Sea Island Rd. A bridge will lead over the narrow inlet to this gated isthmus of an 'island.'

Classic Trip

CHRIS MOORE - EXPLORING LIGHT PHOTOGRAPHY / GETTY IMAGES ©

WHY THIS IS A CLASSIC TRIP
ADAM SKOLNICK, WRITER

Savannah is seldom mentioned when considering America's great cities, but there are few – if any – that are more beautifully planned. It's a city elegant with plazas, shady with oaks, colored with art, both modern and antiquated. South Georgia's charm grows and deepens as you visit humble shrimping ports, vast estuaries, pristine islands and one spectacular driftwood beach.

Top: The picturesque riverfront in Savannah
Left: Forest-covered road through Cumberland Island
Right: Baby alligator, Little St Simons Island

SEAN PAVONE / SHUTTERSTOCK ©

7 Sea Island

Little St Simons it is not. Sea Island, the Golden Isles' other private 'isle,' is much less about raw nature and more about the game of golf. Billed as a five-star golf retreat, it has several restaurants, a 65,000-sq-ft spa and fitness center, tennis and squash courts, and three 18-hole golf courses, which is why it was named one of America's top-75 golf resorts. If you do want to get into nature, join one of its kayaking or fishing trips, go horseback riding, or simply wander down to the beach club, which accesses 5 miles of private beach.

🛏 p155

The Drive » Departing Sea Island, head back to St Simons where you can cross the evocative Sidney Lanier Bridge to the Jekyll Island Causeway, the gateway to Jekyll Island.

DANITA DELIMONT / GETTY IMAGES ©

TRIP HIGHLIGHT

8 Jekyll Island

This glorious island was once the stomping ground for America's rich and famous, and it's not hard to see why. Sixty-five percent undeveloped, woodlands and marshlands dominate the landscape here, peppered with some of the most interesting architecture this side of Charleston. The winter cottages, built between 1884 and 1929, are now the highlight of the **Jekyll Island National Historic**

Landmark District. You may peek inside a few of the fancier buildings on a **Jekyll Island Museum** (☏912-635-4036; www.jekyll island.com/history/museum; 100 Stable Rd; ☺9am-5pm; P ✦) trolley tour (adult/ child $16/7). Alternatively, rent a bike from the hotel. The entire island lends itself to cycling and has more than 20 miles of paved bike paths. Sign up for an after-dark turtle walk at **Georgia Sea Turtle Center** (☏912-635-4444; www.georgiaseaturtlecenter. org; 214 Stable Rd; adult/child

$7/5, tours $22-6; ☺9am-5pm, closed Mon Nov-Mar; ✦), a re-habilitation and research facility working to save Georgia's sea turtles. We love the wide beach and scrubby dunes acces-sible off Borden Lane. It's empty, breezy and perfect, but **Driftwood Beach** is Jekyll's sweet spot. On the island's northeast point, it's saturated with enor-mous washed-up oak trees and is magical at dawn.

🛏 p155

The Drive » Make your way back over the causeway – absorb the last of those supreme estuary and inlet views (for now) and head inland on GA 520 to I-95 south. Exit on Laurel Island Pkwy and follow the signs to St Marys.

9 St Marys

St Marys is a cute little harbor enclave whose raison d'être is to give access to Cumberland Island, but it's attractive in its own right and wor-thy of at least a night. It's sprinkled with historic B&Bs and has a dynamite Greek restaurant. Most importantly, St Marys is home to the **Cumberland Island National Seashore Visitor Center** (☏912-882-4336; www.nps.gov/cuis; 113 St Marys St; ☺8am-4pm), where you can book camp sites, van tours, and transportation to and from the island.

✕ 🛏 p155

⟶ DETOUR: CUMBERLAND ISLAND

Start: 9 St Marys

Cumberland Island (☏912-882-4336; www.nps.gov/cuis; $7), Georgia's largest and southernmost barrier island, is the belle of the ball. Isolated, rugged, and hauntingly pristine, this 57-sq-mile island is brimming with wild marshes, unspoiled beaches and a population and infrastructure lost in time. Think: cultural ruins and ancient oak trees dripping in Spanish moss. John Kennedy Jr was married on the island at the **First African Baptist Church**.

In all, there are 18 miles of roads, best explored on two wheels. You can rent your bike on the ferry for $16 per day, but unless you're on the island for several days of trekking (not a bad idea), the only way to see the whole thing is by booking a van tour (adult/child $15/12) at the **visitor center** in St Marys. Of course, the one drawback of a van tour is that you don't actually visit the beach. If you wish to spend time on the sand, it's best to pedal or stroll. And no matter where or how you travel, be sure to bring food. There are no public restaurants on the island. Book **passage** (☏877-860-6787; www.nps.gov/cuis; round-trip adult/senior/child $28/26/16) well in advance. Walk-in tickets are difficult to wrangle, as there is a limit of 300 visitors per day.

If you'd like to experience Cumberland with a bit more style, continue south on I-95 to Fernandina Beach, FL, where ferries operated by the **Greyfield Inn** (☏904-261-6408; www.greyfieldinn.com; r incl meals $475-600) – Cumberland Island's only hotel – leave three times a day.

Savannah Entrance to the Savannah College of Art and Design (SCAD)

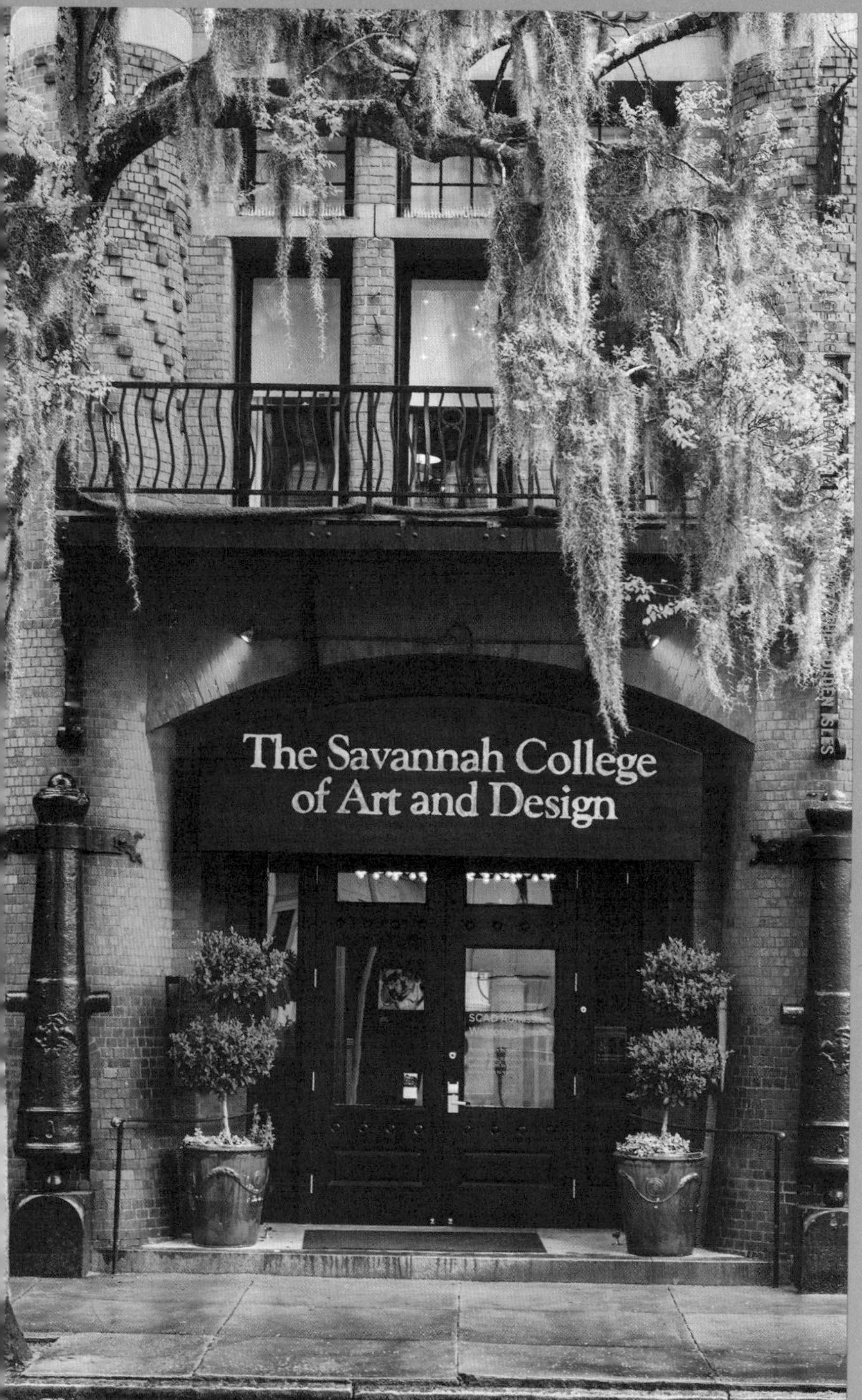
The Savannah College
of Art and Design

Eating & Sleeping

Savannah ➊

✖ Mrs Wilkes Dining Room
Southern US **$$**

(www.mrswilkes.com; 107 W Jones St; lunch adult/child $22/11; ⏲11am-2pm Mon-Fri, closed Jan; 🚸) The line outside can begin as early as 8am at this first-come, first-served Southern comfort-food institution. Once the lunch bell rings and you are seated family-style, the kitchen unloads on you: fried chicken, beef stew, meatloaf, cheese potatoes, collard greens, black-eyed peas, mac 'n' cheese, rutabaga, candied yams, squash casserole, creamed corn *and* biscuits.

⌂ East Bay Inn
Inn **$$**

(☎912-238-1225; www.eastbayinn.com; 225 E Bay St; r/ste from $180/220; 🅿❄🛜🚸) Wedged between corporate rivals this brick behemoth offers just 28 huge rooms all of which have original double-wide wood floors, exposed brick walls, soaring ceilings, slender support columns and flat-screen TVs, along with much charm and warmth to spare.

⌂ Mansion on Forsyth Park
Hotel **$$$**

(☎912-238-5158; www.mansiononforsythpark.com; 700 Drayton St; r weekday/weekend $220/360; 🅿❄@🛜🚸) A choice location and chic design highlight the luxe accommodations on offer at the 18,000-sq-ft Mansion – the sexy bathrooms alone are practically worth the money. The best part of the hotel-spa is the amazing local and international art that crowds its walls and hallways – over 400 pieces in all.

St Simons Island ➎

✖ Palm Coast
Cafe **$**

(☎912-634-7515; www.palmcoastssi.com; 318 Mallery St; mains $8-13; ⏲cafe 8am-3pm, bar to midnight, later on weekends) For simple and affordable eats in the village, choose among the wraps, sandwiches and main salads at this tasty coffeehouse set in a cottage on the main drag. Its cozy bar gets a crowd and it has a rather expansive dining patio out back and rockers on the concrete front porch.

✖ Crab Trap
Seafood **$$**

(☎912-638-3552; www.thecrabtrapssi.com; 1209 Ocean Blvd; dishes $13-26; ⏲5-10pm Mon-Sat; 🚸) A stripped-down seafood house, with pebbled concrete floors, a dank beamed wooden interior and vintage diving and fishing gear on display. Shrimp, oysters, scallops, crab and a single fresh catch of the day are grilled, steamed or fried. The crab soup (read: not bisque!) is locally beloved.

⌂ St Simons Inn by the Lighthouse
Inn **$$**

(☎912-638-1101; www.saintsimonsinn.com; 609 Beachview Dr; r $140-160; 🅿❄🛜🏊) This cute and comfortable good-value inn is accented with white wooden shutters and a general sense of seaside breeziness. It's well located next to the downtown drag and a short pedal from East Beach. Continental breakfast included.

Little St Simons Island ➏

⌂ Lodge on Little St Simons Island
Lodge **$$$**

(☎888-733-5774; www.littlestsimonsisland.com; 1000 Hampton River Club Dr; d from $425; ❄🛜🚸) This isolated historic lodge sits on pristine and private Little St Simons. Stays include accommodations, boat transfers to and from the island, three prepared meals daily, beverages (including soft drinks, beer and wine), all activities (including naturalist-led excursions) and use of all recreation equipment. Rooms have a rustic, cabin vibe, albeit with modern amenities.

Sea Island ⑦

🛏 The Cloister   Resort $$$
(📞855-572-4975; www.seaisland.com; Sea Island Dr; d from $450) Horse stables, a 56,000-sq-ft spa and enough golf to satisfy a PGA tour – no luxurious stone is left unturned at this Mediterranean-inspired resort, where the rooms, atmosphere and rates conspire to put one in mind of the Roman Empire washed ashore in Georgia.

Jekyll Island ⑧

🛏 Villas by the Sea   Villa $
(📞912-635-2521; www.villasbythesearesort. com; 1175 N Beachview Dr; r/condo from $125/235; 🅿 ❄ 🛜 🏊) A nice choice on the north coast close to the best beaches. Rooms are spacious and the one-, two- and three-bedroom condos, set in a complex of lodge buildings sprinkled over a garden, aren't fancy but they're plenty comfy.

🛏 Jekyll Island Club Hotel   Historic Hotel $$
(📞855-535-9547; www.jekyllclub.com; 371 Riverview Dr; d/ste from $200/300, resort fee $15; 🅿 ❄ @ 🛜 🏊) A posh and storied hotel and the backbone of the island, featuring a rambling array of rooms spread out over five historic structures. Each building feels plucked from a novel about Jazz Age decadence, although the current vibe is a little more Hilton Head country club.

St Marys ⑨

🍴 Riverside Cafe   Greek $$
(www.riversidecafesaintmarys.com; 106 St Marys St; mains $8-18; ⊙11am-9pm Mon-Fri, 8:30am-9pm Sat & Sun) A Greek cafe that does a take on the gyro called the Riverside Wrap: pork, lamb and beef are mixed, seasoned and pounded into gyro-like strips (it doesn't have a rotisserie), piled with lettuce, feta and tzatziki, and folded into a fresh pita. The spanakopita is tremendous as well. Come before the ferry and they'll pack a lunch to go.

🛏 Spencer House Inn   Inn $$
(📞912-882-1872; www.spencerhouseinn. com; 200 Osborne St; r $135-245; 🅿 🛜) At this historic inn (c 1872) there are 14 spacious rooms on three floors, with slightly less personality and clutter than other local comers. It's also more up to date with flat-screen TVs and top-end bath products. Staff book ferry reservations, pack lunches for day-trippers and serve a full gourmet breakfast each morning.

Georgia & Alabama Back Roads

12

If you crave life beyond the common stops and exits, it's best to avoid the interstate. Especially in Georgia and Alabama, where unearthed treasures await.

TRIP HIGHLIGHTS

70 miles

Dahlonega
An undercover wine region in the splendid Georgia mountains

Carters Lake ●
2

Gadsden ●

● Jasper

Atlanta ● **START**

5

748 miles

Fort Valley
Because everybody loves peaches!

8

FINISH

Tuscaloosa
A picturesque college town with a football obsession

Tuskegee
African American advancement started here

468 miles

628 miles

4–5 DAYS
748 MILES /
1204KM

GREAT FOR...

BEST TIME TO GO
Spring (March to May) is best in terms of weather, prices and crowds.

 ESSENTIAL PHOTO

Breathtaking views from Dahlonega vineyards over layered mountain ranges.

 BEST FOR OUTDOOR ACTIVITIES

The back roads offer many hiking, paddling and boating options.

Fort Valley Peach trees abound in Georgia's peach capital

157

MICHAEL PIAZZA / GETTY IMAGES ©

12 Georgia & Alabama Back Roads

Have you ever tried to take a road trip sans interstates? It's rather difficult. When President Dwight D Eisenhower hatched the interstate system in 1956, several towns, big and small, and their once-popular attractions, were suddenly off the cross-country map. Yet being left to languish kept things sweet, real and homegrown, while interstate towns often suffered corporate and fast-food overload. Time to get real.

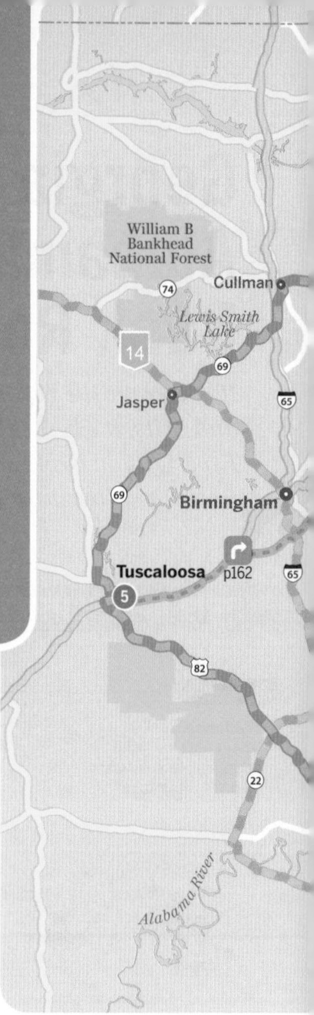

1 Atlanta

Begin in Atlanta where you can catch a breath of urban culture before heading into the Georgia and Alabama backwoods. Midtown is one of Atlanta's most vibrant neighborhoods, and home to the **High Museum of Art** (www. high.org; 1280 Peachtree St NE; adult/child under 5yr $14.50/ free; ◎10am-5pm Tue-Thu & Sat, to 9pm Fri, noon-5pm Sun), with a truly excellent collection of early American modern art from the likes of George Morris and Albert Eugene Gallatin, not to mention post-war work from Mark Rothko. For dinner venture a bit off-center to **Decatur** – which is technically still part of the Atlanta metro area,

yet feels like its own leafy small town. There's the lovely courthouse square, with a gazebo in its heart, dotted with cute shops and special restaurants, imagined by top-level gourmet brains. After dinner, head to **Brick Store Pub** (✆404-687-0990; www. brickstorepub.com; 125 E Court Sq, Decatur; draft beers $5-12; ◎11am-1am Sun & Mon, to 2am Tue-Sat), which draws a cute young crowd midweek, who come for the seven pages of beers! Downstairs serves American-craft brews; the intimate Belgian-beer bar is upstairs.

✗ ⟺ p163, p181

The Drive ≫ Drive north from Atlanta on GA 400, and you'll soon find yourself in a layered

landscape of blue mountains, studded with oaks, pines and vineyards. GA 400 becomes I-19, which you'll follow for about 70 miles to Dahlonega.

TRIP HIGHLIGHT

2 Dahlonega

Here's a super-charming mountain town with a courthouse square dotted with tasting rooms, repre-

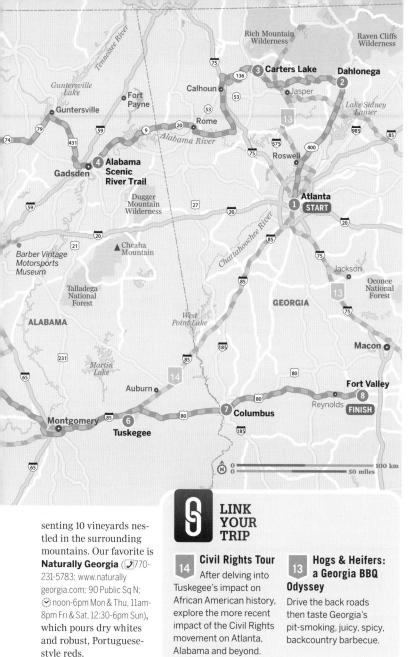

senting 10 vineyards nestled in the surrounding mountains. Our favorite is **Naturally Georgia** (☎770-231-5783; www.naturally georgia.com; 90 Public Sq N; ◷noon-6pm Mon & Thu, 11am-8pm Fri & Sat, 12:30-6pm Sun), which pours dry whites and robust, Portuguese-style reds.

LINK YOUR TRIP

14 Civil Rights Tour

After delving into Tuskegee's impact on African American history, explore the more recent impact of the Civil Rights movement on Atlanta, Alabama and beyond.

13 Hogs & Heifers: a Georgia BBQ Odyssey

Drive the back roads then taste Georgia's pit-smoking, juicy, spicy, backcountry barbecue.

Dahlonega has gold-mining roots and this town prospered with each strike. In 1838 the federal government opened a mint in the town square, where more than $6 million in gold was coined before the operation was closed at the dawn of the Civil War. You can absorb some of that history at the **Dahlonega Courthouse Gold Museum** ([📞]706-864-2257; www.gastateparks.org/dahlonegagoldmuseum; Public Sq; adult/child $7/4.50; [🕐]9am-5pm Mon-Sat, 10am-5pm Sun).

Of course, the most fun to be had here is driving past spectacular mountain scenery on the mountain roads between wineries. We're big fans of **Frogtown Cellars** ([📞]706-865-0687; www.frogtownwine.com; 700 Ridge Point Dr; tastings $15; [🕐]noon-5pm Mon-Fri, to 6pm Sat, 12:30-5pm Sun) – a massive stone lodge where you can taste seven wines for $15. Behind it, **Three Sisters** ([📞]706-865-9463; www.threesistersvineyards.com; 439 Vineyard Way; tastings from $10; [🕐]11am-5pm Thu-Sat, 1-5pm Sun) is a wonderfully unpretentious vineyard where Cheetos, overalls and bluegrass tunes pair just fine with the wine. And if you still can't get enough mountain magic, hit the trail in Amicalola Falls State Park (p185).

[🍴] [🛏] p163, p191

The Drive » The road gets increasingly lonely and luscious as you wind your way west on GA 52 to GA 136, for about 55 miles to Carters Lake.

❸ Carters Lake

An emerald lake nestled in the southern end of the Blue Ridge Mountains, Carters Lake is a haven for boating, bird-watching, hiking and mountain biking. Stop at the **Carters Lake Marina** ([📞]706-276-4891; www.carterslake.com; 575 Marina Rd, Ellijay; pontoon rental half day $225, full day $295-325; [🕐]rentals from 10am-5pm), where you can rent a pontoon boat (no experience necessary) or settle into one of the roomy pine-log cabins with expansive decks overlooking the lake. The most popular hiking trail in the area is the **Amadahy Trail** (3.5 miles, two hours round-trip) offering scenic lake views. For cyclists, the **Ridgeway Mountain Bike Trail** (6 miles, 40 minutes) is a mixture of single-track and narrow logging roads with creek crossings and technical descents.

While the area yields some of the best landscapes in Georgia, it is also the site of one of the most shameful chapters in state history. In 1838, during the height of the Georgia gold rush, local Cherokee families were rounded up and held near the present-day dam. They were forced north, and eventually onto the ill-famed Trail of Tears.

The Drive » There are several back-road options that connect Carters Lake with Gadsen, AL. We suggest you head west on

GA 136, veer south on GA 225, jog left on Hwy 41 then make your way to GA 20, which becomes AL 9 as you cross the border. AL 9 leads to the Alabama Scenic River Trail in Gadsden.

❹ Alabama Scenic River Trail

River rats can paddle part of the Piedmont Section of the 631-mile **Alabama Scenic River Trail** (www.alabamascenicrivertrail.com), which begins at the Alabama–Georgia border and winds its way south towards Gadsden along the Upper Coosa River. You can put in for a half-day paddle on Terrapin Creek, one of the Upper Coosa's tributaries. The **Terrapin Outdoor Center** ([📞]256-447-8383; www.canoeshop.net; 4114 County Rd 175, Piedmont; kayak/canoe rental $25/30; [🕐]9am-5pm Tue-Sun) rents kayaks and canoes, and it has stand up paddle (SUP) boards, too.

The Drive » Head east on Hwy 278 back toward Gadsen then veer north on Hwy 431 over Lake Guntersville, where there's some great lakeside accommodations (p163). Take AL 79 south then AL 74 west to Jasper, where you can pick up AL 69 south to Tuscaloosa.

TRIP HIGHLIGHT

❺ Tuscaloosa

Tuscaloosa is just an hour from Birmingham but it feels a million miles from everywhere, as if farmland and the woods were cleared and a college town dropped into the

Tuskegee Tuskegee Institute National Historic Site

gap. Local life revolves around the **University of Alabama** (www.ua.edu) – and Crimson Tide football. The campus is lovely and leafy: pebbled concrete sidewalks lead past attractive brick buildings to a beautiful quad, featuring an expansive lawn and stand-alone bell tower. Pregame festivities begin here, before the hordes move en masse to **Bryant–Denny Stadium** (☎205-348-3680; www.rolltide.com; 920 Paul W Bryant Dr; ☉tours 11am Mon-Fri): most recently expanded in 2010, it seats more than 101,000 people. Real football fanatics – many

of whom converge from across the state on football Saturdays – will want to explore the **Paul W Bryant Museum** (☎205-348-4668; www.bryant museum.com; 300 Paul W Bryant Dr; adult/senior & child $2/1; ☉9am-4pm). Named in honor of the legendary coach 'Bear' Bryant, this is the Crimson Tide Football Hall of Fame.

✗ ⊨ p163

The Drive » Arguably the prettiest stretch of highway since you left Dahlonega, the narrow Hwy 82, shaded by pines, rolls over foothills and past small farming towns. This is the quintessential back road. In

Montgomery, rejoin I-85N for 32 miles, in to Tuskegee.

- - - - - - - - - - - - - - - -

`TRIP HIGHLIGHT`

❻ Tuskegee

School yourself on African American history at **Tuskegee Institute National Historic Site**, which is home to the **George Washington Carver Museum** (☎334-727-3200; www.nps.gov/tuai; University Campus Ave; ☉9am-4:30pm), devoted to the iconic agricultural pioneer and educator. Don't miss **The Oaks** (☎334-727-3200; www.nps.gov/tuin.com; University Ave; ☉9am-4:30pm, tours

DETOUR:
BARBER VINTAGE MOTORSPORTS
MUSEUM

Start: ⑤ Tuscaloosa

If you're swerving the back roads on two wheels, the **Barber Vintage Motorsports Museum** (☏205-699-7275; www.barbermuseum.org; Leeds, AL; adult/child $15/10; ◷10am-5pm Mon-Sat, noon-5pm Sun Oct-Mar, to 6pm Apr-Sep; P) is a must-visit. More than 1000 motorcycles are stored in this temple to the genre. It was launched by George Barber, a local businessman who loved restoring and racing vintage Porsches. Once his attention turned to motorcycles in 1989, he assembled a restoration team and began collecting in earnest. The sheer range of his collection is mind-boggling. Here is a 1912 Indian, there a 1953 Victoria Bergmeister; there are Harleys, Ducatis and BMWs all from decades long gone, along with plenty of obscure models and brands you may not have heard of. Barber also races these bikes and has a team that wins national championships on the vintage racing circuit. His museum is located on the 740-acre Barber Sports Motorpark, which includes a speedway.

10:30am, 1:30pm, 2:30pm, 3:30pm Tue-Sat), the home of Booker T Washington. Born into slavery, he went on to found the institute and become the university's first president. Five miles outside of town, the **Tuskegee Airmen National Historic Site** (☏334-724-0922; www.nps. gov/tuai; 1616 Chappie James Rd; ◷9am-4:30pm) has been restored to its former glory as the training grounds and airfield for the first African American pilot candidates in the US military – desegregation pioneers who served with distinction in World War II. Several of the original training planes are on display.

The Drive » Head east out of Tuskegee on Hwy 80 for about 45 miles, past the Tuskegee National Forest (the smallest in the USA) and into Columbus, GA.

⑦ Columbus

The main attraction here is the fascinating **National Civil War Naval Museum** (☏706-327-9798; www.portcolumbus. org; 1002 Victory Dr; adult/senior/child $7.50/6.50/6; ◷10am-4:30pm Tue-Sat, 12:30pm-4:30pm Sun & Mon; P ♿) dedicated to the Confederate navy. Check out the CSS *Jackson,* an 1862 ironclad Confederate navy ship that was hauled up after 95 years underwater; and the stunning collection of mid-18th-century American and Confederate flags, unearthed from an attic in – funnily enough – Massachusetts.

The Drive » Skedaddle out of Columbus and stay eastbound on Hwy 80 into a land of peaches and pecans. It's about 75 miles to Fort Valley.

TRIP HIGHLIGHT

⑧ Fort Valley

Fort Valley is the beating heart of Peach County (no, really), the peach capital of the peach state. Your nose, and ample signage, should lead you to **Lane Southern Orchards** (☏800-277-3224; www. lanepacking.com; 50 Lane Rd; tours from $7; ◷9am-6pm; ♿), where more than 3000 acres are dedicated to the cultivation of peaches and pecans. You can stock up on the fruits and nuts themselves, but you may also wish to explore the peach salsa, peach cobbler jam (yum!), peach ice cream, and the peach hot sauce. Learn to embrace the peach! Farm tours are available in June and July when the pickings are at their peak.

Eating & Sleeping

Atlanta ❶

🍴 Leon's Full Service   Fusion $$

(📞404-687-0500; www.leonsfullservice.com; 131 E Ponce de Leon Ave; mains $13-27; ⏰5pm-1am Mon, 11:30am-1am Tue-Thu & Sun, to 2am Fri & Sat; 🛜) Leon's can come across as a bit pretentious, but the gorgeous concrete bar and open floor plan spilling out of a former service station and onto a groovy heated deck with floating beams remains packed at all times. You may find prosciutto wrapped trout and braised short ribs on the changing menu. Everything, from beer, wine and cocktails (spirits are all small-batch craft creations) to the menu, shows attention to detail. No reservations.

🛏 Hotel Artmore   Boutique Hotel $$

(📞404-876-6100; www.artmorehotel.com; 1302 W Peachtree St; r $170-200, ste from $220; P ❄ @ 🛜) This 1924 Spanish-Mediterranean architectural landmark has been completely revamped into an artistic boutique hotel that's become an urban sanctuary for those who appreciate their trendiness with a dollop of discretion. It wins all sorts of accolades: excellent service, a wonderful courtyard with fire pit and a superb location across the street from Arts Center MARTA station.

🛏 Highland Inn   Inn $$

(📞404-874-5756; www.thehighlandinn.com; 644 N Highland Ave; s/d from $75/105; P ❄ 🛜) This European-style 65-room independent inn, built in 1927, has appealed to touring musicians over the years. Rooms aren't huge, but it's as affordably comfortable as you'll get in Atlanta city proper – to say nothing of its great location in the Virginia-Highland area. It's one of the few accommodations in town with single rooms.

🛏 Stonehurst Place   B&B $$$

(📞404-881-0722; www.stonehurstplace.com; 923 Piedmont Ave NE; r $270-370; P ❄ @ 🛜) Built in 1896 by the Hinman family, this elegant B&B has all the modern amenities one could ask for and is well located. It's fully updated with ecofriendly water treatment and heating systems and has original Warhol illustrations on the wall. It's an exceptional choice if you're not on a budget.

Dahlonega ❷

🛏 Hall House Hotel   Inn $$

(📞706-867-5009; www.hallhousehotel.com; 90 Public Sq; r $100-175; ❄ 🛜) A charming historic nest on the square dating to 1881. There are five bright and charming rooms, each uniquely decorated, some with four-poster beds.

Lake Guntersville ❹

🛏 Lodge at Lake Guntersville State Park   Lodge $

(📞256-571-5440; www.alapark.com/lake-guntersville-state-park; 1155 Lodge Dr, Guntersville; r from $104, campsites from $23; P 🐾) This bluff-side resort boasts rooms, lakeside cottages and a 321-site campground.

Tuscaloosa ❺

🍴 Nick's Original Filet House   Steak $

(📞205-758-9316; 4018 Culver Rd; mains $8-17; ⏰5-9pm Mon-Thu, to 10pm Fri & Sat; P) Also known as Nick's in the Sticks, this is a rickety back-road joint if ever there was one, and it's a Tuscaloosa classic. Nestled in the trees about 5 miles out of town, with a flock of signed dollar bills stapled to the ceiling, it does tender filet mignon on the cheap as well as ribeye, and they fry all parts of the chicken (think livers and gizzards). Oh, and about that Nicodemus. Um, it's a drink. Beware the Nicodemus.

🛏 Hotel Capstone   Hotel $$

(📞205-752-3200; www.hotelcapstone.com; 320 Paul Bryant Rd; r from $145; P ❄ 🛜) A decent three-star room, walking distance from the quad and stadium. Digs are spacious with flat-screen TVs, wide desks and a slight corporate vibe. But it's on campus, and has room service and a lobby bar. Reserve well in advance on game day. During the off-season, rates drop by around $50.

Hogs & Heifers: a Georgia BBQ Odyssey

13

There's brisket in Texas, dry rub in Memphis, but in Georgia, the term BBQ is synonymous with chopped or pulled pork, pit roasted, tender, juicy and simmering in succulent sauces.

TRIP HIGHLIGHTS

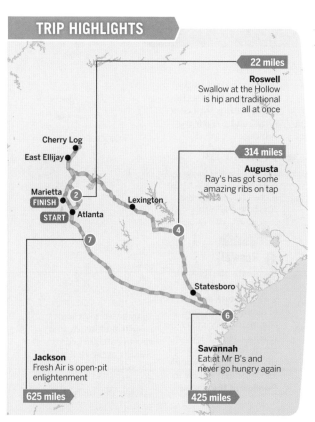

22 miles

Roswell
Swallow at the Hollow is hip and traditional all at once

314 miles

Augusta
Ray's has got some amazing ribs on tap

Cherry Log
East Ellijay

Marietta
FINISH
Lexington
START Atlanta

Statesboro

Jackson
Fresh Air is open-pit enlightenment

625 miles

Savannah
Eat at Mr B's and never go hungry again

425 miles

3 DAYS
710 MILES / 1142KM

GREAT FOR...

BEST TIME TO GO
March to May means milder temps and wildflowers.

ESSENTIAL PHOTO
You, a glistening plate of 'cue, and a jug of rot-your-teeth sweet tea.

BEST FOR SOUTHERN CUISINE
Pork lovers will have a ball discovering and devouring the state's signature meal.

13 Hogs & Heifers: a Georgia BBQ Odyssey

The Deep South's contributions to the American culinary landscape are well documented – fried green tomatoes, fried chicken, collard greens and pecan pie among them – but perhaps no food is more inherently Southern than a juicy plate of smoked meat. Get to know what good is.

Cohutta Wilderness — 515
East Ellijay

75 — 575

Alabama River

Roswell 2
Marietta 8
FINISH 75
Atlanta 1 8
20 START

Chattahoochee River

85

West Point Lake

Flint River

Columbus 12

ALABAMA

1 Atlanta

Don't leave the Atlanta city limits until you sample **Fat Matt's Rib Shack** (📞404-607-1622; www. fatmattsribshack.com; 1811 Piedmont Ave NE; mains $5-14; 🕑11:30am-11:30pm Mon-Thu, to 12:30 Fri & Sat, 1pm-11:30pm Sun). Although it does serve chopped pork we suggest a slab of ribs (though a half slab will probably suffice). Take special note of the Brunswick stew, a delicious side dish best described as barbecue soup. And the best part? It has live blues nightly. Another classic Atlanta haunt is Daddy Dz (p181), a juke joint of a BBQ shack, consistently voted tops

in town, and set smack in downtown. Order the succulent ribs with cornbread, and you'll leave smiling.

🍴 🛏 p171, p181

The Drive » Take Hwy 85 northeast and then take GA 140 northwest to Roswell, about 20 miles from Fat Matt's.

TRIP HIGHLIGHT

2 Roswell

Eventually the Roswell corrals are replaced with the stark angles of planned bedroom-community perimeter fencing...but it's plenty pretty enough to sense the urbane upper-middle appeal, and it's home to **Swallow at the Hollow**

(📞678-352-1975; www. swallowatthehallow.com; 1072 Green St; mains $10.50-25; 🕑11am-9pm Wed, Thu & Sun, to 10pm Fri & Sat; 🅿), many a Georgian son's favorite pit kitchen, and affectionately called 'Swaller at the Haller.' The room – actually, it's a double-wide wooden shack with a tin roof –

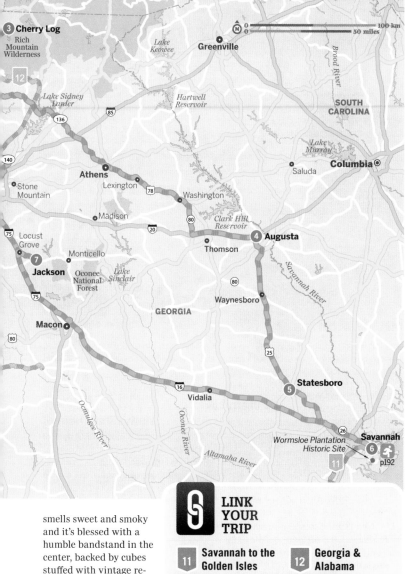

smells sweet and smoky and it's blessed with a humble bandstand in the center, backed by cubes stuffed with vintage records. There are modern accents – the stainless-steel bar (with craft beer on tap), two flat screens for ballgames and ample outdoor seating. All tables are blessed with

LINK YOUR TRIP

11 Savannah to the Golden Isles

Follow the coast down to the shrimping town of Brunswick and across the causeway to the captivating Golden Isles.

12 Georgia & Alabama Back Roads

Now that you've sampled Georgia's down-home cuisine, swerve more of her back roads and soak up the local culture.

the spicy house sauce and house mustard, too. The chopped pork is the thing, but it does ribs, homemade smoked sausage and turkey platters. It even pit-smokes portobello mushrooms for veg-heads, served with smoked gouda and fried green tomatoes. Hey, it's the suburbs!

The Drive » Follow US 140 west to the GA 515, head north to I-575 north and drive approximately 64 miles to Cherry Log. Along the way, you'll find yourself on a gorgeous stretch of road that winds high into wooded Appalachia toward Tennessee.

❸ Cherry Log

Groaning platters of pork, ribs and chicken are served in a log cabin with a chimney pumping out smoky essence of pit BBQ. Jimmy Carter is a fan of the **Pink Pig** (☎706-276-3311; www.budspinkpig.com; 824 Cherry Log St; mains $7.50-15; ⏱11am-9pm Thu-Sun), a fun dining room with exposed beams decked out with colorful signs. In addition to BBQ, it does soul food like chicken and dumplings, chicken livers, cured ham and fried green tomatoes, but the pit is the thing.

The Drive » It's a lovely drive heading southeast via GA 53, GA 136 and GA 15 to Augusta, a distance of some 200 miles.

TRIP HIGHLIGHT

❹ Augusta

Augusta, the second-largest town in Georgia, feels like a quiet village compared to Atlanta. We don't mean this in a negative way; the town spills prettily along the Savannah River and has an understated charm, easily accessible around the Riverwalk Park area. But we're here for the 'cue, which we like to score from **Ray's Smokehouse BBQ** (☎706-

Savannah Southern comfort food at Mrs Wilkes Dining Room

798-7613; www.rayssmoke
housebbq.net; 2817 Deans Bridge
Rd; mains $5-15; ⊘11am-6pm
Thu-Sat), a veritable temple
to the art of making ribs
we would...well, ribs we
would drive across a state
for. Which we kind of just
did. Don't leave without
sampling the sauce, some
fried okra and – why the
hell not? – a bit of banana
pudding for desert.

The Drive ⟩⟩ It's about a 75-
mile drive south along Hwy-25
to Statesboro.

---

⑤ Statesboro

A civil rights case was
once fought over the
integration of **Vandy's**
(☎912-764-2444; www.vandys
bbq.com; 22 W Vine St; mains
$8-14; ⊘6am-2pm Mon-Thu,
to 3pm Fri & Sat; 🛗), a
Statesboro institution
since the 1930s. Simplic-
ity wins here. Its chopped
pork sandwich is served
with a vinegar-and-
mustard-based sauce on
two slices of Sunbeam
white bread baked next
door. The hog is smoked
overnight in a massive
block-and-brick pit out
back to beat the Georgia
heat. And Statesboro
itself is charming and
historic, with a jolt of
contemporary life thanks
to the nearby **Georgia
Southern University**.

You're far east at this
point, so it's a good place
to crash for the night.

The Drive ⟩⟩ From Statesboro
stay on GA 26 east for about
55 miles and you'll wind up
in Savannah, Georgia's most
charming and beautiful city.

TRIP HIGHLIGHT

⑥ Savannah

There are few cities in the
US as glorious as Savan-
nah, a southern charmer
that blends the European
architectural influence
of New Orleans with the
spreading oaks and hospitable smiles of Charleston.
It's artsy, progressive,
walkable (see p192) and

WORMSLOE PLANTATION HISTORIC SITE

On the beautiful Isle of Hope, an island connected to Savannah proper by a low-slung causeway that spans the wetlands and is surrounded by intercostal waterways, the **Wormsloe Plantation Historic Site** (📞912-353-3023; www.gastateparks.org/Wormsloe; 7601 Skidaway Rd; adult/senior/child 6-17yr/child 1-5yr $10/9/4.50/2; ⏰9am-5pm Tue-Sun; 🅿) is one of the most photographed sites in Savannah, and with good reason. The dreamy entrance leads you past the iron gates and beneath a 1.5 mile road that is sheltered by ancient, mossy oaks that appear to be holding hands over the road. Also on-site are 4 miles of trails, an existing antebellum mansion, home to descendants of Noble Jones, and the last colonial ruins in Georgia, along with a colonial site where you can see folks demonstrate blacksmithing and other long-gone trades. Jones arrived in Savannah with General James Oglethorpe, the city's founder, in 1733.

a city you simply must visit at least once – which means you'll probably be back at least twice. Food isn't generally Savannah's strong suit but there is a transcendent hole-in-the-wall tucked down a back alley, hidden among shady squares and elegant mansions. **B's Cracklin' BBQ** (📞912-330-6921; www.bscracklinbbq.com; 12409 White Bluff Rd; mains $9-19; ⏰11am-9pm Tue-Sat, to 6pm Sun; 🅿) is an exemplar of the BBQ genre. Everything on the menu is elevated smoky goodness, and the portions could serve the army of a small nation.

🍴 🛏 p171, p218

The Drive ❯❯ From Savannah, I-16 leads west back up into the foothills, where after 200 miles and three hours you'll find

Jackson, and one of our favorite open pits in the state.

- - - - - - - - - - - - - - - - - -

TRIP HIGHLIGHT

❼ Jackson

Jackson is where you'll find **Fresh Air** (📞770-775-3182; www.freshairbarbecue.com; 1164 Hwy 42; mains $6.50-7.50; ⏰8am-7:30pm Mon-Thu, to 8:30pm Fri & Sat, to 8pm Sun; 🚼), the Holy Grail of Georgia BBQ, a gloriously warm and friendly pioneer-style, wooden roadside shack. The outdoor seating area in front is covered in sawdust. Fresh Air only does three things: chopped pork, Brunswick stew and coleslaw. No ribs. No shoulder. The hams spend a full 24 hours in the smoker, which is the way it's been done

since 1929. The result is transcendent, vinegary BBQ that is even better with a dash of that hot sauce. Congratulations, you have reached swine nirvana.

The Drive ❯❯ If you depart late afternoon, the 70-mile drive from Jackson through Georgia's gentle foothills to the Atlanta area is rather glorious, what with the pale sun flickering through slender stands of feathery pines along I-75.

- - - - - - - - - - - - - - - - - -

❽ Marietta

This culinary odyssey ends in Marietta, just north of Atlanta, at **Sam's BBQ1** (📞770-977-3005; www.bbq1.net; 4944 Lower Roswell Rd; mains $6-17; ⏰11am-7:30pm Mon-Thu, to 8pm Fri & Sat, to 3pm Sun; 🅿🚼), run by grill master Sam Huff, who makes pork so tender, sweet and satisfying he has been immortalized in song (and on the Food Network). He smokes pork, chicken, brisket, ribs, sausages and turkey. But like elsewhere, pork is king, and he has the awards to prove it. If you can't bear to leave the Georgia flavor behind as you head out of state, make sure you sign up for Huff's **Pork U** (as in university), a one-day open-pit cooking intensive where you will learn how to roast a whole hog and craft a damn fine sauce, to boot. You've had the rest, now learn to make the best.

Eating & Sleeping

Atlanta ❶

✕ Leon's Full Service — Fusion $$

(☎404-687-0500; www.leonsfullservice.com; 131 E Ponce de Leon Ave; mains $13-27; ⊗5pm-1am Mon, 11:30am-1am Tue-Thu & Sun, to 2am Fri & Sat; 🛜) Leon's can come across as a bit pretentious, but the gorgeous concrete bar and open floor plan spilling out of a former service station and onto a groovy heated deck with floating beams remains packed at all times. You may find prosciutto wrapped trout and braised short ribs on the changing menu. Everything, from beer, wine and cocktails (spirits are all small-batch craft creations) to the menu, shows attention to detail. No reservations.

🛏 Hotel Artmore — Boutique Hotel $$

(☎404-876-6100; www.artmorehotel.com; 1302 W Peachtree St; r $170-200, ste from $220; P ❄ @ 🛜) This 1924 Spanish-Mediterranean architectural landmark has been completely revamped into an artistic boutique hotel that's become an urban sanctuary for those who appreciate their trendiness with a dollop of discretion. It wins all sorts of accolades: excellent service, a wonderful courtyard with fire pit and a superb location across the street from Arts Center MARTA station.

🛏 Highland Inn — Inn $$

(☎404-874-5756; www.thehighlandinn.com; 644 N Highland Ave; s/d from $75/105; P ❄ 🛜) This European-style 65-room independent inn, built in 1927, has appealed to touring musicians over the years. Rooms aren't huge, but it's as affordably comfortable as you'll get in Atlanta city proper – to say nothing of its great location in the Virginia-Highland area. It's one of the few accommodations in town with single rooms.

🛏 Stonehurst Place — B&B $$$

(☎404-881-0722; www.stonehurstplace.com; 923 Piedmont Ave NE; r $270-370; P ❄ @ 🛜) Built in 1896 by the Hinman family, this elegant B&B has all the modern amenities one could ask for and is well located. It's fully updated with ecofriendly water treatment and heating systems and has original Warhol illustrations on the wall. It's an exceptional choice if you're not on a budget.

Savannah ❻

✕ Mrs Wilkes Dining Room — Southern US $$

(www.mrswilkes.com; 107 W Jones St; lunch adult/child $22/11; ⊗11am-2pm Mon-Fri, closed Jan; 👪) The line outside can begin as early as 8am at this first-come, first-served Southern comfort-food institution. Once the lunch bell rings and you are seated family-style, the kitchen unloads on you: fried chicken, beef stew, meatloaf, cheese potatoes, collard greens, black-eyed peas, mac 'n' cheese, rutabaga, candied yams, squash casserole, creamed corn *and* biscuits.

🛏 East Bay Inn — Inn $$

(☎912-238-1225; www.eastbayinn.com; 225 E Bay St; r/ste from $180/220; ❄ 🛜 👪) Wedged between corporate rivals this brick behemoth offers just 28 huge rooms all of which have original double-wide wood floors, exposed brick walls, soaring ceilings, slender support columns and flat-screen TVs, along with much charm and warmth to spare.

🛏 Mansion on Forsyth Park — Hotel $$$

(☎912-238-5158; www.mansiononforsythpark. com; 700 Drayton St; r weekday/weekend $220/360; P ❄ @ 🛜 👪) A choice location and chic design highlight the luxe accommodations on offer at the 18,000-sq-ft Mansion – the sexy bathrooms alone are practically worth the money. The best part of the hotel-spa is the amazing local and international art that crowds its walls and hallways – more than 400 pieces in all.

Civil Rights Tour

14

Feel and absorb the history of the American Civil Rights movement as you follow in the footsteps of the legendary Dr Martin Luther King Jr from Atlanta to Memphis.

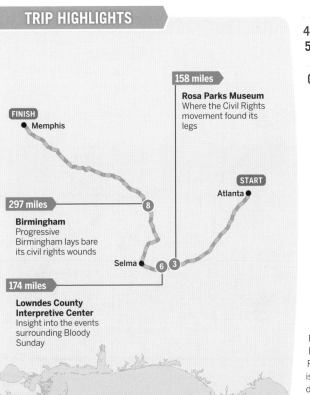

TRIP HIGHLIGHTS

158 miles

Rosa Parks Museum
Where the Civil Rights movement found its legs

FINISH
Memphis

START
Atlanta

297 miles

Birmingham
Progressive Birmingham lays bare its civil rights wounds

Selma

174 miles

Lowndes County Interpretive Center
Insight into the events surrounding Bloody Sunday

**4 DAYS
568 MILES / 914KM**

GREAT FOR...

BEST TIME TO GO
Dodge summer crowds from April to June.

ESSENTIAL PHOTO
The Edmund Pettus Bridge at sunset has an eerie, solemn beauty.

BEST FOR HISTORY
Following the Birmingham Civil Rights Memorial Trail is sure to spark some deep conversation.

Birmingham Sign marking the historic 16th St Baptist Church

173

14 Civil Rights Tour

To trace the solemn, sad, yet triumphant road of American civil rights activists is to explore the very worst and the incomparable best of America. Martin Luther King Jr's journey from his Atlanta birth and biblical upbringing to his assassination in Memphis visits the stages of Montgomery, Selma and Birmingham and reveals, within the human experience, an infinite capacity to love, endure and cultivate strength and faith no matter what.

❶ Atlanta

The story begins in Atlanta, where the **Sweet Auburn** neighborhood was already a bustling, affluent, middle-class beacon of African American advancement in the oppressive, segregated South when a preacher's son, Martin Luther King Jr, was born here on January 15, 1929. You can visit the **Martin Luther King Jr Birthplace** (☎404-331-5190; www.nps.gov/malu; 501 Auburn Ave; ☺10am-4pm) on a guided tour, one of several sights that form

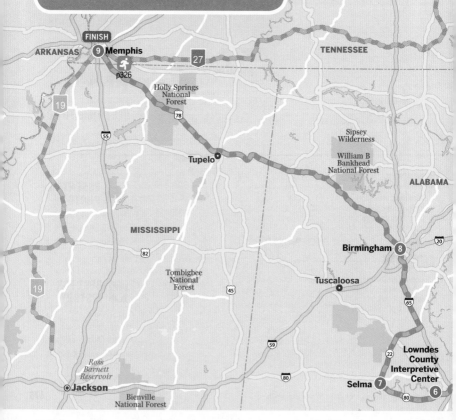

the **Martin Luther King Jr National Historic Site** ([📞]404-331-5190; www.nps.gov/malu; 450 Auburn Ave; [🕐]9am-5pm; [P] [♿]), Atlanta's civil rights nexus. First, get a powerful civil rights primer at the **visitor center**, where dehumanizing segregation-era laws are etched into glass. Across the street is the **First Ebenezer Baptist Church** ([📞]404-331-5190; www.nps.gov/malu; 407 Auburn Ave NE; [🕐]9am-5pm), where King's father led the congregation, and his mother directed the choir. Sit on a wooden pew and listen to Dr King's voice echo through the serene sanctuary of a 1963 time capsule. Nearby, King is entombed in the courtyard behind the nonprofit **King Center for Nonviolent Social Change** ([📞]404-526-8900; www.thekingcenter.org; 449 Auburn Ave NE; [🕐]9am-5pm, to 6pm summer), where there's a small gallery on the 2nd floor worth seeing.

[🍴][🛏] p163, p181

The Drive » It's a two-hour drive south on I-85 across the state line and into Alabama to reach Tuskegee.

② Tuskegee

Before the Civil Rights movement of the 1950s and 1960s, there were the Tuskegee Airmen. Also known as the Red Tails, these African American fighter pilots – America's first – shattered the glass ceiling and received their training at what is now the **Tuskegee Airmen National Historic Site** ([📞]334-724-0922; www.nps.gov/tuai; 1616 Chappie James Rd; [🕐]9am-4:30pm) in July 1941. The first graduating class had 13 cadets, but eventually over 300 African American pilots were trained here and served overseas. Their legacy is important because African American soldiers who had served in Europe enjoyed freedoms there

LINK YOUR TRIP

19 **The Blues Highway**
From Memphis, get on Hwy 66 and delve into the Mississippi Delta, where like a diamond from coal, Mississippi's institutionalized poverty, segregation and oppression birthed the blues and American popular music.

27 **Memphis to Nashville**
After getting a taste of the blues, head east to Nashville and enjoy some honky-tonk enlightenment.

- ③ Rosa Parks Museum
- ④ Dexter Avenue King Memorial Church
- ⑤ Civil Rights Memorial Center
- ② Tuskegee
- Columbus
- Montgomery
- Macon
- Atlanta ① START
- GEORGIA
- Chattanooga
- NORTH CAROLINA
- Cohutta Wilderness
- Tennessee River
- Dugger Mountain Wilderness
- Cheaha Mountain
- Talladega National Forest
- 100 km / 50 miles

that they were denied at home, and many began to work diligently for desegregation upon returning to the South after the war. Tuskegee is also the home of Booker T Washington's **Tuskegee Institute**, which was America's first African American teacher's college, as well as a noted agricultural institute. George Washington Carver – the famed agricultural pioneer who developed alternative crops to cotton such as peanuts and soy – taught and published here for 47 years; there is a museum (p161) dedicated to him.

The Drive » Continue southwest on I-85 for another 45 minutes to reach Montgomery, Alabama's capital city.

TRIP HIGHLIGHT

❸ Rosa Parks Museum

It was in Montgomery where the Civil Rights movement truly found its footing in 1955, when a secretary for the local chapter of the National Association for the Advancement of Colored People (NAACP), Rosa Parks, refused to give up her seat to a white passenger on a city bus. This iconic moment is re-created at the **Rosa Parks Museum** (☎334-241-8615; www.troy.edu/rosaparks; 251 Montgomery St; adult/child 4-12yr $7.50/5.50; ⏰9am-5pm Mon-Fri, 9am-3pm Sat; 🚸), located in the former site of the Empire Theater, in

front of which Parks took her defiant stand. Parks wasn't the first to engage in this sort of civil disobedience. In fact she was well trained in the discipline, along with some of her NAACP colleagues, at a retreat held not long before her admirable defiance. Yet her actions and subsequent arrest became national news when they sparked the Montgomery bus boycott, led by an as-yet-unknown, 26-year-old preacher named Martin Luther King Jr.

🍴 p181

The Drive » You can just as easily walk the two blocks northeast on Montgomery to the traffic circle, and hang a right on Dexter Ave. Continue for five blocks.

----

❹ Dexter Avenue King Memorial Church

When Martin Luther King arrived in Montgomery, he was appointed to the position of parson at the **Dexter Avenue congregation** (☎334-356-3494; www.dexterkingmemorial.org; 454 Dexter Ave; adult/child 3-12yr $10/6; ⏰10am-3pm Tue-Fri, to 1pm Sat) due to his obvious intellectual abilities, then to leader of the bus boycott due to his low profile at the time. King employed a mix of Christian theology, nonviolent philosophy and pointed political activism; as local blacks began using carpools to get to

Selma Edmund Pettus Bridge

ECHOES OF A KING

Martin Luther King Jr, the quintessential figure of the American Civil Rights movement and arguably America's greatest leader, was born in 1929, the son of an Atlanta preacher and choir leader. His lineage was significant not only because he followed his father to the pulpit of Ebenezer Baptist Church, but also because his political speeches rang out with a preacher's inflections.

Following his successful leadership of the year-long 'bus boycott' in Montgomery, AL, in 1955, King emerged as an inspiring moral voice.

King espoused a nonviolent approach to racial equality and peace, which he borrowed from Gandhi and used as a potent weapon against hate, segregation and racially motivated violence. He was assassinated on a Memphis hotel balcony in 1968, four years after receiving the Nobel Peace Prize and five years after giving his legendary 'I Have a Dream' speech in Washington, DC.

King remains one of the most recognized and respected figures of the 20th century. Over 10 years he led a movement that fought a system of statutory discrimination in existence since the country's founding.

work, city leaders – and soon, the world – began to take notice of the tensions stirring in Alabama.

During that time, King's modest home, today the **Dexter Avenue Parsonage** (☎334-261-3270; www.dexterkingmemorial. org; 309 S Jackson St; adult/ child $7.50/5.50; ⊕10am-3pm Tue-Fri, to 1pm Sat; **P**), was bombed, and King was arrested for the first time along with 88 others when local authorities attempted to outlaw the boycott. But the movement would not be deterred and on November 13, 1956, the Supreme Court ruled segregation of city buses unconstitutional. King scored his first major victory, and the leadership behind this boycott would soon form the Southern Christian Leadership Conference (SCLC), a major engine driving a movement that would grow in scope and power.

The Drive » Take Dexter Ave to Decatur St. Make a right, walk one block to Washington Ave, and make another right.

- - - - - - - - - - - - - - - - - -

⑤ Civil Rights Memorial Center

Closer to the Alabama Capitol steps is the **Civil Rights Memorial Center** (☎334-956-8200; www.spl center.org/civil-rights-memorial; 400 Washington Ave; memorial free, museum adult/child $2/free; ⊕memorial 24hr, museum 9am-4:30pm Mon-Fri, 10am-4pm Sat). The memorial is a circular fountain designed by Maya Lin – who also designed the Vietnam Veterans Memorial – and a haunting remembrance of 40 martyrs of the movement, all activists or citizens murdered for their convictions, deeds or simply their color. Some of the names like Emmet Till and Medgar Evers are relatively well known,

others are much less heralded and their stories just as tragic. Inside the center are interactive displays that provide context for each victim. The museum is a project of the **Southern Poverty Law Center**, the legendary nonprofit credited with bankrupting the Ku Klux Klan after it was held responsible for a racially motivated murder in 1987.

The Drive » Hwy 80 is a straight shot west into Alabama's old cotton country. You are now traveling one of the Civil Rights movement's darkest and most divisive roads, and it leads to Selma. After 30 miles, you'll reach the Lowndes County Interpretive Center.

- - - - - - - - - - - - - - - - - -

TRIP HIGHLIGHT

⑥ Lowndes County Interpretive Center

The **Selma to Montgomery National Historic Trail** (Hwy 80; www.nps. gov/semo) commemorates the 1965 Voting Rights March, one of the most violent and contentious of Alabama's civil rights confrontations. During voting-rights activities in nearby Dallas County, a young activist, Jimmie Lee Jackson, was shot and killed at point-blank range while attempting to shelter his mother from police batons during a peaceful march. In his memory, the Dallas County Voting Rights League decided to walk from Selma to Montgomery to highlight police brutality, and invited King and the SCLC to join them. But another violent police crackdown in Selma halted the march. A second attempt was made, but King turned the marchers back fearing for their safety. Finally, the march succeeded on its third attempt. Halfway between Montgomery and Selma, the **Lowndes County Interpretive Center** (☏334-877-1983; www.nps.gov/semo; 7002 US Hwy 80; ⌚9am-4:30pm Mon-Sat; [P]) is a wonderfully done museum, where a 25-minute documentary delves into the march. This site was also integral to the next phase of the movement. The seeds of Black Power were sown here after the march was over.

The Drive » Stay on Hwy 80 east for about 21 miles until you reach Selma.

- - - - - - - - - - - - - - - - - -

❼ Selma
On March 7, 1965, aka 'Bloody Sunday,' Alabama State troopers and recently deputized local white men attacked 500 peaceful marchers on the **Edmund Pettus Bridge** (Broad St & Walter Ave) with clubs and tear gas. The whole thing was captured on video, marking one of the first times Americans outside the South had

LOWNDES COUNTY & BLACK POWER

The march from Selma to Montgomery was a watershed moment in the Civil Rights movement, and not simply because of the violence that turned stomachs around the world. It also sparked a rupture between the Student Nonviolent Coordinating Committee (SNCC) and Martin Luther King's Southern Christian Leadership Conference (SCLC).

The SNCC was first on the ground in Selma, and was supporting the Dallas County Voting Rights League when Jimmie Lee Jackson was shot and killed. It invited the SCLC to join them because King's stature allowed them to raise money and receive maximum media attention. Yet some younger SNCC activists, including Stokley Carmichael (who would go on to be a founding member of the Black Panther Party), bristled at what they saw as a takeover of their organizing work, and were especially peeved when King turned the marchers around during their second attempt to cross the Edmund Pettus Bridge. When they eventually passed through Lowndes County on their way to Montgomery, Carmichael promised local folks that SNCC would be back. He kept his promise, and their ensuing voter registration drive saw the number of Lowndes County blacks registered to vote increase from 70 to 2,600 – 300 more than white registered voters. The new party, the Lowndes County Freedom Organization, was the first to employ a black panther as its logo.

The success of Carmichael's registration drive had a ripple effect. Locally, about 40 share-cropping families were evicted from their land by their white landlords after the ensuing election. So they set up a tented camp and lived on what is now home to the Lowndes County Interpretive Center. On a national level, within a year, the existing SNCC leadership – closely allied with Dr King – was ousted in favor of Carmichael, who made more waves when he delivered his first 'Black Power' speech in Greenwood, MS, in 1966.

witnessed the horrifying images of the struggle. Shock and outrage was widespread, and support for the movement grew. Eventually President Lyndon Johnson ordered the Alabama National Guard to protect what became over 8000 marchers (Joan Baez famously walked among them) who poured in from across the country to walk the 54 miles in four days, beginning on March 16 and culminating with a classic King speech on the capitol steps. The **National Voting Rights Museum** (☏334-418-0800; www.nvrmi.com; 6 US Highway 80 East; adult/senior & student $6.50/4.50; ☺10am-4pm Mon-Thu, by appt only Fri-Sun; **P**) is near the base of the bridge. The bulk of the organizing took place at the striking brick-red Victorian church, **Brown Chapel** (☏334-874-7897; 410 Martin Luther King St).

The Drive » From Selma, head east on AL 22, skirt the pine-dappled lake at Paul M Grist State Park, then veer north on AL 191 before merging with Hwy 31 and I-65 north into Birmingham, a total distance of about 90 miles.

TRIP HIGHLIGHT

❽ Birmingham

Progressive Birmingham was not always so inviting. When Bull Conner was the sheriff, civil rights activists, led by Dr King, embarked on a desegregation campaign downtown that employed masses of

'foot soldiers' – local activists, often high school students, who flooded local jails. Eventually, the Birmingham police responded to civil disobedience with water cannons and attack dogs, creating images that horrified the world, and which are subsequently immortalized via conceptual sculpture in **Kelly Ingram Park** (1600 5th Ave N). The campaign also gave us King's famed 'Letter from Birmingham Jail.'

All of this history is on display at the superb **Birmingham Civil Rights Institute** (☏866-328-9696; www.bcri.org; 520 16th St N; adult/child $12/5, Sun by donation; ☺10am-5pm Tue-Sat, 1-5pm Sun). The seven-block **Birmingham Civil Rights Memorial Trail** (www.bcri. org; 520 16th St N), installed in 2013 for the 50th anniversary of the campaign, depicts 22 moving scenes with statues and photography. It begins at the BCRI. The saddest and most enduring memories from that struggle remain the murder of four little girls, killed when the **16th Street Baptist Church** (☏205-251-9402; www.16thstreetbaptist.org; cnr 16th St & 6th Ave N; $5; ☺ministry tours 10am-3pm Tue-Fri, by appt only 10am-1pm Sat) was bombed by the Klan during Sunday School.

✗ ᕾ p181

The Drive » From Birmingham take Hwy 78 west for 219 miles through the Holly

Springs National Forest and merge onto I-240, which snakes into Memphis.

❾ Memphis

It was here that King's crusade was abruptly halted in April 1968, when he visited Memphis in support of the black sanitation-workers strike. The visit was tense, and King's entourage noticed he was more nervous than usual. On April 3 he spoke prophetically at the Mason Temple: 'Well, I don't know what will happen now. We've got some difficult days ahead. But it really doesn't matter with me now, because I've been to the mountaintop,' continuing on to say he'd seen the promised land, and that if he didn't make it there, he was sure his people would.

The next day, as he stood on the balcony outside room 306 at the **Lorraine Motel** on the south end of downtown Memphis, James Earl Ray shot him in the neck and face. He collapsed, one foot hanging off the railing, and died. Both the Lorraine Motel and the boarding house from where the shot was allegedly fired are now part of the **National Civil Rights Museum** (www.civilrightsmu seum.org; 450 Mulberry St; adult $15, child $12; ☺9am-5pm Mon & Wed-Sat, 1-5pm Sun), which you can visit on our Memphis walking tour (p326).

✗ ᕾ p181, p237, p275, p312, p322

Eating & Sleeping

Atlanta ❶

🍴 Daddy Dz   Barbecue $$

(📞404-222-0206; www.daddydz.com; 264 Memorial Dr SE; sandwiches $7-13, plates $13-23; 🕐11am-10:30pm Mon-Thu, to 11pm Fri & Sat, noon-9pm Sun; P) A juke joint of a BBQ shack, consistently voted one of the tops in town, and set smack in downtown. From the graffiti murals on the red, white and blue exterior, to the all-powerful smoky essence, to the reclaimed booths on the covered patio, there is soul to spare. Order the succulent ribs with cornbread, and you'll leave smiling.

🛏 Hotel Artmore   Boutique Hotel $$

(📞404-876-6100; www.artmorehotel.com; 1302 W Peachtree St; r $170-200, ste from $220; P ✳ @ 🛜) This 1924 Spanish-Mediterranean architectural landmark has been completely revamped into an artistic boutique hotel that's become an urban sanctuary for those who appreciate their trendiness with a dollop of discretion. It wins all sorts of accolades: excellent service, a wonderful courtyard with fire pit and a superb location across the street from Arts Center MARTA station.

Montgomery ❸

🍴 Farmer's Market Cafe   Southern US $

(📞334-262-1970; www.farmersmarketcafe.net; 315 N McDonough St; meals $6-10; 🕐5:30am-2pm Mon-Fri) This oversized downtown cafeteria serves up God-fearing Southern home cooking at recession-friendly prices according to the meat/veggie combo of your choice. Don't skip the grits casserole.

Birmingham ❽

🍴 Bottega   Italian $$$

(📞205-939-1000; www.bottegarestaurant.com; 2240 Highland Ave S; dinner $21-39; 🕐5:30-10pm Tue-Sat; P) Enjoy a spot of Birmingham posh at this fine Italian establishment in the Highlands, one of three stellar restaurants owned by chef Frank Stitt. The Parmesan soufflé is a signature starter, and they do a nice spaghetti with scallops and a popular hanger steak. Make reservations.

Right next door is **Café Bottega**, a more casual iteration of the restaurant with lower prices that draws preppy, seersucker-wearing crowds for lunch and dinner. Try the creative pizzas like crawfish and conecuh sausage, or the *piadina* (a type of Italian flatbread) with watercress, mint, dill, walnuts and radish.

🛏 Redmont Hotel   Historic Hotel $$

(📞205-957-6828; www.redmontbirmingham.com; 2101 5th Ave N; r/ste from $170/230; ✳ @ 🛜) The piano and chandelier in the lobby of this 1925 hotel lend a certain historical, old-world feel, and all deluxe rooms were just renovated, giving it a modern edge. The spacious rooftop bar doesn't hurt, either. It's walking distance to the civil rights sights.

Memphis ❾

🍴 Cozy Corner   Barbecue $

(www.cozycornerbbq.com; 735 N Pkwy; plates $6-14; 🕐11am-9pm Tue-Sat) Slouch in a torn vinyl booth and devour an entire barbecued Cornish game hen ($11.75), the house specialty at this recently renovated cult favorite. Ribs and wings are spectacular too, and the fluffy, silken sweet-potato pie is an A-plus specimen of the classic Southern dessert.

🛏 Talbot Heirs   Guesthouse $$

(📞901-527-9772; www.talbothouse.com; 99 S 2nd St; ste $160-200; ✳ @ 🛜) Inconspicuously located on the 2nd floor of a busy downtown street, this cheerful guesthouse is one of Memphis' best kept and most unique secrets. Spacious suites, all with recently modernized bathrooms, are more like hip studio apartments than hotel rooms, with Asian rugs, funky local artwork and kitchens stocked with (included!) snacks. Big stars like Harvey Keitel, Matt Damon and John Grisham have nested here, as well as Bobby Whitlock of Derek and the Dominos fame, who signed a piano.

Appalachian Trail

15

*Georgia, Tennessee and North Carolina each
claim a section of the 2175-mile Maine-to-
Georgia trail. On this journey you'll get a taste
of the trail and the charming towns alongside it.*

TRIP HIGHLIGHTS

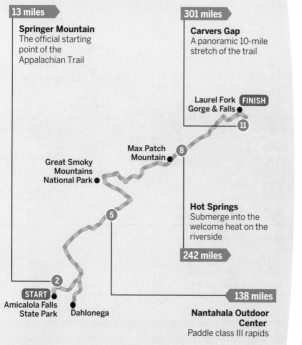

13 miles

Springer Mountain
The official starting
point of the
Appalachian Trail

301 miles

Carvers Gap
A panoramic 10-mile
stretch of the trail

Laurel Fork FINISH
Gorge & Falls
⑪

Max Patch ⑧
Mountain

**Great Smoky
Mountains
National Park** ●

⑤

Hot Springs
Submerge into the
welcome heat on the
riverside

242 miles

②

START
Amicalola Falls ●
State Park **Dahlonega**

138 miles

**Nantahala Outdoor
Center**
Paddle class III rapids

**5–7 DAYS
343 MILES /
552KM**

GREAT FOR...

BEST TIME TO GO

From April to October
snow has melted, or
has not yet begun
to fall.

ESSENTIAL PHOTO

Max Patch Mountain
offers signature views
of the lower portion of
the AT.

BEST FOR OUTDOORS

The AT is the original
long-distance hiking
trail.

Appalachian Trail Hking through Roan Mountain State Park

15 Appalachian Trail

Originally the idea of one man, Benton MacKaye, as an antidote to the busy, urban lifestyle of the East Coast in the 1920s, the Appalachian Trail (known as the AT) was completed in 1937. The entire route is marked by a series of 2in x 6in white blazes, and is for foot traffic only. Our trip will allow you to experience the trail with a minimum of sufferance.

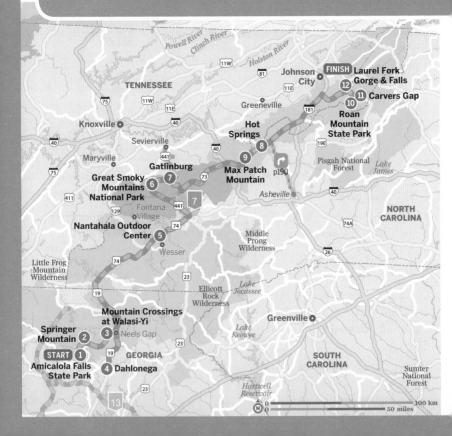

❶ Amicalola Falls State Park

There is no better way to get a feel for the grandeur of the Appalachian Trail than at its Georgian gateway, **Amicalola Falls State Park** (☏706-265-4703; www.gastateparks.org/amicalolafalls; 280 Amicalola Falls State Park Rd, Dawsonville; per vehicle $5; ⏰7am-10pm; **P**). Amicalola, a Cherokee Indian word meaning 'tumbling waters,' is an appropriate name for these 729ft falls – the tallest cascade east of the Mississippi River. The park offers more than 12 miles of hiking trails, including the 8.5 mile **Approach Trail**, past the falls to Springer Mountain, where the Appalachian Trail officially begins.

LINK YOUR TRIP

7 The Great Smokies

If you want still more mountain madness, explore the glory of the Smoky Mountains.

13 Hogs & Heifers: A Georgia BBQ Odyssey

Take a detour from Dahlonega and explore the soulful, smokey sustenance that is Georgia barbecue.

Get set up with maps and local hiking tips at the **Amicalola Falls State Park Visitors Center**, which also offers exhibits and a gift shop.

🛏 p191

The Drive ❯❯ Thru-hikers can trek here from Amicalola Falls State Park, but if the 604-step staircase freaks you out, take GA 52E to Winding Stair Gap Rd, and you find some nice views of Springer Mountain.

TRIP HIGHLIGHT

❷ Springer Mountain

The Appalachian Trail officially starts on top of this mountain, marked with a plaque: 'A footpath for those who seek fellowship with the wilderness.'

Most thru-hikers (or '2000 milers,' as those who walk the Appalachian Trail in a single journey are known) usually start here, at the Georgia terminus (about two hours north of Atlanta), in the late spring, and finish five to seven months later on Mt Katahdin in Maine, 2175 miles to the north. About 400 to 600 registered hikers complete the journey each year, about a quarter of those who set out. Altogether, only a little more than 10,000 brave and hearty trekkers have ever completed the journey. A few of those thru-hike the entire route in one go, but many hike the trail in sections – a few months, or weeks, at a time.

The Drive ❯❯ Thirty miles north of Springer Mountain by foot is your first stop in civilization, but if you're on wheels, it's 65 miles by car down graded roads. Take Service Road 42, make a right on GA 60 and a left on GA 19. Always check road conditions before starting off. Sometimes roads are closed or impassable due to weather.

---

❸ Mountain Crossings at Walasi-Yi

Mountain Crossings at Walasi-Yi (☏706-745-6095; www.mountaincrossings.com; 9710 Gainesville Hwy, Blairsville; per person per night $18; ⏰store 8:30am-5pm Mon-Thu, to 6pm Fri-Sun) is the one and only constructed intrusion on the trail. Of course, parched and sore hikers will be happy it isn't a mirage, as they follow the AT directly through the store, which has served as an outfitter to AT hikers since it was completed by the New Deal's Civilian Conservation Corps in 1937. There are hostel beds for those who'd like to do the first part of the trail and then hike (or hitchhike) back to Springer Mountain. And if you're a thru-hiker and have already blown through gear or forgotten something vital, they'll have it here.

The Drive ❯❯ Take Hwy 19 for about 22 miles from Mountain Crossings to Dahlonega.

Classic Trip

---

④ Dahlonega

In the 1820s the Dahlonega area was the site of the country's first gold rush. Its story is told inside the oldest courthouse in Georgia, built in 1836, and home of the **Dahlonega Courthouse Gold Museum** (📞706-864-2257; www.gastateparks.org/dahlonegagoldmuseum; Public Sq; adult/child $7/4.50; ⊙9am-5pm Mon-Sat, 10am-5pm Sun). But the new boom can be seen in the thousands of acres of vineyards that lace the surrounding mountainsides. **Naturally Georgia** (📞770-231-5783; www. naturallygeorgia.com; 90 Public Sq N; ⊙ noon-6pm Mon & Thu, 11am-8pm Fri & Sat, 12:30-6pm Sun), on the courthouse square, is a combined tasting room and art gallery where they pour surprisingly good dry whites and Portuguese reds from Tiger Mountain (you can find them in Whole Foods) and Crane Creek (a vintner who only sells locally). Or you could simply head to one of 10 nearby vineyards for a tasting. **Frogtown Cellars** (📞706-865-0687; www.frogtownwine.com; 700 Ridge Point Dr; tastings $15; ⊙noon-5pm Mon-Fri, to 6pm Sat, 12:30-5pm Sun) is a beautiful winery and has a killer deck on which to sip libations and nibble cheese. Nearby **Three Sisters** (📞706-865-9463; www.threesistersvineyards.com; 439 Vineyard Way; tastings from $10; ⊙11am-5pm Thu-Sat, 1-5pm Sun) is as unpretentious as it is quirky, where fine wine is paired with bluegrass, overalls and Cheetos.

✕ 🛏 p163, p191

The Drive » It's a gorgeous 90-mile drive up GA 19 through Vogel State Park and the Blue Ridge Mountains into North Carolina. Hang a right on Hwy 74 to Bryson City.

TRIP HIGHLIGHT

⑤ Nantahala Outdoor Center

Go wild at your next stop, the **Nantahala Outdoor Center** (NOC; 📞828-785-5082, 828-785-4850; www.noc.com; 13077 Hwy 19 W; ducky rental per day $35, guided trips $50-200; ⊙8am-8pm Jun-Jul, earlier Aug-May), where the Appalachian Trail and Nantahala River meet. Nestled in a steep gorge, the river offers 8 miles of easy class II rapids before splashing through exciting class III white water at **Nantahala Falls**. The NOC is a campus, with an outdoor store, an adventure center and a lodge. It also has free trail maps and tips. The AT cuts through the parking lot beside the outdoor store then crosses the river on the pedestrian bridge. From the NOC it's a 4-mile (strenuous!) hike to **Jump Up**, a rocky outcrop boasting outstanding views, or a 6.5-mile hike to the top of **Wesser Bald** (4627ft) and the former fire tower, now an observation deck, offering panoramic views of the Great Smoky Mountains. Hiking north, it's a longer, more strenuous hike (8.1 miles) to the summit of **Cheoah Bald** (5062ft), which offers splendid panoramas of the Southern Appalachians. There are AT sleeping shelters all along the trails for overnight hikers.

The Drive » It's a lovely 65 miles up Hwy 74E to Hwy 441N into Tennessee and the Great Smoky Mountains National Park.

---

⑥ Great Smoky Mountains National Park

This 815-sq-mile park is America's most visited but studies have shown that 95% of visitors never venture further than 100 yards from their cars, so it's easy to leave the teeming masses behind.

WARNING

Always check road conditions before starting off. Sometimes roads are closed or impassable due to weather, especially in the winter and spring.

In total there are 842 miles of trails in the Great Smoky Mountains National Park, including 73 miles of the Appalachian Trail which acts as a natural border between North Carolina and Tennessee. **Clingmans Dome** (6643ft) is almost dead center in the park, and is its highest point. The easiest way to get here is to take Hwy 441 to Clingmans Dome Road – a 7-mile spur road that ends in a paved parking lot. From there it's a mere half-mile walk to the peak. The **Sugarlands Visitor Center** (☏865-436-1291; www.nps.gov/grsm; 107 Park Headquarters Rd; ◷8am-7:30pm Jun-Aug, hours vary Sep-May) is a great resource for travelers. You can get backcountry permits ($4 per night) and reserve your campsite here. It has loads of maps and advice, and behind the visitor center is a mile-long nature trail to the modest but lovely **Cataract Falls**.

The Drive » It's just 3 quick miles down Hwy 441 from the Sugarlands Visitor Center to downtown Gatlinburg.

⑦ Gatlinburg

Wildly kitschy Gatlinburg hunkers at the entrance of the Great Smoky Mountains National Park, waiting to stun hikers with the scent of fudge and cotton candy. Tourists flock here to ride the gondola, shop for Confederate-flag

TOP TIP:
CLINGMANS DOME

Although it may be tempting to take the lazy alternative (ie drive), it is much sweeter to sweat your way to the summit. Especially since you'll be hiking a 7.7-mile slice of the Appalachian Trail, which begins in Newfound Gap. Sure, it parallels the road in sections, but don't let that dissuade you, and if you'd rather not walk down the mountain, you can easily hitch a ride back.

undershorts, get married at the many wedding chapels and play hillbilly mini-golf. Love it or hate it, the entire village is a gin-u-wine American roadside attraction. The best activity here is the **Ober Gatlinburg Aerial Tramway** (☏865-436-5423; www.obergatlinburg.com; 1001 Parkway; adult/child $13/10.50; ◷9:30am-9:40pm Mon-Thu, 7:30am-10:40pm Fri & Sat, to 6:20pm Sun with seasonal variations). A ski or snow tube area in the winter and an alpine slide in the summer time, families love the ride to the lodge at the top of the mountain in the glassed-in gondola, and enjoy coming down even more. **Ole Smoky Moonshine Holler** (www.olesmokymoonshine.com; 903 Parkway; ◷10am-10pm) is a stone-and-wood moonshine distillery where you may peer over oak barrels and copper boilers then taste that fiery hooch. Don't bother with the flavored varietals. It's all about the White Lightnin'.

✕ 🏠 p112, p191

The Drive » Take TN 73 east to the TN 32 into Newport, where you'll turn onto the Hwy 70 east into the Cherokee National Forest and back over the North Carolina state line.

TRIP HIGHLIGHT

⑧ Hot Springs

Hot Springs is known for its steaming, frothing mineral water upwelling from the earth to heal you. **Hot Springs Spa & Mineral Baths** (☏828-622-7676; www.nchotsprings.com; 315 Bridge St; mineral hot tubs from $20, massage $55-150; ◷noon-10pm Mon-Thu, 10am-midnight Fri-Sun) has 17 outdoor riverfront hot tubs fed by natural springs that range from 100°F (37°C) to 104°F (40°C), plus massage rooms and a pre- or post-massage fire pit for relaxing. Want to hit the river? **Hot Springs Rafting Company** (☏877-530-7238; www.hotspringsraftingco.com; 22 US 25; trips adult/child from $45/40; ◷9am-6pm) will set you up. Take a 5-mile guided trip down the French Broad River on class IIs

DOUG ASH / GETTY IMAGES ©

Classic Trip

KELLYVANDELLEN / GETTY IMAGES ©

MAINE TO GEORGIA

WHY THIS IS A CLASSIC TRIP
TRISHA PING,
DESTINATION
EDITOR

Offering verdant mountain vistas, winding roads, Olympic-class rapids and shaded forest trails, this area of the Appalachians is a stunner. Mountainside wineries and charming small towns are the icing on the cake. Whether you thru-hike, rev up the convertible or combine the two, your Appalachian journey is a guaranteed good time.

Above left: Sunrise over the trail near Max Patch
Mountain
Left: Stone marker at the start of the trail near
Springer Mountain
Right: Nantahala Falls

SKISERGEJ / GETTY IMAGES ©

and IIIs, or brave a 9-mile trip with class IVs. To float at your own pace, hop into a funyak (an inflatable, open-cockpit kayak; adult/child $35/30) or inner tube ($15).

❌ 🛏 p191

The Drive ›› It's a brilliant 45-minute mountain drive from the springs to a bald peak. Take NC 209 south for about 7 miles from Hot Springs, turning west on NC 1175 for 5.3 miles then turn onto Max Patch Rd (NC 1182). The parking area at the foot of the bald is 3 miles down Max Patch Rd.

⑨ Max Patch Mountain

While there is pleasant hiking both north and south, the 1.6-mile round-trip hike, accessed from a trailhead on Max Patch Rd, offers the best payoff for the least amount of sweat. The **Short Loop Trail** winds up the Appalachian Trail's southernmost bald, Max Patch Mountain. From atop the grassy summit there are panoramic views of the Blacks, Balds and Balsams, and the Great Smoky Mountains, of course. On a clear day you can even see the highest point in the eastern US – **Mt Mitchell** (6684ft). Add another mile, pick up the peak, and enjoy even more scenic beauty on the **Long Loop Trail**.

The Drive ›› Hop over the border to Tennessee, then continue another 50 miles on

TN 352 and I-26. Take exit 32 to reach Roan Mountain State Park.

----

⑩ Roan Mountain State Park

Roan Mountain State Park (☎800-250-8620; www.tnstateparks.com/parks; 1015 Hwy 143; ⊙8:30am-4pm) encompasses 2006 acres of southern Appalachian forest at the base of 6285ft Roan Mountain. On the top of Roan Mountain, straddling the Tennessee–North Carolina border, are the ruins of the old **Cloudland Hotel** site. The 300-room hotel was built in 1885 by Civil War general John T Wilder. Legend has it that North Carolinian sheriffs would hang out in the saloon, waiting for drinkers from the Tennessee side to stray across the line, as North Carolina was a dry state back then. There's also a great 4.6-mile round-trip hike to **Little Rock Knob** (4918ft) through hardwood forests, with epic cliff-top views into Tennessee.

📖 p191

The Drive » Just 8 miles past Roan Mountain State Park on NC 143 you'll reach Carvers Gap.

TRIP HIGHLIGHT

⑪ Carvers Gap

Carvers Gap is where a set of log steps leads to a section of the Appalachian Trail which crosses a 10-mile series of so-called grassy balds – treeless mountains with unobstructed views over Tennessee's Blue Ridge Mountains. Theories for their evolution include everything from extensive grazing to their creation by aliens. Uh-huh. To the south, the Appalachian Trail climbs to the high point of the Roan Mountain ridge, the 6285ft **Roan High Knob**.

The Drive » It's just a 27-mile drive through the Cherokee National Forest between trailheads. Take NC 143 north and turn left on TN 37 north.

----

⑫ Laurel Fork Gorge & Falls

Two moderate hikes lead to Laurel Fork Gorge and Falls. The vertical walls of the gorge rise 100ft on either side of the AT, the only trail through. You can access the gorge and the 40ft falls on one of two feeder trails. The first is a 5-mile round-trip, and the other 2.6 miles. To hike the former, access the blue-blazed **Hampton Blueline Trail** where I-321 crosses Laurel Fork in Hampton, TN (there's a parking lot for hikers here). The shorter hike can be reached by taking TN 67 from Hampton to Braemar, where you can pick up USFS 50 (Dennis Cove Rd) for the 3 miles to the parking area on the left. With the exception of the steep and rocky descent to the falls – which can be treacherous – the walks are quite flat and easy.

DETOUR:
ASHEVILLE

From: ⑧ **Hot Springs, NC**

With its homegrown microbreweries, decadent chocolate shops and stylish New Southern eateries, Asheville is one of the trendiest small cities in the east. Glossy magazines swoon for the place, but don't be put off by the hipsters and the flash. At heart, Asheville is still an overgrown mountain town, an oasis for hikers, musicians and artists, and more than a few hard-core hippies. For where to eat and stay in Asheville, see p100.

Eating & Sleeping

Amicalola Falls State Park ❶

🛏 Amicalola Falls Lodge　　Lodge $$

(📞800-573-9656; www.amicalolafalls.com; 418 Amicalola Falls State Park Rd, Dawsonville; campsites from $30, r & cottages $140-240; 🅿 ❄ @) This lodge is a full-service hotel with beautiful views from every room; the rustic cottages sleep four to 10. You can eat buffet-style at the on-site Maple Restaurant, and take advantage of local zip lines, archery courses and other adventure activities.

🛏 Len Foote Hike Inn　　Lodge $$

(📞800-581-8032; www.hike-inn.com; 280 Amicalola Falls State Park Rd, Dawsonville; s/d $120/175) You will be far from the rat race at this hike-in-only lodge, 5 miles from the nearest road. You'll need to carry in everything, haul out your own trash and reserve in advance. Rooms are comfortable and cozy – a welcome break from the trails – and two hot meals are served each day.

Dahlonega ❹

🍴 Back Porch Oyster Bar　　Seafood $$

(📞706-864-8623; www.backporchoysterbar. net; 19 N Chestatee St; mains $9-31; ⏲11:30am-9pm Mon-Thu, to 10pm Fri & Sat, to 8pm Sun; 🛜) Oysters, ahi and clams are among the bounty flown in daily to be shucked, seared and steamed at this neighborhood fish house. A front porch overlooking the square is perfect for taking it in.

🛏 Hiker Hostel　　Hostel $

(📞770-312-7342; www.hikerhostel.com; 7693 Hwy 19 N; dm/r $25/70, cabins $90-110; 🅿 ❄ @ 🛜) Seven miles or so from town, this hostel is owned by an avid pair of cycling and outdoors enthusiasts, and caters to those looking to explore the Appalachian Trail. The hostel is a converted log cabin; each bunk room has its own bath and it is wonderfully neat and clean.

Gatlinburg ❼

🍴 Wild Boar Saloon & Howard's Steakhouse　　Steak $$

(📞865-436-3600; www.facebook.com/ TheWildBoarSaloon; 976 Parkway; mains $10-37; ⏲11am-11pm Apr-Jan, to 9pm winter; 🛜) Since 1946 this dark creekside saloon has been serving burgers, ribs and a tasty pulled-pork shoulder drenched in homemade sauce, and is known for its steaks and Bloody Marys. The creekside patio is a winner on a warm day.

🛏 Bearskin Lodge　　Lodge $$

(📞877-795-7546; www.thebearskinlodge.com; 840 River Rd; d $79-220; 🅿 ❄ 🛜 ♿) This shingled riverside lodge is blessed with timber accents and a bit more panache than other Gatlinburg comers. All of the 96 spacious rooms have flat-screen TVs and some come with gas fireplaces and private balconies jutting over the river.

Hot Springs ❽

🍴 Smoky Mountain Diner　　Diner $

(70 Lance Ave; breakfast $2-16, mains $2-17; ⏲6am-4pm Mon-Tue, 6am-7pm Wed-Fri, 6:30am-7pm Sat, 6:30am-2pm Sun) Located directly on the Appalachian Trail running through town. Fuel up for a day of hiking with one of the giant egg dishes. Reenergize with burgers, meatloaf or fried chicken when you return. Save room for pie.

🛏 Mountain Magnolia Inn　　Inn $$

(📞828-622-3543; www.mountainmagnoliainn. com; 204 Lawson St; r $105-260) Built in 1868, this upscale inn gives guests an opportunity to enjoy the health-giving properties of the springs, while its restaurant completes the experience with high-end organic-driven fare (mains $26 to $32). Some rooms are in buildings off-site. Through-hikers are offered a steal of a deal: $75 for a single, $150 for a double.

Roan Mountain State Park ❿

🛏 Roan Mountain State Park Lodge　　Lodge $

(📞800-250-8620; https://tnstateparks.itinio. com/roan-mountain/cabins; 1015 Hwy 143; campsites $13-31, cabins $85-150; ⏲year-round, tent camping Apr-Nov) Book a campsite or cabin amid one of the park's most beautiful locations.

STRETCH YOUR LEGS
SAVANNAH

Start/Finish Sentient Bean, Forsyth Park

Distance 3.3 miles

Duration Three hours

Savannah is a living museum of Southern architecture and antebellum charm. Gorgeous and full of Old South charisma, its historical heart is freckled with pleasant squares shaded by spreading oaks dripping with Spanish moss. This town was made for walking.

Take this walk on Trips

Sentient Bean

Savannah is a coffee-loving town, and there's no better place to start your morning than Sentient Bean (www.sentientbean.com; 13 E Park Ave; ⊘7am-9pm; 🛜), a fabulous, bohemian cafe with terrific coffee, gourmet scones, hipster clientele and baristas with attitude (the good kind). Plus, it's just across the street from Forsyth Park.

The Walk » Step across the street and stroll through Savannah's most central, and most beautiful, park.

Forsyth Park

Gushing with fountains, draped with mossy oaks, unfurled with vast lawns and basketball and tennis courts, this is one dynamite city park. The **visitor center** has a number of brochures and maps that delve into local architecture and history and is worth stopping by. You also might consider staying the night at the hip and swanky Mansion on Forsyth Park (p171).

The Walk » From the north end of the park continue straight to elegant Monterey Sq, your first of such rectangular oases of European charm.

Mercer-Williams House

The location of an infamous homicide, the **Mercer-Williams House** (☑912-236-6352; www.mercerhouse.com; 429 Bull St; adult/student $12.50/8; ⊘10:30am-4:10pm Mon-Sat, noon-4pm Sun) was purchased and restored by eccentric art dealer Jim Williams in 1969. Inside you'll find the room in which Danny Hansford was murdered in 1981. That story is at the heart of *Midnight in the Garden of Good and Evil,* the book and subsequent film that put Savannah (and Kevin Spacey) on the map.

The Walk » From Monterey Sq, take Bull St north for four blocks, past a row of historic homes to E Charlton St on Madison Sq.

Shop SCAD

Creative impulse charges through Savannah's veins, thanks in large part

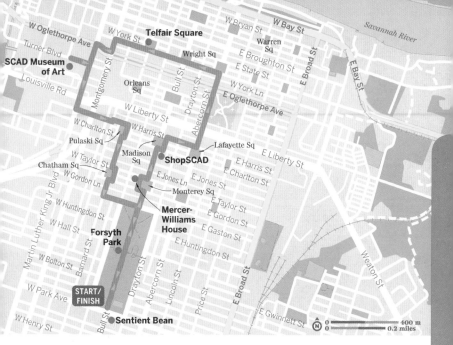

to the **Savannah College of Art and Design** (SCAD). SCAD students are legion, its graduates often settling in town to paint or open flower shops, textile depots or design businesses. All the wares on sale at **ShopSCAD** (☑912-525-5180; www.shopscadonline.com; 340 Bull St; ⏰9am-5:30pm Mon-Fri, 10am-6pm Sat, noon-5pm Sun) – the throw pillows, the canvases and art books, the jewelry and T-shirts – were imagined by SCAD students, alumni or faculty.

The Walk ⟫ Make a right on Harris St and wander past Lafayette Sq (one of our favorites) then make a left on Abercorn St.

Telfair Square

Two of Savannah's most popular museums are set around this leafy residential plaza. The **Telfair Academy of Arts & Sciences** (☑912-790-8800; www. telfair.org; 121 Barnard St; adult/child $20/15; ⏰noon-5pm Sun & Mon, 10am-5pm Tue-Sat) is filled with 19th-century American art and silver, and a smattering of European pieces. Nearby, Jepson Center

for the Arts (p146) has 20th- and 21st-century art.

The Walk ⟫ Take York St west to Montgomery, head south one block to Oglethorpe and head west again. Cross Martin Luther King Jr Blvd, one of town's major thoroughfares, and walk two long blocks south to Turner Blvd.

SCAD Museum of Art

More than the sum of its parts, the SCAD Museum of Art (p146) is a brick, steel, concrete and glass long-house carved with groovy, creative sitting areas inside and out, and filled with fun rotating exhibitions. We saw an installation of video screens strobing various karaoke interpretations of Madonna's *Lucky Star*. It has intriguing mixed-media pieces, and an inviting cafe.

The Walk ⟫ Your 1.25 mile walk back to the start follows MLK Blvd to Harris St. Make a left to Barnard, and head south, through Pulaski and Chatham Sqs. Make a left on Gaston to re-enter Forsyth Park.

Mississippi, Louisiana & Arkansas

Venture into these three distinct, alluring states, and you may just fall in love. Arkansas flaunts granite bluffs, scenic rivers, quirky mountain towns and narrow trails that lead to the edge of heaven. In sultry Mississippi, juke joints hum until the wee hours, historic Oxford is the kind of fun-yet-refined college town that reels you in, and the Natchez Trace Parkway is simply the most beautiful highway in the South. Then let Louisiana satiate you with the naughty flavor, period architecture and addictive soundtrack of New Orleans. Outside the Crescent City limits explore a fertile maze of plantations, misty bayous and swamps, and tasty Cajun towns. The complex, tortured, musical, joyful Southern soul will be laid bare here, and you'll leave inspired.

Whitaker Point Granite table-top high above the Buffalo River region
BRANDON ALMS / SHUTTERSTOCK ©

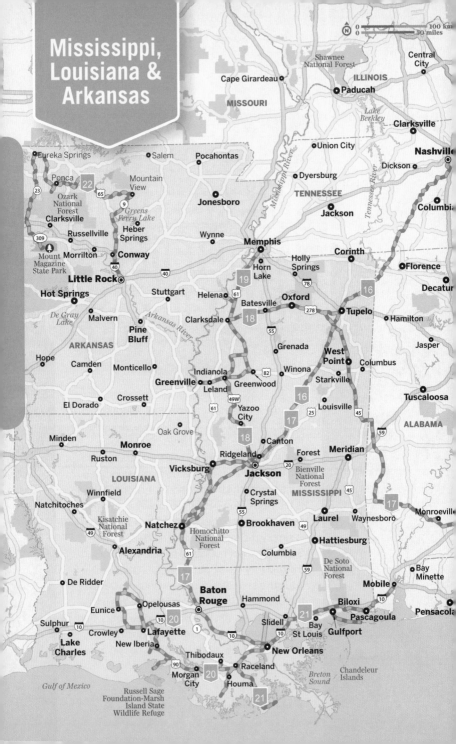

Mississippi, Louisiana & Arkansas

Natchez Trace Parkway 3 Days
16
The journey south from Nashville stuns with
natural beauty and American history. (p199)

17 **Southern Gothic Literary Tour 7 Days**
Trace the backstories of the South's most revered
literary legends. (p211)

18 **Historical Mississippi 3 Days**
Mississippi's complex history is on display from
Oxford to Vicksburg to Natchez. (p221)

 The Blues Highway 3 Days
19
A soulful ramble to the roots of American popular
music. (p229)

20 **Cajun Country 4 Days**
Explore bayous, dance halls, crawfish boils and
folk ways in Louisiana's idiosyncratic Acadiana
region. (p239)

21 **Gulf Coast 4 Days**
Glimpse the Gulf from Louisiana wetlands, Mississippi beaches and industrial Alabama ports.
(p247)

22 **Back Roads Arkansas 4 Days**
Hike, paddle, zip and drive through Arkansas'
soul-stirring countryside. (p255)

 DON'T MISS

French Quarter
Wrought-iron balconies,
ivy creeping over brick,
Creole, Spanish and
Caribbean architecture;
the French Quarter is
timeless. Explore on
Trips **17** **21** **28**

Rowan Oak
William Faulkner lived
here, on this peaceful
Oxford estate, for most
of his literary career. See
it on Trips **17** **18**

Clarksdale
The hub of the
Mississippi Delta, with
a spectacular juke joint
and comfortable digs
from where you explore
the blues. Visit on Trips
18 **19** **28**

Natchez
An antebellum time
capsule? A laid-back
river town? A charming
respite for a few
days of strolling and
contemplation? Yes. All
of it. Experience on Trips
17 **18** **28**

Buffalo River
Scenic and protected,
the crystalline Buffalo
winds along majestic
bluffs yet is mellow
enough for beginners.
Paddle it on Trip **22**

New Orleans Streetcars

197

Classic Trip

Natchez Trace Parkway

16

With emerald mounds, opulent mansions and layers of American history, the Natchez Trace Parkway winds 444 gorgeously wooded miles from Nashville all the way to southern Mississippi.

TRIP HIGHLIGHTS

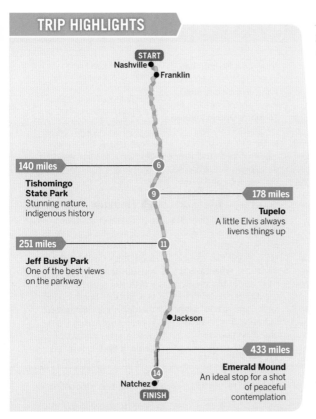

START
Nashville ●
● Franklin

140 miles ⑥

Tishomingo State Park
Stunning nature, indigenous history

⑨ **178 miles**

Tupelo
A little Elvis always livens things up

251 miles ⑪

Jeff Busby Park
One of the best views on the parkway

● Jackson

433 miles

Emerald Mound
An ideal stop for a shot of peaceful contemplation

⑭
Natchez ●
FINISH

**3 DAYS
444 MILES / 714KM**

GREAT FOR...

BEST TIME TO GO
The climate is lovely in spring (April to June) and fall (September to November).

 ESSENTIAL PHOTO
Emerald Mound, second-largest Native American mound in the world, is magical just before sunset.

 BEST FOR HISTORY
Glimpse indigenous ways and echoes of a pioneering past.

Natchez Trace Parkway The iconic Double-Arch Bridge

Classic Trip

16 Natchez Trace Parkway

America grew from infancy to childhood then adolescence in the late 18th and 19th centuries. Early American settlers explored, expanded and traded, clashed with Native Americans, and confronted their own shadow during the Civil War. Evidence of this drama can be found along the Natchez Trace, but before you begin, hit the honky-tonks and enjoy a little night music.

❶ Nashville

Although this leafy, sprawling Southern city – with its thriving economy and hospitable locals – has no scarcity of charms, it really is all about the music. Boot-stomping honky-tonks lure aspiring stars from across the country in the hopes of ascending into royalty, of the type on display at the **Country Music Hall of Fame**, which you can visit on our walking tour (p324). Don't miss **Bluebird Cafe** (☎615-383-1461; www.bluebirdcafe. com; 4104 Hillsboro Rd; cover free-$30): tucked into a suburban strip mall, this singer-songwriter haven was made famous in the recent television series

Nashville. No chitchat or you will get bounced. Enjoy a less-controlled musical environment at **Tootsie's Orchid Lounge** (☎615-726-7937; www. tootsies.net; 422 Broadway; ⏰10am-2:30am), a glorious dive smothered with old photographs and hand-bills from the Nashville Sound glory days. Blue-grass fans will adore **Station Inn** (☎615-255-3307; www.stationinn.com; 402 12th Ave S; ⏰open mike 7pm, live bands 9pm), where you'll sit at one of the small cocktail tables, swill beer (only), and marvel at the lightning fingers of fine bluegrass players.

🍽 🛏 p208, p312

The Drive » The next day head south, and you will

traverse the Double-Arch Bridge, 155ft above the valley, before settling in for a pleasant country drive on the parkway. You'll notice dense woods encroaching and arching elegantly over the baby-bottom-smooth highway for the next 444 miles. It's about 10 miles from Nashville to Franklin.

❷ Franklin

Before you embark on the Trace, make a little side trip to Franklin. Although it's just 10 miles outside of Nashville, it's worth stopping in this tiny historic hamlet. The Victorian-era downtown is charming and the nearby artsy enclave of **Leiper's Fork** is fun and eclectic. But you're in the area to check out one of the Civil War's bloodiest

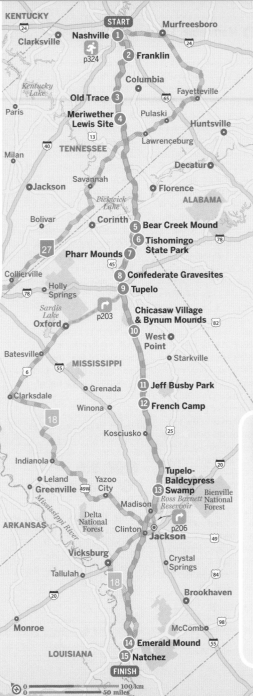

battlefields. On November 30, 1864, 37,000 men (20,000 Confederates and 17,000 Union soldiers) fought over a 2-mile stretch of Franklin's outskirts. Nashville's sprawl has turned much of that battlefield into suburbs, but the **Carter House** (615-791-1861; www.boft. org; 1140 Columbia Ave; adult/ child 6-15yr/child under 6yr $18/8/free; 9am-5pm Mon-Sat, 11am-5pm Sun;) property is a preserved 8-acre chunk of the **Battle of Franklin**. The house is still riddled with 1000-plus bullet holes.

The Drive » The parkway carves a path through dense woodland as you swerve past another historic district at Leiper's Fork, before coming to the first of several Old Trace turnouts after approximately 40 miles.

LINK YOUR TRIP

18 Historical Mississippi

Don't abandon the past in Natchez, but continue your odyssey through the deep roots of Mississippi's complex history.

27 Memphis to Nashville

Follow this trip in reverse, starting in Nashville and making your way to Beale St, Memphis.

Classic Trip

❸ Old Trace

At Mile 403.7 (yes that's right – don't worry about the 'backward' mile markers; we think a north–south route works best) you'll find the first of several sections of the Old Trace.

In the early 19th century, Kaintucks (boats-people from Ohio and Pennsylvania) floated coal, livestock and agricultural goods down the Ohio and Mississippi Rivers aboard flat-bottom boats. Often their boats were emptied in Natchez, where they disembarked and began the long walk home up the Old Trace to Nashville, where they could access established roads further north. This walking path intersected Choctaw and Chicasaw country, which meant it was hazardous. In fact, indigenous travelers were the first to beat this earth. You can walk a 2000ft section of that original trail at this turnout.

The Drive » There's beaucoup beauty on a 20-mile stretch of road, as the parkway flows past Jackson Falls and the Baker Bluff overlook, which offers views over the Duck River.

❹ Meriwether Lewis Site

At Mile 385.9 you'll come to the Meriwether Lewis Site, where the famed explorer and first governor of the Louisiana territory died mysteriously at nearby **Grinders Inn**. His fateful journey began in September 1809, and his plan was to travel to Washington, DC, to defend his spending of government funds (think of it as an early-days subpoena before a Congressional committee). At Fort Pickering, a remote wilderness outpost near modern-day Memphis, he met up with a Chicasaw agent named James Neely, who was to escort the Lewis party safely through Chicasaw land. They traveled north, through the bush, and along the Old Trace to **Grinder's Stand**, and checked into the inn run by the pioneering Grinder family. Mrs Grinder made up a room for Lewis and fed him, and after he retired, two shots rang out. The legendary explorer was shot in the head and chest and died at 35. Lewis' good friend, Thomas Jefferson, was convinced it was suicide. His family disagreed.

The Drive » It's about 77 miles to your next stop. Continue on and you will cross into Alabama at Mile 341.8, and Mississippi at Mile 308.

❺ Bear Creek Mound

Just across the Alabama state line and in Mississippi, at Mile 308.8, you'll find Bear Creek Mound, an ancient indigenous ceremonial site. There are seven groups of Indian mounds found along the parkway, all of them in Mississippi. They varied in shapes from Mayan-like pyramids to domes to small rises, and were used for worship and burying the dead; some were seen as power spots for local chiefs who sometimes lived on top of them. That was arguably the case at Bear Creek, which was built between 1100 and 1300 AD. Archaeologists are convinced that there was a temple and/or a chief's dwelling on the top of the rise.

The Drive » The highway bisects Tishomingo State Park at Mile 304.5.

TRIP HIGHLIGHT

❻ Tishomingo State Park

This state park is named for the Chicasaw Indian Chief Tishomingo. If you're taking it slow, you may want to **camp** (📞662-438-6914; www.mississippistateparks.reserveamerica.com; Mile 304.5 Natchez Trace Pkwy; campsite $18; ⏱24hr; 🚻🐾) here, among the evocative, moss-covered sandstone cliffs and rock formations, fern gullies and waterfalls of Bear Creek canyon. Hiking trails abound, canoes are available for rent if you wish to paddle **Bear Creek**, and spring wildflowers bloom once the weather warms. It's a special oasis, and one that was utilized by the Chicasaw and their Paleo Indian antecedents. There is evidence of their civilization in the park dating back to 7000 BC.

The Drive ⟫ Just under 20 miles of more wooded beauty leads from Tishimongo State Park to the next in a series of Native American mounds at Mile 286.7.

⑦ Pharr Mounds

The Pharr Mounds is a 2000-year-old, 90-acre complex of eight indigenous burial sites. Four of them were excavated in 1966 and found to have fireplaces and low platforms where the dead were cremated. Ceremonial artifacts were also found, along with copper vessels, which raised some eyebrows. Copper is not indigenous to Mississippi, and its presence here indicated an extensive trade network with other nations and peoples.

The Drive ⟫ About 17 miles on, at Mile 269.4, you'll come across a turnout that links up to another section of the Old Trace and offers a bit more recent history.

⑧ Confederate Gravesites

Just north of Tupelo, on a small rise overlooking the Old Trace, lies a row of 13 graves of unknown Confederate soldiers. What led to their fate has been lost in time, but theories range from their having died during the Confederate retreat from Corinth, MS, following the legendary Battle of Shiloh. Others believe they were wounded in the nearby Battle of Brice's Crossroads, and buried by their brothers, here.

The Drive ⟫ Less than 10 miles later you will loop into the comparatively large hamlet of Tupelo, at Mile 266, where you can gather road supplies for the southward push.

TRIP HIGHLIGHT

⑨ Tupelo

Here, the **Natchez Trace Parkway Visitors Center** (☑800-305-7417, 662-680-4025; www.nps.gov/natr; Mile 266 Natchez Trace Pkwy; ⊙8am-5pm, closed Christmas; 🚹 👶) is a fantastic resource with well-done natural- and American-history displays, and detailed parkway maps. Music buffs will know that Tupelo is world famous for its favorite son. **Elvis Presley's Birthplace** (☑662-841-1245; www.elvispresleybirthplace. com; 306 Elvis Presley Dr; adult/senior/child $17/14/8, house only adult/child $8/5; ⊙9am-5pm Mon-Sat, 1-5pm Sun; ℗) is a pilgrimage site for those who kneel before the King. The original structure has a new roof and furniture, but no matter the decor, it was within these humble walls that Elvis was born on January 8, 1935, where he learned to play the guitar and began to dream big. His family's church, where Elvis was first bit by the music bug, has been transported and restored here, as well.

DETOUR:
OXFORD

Start: ⑨ Tupelo

If you plan on driving the entire Natchez Trace from Nashville to Natchez, you should make the 50-mile detour along Hwy 6 to Oxford, MS, a town rich in culture and history. This is Faulkner country, and Oxford is a thriving university town with terrific restaurants and bars. Don't miss the catfish dinner at Taylor Grocery (p218), 15 minutes south of Oxford, via County Rd 303.

Classic Trip

LEAH SMALLEY / SHUTTERSTOCK ©

WHY THIS IS A CLASSIC TRIP
ADAM SKOLNICK, WRITER

When you combine abundant, natural beauty with the type of deep history that folds into anthropology, and add to that a smooth road (which makes for terrific cycling), nearby hiking trails, rivers and streams, you have 444 miles of enriching, vacation reverie at your disposal.

Top: French Camp Museum, French Camp
Left: Nine-banded armadillo, a Natchez Trace Parkway resident
Right: Emerald Mound indigenous site

DANITA DELIMONT / GETTY IMAGES ©

FRANK KEATING / GETTY IMAGES ©

The Drive >> Just barely out of Tupelo, at Mile 261.8, is Chicasaw Village. The Bynum Mounds are another nearly 30 miles south. You'll see the turnoff just after leaving the Tombigbee National Forest.

----

⑩ Chicasaw Village & Bynum Mounds

South from Tupelo, the Trace winds past the Chickasaw Village Site, where you'll find displays documenting how the Chickasaw lived and traveled during the fur-trade heydays of the early 19th century. It was 1541 when Hernando de Soto entered Mississippi under the Spanish flag. They fought a bitter battle, and though De Soto survived, the Chickasaw held strong. By the 1600s the English had engaged the Chickasaw in what became a lucrative fur trade. Meanwhile, the French held sway just west in the massive Louisiana territory. As an ally to England, the Chickasaw found themselves up against not only the French, but their Choctaw allies.

Further down the road are the site of six 2100-year-old Bynum Mounds. Five were excavated just after WWII, and copper tools and cremated remains were found. Two of the mounds have been restored for public viewing.

Classic Trip

The Drive » It's about 39 miles from the Bynum Mounds to Jeff Busby Park, which can be found at Mile 193.1.

TRIP HIGHLIGHT

⑪ Jeff Busby Park

Don't miss this hilltop park with picnic tables and a fabulous overlook taking in low-lying, forested hills that extend for miles, all the way to the horizon. Exhibits at the top include facts and figures about local flora and fauna, as well as a primer on indigenous tools. **Little Mountain Trail**, a half-mile loop that takes 30 minutes to complete, descends from the parking lot into a shady hollow. Another half-mile spur trail branches from that loop to the campground below.

The Drive » Thirteen miles down the road, at Mile 180, the forest clears and an agrarian plateau emerges, jade and perfect, as if this land has been cultivated for centuries.

⑫ French Camp

The site of a former French pioneer settlement, here you can tour an antebellum two-story home, built by Revolutionary War veteran Colonel James Drane. An end table is set for tea, aged leather journals are arranged on the desk and Drane's original US flag is in an upstairs bedroom along with an antique loom.

Even more noteworthy is the ornate stagecoach of Greenwood LeFlore, which carried the last chief of the Choctaw nation east of the Mississippi on his two trips to Washington to negotiate with President Andrew Jackson. For more recent French camp history you can peruse the **French Camp Museum**. Set in a vintage log cabin, there are a number of historic photos on the porch, as well as framed newspaper articles and maps in the museum itself.

🛏 p209

The Drive » As you head south, the forest clears for snapshots of horses in the prairie, before the trees encroach again and again. The next stop is about 55 miles down the Trace.

⑬ Tupelo-Baldcypress Swamp

At Mile 122, you can examine some of these trees up close as you tour the stunning Tupelo-Baldcypress Swamp. The 20-minute **trail** snakes through an abandoned channel and continues on a boardwalk over the milky green swamp shaded by water tupelo and bald cypresses. Look for turtles on the rocks and gators in the murk.

The Drive » The swamp empties into the Ross R Barnett Reservoir, which you'll see to the east as you speed toward and through the state capital

---

↱ **DETOUR:**
JACKSON

Start: ⑬ **Tupelo-Baldcypress Swamp**
Twenty-two miles south of the swamp, and just a bit further along the interstate, is Mississippi's capital. With its fine downtown museums and artsy-funky **Fondren District** – home to Mississippi's best kitchen – Jackson offers a blast of Now if you need a pick-me-up. The city's two best sites are the Mississippi Museum of Art (p216), which promotes homegrown artists and offers rotating exhibitions, and the Eudora Welty House (p216). This is where the literary giant, and Pulitzer Prize winner, crafted every last one of her books. And do not leave town without enjoying lunch or dinner at Walker's Drive-In (p218). For where to eat and sleep, see p218 and p227.

of Jackson. The next intriguing sight is just 10.3 miles from Natchez, accessible by graded road that leads west from the parkway.

TRIP HIGHLIGHT

14 Emerald Mound

Emerald Mound is by far the best of the indigenous mound sites. Using stone tools, pre-Columbian ancestors to the Natchez people graded this 8-acre mountain into a flat-topped pyramid. It is now the second-largest mound in America. There are shady, creekside picnic spots here, and you can and should climb to the top where you'll find a vast lawn along with a diagram of what the temple may have looked like. It would have been perched on the secondary and highest of the mounds. A perfect diversion on an easy spring afternoon just before the sun smolders, when birdsong rings from the trees and comingles with the call of a distant train.

The Drive ›› Drive on for about 22 more miles. As you approach Natchez, the mossy arms of southern oaks spread over the roadway, and the air gets just a touch warmer and more moist. You can almost smell the river from here.

----

15 Natchez

When the woods part, revealing historic antebellum mansions, you have reached Natchez, MS. In the 1840s, Natchez had more millionaires per capita than any city in the world (because the plantation owners didn't pay their staff). Yes, old cotton money built these homes with slave labor, but they are graced all the same with an opulent, *Gone With the Wind* charm. 'Pilgrimage season' is in the spring and fall, when the mansions open for tours, though some are open year-round. The brick-red **Auburn Mansion** (📞601-446-6631; www.auburnmuseum.org; 400 Duncan Ave; adult/child $15/10; ⏰11am-3pm Tue-Sat, last tour departs 2:30pm; 🚻) is famous for its freestanding spiral staircase. Built in 1812, the architecture here influenced countless mansions throughout the South.

Natchez has dirt under its fingernails, too. When Mark Twain came through town (and he did on numerous occasions), he crashed in a room above the local watering hole. Under the Hill Saloon (p217), across the street from the mighty Mississippi River, remains the best bar in town, with terrific (and free) live music on weekends.

🍴 🛏 p209

Eating & Sleeping

Nashville ❶

✗ Prince's Hot Chicken   Fast Food $

(123 Ewing Dr; quarter/half/whole chicken $5/11/22; ⏱11:30am-10pm Tue-Thu, 11:30am-4am Fri, 2pm-4am Sat; P) Tiny, faded, family-owned Prince's serves Nashville's most legendary 'hot chicken.' It's set in a gritty, northside strip mall and attracts everyone from hipsters to frat boys to entire immigrant families to local heads to hillbillies. Fried up mild (total lie), medium (what a joke), hot (verging on insanity), Xhot (extreme masochism) and XXXHot (suicide), its chicken will burn a hole in your stomach, and take root in your soul. Cash only.

✗ City House   Southern US $$

(☎615-736-5838; www.cityhousenashville.com; 1222 4th Ave N; mains $15-29; ⏱5-10pm Mon & Wed-Sat, to 9pm Sun) This signless brick building in Nashville's smart Germantown district hides one of the city's best restaurants. The food, cooked in an open kitchen in the warehouse-like space, is a crackling bang-up of Italy meets New South. On offer are tangy kale salads, a tasty smoked lamb with chard, lemon and pecorino, pastas featuring twists like octopus ragu, or baked grits in cauliflower ragu. The folk at City House cure their own sausage and salamis, and take pride in their cocktail and wine list. Save room for dessert. Sunday supper features a stripped-down menu. The bar, pizza counter and screened-in porch are saved for walk-ins.

✗ Monell's   Southern US $$

(☎615-248-4747; www.monellstn.com; 1235 6th Ave N; all you can eat $14-21; ⏱8am-3pm Mon, 8am-3pm & 5-8:30pm Tue-Sat, 8am-4pm Sun) In an old brick house just north of downtown, Monell's is beloved for down-home Southern food served family style. This is not just a meal, it's an experience, as platter after platter of

skillet-fried chicken, pulled pork, corn pudding, baked apples, mac 'n' cheese and mashed potatoes keep coming...and coming. Clear your afternoon schedule!

🛏 Hutton Hotel   Boutique Hotel $$

(☎615-340-9333; www.huttonhotel.com; 1808 West End Ave; r from $279; P ❄ @ 🛜) One of our favorite Nashville boutique hotels riffs on mid-century modern design with bamboo-paneled walls and reclaimed WWI barn wood flooring. Sizable rust- and chocolate-colored rooms are well appointed with electrically-controlled marble rain showers, glass washbasins, king beds, ample desk space, wide flat-screens and high-end carpet and linens. Don't miss daily complimentary happy hours with local wineries, distilleries and breweries. Sustainable luxury abounds. Take a free spin in the hotel's electric Tesla!

🛏 Hotel Indigo   Boutique Hotel $$

(☎615-891-6000; www.hotelindigo.com; 301 Union St; r from $189; P ❄ @ 🛜) Part of a boutique international chain, the Indigo has a fun, pop-art look, with 161 rooms (30 of which are brand new). Avoid the original (but tacky) Terrazo floor rooms in favor of those spacious King Rooms, with brand new hardwood floors, high ceilings, flat-screens, leather headboards and office chairs.

🛏 Union Station Hotel   Hotel $$$

(☎615-726-1001; www.unionstationhotel nashville.com; 1001 Broadway; r from $300; P ❄ 🛜) This soaring Romanesque gray stone castle was Nashville's train station back in the days when rail travel was a grand affair; today it's downtown's most iconic hotel. The vaulted lobby is dressed in peach and gold with inlaid marble floors and a stained-glass ceiling. All rooms have just been tastefully modernized with new smart TVs, cowhide headboards and chicken wire chandeliers (upper floors).

French Camp 12

🛏 French Camp B&B   B&B $$

(📞662-547-6835; www.frenchcamp.org; Mile
180.7 Natchez Trace Pkwy; r $95-145; P ❄ 🐾)
Stay the night in a log cabin built on a former
French pioneer site that was further developed
by a Revolutionary War hero. Rustic rooms and
cabins will have you feeling close to nature –
which is plentiful, gorgeous and all around you.

Natchez 15

✗ Magnolia Grill   Southern US $$

(📞601-446-7670; www.magnoliagrill.com; 49
Silver St; mains $13-22; ⏲11am-9pm, to 10pm Fri
& Sat; 🐾) Down by the riverside, this attractive
wooden storefront grill with exposed rafters and
outdoor patio is a good place for a pork tenderloin
po'boy, or a fried crawfish spinach salad.

✗ Cotton Alley   Cafe $$

(📞601-442-7452; www.cottonalleycafe.com; 208
Main St; mains $10-20; ⏲11am-2pm & 5:30-9pm
Mon-Sat) This cute whitewashed dining room

is chockablock with knickknacks and artistic
touches and the menu borrows from local tastes.
Think: grilled chicken sandwich on Texas toast
and jambalaya pasta, but it does a nice chicken
Caesar and a tasty grilled salmon salad too.

🛏 Mark Twain
Guesthouse   Guesthouse $

(📞601-446-8023; www.underthehillsaloon.com;
33 Silver St; r without bath $65-85; ❄ 🔊) Mark
Twain used to crash in room 1, above the bar
at the current Under the Hill Saloon (p217),
when he was a riverboat pilot passing through
town. There are three rooms in all, sharing one
bath and laundry facilities.

🛏 Historic Oak
Hill Inn   Inn $$

(📞601-446-2500; www.historicoakhill.
com; 409 S Rankin St; r $135-160, ste $235;
P ❄ 🔊) Ever wish you could sleep in one of
those historic homes? At the Historic Oak Hill
Inn, you can sleep in an original 1835 bed and
dine on pre–Civil War porcelain under 1850
Waterford crystal gasoliers – it's all about purist
antebellum aristocratic living at this classic
Natchez B&B.

Southern Gothic Literary Tour

17

To serve regional drama (obscene riches, crippling poverty, brutal racial oppression), garnished with sweltering nights and powerful storms, is to become a giant in the South's very own literary genre.

TRIP HIGHLIGHTS

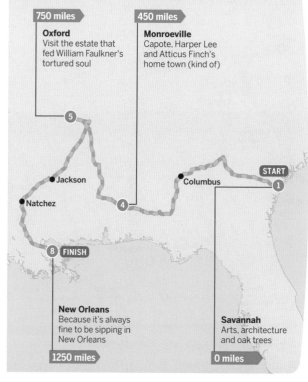

750 miles

Oxford
Visit the estate that fed William Faulkner's tortured soul

450 miles

Monroeville
Capote, Harper Lee and Atticus Finch's home town (kind of)

5

Jackson

START

Natchez

Columbus

4

8 FINISH

New Orleans
Because it's always fine to be sipping in New Orleans

Savannah
Arts, architecture and oak trees

1250 miles

0 miles

7 DAYS
**1250 MILES /
2011KM**

GREAT FOR...

BEST TIME TO GO
March to June: the trees bud, flowers bloom and the climate is mild and perfect.

ESSENTIAL PHOTO
Faulkner's wooded lair on a gorgeous Oxford estate.

BEST FOR ARTS & ARCHITECTURE
Delve into the archives for the roots of some of America's finest authors.

Savannah Riverboat moored at sunrise

211

17 Southern Gothic Literary Tour

The South has produced some of America's most glorious writers, novels and characters. William Faulkner, Tennessee Williams, Carson McCullers and Flannery O'Connor have roots in Southern soil, as do the unforgettable Vampire Lestat, the brave Atticus Fitch, and wily Huckleberry Finn and his friend Jim. The Great American Novel was invented here, and the Southern Gothic genre has flourished. There have been countless bestsellers and Pulitzers and one Nobel Prize.

TRIP HIGHLIGHT

① Savannah

Our journey begins at *Midnight in the Garden of Good and Evil*, also known as Savannah, GA. This opulent, historic town is nestled on the Savannah River, 18 miles from the Atlantic. Lowcountry swamps and massive oaks heavy with Spanish moss surround its countless antebellum mansions and Colonial relics; explore it on our walking tour (p192). It's a beautiful place, and you're here because of one

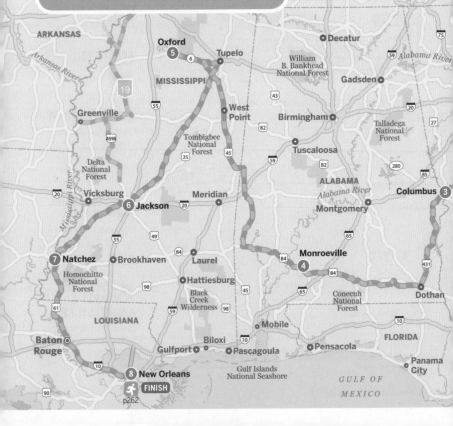

of the more recent books on our list. *Midnight* was written by John Berendt in 1994, and though it's classified as nonfiction, it reads like a novel. Written in the Southern Gothic tone, this distinctively 1980s tale revolves around the murder of a local hustler, Danny Hansford, by respected art dealer Jim Williams – an event that triggered four murder trials. Williams lived in the **Mercer-Williams House** (☎912-236-6352; www.mercerhouse.com; 429 Bull St; adult/student $12.50/8; ☺10:30am-4:10pm Mon-Sat,

noon-4pm Sun), where Hansford was killed. Williams died in 1990 and the house opened for tours in 2004. The 'garden of good and evil' refers to Savannah's **Bonaventure Cemetery** (☎912-651-6843, Historical Society 912-412-4687; www.bonaventurehistorical.org; 330 Bonaventure Rd; ☺8am-5pm; P). Serious lit buffs should also stop by the **Flannery O'Connor Childhood Home** (☎912-233-6014; www.flanneryoconnorhome.org; 207 E Charlton St; adult/student $6/5; ☺1-4pm Fri-Wed, closed Thu) on beautiful Lafayette Sq.

✕ ⌖ p154, p218

The Drive » Take I-16W for 112 miles, to GA 19 north for 3 miles, to Hwy 441N for 44 miles to reach Andalusia.

----

❷ Andalusia

Flannery O'Connor was raised on the 544-acre estate **Andalusia** (☎478-454-4029; www.andalusiafarm.org; 2628 N Columbia St, Milledgeville; admission by donation; ☺10am-5pm Thu-Sun; P) when her family moved from Savannah. After attending the Writers Workshop at the University of Iowa, she returned here to write. Her acclaimed short-story collection, *A Good Man is Hard to Find,* was published in 1955. Like her father, she died of lupus. She was just 39. Before she died she published two novels and two short-story collections. She won the

LINK YOUR TRIP

19 **The Blues Highway**
An easy adjunct would be to follow Hwy 61 from Jackson into Clarksdale – the beating heart of the Mississippi Delta, the birthplace of the blues and American popular music.

11 **Savannah to the Golden Isles**
From Savannah follow the coast to a host of wild and beautiful beaches.

National Book Award for her compilation *The Complete Stories,* published posthumously. Set amid beautiful wooded, rolling hills, her home is open for walk-in tours five days a week.

The Drive » From Andalusia, McCullers fans should make their way back to I-16W, merge onto I-75S and exit onto GA 22/Hwy 80W. Follow this to GA 208W, leading to GA 315W into Columbus after about 140 miles.

----

③ Columbus

Carson McCullers, Tennessee Williams' favorite protégée, was born here and her home town served as inspiration for the mill town depicted in her first and greatest novel, *The Heart is a Lonely Hunter.* It's a beautifully sad yet ultimately hopeful tome about an enlightened deaf man and his various friends and confidantes (including an adolescent girl, an African American doctor, a business owner and a hard-drinking communist) during the Great Depression. These days, McCullers' **childhood home** (📞706-565-1200; www.mccullerscenter.org; 1519 Stark Ave; $5; ☺ by appointment; **P**) is open for tours, and it's the base of operations for the **Carson McCullers Center**, which runs a McCullers-based archive and offers fellowships to aspiring writers and artists. Call at least

a day ahead to tour the home.

The Drive » Take Hwy 431S for 99 miles to the small town of Dothan, where you'll catch Hwy 84 and take it 22 miles until it meets AL 36. Hang a right and you'll reach Monroeville.

TRIP HIGHLIGHT

④ Monroeville

Monroeville is a small Alabama town that gave us both Truman Capote, the progenitor of the nonfiction novel, and his childhood friend Harper Lee. *To Kill a Mockingbird,* written by Lee in the Southern Gothic style, takes aim at the institutional racism of the South. A runaway hit, it earned her the 1961 Pulitzer Prize, and takes place in the fictional town of Maycomb, a mirror image of Monroeville. The plot revolves around the trial of a young black man who is wrongfully accused of raping a white woman during the Great Depression. It's narrated by six-year-old Scout Finch, whose dad, Atticus, risks his and his family's safety to defend his railroaded client. If you've never read it, this book is an absolute must. Each May, curtains rise on a production of *To Kill A Mockingbird* at the **Old Courthouse Museum** (📞251-575-7433; www.monroecountymuseum.org; 31 N Alabama Ave; museum admission $5, play tickets $55; ☺10am-4pm Tue-Fri, to 1pm Sat), which also has per-

PETER JOHANSKY / GETTY IMAGES ©

manent exhibits on both Lee and her pal, Capote.

It's worth noting the controversial 'sequel' to *Mockingbird, Go Set a Watchman,* is also set in Maycomb/Monroeville. Many believe that novel – which paints a considerably darker picture of Atticus Finch – was published under dodgy circumstances, at a time when Harper Lee was

Savannah Bonaventure Cemetery, inspiration for John Berendt's *Midnight in the Garden of Good and Evil*

elderly and being taken advantage of (an Alabama state investigation concluded she was in control of her faculties regarding publication of the novel). Others believe *Watchman* was less a sequel, and more an unedited first draft of *Mockingbird*, and has been dubiously marketed as a companion piece to that novel.

The Drive » When the curtain drops, find Hwy 45 north and take the long drive – about 280 miles – to MS 6 and Oxford, MS.

TRIP HIGHLIGHT

5 Oxford

Nobel Prize winner William Faulkner may be long dead, but he still owns this town, home to the lovely **University of Mississippi** (www.

olemiss.edu). **Rowan Oak** (☏662-234-3284; www. rowanoak.com; Old Taylor Rd; adult/child $5/free; ☉10am-4pm Tue-Sat, 1-4pm Sun Sep-May, 10am-6pm Tue-Sat, 1-6pm Sun Jun-Aug), Faulkner's fine, 33-acre estate, nurtured many novels, but required him to slum in Hollywood as a studio-owned screenwriter to pay it off. Ninety percent of Rowan Oak's original furnishings are intact – you'll see Faulkner's prized typewriter, rusted golf clubs, and an outline for a never-written fable written on the walls. His 1950 Nobel Prize is on permanent display at the **Center for Southern Culture** (✆662-915-5993; www.southernstudies.olemiss. edu; Barbard Observatory; ⊗8am-9pm Mon-Thu, to 4pm Fri, to 5pm Sat, 1-5pm Sun). It also has a copy of his Nobel acceptance speech, which became an instant classic. Oxford isn't all about the past. **Square Books** (✆662-236-2262; www.squarebooks.com; 160 Courthouse Sq; ⊗9am-9pm Mon-Sat, to 6pm Sun) is one of the very best indie bookstores in the US. Visiting authors read from their newly published works on the regular, and autographed copies of hot novels abound. There's a Faulkner section upstairs, next to the cafe.

✗ ⊫ p218, p227

The Drive ≫ After enjoying Oxford, detour through Tupelo, the birthplace of King Presley, and hop on the Natchez Trace Pkwy through a glorious oak-and-swamp-studded countryside, before buzzing east on I-20 to Jackson. This stretch lasts about 230 miles.

- - - - - - - - - - - - - - - - - -

❻ Jackson

Mississippi's capital is clean, historic and resolute. Eudora Welty, one of the state's great writers and a Pulitzer Prize winner, lived here all her life. She moved into what is now the **Eudora Welty House** (✆601-353-7762; www.eudorawelty.org; 1119 Pinehurst St; adult/student/child $5/3/free; ⊗tours 9am, 11am, 1pm & 3pm Tue-Fri) when she was 16 and penned every one of her books in the study, where readers and visitors would descend unannounced (and were always welcomed). She cut and pinned up her manuscripts, in what was her own (pre-Nabokov) revision system. Noted author, traveler and

thinker Richard Wright was also a Jackson native. Best known for his story collection *Uncle Tom's Children,* based in part on lynchings in Mississippi, he was an important writer and devoted communist living in New York by the time he was 30. Eventually he moved to Europe, where he mingled with Sartre and Camus and died too soon at 52. Wright was the valedictorian of Jackson's first African American School (p225). Wright's and Welty's insightful words grace the eaves at the worthwhile **Mississippi Museum of Art** (✆601-960-1515; www.msmuseumart.org; 380 South Lamar St; exhibitions $5-12; ⊗10am-5pm Tue-Sat, noon-5pm Sun).

✗ ⊫ p218, p227

The Drive ≫ Merge back onto I-20 west to the Natchez Trace Pkwy, and follow that green band of historical beauty for a little over 100 miles until it ends in Mark Twain's old haunt.

- - - - - - - - - - - - - - - - - -

❼ Natchez

Natchez is one of the only antebellum towns left standing in the South, mostly because when Sherman and his Union troops marched in, the locals served them sweet tea and Southern hospitality. A hundred-and-fifty years later and Natchez attracts visitors from around the world to its historic antebellum mansions. Especially during pilgrimage season. But if slaver

SOUTHERN GOTHIC EXPOSED

Gothic literature was born in England, when 18th-century writers took on themes of horror, the macabre, tragedy and romance, often incorporating medieval tropes and clichés. Southern writers, for the most part, muted the supernatural in their work. Instead they plumbed the characters and communities damaged by a regional history of white Christian supremacy, frosted with an 'everything is just fine as it is' veneer. Writers knew that such social tension led to years of brutality, as well as economic and moral bankruptcy, because they lived it. Which makes their stories more dramatic and poignant.

wealth leaves you cold (or angry, or both), head down to the riverside.

The Mississippi River forms a natural border, dividing Mississippi and Louisiana, and is another of Natchez' main attractions. Back when Mark Twain was steamboat pilot Samuel Clemens, he cruised through town countless times and did his drinking at the **Under the Hill Saloon** (☏601-446-8023; 25 Silver St; ⏱10am-late), which is still a local hot spot with live music on weekends. And when he had had enough, he often crashed upstairs. Of course, Mark Twain moved on from the riverboat to become the inventor of the Great American Novel (or so he has been credited) with the publication of *The Adventures of Huckleberry Finn,* which followed Huck and Jim as they floated downriver on a raft, searching for freedom.

✕ ⛺ p209, p219

The Drive » Eventually, all southern roads pass through New Orleans, and the literary one is no exception. From Natchez drive south on Hwy 61 until it merges with I-110E in Baton Rouge and then I-10E towards New Orleans – a total jaunt of around 170 miles.

- - - - - - - - - - - - - - - - - -

TRIP HIGHLIGHT

❽ New Orleans

This is the town of Tennessee Williams, Anne Rice and Ignatius J Reilly. Many of the city's literary sites are concentrated

ADAPTATION

The book is always better, but that doesn't mean we don't love movies. Here are three Southern Gothic dramas that made the leap with style:

» *A Streetcar Named Desire* (1951) Brando's Stanley Kowalski loves STELLA! Four Oscars, Marlon becomes a star.

» *To Kill a Mockingbird* (1962) Oscar-winning best actor, Gregory Peck, is Atticus Finch.

» *Interview With a Vampire* (1994) An unintentional comedy. Tom Cruise and Brad Pitt vamp around New Orleans in wigs and makeup.

in the French Quarter. **Lafitte's Blacksmith Shop** (☏504-593-9761; www. lafittesblacksmithshop.com; 941 Bourbon St; ⏱10:30am-3am), a stone shack on the corner of Bourbon St, claims to be the oldest bar in the USA. Tennessee Williams used to party here with fellow artists while a pianist played whatever sheet music Williams brought in that day. Nearby **Napoleon House** (☏504-524-9752; www.napole onhouse.com; 500 Chartres St; ⏱11am-10pm Sun-Thu, to 11pm Fri & Sat), an attractive bar set in a courtyard building erected in 1797, was another drinking haunt of Williams; on hot days you can sit in the courtyard, order a scoop of shrimp remoulade served in a half avocado and dream sultry literary dreams. Or consider a stop at **Faulkner House Books** (☏504-524-2940; www. faulknerhousebooks.com; 624 Pirate's Alley; ⏱10am-6pm), a lovely old bookshop that once housed the Southern literary icon himself, or

the Hotel Monteleone (p219), which has hosted dozens of authors, including Ernest Hemingway, Truman Capote and Tennessee Williams.

If you prefer sexed-up vampires who are into rock and roll and a bit of evil, check out **Lafayette Cemetery No 1** (Washington Ave, at Prytania St; ⏱7am-3pm). Shaded by magnificent groves of lush greenery, this Garden District landmark was a favorite haunt (pun intended) of Anne Rice, and has featured prominently in many vampire and witches of Mayfair novels. You'll notice many German and Irish names on the aboveground graves, testifying that immigrants were devastated by 19th-century yellow-fever epidemics. Not far from the entrance is a tomb containing the remains of an entire family that died of the fever.

See New Orleans on our walking tour, p262.

✕ ⛺ p219, p253, p323

Eating & Sleeping

Savannah ❶

✖ Mrs Wilkes Dining Room
Southern US $$

(www.mrswilkes.com; 107 W Jones St; lunch adult/child $22/11; ⏰11am-2pm Mon-Fri, closed Jan; 🚸) The line outside can begin as early as 8am at this first-come, first-served Southern comfort-food institution. Once the lunch bell rings and you are seated family-style, the kitchen unloads on you: fried chicken, beef stew, meatloaf, cheese potatoes, collard greens, black-eyed peas, mac 'n' cheese, rutabaga, candied yams, squash casserole, creamed corn *and* biscuits.

✖ Local11Ten
Modern American $$$

(📞912-790-9000; www.local11ten.com; 1110 Bull St; mains $26-45; ⏰6-10pm; 🍴) Upscale, sustainable, local and fresh: these elements help create an elegant, well-run restaurant that's easily one of Savannah's best. Start with a deconstructed rabbit ravioli, then move on to the fabulous seared sea scallops in mint beurre blanc or the harissa-marinated bison hanger steak and a salted caramel pot de crème for a happy ending. Wait. Scratch that. The menu already changed.

🛏 East Bay Inn
Inn $$

(📞912-238-1225; www.eastbayinn.com; 225 E Bay St; r/ste from $180/220; 🅿🕸🛜🐾) Wedged between corporate rivals this brick behemoth offers just 28 huge rooms all of which have original double-wide wood floors, exposed brick walls, soaring ceilings, slender support columns and flat-screen TVs, along with much charm and warmth to spare.

Oxford ❺

✖ Taylor Grocery
Seafood $$

(📞662-236-1716; www.taylorgrocery.com; 4 1st St; dishes $9-15; ⏰5-10pm Thu-Sat, to 9pm Sun; 🅿) Be prepared to wait – and to tailgate in the parking lot – at this splendidly rusticated catfish haunt. Order fried or grilled (either way, it's amazing) and bring a marker to sign

your name on the wall. It's about 7 miles from downtown Oxford, south on Old Taylor Rd.

✖ City Grocery
American $$$

(📞662-232-8080; www.citygroceryonline.com; 152 Courthouse Sq; mains $26-32; ⏰11:30am-2:30pm Mon-Sat, 6-10pm Mon-Wed, to 10:30pm Thu-Sat, 11am-2:30pm Sun) Chef John Currance won a James Beard award and quickly set about dominating the Oxford culinary scene. City Grocery is one of his finest restaurants, offering a menu of haute Southern goodness like rice grits risotto and lard-braised hangar steak. The upstairs bar, decked out with local folk art, is a treat. Reservations recommended.

🛏 Inn at Ole Miss
Hotel $$

(📞662-234-2331; www.theinnatolemiss.com; 120 Alumni Dr; r from $99-149; 🅿🕸@🛜🐾) Unless it's a football weekend, in which case you'd be wise to book well ahead, you can usually find a nice room at this 180-room hotel and conference center right on the Ole Miss Grove. Although it's not super personal, it's comfortable, well-located and walkable to downtown.

Jackson ❻

✖ Walker's Drive-In
Southern US $$$

(📞601-982-2633; www.walkersdrivein.com; 3016 N State St; mains lunch $8-17, dinner $29-37; ⏰11am-2pm Mon-Fri & from 5:30-10pm Tue-Sat) This retro masterpiece has been restored with love and infused with new Southern foodie ethos. Lunch is diner 2.0 fare with grilled redfish sandwiches, tender burgers and grilled oyster po'boys, as well as an exceptional seared, chili-crusted tuna salad, which comes with spiced calamari and seaweed.

✖ Mayflower
Seafood $$$

(📞601-355-4122; www.mayflowercafems.com; 123 W Capitol St; mains $21-29; ⏰11am-10pm Mon-Fri, 4:30-10pm Sat) It looks like just another downtown dive, but it's a damn fine seafood house. Locals swear by the broiled redfish and the Greek salad, which becomes a meal when you add pan-seared scallops (sensational!). Everything is obscenely fresh.

Fairview Inn
Inn $$$

(☎601-948-3429; www.fairviewinn.com; 734 Fairview St; ste $200-340; P ❄ @ 🛜) For a colonial-estate experience, the 18-room Fairview Inn, set in a converted historic mansion, will not let you down. The antique decor is stunning rather than stuffy and tastefully deployed across each individually appointed room. It also has a full spa.

Natchez ❼

✕ Magnolia Grill
Southern US $$

(☎601-446-7670; www.magnoliagrill.com; 49 Silver St; mains $13-22; ⏱11am-9pm, to 10pm Fri & Sat; 🚻) Down by the riverside, this attractive wooden storefront grill with exposed rafters and outdoor patio is a good place for a pork tenderloin po'boy, or a fried crawfish spinach salad.

⌂ Historic Oak Hill Inn
Inn $$

(☎601-446-2500; www.historicoakhill.com; 409 S Rankin St; $135-160, ste $235; P ❄ 🛜) Ever wish you could sleep in one of those historic homes? At the Historic Oak Hill Inn, you can sleep in an original 1835 bed and dine on pre–Civil War porcelain under 1850 Waterford crystal gasoliers – it's all about purist antebellum aristocratic living at this classic Natchez B&B.

New Orleans ❽

✕ Sylvain
Louisianan $$

(☎504-265-8123; www.sylvainnola.com; 625 Chartres St; mains $14-29; ⏱5:30-11pm Mon-Thu, to midnight Fri & Sat, to 10pm Sun, 10:30am-2:30pm Fri-Sun) This rustic yet elegant gastropub draws inspiration from the dedication to local ingredients demonstrated by chefs like Thomas Keller. The focus is Southern haute cuisine and excellent cocktails; the duck confit served on a bed of black-eyed peas is indicative of the gastronomic experience: rich, refined and delicious.

⌂ Hotel Maison de Ville
Historic Hotel $$$

(☎504-324-4888; www.hotelmaisondeville.com; 727 Toulouse St; r from $275; ❄ 🛜) A series of remodeled suits, cottages and apartments form this graceful hotel, which includes the one- and two-bedroom Audubon Cottage suites (where artist John J Audubon stayed and painted while in town). It's a quintessential French Quarter property, dripping with tropical historical accents and built around a lushly landscaped courtyard that feels plucked out of time.

⌂ Hotel Monteleone
Hotel $$$

(☎504-523-3341; www.hotelmonteleone. com; 214 Royal St; r $190-270, ste from $370; ❄ 🛜👶) Perhaps the city's most venerable hotel, the Monteleone is also the Quarter's largest. Not long after it was built, preservationists put a stop to building on this scale below Iberville St. Since its inception in 1866, the hotel has lodged literary luminaries including William Faulkner, Truman Capote and Rebecca Wells. Rooms exude an old-world appeal with French toile and chandeliers.

Historical Mississippi

Over the course of its history, Mississippi has proven to be beautiful and wild, serene and violent, complex yet simple. To explore its turbulent past is to discover Mississippi now.

18

TRIP HIGHLIGHTS

64 miles

Clarksdale
Home of Red's, a classic Mississippi Delta juke joint

2

1 START

272 miles

6

Jackson

Vicksburg
Gravitas and Mississippi River beauty

FINISH Natchez

Oxford
Our favorite town in Mississippi for good reason

0 miles

3 DAYS
354 MILES / 570KM

GREAT FOR...

BEST TIME TO GO
Best in spring and fall for milder temperatures.

ESSENTIAL PHOTO

Rowan Oak makes for a wonderful late-afternoon photo shoot.

BEST FOR HISTORY

From Indian mounds to the birth of the blues to the Civil Rights movement, Mississippi is ripe with compelling stories.

Vicksburg Twin bridges across the Mississippi River

Historical Mississippi

Stroll in the footsteps of literary masters and civil rights heroes, consider the origins of American popular music, and hear gun shots ring and see crosses burn in the mind as you stroll blood-soaked battlefields and consider the state's once-impenetrable segregation stranglehold. Mississippi's history will never be easy to reconcile, but its stories — its people — are forever compelling.

TRIP HIGHLIGHT

❶ Oxford

Oxford is one of those rare towns that seeps into your bones and never leaves. Local life revolves around the quaint-yet-hip square, where you'll find inviting bars, wonderful food and decent shopping, and the rather regal **University of Mississippi** (www.olemiss.edu), aka Ole Miss. All around and in-between are quiet residential streets, sprinkled with antebellum homes and shaded by majestic oaks. Oh, and

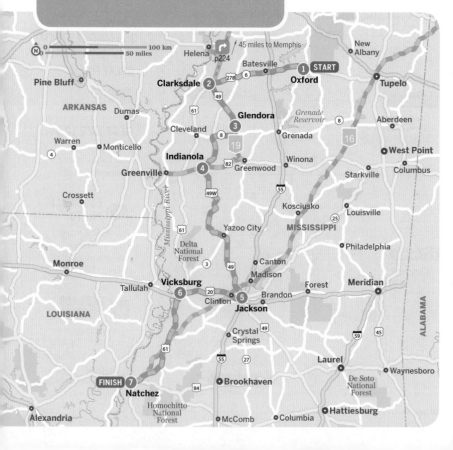

there's history to spare. Begin at the **Grove**, the heart of Ole Miss and site of one of the Civil Rights movement's iconic scenes. The Center for Southern Culture (p216) archive, on the 3rd floor of the JD Williams Library, displays William Faulkner's correspondence along with his 1950 Nobel Prize. A half-mile trail leads from the **University of Mississippi Museum** (www.museum.olemiss. edu; University Ave at 5th St; ⊙10am-6pm Tue-Sat), where you'll find a collection of early astronomical marvels, Choctaw lacrosse sticks, Confederate soldier gear and original Man Ray and Georgia O'Keefe canvases, through the woods to Rowan Oak (p215), the

LINK YOUR TRIP

16 Natchez Trace Parkway

The 444-mile parkway connecting Natchez with Nashville is one of the nation's most beautiful roads, and offers more history if you're still hungry for stories.

19 The Blues Highway

Jump from the history book to the origins of American popular music on this journey through the Mississippi Delta.

former home of Faulkner. Ninety percent of the original furnishings are intact. Including his typewriter.

 p218, p227

The Drive » It's just over an hour's drive east on MS 6/ Hwy 278 through rolling hills into Clarksdale and the Mississippi Delta.

TRIP HIGHLIGHT

② Clarksdale

You can't explore Mississippi history without paying homage to the birthplace of American music. Blues legend Robert Johnson is said to have sold his soul to the devil down at the **Crossroads** (Hwy 61 & Hwy 49), the junction of Hwy 61 (the Blues Highway) and Hwy 49 in Clarksdale. Clarksdale is the hub of Delta-blues country and its most comfortable and vibrant base. Here you can visit Muddy Waters' childhood cabin at the **Delta Blues Museum** (☎662-627-6820; www. deltabluesmuseum.org; 1 Blues Alley; adult/senior & student $10/5; ⊙9am-5pm Mon-Sat Mar-Oct, from 10am Nov-Feb; ℗), and see modern-day bluesmen howl at **Red's** (☎662-627-3166; 395 Sunflower Ave; cover $7-10; ⊙live music 9pm Fri & Sat). WC Handy was the first songwriter who finally put the 12-bar blues down on paper, several years after he first heard a nomadic guitar man strumming

in tiny **Tutwiler** in 1903. The convergence of musician and songwriter is remembered with a mural along the Tutwiler Tracks (p233).

 p227, p237, p322

The Drive » From Clarksdale, take Hwy 49 south for 13 miles to 49 east, which diverges from 49 west for 13 miles, though both run north and south. Yes, it's confusing, but 16 miles later you will land in Glendora.

----

③ Glendora

Sixteen miles south of Tutweiler is another small Delta town, but Glendora's legacy is much darker. It was here on August 28, 1955, that Emmett Till was kidnapped and murdered following a brief encounter with a white woman in a local store. Born in Chicago and just 14 years old, he was ignorant of the local racial mores, and supposedly said, 'Bye, baby,' to a white woman – Carolyn Bryant – on a dare; in 2008, Bryant admitted much of her testimony in the case was false.

Days later, Till was murdered by Bryant's husband and half-brother-in-law, who were swiftly acquitted of the crime, though there was never any argument that they did it. After Till's mother ordered an open casket at his funeral, so all could see how badly he had been beaten, his case became national news, and a rallying cry for civil rights activists throughout the South. You can learn more about the case at the **Emmett Till Museum** (☎662-483-0048; www.emmett-till.org; 120 N Court St, Sumner; hours vary; ☻8am-5pm Mon-Fri), which is as much an interactive narrative experience as it is a tour.

The Drive ≫ Take Hwy 49E south for 8 miles to MS 8 west to Hwy 49W, which runs south through the plains for 24 miles until it intersects with Hwy 82 in Indianola.

WESLEY HITT / GETTY IMAGES ©

④ Indianola

Indianola is a rather prosperous middle-class town in the delta with a corporate bloom on Hwy 82, and wide, lovely leafy streets dotted with well-kept single-family homes around downtown, where BB King used to play guitar for passersby. The late BB King is Indianola's favorite son, and you'll see his likeness on murals, and on a plaque on his favorite street corner, and learn all about his difficult, triumphant life at the **BB King Museum and Delta Interpretive Center** (☎662-887-9539; www.bbkingmuseum.org; 400 2nd St; adult/student/child $15/10/free; ☻10am-5pm Tue-Sat, noon-5pm Sun-Mon, closed Mon Nov-Mar; **P**). The region's very best museum offers engaging interactive exhibits that illuminate the various musical influences on the Delta blues sound, and on King's music in particular. It's a must-see for music geeks.

The Drive ≫ Drive south on Hwy 49 for 100 miles to Jackson.

---

⑤ Jackson

Mississippi's capital and largest city has plenty of history to explore, and

---

DETOUR: MEMPHIS

Start: ② Clarksdale

Easily accessible to both Oxford and Clarksdale, Memphis is a thriving city with a blues history to match Mississippi. Set right on the river, the musical roots here (Stax Records, Sun Studios, Graceland) are what attract the tourists, but the warmth and hospitality of the locals is why you'll fall in like or love. For where to eat and sleep in Memphis, see p181, p237, p275, p312 and p322.

Oxford University of Mississippi campus

the **Old Capitol Museum**
(📞601-576-6920; www.mdah.
ms.gov/oldcap; 100 State St;
🕐9am-5pm Tue-Sat, 1-5pm
Sun) is a good place to
start. It tells the story of
the Greek Revival build-
ing itself, and in so doing
touches on Mississippi
history. You'll learn that
15 lawmakers opposed se-
cession in the run-up to
the Civil War, and there
are some interesting
exhibits on reconstruc-
tion and what were the
nation's harshest 'Black
Codes,' the gateway to
full segregation.

The Mississippi
Museum of Art (p216)
includes 200 works

from Mississippi artists.
Our favorites were the
photographs of literary
scions Eudora Welty and
William Faulkner, and
another of Quincy Jones
and Elvis crooning at a
Tupelo concert. Housed
in Mississippi's first
public school for African
American kids is the
**Smith Robertson Mu-
seum** (📞601-960-1457; www.
jacksonms.gov; 528 Bloom
St; adult/child $4.50/1.50;
🕐9am-5pm Mon-Fri, 10am-
1pm Sat; 🅿), the alma
mater of author Richard
Wright. It offers insight
and explanation into the
pain and perseverance
of the African American

legacy in Mississippi. And
then there's the Eudora
Welty House (p216), a
must for literature buffs.

✗ ⤷ p218, p227

The Drive ≫ It's just 44 quick
miles west from Jackson to
Vicksburg on I-20.

- - - - - - - - - - - - - - - - - - - -

TRIP HIGHLIGHT

6 Vicksburg
Vicksburg is famous for
its strategic location in
the Civil War, thanks to
its position on a high
bluff overlooking the Mississippi River, and his-
tory buffs dig it. General
Ulysses S Grant besieged
the city for 47 days, until

18

JAMES MEREDITH

The generally peaceful and serene **Grove** was the site of a riot on September 21, 1962, when a violent mob of segregationists descended to prevent James Meredith, the school's first-ever African American student, from enrolling for the semester. With the Mississippi governor siding with the mob, the Kennedy administration called in 500 federal marshals and federalized the national guard to tamp down the rioters and ensure Meredith's safety. Those troops remained on campus when Meredith and state NAACP chairman, Medgar Evers (who would later be assassinated), marched through thousands of vitriolic segregationists to break the Ole Miss color barrier on October 1, 1962. Meredith went on to march 220 miles across the state, from Memphis to Jackson, in a 1966 protest against racial violence. Some of his correspondence is on display at the **Center for Southern Culture** (p216).

its surrender on July 4, 1863, at which point the North gained dominance over North America's greatest river. The **Vicksburg National Military Park** (601-636-0583; www.nps.gov/vick; 3201 Clay St; per bicycle/car $5/15; 8am-5pm;) honors that battle. You can drive, or pedal (if you're traveling with bicycles), along the 16-mile **Battlefield Drive**, which winds past 1330 monuments and markers – including statues, battle trenches, a restored Union gunboat and a National Cemetery. Vicksburg's historic riverside core is rather pretty, and worth a look. You'll find regal old homes lined up on terraced bluffs with views of slender wooded islands forming natural inlets, which loom at arm's length along with those riverboat casinos. As long as you're downtown don't miss the **Attic**

Gallery (601-638-9221; 1101 Washington St; 10am-5pm Mon-Sat). It features virtuoso regional artists, and a funky collection of folk art and jewelry.

p227, p322

The Drive » Hop on Hwy 61, which follows the Mississippi River (though not always so closely) for about 72 miles down to Natchez.

- - - - - - - - - - - - - - - - - -

❼ Natchez

Adorable Natchez stews together a wide variety of humans, from gay log-cabin republicans to intellectual liberals, to down-home folks. Perched on a bluff overlooking the Mississippi, it attracts tourists in search of antebellum history and architecture – 668 antebellum homes pepper the oldest Western settlement on the Mississippi River (beating New Orleans by two years). Although

most such towns were torched by Union troops, Natchez was spared thanks to some rather hospitable local ladies who invited the troops in for rest and relaxation (at least according to legend). The **Visitor and Welcome Center** (800-647-6724; www.visitnatchez.org; 640 S Canal St; 8:30am-5pm Mon-Sat, 9am-4pm Sun) is a large, well-organized tourist resource with little exhibits of area history and a ton of information on local sites. During the 'pilgrimage' seasons in spring and fall, local mansions are opened to visitors, though some properties, such as the Auburn Mansion (p207), are open year-round. Natchez is also the end (or is it the beginning?) of the scenic 444-mile Natchez Trace Pkwy.

p209 , p227

Eating & Sleeping

Oxford ❶

✕ City Grocery   American $$$

(☎662-232-8080; www.citygroceryonline.com;
152 Courthouse Sq; mains $26-32; ⊕11:30am-
2:30pm Mon-Sat, 6-10pm Mon-Wed, to 10:30pm
Thu-Sat, 11am-2:30pm Sun) Chef John Currance
won a James Beard award and quickly set about
dominating the Oxford culinary scene. City
Grocery is one of his finest restaurants, offering
a menu of haute Southern goodness like rice
grits risotto and lard-braised hangar steak. The
upstairs bar, decked out with local folk art, is a
treat. Reservations recommended.

🛏 5 Twelve   B&B $$

(☎662-234-8043; www.the5twelve.com; 512
Van Buren Ave; r $140-200, studio $200-
250; 🅿 ❄ 📶) This six-room B&B has an
antebellum-style exterior and modern interior
(think Tempur-Pedic beds and flat-screen TVs).
Room rates include full Southern breakfast
to order. It's an easy walk from shops and
restaurants, and the hosts will make you feel
like family.

Clarksdale ❷

✕ Yazoo Pass   Cafe $$

(☎662-627-8686; www.yazoopass.com; 207
Yazoo Ave; mains lunch $6-10, dinner $13-26;
⊕7am-9pm Mon-Sat; 📶) A contemporary
space where you can enjoy fresh scones
and croissants in the mornings, a salad bar,
sandwiches and soups at lunch, and pan-seared
ahi, filet mignon, burgers and pastas at dinner.

🛏 Shack Up Inn   Inn $$

(☎662-624-8329; www.shackupinn.com;
001 Commisary Circle, off Hwy 49; d $75-165;
🅿 ❄ 📶) At the Hopson Plantation, this
self-titled 'bed and beer' allows you to stay
in refurbished sharecropper cabins or the
creatively renovated cotton gin. The cabins have
covered porches and are filled with old furniture
and musical instruments.

Jackson ❺

✕ Walker's Drive-In   Southern US $$$

(☎601-982-2633; www.walkersdrivein.com;
3016 N State St; mains lunch $8-17, dinner $29-
37; ⊕11am-2pm Mon-Fri & from 5:30-10pm Tue-
Sat) This retro masterpiece has been restored
with love and infused with new Southern foodie
ethos. Lunch is diner 2.0 fare with grilled redfish
sandwiches, tender burgers and grilled oyster
po'boys, as well as an exceptional seared, chili-
crusted tuna salad, which comes with spiced
calamari and seaweed.

🛏 Old Capitol Inn   Boutique Hotel $$

(☎601-359-9000; www.oldcapitolinn.com; 226
N State St; r/ste from $99/145; 🅿 ❄ @ 📶 ☒)
This 24-room, boutique hotel, located near
museums and restaurants, is terrific. Rooms
are comfortable and uniquely furnished, and a
full Southern breakfast (and early-evening wine
and cheese) is included. The rooftop garden
includes a hot tub.

Vicksburg ❻

🛏 Corners Mansion   B&B $$

(☎601-636-7421; www.thecorners.com; 601
Klein St; r $125-170; 🅿 ❄ 📶) The best part of
this wedding-cake 1873 B&B is looking over the
Yazoo and Mississippi Rivers from your porch
swing. The gardens and Southern breakfast
don't hurt either.

Natchez ❼

✕ Magnolia Grill   Southern US $$

(☎601-446-7670; www.magnoliagrill.com; 49
Silver St; mains $13-22; ⊕11am-9pm, to 10pm Fri
& Sat; 👶) Down by the riverside, this attractive
wooden storefront grill with exposed rafters
and outdoor patio is a good place for a pork
tenderloin po'boy, or a fried crawfish spinach
salad.

Classic Trip

The Blues Highway

Listen to living blues legends howl their sad enlightenment and pay homage to the music that saturated northern Mississippi for a century and bloomed into rock and roll.

19

TRIP HIGHLIGHTS

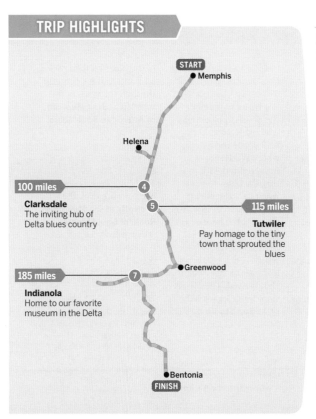

START ● Memphis

Helena

100 miles
4
5

Clarksdale
The inviting hub of Delta blues country

115 miles

Tutwiler
Pay homage to the tiny town that sprouted the blues

● Greenwood

185 miles
7

Indianola
Home to our favorite museum in the Delta

● Bentonia
FINISH

3 DAYS
350 MILES / 563KM

GREAT FOR...

BEST TIME TO GO
Blues festivals bloom in the Delta in May and June, and October is an obscenely pleasant month.

 ESSENTIAL PHOTO
Snap Red's smoky glow while a bluesman wails on stage.

 BEST FOR MUSIC
The Mississippi Delta is cultural immersion – with an epic soundtrack.

Indianola Replica of Lucille, BB King's guitar, at the BB King Museum and Delta Interpretive Center

229

Classic Trip

19 The Blues Highway

In the plains, along Hwy 61, American music took root. It arrived from Africa in the souls of slaves, morphed into field songs, and wormed into the brain of a sharecropping troubadour waiting for a train. In Clarksdale, at the crossroads, Robert Johnson made a deal with the devil and became America's first guitar hero. But to fully grasp its influence, start in Memphis.

① Memphis

The Mississippi Delta and Memphis have always been inextricably linked. Memphis was a beacon for the Delta bluesmen, both because it's the region's biggest city, but also because Memphis meant a certain amount of freedom, African American–owned businesses, and the bright lights and foot-stomping crowds of Beale St, which is still rocking (check it out on our walking tour, p326). **Rum Boogie** (www.rumboogie. com; 182 Beale St; ⏰11am-1am) is a Cajun-themed blues bar with a terrific house band. The original **BB King's** (☎901-524-5464; www.bbkingclubs.com; 143 Beale St; ⏰11am-11:30pm Mon-Thu, noon-2am Fri, 11am-midnight Sat, 11am-11pm Sun) is a living monument to the Mississippi genius who made good here. And it was in Memphis where WC Handy was first credited with putting the blues to paper when he wrote 'Beale Street Blues' in 1916. You can visit the **house** (www.wchandymemphis.org; 352 Beale St; adult/child $6/4; ⏰11am-4pm Tue-Sat winter, 10am-5pm summer) where Handy lived. The Mississippi Delta legacy bubbles up at **Sun Studio** (☎800-441-6249; www.sunstudio.com; 706 Union Ave; adult/child $12/free; ⏰10am-6:15pm), where you can tour the label that launched Elvis – whose interpretation of the blues birthed rock and roll. And it's running through the veins of the wonderful **Stax Museum of American Soul Music** (☎901-942-7685; www.staxmuseum.com; 926 E McLemore Ave; adult/child $13/10; ⏰10am-5pm Tue-Sat, 1-5pm Sun). Those connections are explained perfectly at the **Memphis Rock 'n' Soul Museum** (www.memphisrocknsoul.org; 191 Beale St; adult/child $12/9; ⏰10am-7pm).

✕ ⌂ p181, p237, p275, p312, p322

The Drive » Hwy 61 begins in Memphis, where it is a wide avenue snaking through the city's rough seam. Eventually urbanity gives way to flat farmland, and the highway goes rural as you enter Mississippi. It's about 30 miles to Tunica.

2 Tunica

A collection of casinos rests near the riverbanks in Tunica, Hwy 61's most-prosperous and least-authentic town. Nevertheless, it is the gateway to the blues and home to their juke-joint mock-up of a **Visitor Center** (☎888-488-6422; www.tunicatravel.com; 13625 US 61, Robinsonville; ⏰8am-5:30pm Mon-Fri, from 10am Sat, 1-5pm Sun), where a cool interactive digital guide comes packed with information on famed blues artists and the **Mississippi Blues Trail** itself. It's a good place to get inspired about what you are about to experience, and perhaps do some plotting and planning.

LINK YOUR TRIP

18 Historical Mississippi

Continue your journey through the Mississippi mind by taking in the towns of Oxford, Jackson, Vicksburg and Natchez and exploring the past and present all at once.

27 Memphis to Nashville

Head from the rhythm-and-blues haunts of Beale St to the down-home honky-tonks that put Nashville on the map.

Unless you play cards, however, Tunica is not otherwise noteworthy.

The Drive ≫ Continue on the arrow-straight road for 19 miles, then veer west on Hwy 49 and drive 10 miles over the Mississippi River into Helena, AR.

---

❸ Helena

Helena, AR, a depressed mill town 32 miles north and across the Mississippi River from Clarksdale, was once the home of blues legend Sonny Boy Williamson. He was a regular on *King Biscuit Time,* America's original blues radio show. It still broadcasts out of the **Delta Cultural Center** (☏870-338-4350; www.deltaculturalcenter.com; 141 Cherry St; ⏲9am-5pm Tue-Sat; Ⓟ), a worthwhile

blues museum. Down the street you'll find the Delta's best record store, **Bubba's Blues Corner** (☏870-338-3501; 105 Cherry St; ⏲9am-5pm Tue-Sat). Delightfully disorganized, it's supposedly a regular stop on Robert Plant's personal blues pilgrimages. Bubba himself is warm and friendly and offers a wealth of knowledge. If the shop isn't open when you fall by, give Bubba a ring, and he'll happily open up. The King Biscuit Blues Festival (p236) is held over three days each October.

The Drive ≫ Hwy 49 converges with the Hwy 61 in Mississippi, and from there it's 30 miles south until you reach the Crossroads. Peeking out above the trees on the northeast corner of Hwy 61 and Hwy 49, where the roads diverge once again, is the landmark weathervane of three interlocking blue guitars. You have arrived in the Delta's beating heart.

TRIP HIGHLIGHT

❹ Clarksdale

Clarksdale is the Delta's most useful base – with more comfortable hotel rooms and modern, tasteful kitchens here than the rest of the Delta combined. It's also within a couple of hours of all the blues sights. If you want to know who's playing where, come see Roger Stolle at **Cat Head** (☏662-624-5992; www.cathead.biz; 252 Delta Ave; ⏲10am-5pm Mon-Sat). He also sells a good range of blues souvenirs, and is the main engine behind the annual Juke Joint Festival (p236). Wednesday through Saturday, live music sweeps through Clarksdale like a summer storm. Morgan Freeman's **Ground Zero** (☏662-621-9009; www.groundzeroblues club.com; 252 Delta Ave; ⏲11am-2pm Mon & Tue, to 11pm Wed & Thu, to 2am Fri & Sat) has the most professional

BB KING'S BLUES

BB King grew up in the cotton fields on the outskirts of Indianola, a leafy middle-class town, and it didn't take long before he learned what it meant to have the blues. His parents divorced when he was four, and his mother died when he was nine. His grandmother passed away when he was 14. All alone, he was forced to leave Indianola – the only town he ever knew – and live with his father in Lexington, MS. He quickly became homesick, and made his way back, riding his bicycle for two days to return to Indianola. As a young man he was convinced he would become a cotton farmer. There weren't many other possibilities to consider. Or so he thought. When he went to Memphis for the first time in the 1940s, his world opened. From there he drifted into West Memphis, AR, where he met Sonny Boy Williamson, who put the young upstart on the radio for the first time, launching his career. When King died in 2015, it felt as if the entire Delta took a few days to mourn the loss of a legend.

bandstand and sound system, but it will never compare to Red's (p223), a funky, red-lit, juke joint run with in-your-face charm by Red himself. He'll fire up his enormous grill outside on special occasions. The Delta Blues Museum (p223), set in the city's old train depot, has a fine collection of blues memorabilia, including Muddy Waters' reconstructed Mississippi cabin. The creative, multimedia exhibits also honor BB King, John Lee Hooker, Big Mama Thornton and WC Handy.

✕ ⌂ p227, p237, p322

The Drive >> From Clarksdale, take Hwy 49 south from the Crossroads for 15 miles to the tiny town of Tutwiler.

TRIP HIGHLIGHT
⑤ Tutwiler

Sleepy Tutwiler is where WC Handy heard that ragged guitar man in 1903. Handy, known as the 'father of the blues,' was inspired to (literally) write the original blues song, in 12 bars with a three chord progression and AAB verse pattern, in 1912, though he wasn't widely recognized as an originator until 'Beale Street Blues' became a hit in 1916. That way-back divine encounter, which birthed blues and jazz, is honored along the **Tutwiler Tracks** (Front & Hancock Sts; ⓘ), where the train station used to be.

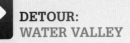

DETOUR:
WATER VALLEY

Start: ⑤ Tutwiler
From Tutwiler, take MS 32 east for about 55 miles to reach Water Valley, a town that's about as pretty as its name implies. This was once a depressed railroad hub, but young professionals and artists from Oxford – just 20 miles north – came here attracted by a glut of gorgeous, if crumbling, historical homes. Veritable mansions were bought and restored for the cost of less than a year's rent in New York, yielding a small-town civic revival that's a joy to soak up. Wander along Main St and pop into galleries and restaurants, or marvel at the architecture of restored homes on Leland and Panola streets.

The mural also reveals the directions to **Sonny Boy Williamson's Grave** (off Prairie Rd, 34.018481, -90.457624). He's buried amid a broken-down jumble of gravestones and Williamson's headstone is set back in the trees. Rusted harmonicas, candles and half-empty whiskey bottles have been left here out of respect.

The Drive >> Continue on the other blues highway, Hwy 49 south, through more farmland

for 42 miles, across the Yazoo River and into the tiny town of Greenwood.

---

⑥ Greenwood

Greenwood is the Delta's most prosperous town that doesn't involve slot machines. The financial backbone here is the Viking Range Corporation which builds its magnificent cooking ranges in town and whose wares you can buy in upmarket showrooms. There is also

---

KING BISCUIT TIME

Sonny Boy Williamson was the host of *King Biscuit Time* when BB King was a young buck. King recalls listening to the lunch-hour program, and dreaming of possibilities. When he moved to Memphis as a teenager and began playing Beale St gigs, Williamson invited King to play on his radio show, and a star was born. Williamson remained an important mentor for King as his career took off. The radio show, which begins weekdays at 12:15pm, is still running, and has been hosted by Sunshine Sonny Payne since 1951.

Classic Trip

WHY THIS IS A CLASSIC TRIP
ADAM SKOLNICK, WRITER

The story of America is one of arrival from elsewhere, suffering at the mercy of nature, or an oppressor, or time, and it's a story of rebirth. The blues is America's soundtrack. Beautiful and wild, it thrums up in those darkest hours and explodes as a catharsis. It's a painkiller, a purification. In the moment, it feels like liberation. It's a sound that revolutionized America. And it happened here.

Top: Beale St, Memphis
Left: Delta Blues Museum, Clarksdale
Right: James 'Chicken' Dooris performs at Ground Zero, Clarksdale

a fantastic cafe and a fine hotel – the best in the Delta – within these city limits. As far as history goes, Greenwood happens to be the hometown of Byron De La Beckwith, the murderer of Medgar Evers and, at the time of his crime, a member of the local White Citizens Council.

✕ ⊨ p237

The Drive » From Greenwood, take Hwy 82 east for 30 miles, over the Yazoo River, through leafy horse country, and through an ugly commercial bloom of big chain stores and kitchens, into Indianola.

TRIP HIGHLIGHT

7 Indianola

You have reached the home town of arguably the Delta's biggest star. When BB King was still a child, Indianola was home to **Club Ebony** (404 Hannah St; ⊙ from 8pm Thu), a fixture on the so-called 'chitlin circuit.' Ebony gave BB his first steady work, and hosted legends like Howlin' Wolf, Muddy Waters, Count Basie and James Brown. The corner of Church and 2nd is where BB used to strum his beloved guitar, Lucille, for passersby. Nearby, the BB King Museum and Delta Interpretive Center (p224) is set in a complex around the old Indianola cotton gin. The experience starts with a 12-minute film covering King's work. Afterward you are free to roam halls

235

Classic Trip

packed with interactive exhibits, tracing King's history and his musical influences – African, gospel and country. Other interactive exhibits demonstrate his influence on the next generation of artists, including Jimi Hendrix and the Allman Brothers. Oh, and BB's 12 Grammy awards are here, too.

The Drive » From Indianola, go west through 15 miles of fast-food jumble along Hwy 82 into Leland.

- - - - - - - - - - - - - - - -

8 Leland

Leland is a small, down-on-its-luck town, but one with a terrific museum. The **Hwy 61**

Blues Museum (☎662-686-7646; www.highway-61blues.com; 307 N Broad St; $7; ◷10am-5pm Mon-Sat) offers details on local folks like Ruby Edwards and David 'Honeyboy' Edwards.

Luminary Jim Henson, the creator of the Muppets, is also from Leland, and his life and work are celebrated at the Jim Henson Exhibit on the bank of Deer Creek.

The Drive » Head west on Hwy 82 for 25 miles until it ends near the river.

- - - - - - - - - - - - - - - -

9 Greenville

The Mississippi River town of Greenville was a fixture on the riverboat route and has long been a gambling resort area. For years it supported blues and jazz musicians who played the resorts.

Although it's scruffy around the edges, Greenville can be pleasant along the river. But the real reason to visit is to try the steaks, tamales and chili at **Doe's Eat Place** (☎662-334-3315; www.doeseatplace.com; 502 Nelson St; mains $22-40; ◷5-9pm Mon-Sat) – a classic hole-in-the-wall joint you may never forget.

The Drive » Return to Indianola then drive south on Hwy 49W to humble Bentonia; it's about a 90-mile drive.

- - - - - - - - - - - - - - - -

10 Bentonia

Bentonia, once a thriving farming community, now has fewer than 100 people and the downtown is gutted, but it's still home to one of Mississippi's most historic jukes. The Holmes family opened the **Blue Front** (☎662-528-1900; www.facebook.com/bluefrontcafeblues; 107 E Railroad Ave; ◷9am-8pm Mon-Thu, to 10pm Fri & Sat, 1-8pm Sun) during the Jim Crow period, when African Americans weren't even allowed to sip Coca-Cola. The Holmes sold house-stilled corn liquor (to blacks and whites) during Prohibition and welcomed all the Delta blues artists of the day: Sonny Boy, Percy Smith and Jack Owens among them. The joint still opens in the evenings, but live blues only blooms during Bentonia's annual festival when the town comes back to life, if ever so briefly.

FAVORITE BLUES FESTS

To make the most of your music-loving dollar, hit the Delta during one of its many blues festivals. Rooms can be scarce. Book well in advance.

Juke Joint Festival (www.jukejointfestival.com; tickets $15; ◷Apr) Clarksdale

Bentonia Blues Festival (☎662-763-5306; www.facebook.com/BentoniaBluesFestival; tickets $10; ◷mid-Jun) Bentonia

Sunflower River Blues & Gospel Festival (www.sunflowerfest.org; ◷Aug) Clarksdale

Mighty Mississippi Music Festival (Warfield Point Park; weekend pass adult/student/child $70/35/20; ◷late Sep) Greenville

King Biscuit Blues Festival (☎870-572-5223; www.kingbiscuitfestival.com; tickets $45; ◷Oct) Helena

Eating & Sleeping

Memphis ❶

✕ Arcade   Diner $

(www.arcaderestaurant.com; 540 S Main St;
mains $7-10; ⏰7am-3pm Sun-Wed, to 11pm
Thu-Sat) Step inside this ultra-retro diner,
Memphis' oldest, and wander to the Elvis booth,
strategically located near the rear exit. The King
used to sit here and eat griddle-fried peanut
butter and banana sandwiches and would bolt
out the door if fan-instigated pandemonium
ensued. Crowds still pack in for sublime
sweet-potato pancakes – as fluffy, buttery and
addictive as advertised.

✕ Gus's World Famous
Fried Chicken   Fast Food $

(www.gusfriedchicken.com; 310 S Front St;
plates $6-12; ⏰11am-9pm Sun-Thu, to 10pm Fri
& Sat) Fried-chicken connoisseurs across the
globe twitch in their sleep at night, dreaming
about the gossamer-light fried chicken at this
downtown concrete bunker, with a fun, neon-lit
interior and vintage jukebox. On busy nights,
waits can top an hour.

✕ Charlie Vergos'
Rendezvous   Barbecue $$

(☎901-523-2746; www.hogsfly.com; 52 S 2nd
St; mains $8-20; ⏰4:30-10:30pm Tue-Thu,
11am-11pm Fri, from 11:30am Sat) Tucked in its
own namesake alleyway off Monroe Ave, this
subterranean institution sells an astonishing
5 tons of its exquisite dry-rubbed ribs weekly.
The ribs don't come with any sauce, but the
pork shoulder does, so try a combo and you'll
have plenty of sauce to enjoy. The beef brisket is
also tremendous. Expect a wait.

⍟ Madison Hotel   Boutique Hotel $$$

(☎901-333-1200; www.madisonhotelmemphis.
com; 79 Madison Ave; r from $279;
P ❄ @ 🛜 ♨ 🐾) If you're looking for a sleek
treat, check into these swanky, music-themed
boutique sleeps. The rooftop Sky Terrace ($10
for non-guests) is one of the best places in town
to watch a sunset, and stylish rooms have nice
touches like hardwood entryways, high ceilings
and Italian linens. Parking is $29.

Clarksdale ❹

✕ Abe's Bar-B-Q   Barbecue $

(☎662-624-9947; www.abesbbq.com; 616 State
St; sandwiches $4-6, plates $6-14; ⏰10am-
8:30pm Mon-Sat, to 8pm Sun; P 🚻) Abe's has
served zesty pork sandwiches, vinegary slaw
and slow-burning tamales at the Crossroads
since 1924.

⍟ Lofts at the Five
& Dime   Apartment $$

(☎888-510-9604; www.fiveanddimelofts.com;
211 Yazoo St; lofts from $150; ❄ 🛜) Set in a
1954 building are plush, loft-style apartments
with molded-concrete counters in the full
kitchen, massive flat-screens in the living room
and bedroom, terrazzo showers, and free sodas
and water throughout your stay. They sleep up
to four people comfortably.

Greenwood ❻

✕ Delta Bistropub   Southern US $$

(☎662-459-9345; www.deltabistro.com; 222
Howard St; mains $13-26; ⏰11am-2pm & 5-9pm
Tue-Fri, 11am-9pm Sat) A tasty upmarket cafe
serving Southern treats like fried catfish and
barbecue shrimp po'boys and crab bisque, as
well as fine departures like local shrimp with
lemon zest and fried basil, and a seared duck
breast served with pork belly and grilled baby
asparagus. This is the best kitchen in the Delta.

⍟ Alluvian   Boutique Hotel $$$

(☎662-453-2114; www.thealluvian.com; 318
Howard St; r $200-235, ste $300; P ❄ @ 🛜)
This stunning four-star boutique hotel includes
a gallery of Delta art, a gushing fountain in the
courtyard, and spacious rooms and suites with
all the trimmings: soaker tubs, high ceilings,
granite washbasins and checkerboard parlor
floors in the bathrooms. Some rooms have
courtyard views. Others overlook downtown
Greenwood. Book ahead.

Cajun Country

Enter a maze of bayous, lakes, swamps and prairies where the crawfish boils, and all-night jam sessions and dance parties don't end.

20

TRIP HIGHLIGHTS

160 miles

Chicot State Park
Wander between bayous and cypress stands

105 miles

Breaux Bridge
Dine on decadent Cajun fare

3
Mamou

2

6
FINISH

New Iberia

Morgan City

Thibodaux
START

230 miles

Lafayette
Split time between live music and Cajun cuisine

4 DAYS
230 MILES / 370KM

GREAT FOR...

BEST TIME TO GO

March to June is festival season in Acadiana; warm weather and lots of parties.

ESSENTIAL PHOTO

Cajun concerts rock Fred's Lounge every Saturday morning.

BEST FOR CULTURE

The unique folkways of Acadiana permeate south Louisiana.

Lake Martin Home to the great egret

20 | Cajun Country

Cross into south Louisiana, and you venture into a land that's intensely, immediately unique. You will drive past dinosaur-laced wetlands where standing water is uphill from the floodplain, through villages where French is still the language of celebration, and sometimes, the home, and towns that love to fiddle, dance, two-step and, most of all, eat well. Bienvenue en Louisiane: this is Cajun Country, a waterlogged, toe-tapping nation unto itself.

➊ Thibodaux

Thibodaux (tib-ah-*doe*), huddled against the banks of **Bayou Lafourche**, is the traditional gateway to Cajun country for those traveling from New Orleans. Thanks to a city center lined with historic homes, it's a fair bit more attractive than nearby Houma, which is often also cited as a major Cajun Country destination but is in reality more of a charmless oil town. The main attraction in Thibodaux is the **Wetlands Acadian Cultural Center** (☎985-448-1375; www.nps.gov/jela; 314 St Mary St; ◷9am-7pm Mon & Tue, to 5pm Wed-Fri; 👶🏻 📷), part of the Jean Lafitte National Park system. NPS rangers lead boat tours from here into the bayou during spring and fall; you can either chug to the **ED White Plantation** home on Wednesday (10am to noon; $5) or head to the **Madewood Plantation** on Saturday (10am to 2:30pm; $32), where you're given a house tour and lunch. The center also hosts an excellent on-site museum and helpful staff who provide free walking tours of Thibodaux town (2pm, Monday, Tuesday and Thursday). If you're lucky, you'll land here on a Monday evening, when Cajun musicians jam out (5:30pm to 7pm).

✗ p245

The Drive ⟫ Get on Hwy 90 and drive to Breaux Bridge. It's about two hours nonstop, but don't be afraid to occasionally peel off and check out some side roads.

TRIP HIGHLIGHT

➋ Breaux Bridge

Little Breaux Bridge boasts a pretty 'downtown' of smallish side

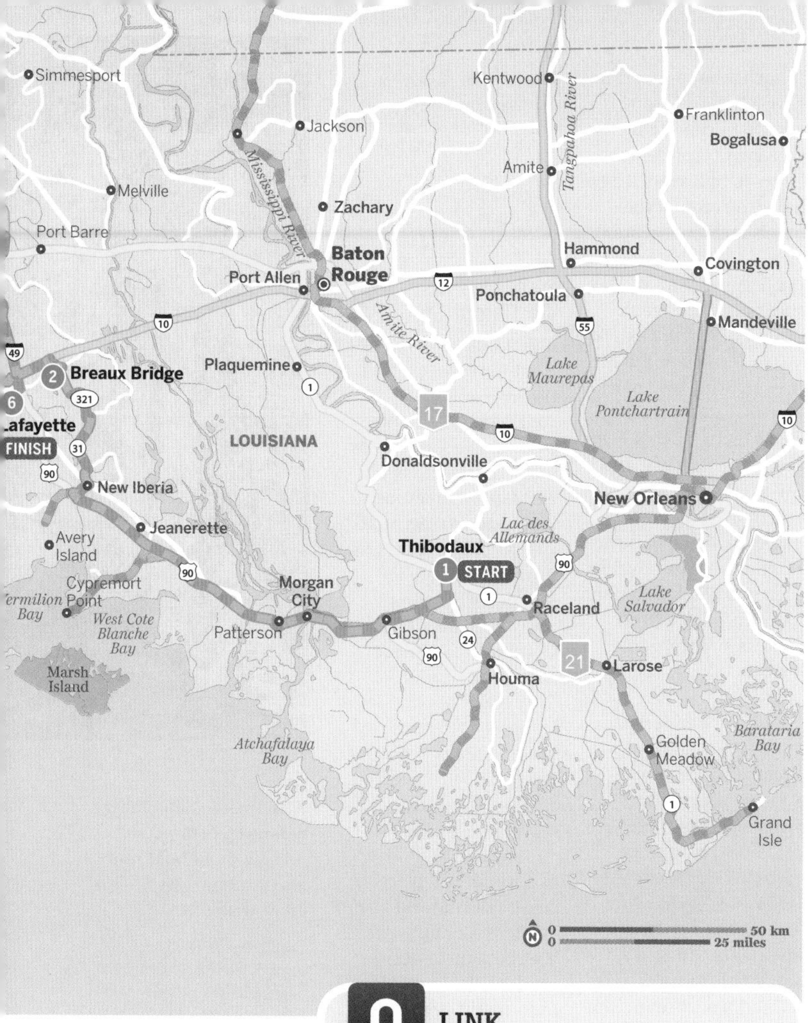

streets, Cajun hospital-
ity and a silly amount
of good food. Your main
objective is to eat at the
ridiculously delicious
Café des Amis (p245),
where sinfully good
Cajun fare is often served
alongside local live music.
The shows are scheduled
for Wednesday nights and
Sunday mornings (zydeco

LINK YOUR TRIP

17 Southern Gothic Literary Tour

Search for stories amid
the storied streets of
New Orleans while night
falls over her Gothic
neighborhoods.

21 Gulf Coast

Go to Grand Isle
and follow the Gulf
Coast, from Louisiana's
wetland-speckled shores
to sugar-sand beaches.

brunch!), but performers have a habit of dropping in unexpectedly. Otherwise there's not a lot to do in Breaux Bridge but stroll around the handsome town center and, if you're here during the first weekend in May, check out the **Breaux Bridge Crawfish Festival**.

Three miles south of Breaux Bridge is **Lake Martin** (Lake Martin Rd), a bird sanctuary that hosts thousands of great and cattle egrets, blue heron and more than a few gators. A small walkway extends over the algae-carpeted black water and loops through a pretty cypress swamp, while birds huddle in nearby trees.

Stop by **Henderson**, 8 miles northeast of Breaux Bridge. On Sunday afternoons, **Whiskey River** (☏337-228-8567; www.whiskeyriverla.com; 1365 Henderson Levee Rd; cover varies; ☉3-9pm Sun) rocks to zydeco and Cajun tunes. It's a small house, and it gets packed. Locals dance on tables, on the bar and in the water. Nearby **Pat's** (☏337-228-7512; www.patsfishermanswharf.com; 1008 Henderson Levee Rd; mains $12-26; ☉11am-9:30pm Sun-Thu, to 10:30pm Fri & Sat; **P**) serves decent seafood of the fried variety, and dancing of the two-step and Cajun genre.

✖ ⊨ p245

The Drive ≫ From Breaux Bridge you can take Hwy 49 north for about 24 miles, then Hwy 167 north to Ville Platte, then LA 3042 to Chicot State Park, a total trip time of about 80 minutes.

TRIP HIGHLIGHT

❸ Chicot State Park

Cajun Country isn't just a cultural space – it's a physical landscape as well, a land of shadowy, moss-draped pine forest and slow-water bayous and lakes. Sometimes it can be tough seeing all this from the roadways, as roads have understandably been built away from floodable bottomlands. **Chicot State Park** (☏337-363-2403, 888-677-2442; www.crt.louisiana.gov/louisiana-state-parks/parks/chicot-state-park; 3469 Chicot Park Rd, Ville Platte; per person $3; ☉6am-9pm Sun-Thu, to 10pm Fri & Sat; **P** ♿ 🎣) is a wonderful place to access the natural beauty of Cajun Country. An excellent interpretive center is fun for kids and informative for adults, and deserves enormous accolades for its open, airy design. Miles of **trails** extend into the nearby forests, cypress swamps and wetlands. If you can, stay for early evening; the sunsets over the Spanish-moss-draped trees that fringe **Lake Chicot** are superb. There are **campsites** ($16 per night October to March,

JAYL / SHUTTERSTOCK ©

$20 April to September), **cabins** (six-/15-person $85/120) and **boat rentals** (per hour/day $5/20) all available.

The Drive ≫ Head back towards Ville Platte, then turn onto LA 10 west. After 7 miles turn south onto LA 13; it's about 4 miles more to Mamou.

❹ Mamou

Deep in the heart of Cajun Country, Mamou is a typical south Louisiana small town six days of the week, worth a peek and a short stop before rolling to Eunice. But on Saturday mornings, Mamou's hometown

242

Chicot State Park Bald cypress swamp

hangout, little **Fred's Lounge** (420 6th St; ⊙8:30am-2pm Sat), becomes the apotheosis of a Cajun dancehall.

OK, to be fair: Fred's is more of a dance shack than hall. It's a little bar and it gets more than a little crowded from 8:30am to 2pm-ish, when owner 'Tante' (auntie) Sue and her staff host a Francophone-friendly music morning, with bands, beer, cigarettes and dancing (seriously, it gets smoky in here. Fair warning). Sue herself will often take to the stage to dispense wisdom and song in Cajun French, all

while taking pulls off a bottle of brown liquor she keeps in a pistol holster.

The Drive » Eunice is only 11 miles south of Mamou; just keep heading straight on LA 13.

- - - - - - - - - - - - - - - -

⑤ Eunice

Eunice lies in the heart of the Cajun prairie, its associated folkways, and music. Musician Mark Savoy builds accordions at his **Savoy Music Center** (📞337-457-9563; www.savoymusiccenter.com; 4413 Hwy 190; ⊙9am-5pm Tue-Fri, to noon Sat), where you can also pluck some CDs and catch a Saturday-morning jam

session. Saturday night means the **Rendez-Vous Cajuns** are playing the **Liberty Theater** (📞337-457-6577; www.eunice-la.com/index.php/things-to-do/liberty-schedule; 200 Park Ave; $5; ⊙6-7:30pm), which is just two blocks from the **Cajun Music Hall of Fame & Museum** (📞337-457-6534; www.cajunfrenchmusic.org; 230 S CC Duson Dr; ⊙9am-5pm) – a small affair, to be sure, but charming in its way. The NPS-run **Prairie Acadian Cultural Center** (📞337-457-8499; www.nps.gov/jela; 250 West Park Ave; ⊙9:30am-4:30pm Wed-Fri, to 6pm Sat) is another worthy stop, and

CAJUNS & CREOLES

A lot of tourists in Louisiana use the terms 'Cajun' and 'Creole' interchangeably, but the two cultures are different and distinct. 'Creole' refers to descendants of the original European settlers of Louisiana, a blended mix of mainly French and Spanish ancestry. The Creoles tend to have urban connections to New Orleans and considered their own culture refined and civilized. Many (but not all) were descended from aristocrats, merchants and skilled tradespeople.

The Cajuns can trace their lineage to the Acadians, colonists from rural France who settled Nova Scotia. After the British conquered Canada, the proud Acadians refused to kneel to the new crown, and were exiled in the mid-18th century – an act known as the Grand Dérangement. Many exiles settled in south Louisiana; they knew the area was French, but the Acadians ('Cajun' is an English bastardization of the word) were often treated as country bumpkins by the Creoles. The Acadians-cum-Cajuns settled in the bayous and prairies, and to this day self-conceptualize as a more rural, frontier-stye culture.

Adding confusion to all of the above is the practice, standard in many post-colonial French societies, of referring to mixed-race individuals as 'creoles.' This happens in Louisiana, but there is a cultural difference between Franco-Spanish Creoles and mixed-race creoles, even as these two communities very likely share actual blood ancestry.

often hosts music nights and educational lectures.

The Drive » Head east on Hwy 190 (Laurel Ave) and turn right onto LA 367. Follow LA 367 for around 19 miles (it becomes LA 98 for a bit), then merge onto I-10 eastbound. Follow I-10 for around 14 miles, then take exit 101 onto LA 182/N University Ave; follow it into downtown Lafayette.

- - - - - - - - - - - - - - - - - -

TRIP HIGHLIGHT

❻ Lafayette

Lafayette, capital of Cajun Country and fourth-largest city in Louisiana, has a wonderful concentration of good eats and culture for a city of its size (around 120,000). On most nights you can catch fantastic zydeco, country, blues, funk, swamp rock and even punk blasting out of the excellent **Blue Moon Saloon** (🖉337-234-2422; www.bluemoonpresents.com; 215 E Convent St; cover $5-8; 🕑5pm-2am Tue-Sun); the crowd here is young, hip and often tattooed, but they'll get down to a fiddle as easily as drum-and-bass. During the last weekend in April Lafayette hosts **Festival International de Louisiane** (www.festivalinternational.org; 🕑Apr), the largest Francophone musical event in the Western Hemisphere.

Vermilionville (🖉337-233-4077; www.bayouvermiliondistrict.org/vermilionville; 300 Fisher Rd; adult/student $10/6, boat tour $12/8; 🕑10am-4pm Tue-Sun; P 🚻), a restored/re-created 19th-century Cajun village, wends its way along the bayou near the airport. Costumed docents explain Cajun, Creole and Native American history, local bands perform on Sundays and boat tours of the bayou are offered. The not-as-polished **Acadian Village** (🖉337-981-2364; www.acadianvillage.org; 200 Greenleaf Dr; adult/student $8/6; 🕑10am-4pm Mon-Sat; P 🚻) offers a similar experience, minus the boat tours. Next to Vermilionvile, the NPS runs the **Acadian Cultural Center** (🖉337-232-0789; www.nps.gov/jela; 501 Fisher Rd; 🕑9am-4:30pm Tue-Fri, 8:30am-noon Sat; P 🚻), containing exhibits on Cajun life; it's a little dry compared to the above, but still worth a visit.

✕ 🛏 p245

Eating & Sleeping

Thibodaux ①

✖ Fremin's   Cajun $$

(☎985-449-0333; www.fremins.net; 402 W
Third St; mains $12-37; ☻11am-2pm Tue-Fri,
5-9pm Tue-Thu, to 10pm Fri & Sat) Fremin's is
one of the great-granddaddies of high-end,
classic Cajun cuisine. The menu doesn't change
much, and while there are some items that
could use an update, overall this is a solid menu.
Case in point: soft-shell crab served over pasta
with a very good mushroom brandy sauce.

Breaux Bridge ②

✖ Café des Amis   Cajun $$

(☎337-332-5273; www.cafedesamis.com; 140 E
Bridge St; mains $17-26; ☻11am-2pm Tue, 11am-
9pm Wed & Thu, 7:30am-9pm Fri & Sat, 8am-2pm
Sun; 🖐) In the compact, crawfish lovin'
town of Breaux Bridge, you'll find this utterly
unexpected cafe, where you can relax amid
funky local art as waiters trot out sumptuous
weekend breakfasts, all set to live zydeco music
on Saturday morning. Dig in to Cajun classics
with a contemporary twist like pecan-crusted
catfish or eggs with crawfish étoufée.

🛏 Bayou Cabins   Cabin $

(☎337-332-6158; www.bayoucabins.com; 100 W
Mills Ave; cabin $80-150; P 🛜) The wonderful
Bayou Cabins, situated on Bayou Teche, feature
14 completely individualized cabins, some with
1950s retro furnishings, others decked out
in regional folk art. The included breakfast is
delicious, but the smoked meats may shave a
few years off your life.

Lafayette ⑥

✖ Dwyer's   Diner $

(☎337-235-9364; 323 Jefferson St; mains
$6-14; ☻6am-2pm; 🖐) This family-owned joint
serves Cajun diner fare, finally bringing gumbo
for lunch and pancakes for breakfast into one
glorious culinary marriage. It's especially fun on
Wednesday mornings when a French-speaking
table is set up and local Cajuns shoot the breeze
in their old-school dialect. Rotating lunch mains
include smothered pork chops, fried chicken
and shrimp stew.

✖ French Press   Breakfast $

(☎337-233-9449; www.thefrenchpresslafayette.
com; 214 E Vermillion; mains $9-15; ☻7am-2pm
Mon-Fri, 9am-2pm Sat & Sun; 🛜) This French-
Cajun hybrid is one of the best culinary things
going in Lafayette. Breakfast is mind-blowing,
with a sinful Cajun Benedict (boudin instead of
ham), cheddar grits (that will kill you dead) and
organic granola (to offset the grits). Lunch ain't
half bad either; the fried shrimp melt, doused in
Sriracha mayo, is gorgeously decadent.

🛏 Blue Moon
Guest House   Guesthouse $

(☎337-234-2422; www.bluemoonpresents.
com; 215 E Convent St; dm $18, r $70-90;
P ❄ @ 🛜) This tidy home is one of
Louisiana's travel gems: an upscale hostel-like
hangout just walking distance from downtown.
Snag a bed and you're on the guest list for
Lafayette's most popular down-home music
venue (p244), located in the backyard. The
friendly owners, full kitchen and camaraderie
among guests create a unique music-meets-
migration environment catering to backpackers,
flashpackers and those in transition
(flashbackpackers?). Prices skyrocket during
festival time. Decidedly not quiet.

Gulf Coast

One of the nation's prettiest stretches of coast is criminally neglected by travelers – challenge the status quo and explore a quilt of wetlands, pine forests, bayous and white-sand beaches.

21

TRIP HIGHLIGHTS

0 miles

New Orleans
Because even a hint of NOLA is always welcome

648 miles

Mobile
Antebellum homes and shady live oak trees

FINISH
8

Biloxi
Gulfport
6

3

1
START

Grand Isle

Avery Island
Explore the island's eccentric botanical beauty

168 miles

Gulf Islands National Seashore
Untouched barrier islands worth seeking out

586 miles

---

4 DAYS
648 MILES / 1043KM

GREAT FOR...

BEST TIME TO GO
From April to June, the sun is shining again, and the heat has yet to bear down.

ESSENTIAL PHOTO
Snap the waters of Cypremort Point State Park at sunset.

BEST FOR OUTDOOR ACTIVITIES
Poke around wetlands, bayous, marshes and beaches.

21 Gulf Coast

Florida gets all the good press when it comes to Southern coastline, but the Gulf laps the beaches of Louisiana, Mississippi and, ever so briefly, Alabama too. And while it has been used and abused and even ended up in the (bad) news more than once during the past decade, there are plenty of overlooked pockets of charm, beauty and history to occupy you.

TRIP HIGHLIGHT

❶ New Orleans

Few destinations have as many ways to creatively kill time as the Crescent City. It's deep in history and architecture, has sensational food, and there's more great, free live music here than anywhere else. Begin with a tipple at Lafitte's Blacksmith Shop (p217), set in one of the few 18th-century cottages to survive the French Quarter fires during the Spanish era. Then quickly seek some cleansing night music. **Preservation**

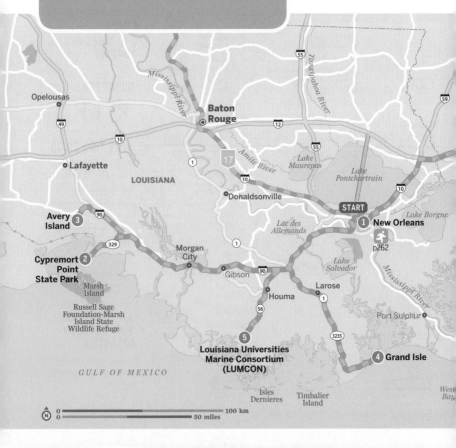

Hall (🖉504-522-2841; www.preservationhall.com; 726 St Peter St; cover $15 Sun-Thu, $20 Fri & Sat, reserved seats $34-45; ⊙shows 8pm, 9pm & 10pm Mon-Wed, 6pm, 8pm, 9pm & 10pm Thu-Sun) is the place to hear authentic New Orleans jazz by local masters. When darkness deepens head to **Frenchmen Street** (from Esplanade Ave to Royal St) in **Fauborg Marigny** – a haven for terrific live music with a more evolutionary bent. The **St Charles Avenue Streetcar** (🖉504-248-3900, TTY 504-827-7832; www.norta.com; per ride $1.25; 🚹) will take you up and down this famous avenue, through the CBD, to the **Garden District** and **Uptown** mansions. Out in Mid-City, by scenic **Bayou St John**, you can peruse the **New Orleans Museum of Art** (NOMA; 🖉504-658-4100; www.noma.org; 1 Collins Diboll Circle; adult/child 7-17yr $12/6; ⊙10am-6pm Tue-Thu, to 9pm Fri, 10am-5pm Sat, 11am-5pm Sun) or just stroll beneath the old, mossy oaks in **City Park** (🖉504-482-4888; www.neworleanscitypark.com; Esplanade Ave & City Park Ave; 🅿). Explore further on our walking tour, p262.

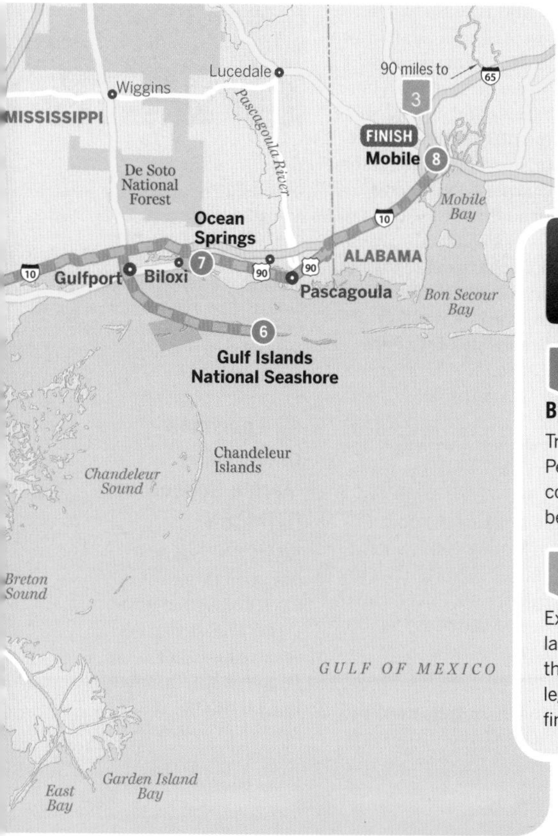

🍴 🛏 p219, p253, p323

The Drive >> Take Avery Island road (LA 329) to New Iberia town, then hop on LA 83 and take that south. After about 15 miles you'll take a right in LA 319; from here it's about 5.5 miles to Cypremort Point.

❷ Cypremort Point State Park

You can't get more end of the road than **Cypremort Point** (🖉337-867-4510; 306 Beach Lane; adult/senior & child under 3yr $3/free; ⊙7am-9pm, to 10pm Fri & Sat; 🅿 🚹 🐾), a lonely, windswept promontory of land buffeted by wind, seagull calls and foam spray off the Gulf of Mexico. There's a little artificial beach and some picnic tables, but we mainly like coming here for the long, slightly surreal drive over

Lucedale
90 miles to 🛣65
3
Wiggins
MISSISSIPPI
Pascagoula River
FINISH
Mobile 8
De Soto National Forest
Mobile Bay
Ocean Springs
🛣10
ALABAMA
🛣10 Gulfport Biloxi 🛣90 🛣90 7
Pascagoula
Bon Secour Bay
6
Gulf Islands National Seashore
Chandeleur Islands
Chandeleur Sound
Breton Sound
GULF OF MEXICO
East Bay
Garden Island Bay

LINK YOUR TRIP

3 North Florida Backwaters & Byways

Traverse Mobile Bay into Pensacola and follow the coastline as it arcs and bends southward.

17 Southern Gothic Literary Tour

Explore the South's literary landscape as you investigate the roots and admire the legacy of some of America's finest scribes.

miles and miles of breeze-bent marshland and still piney woods.

The Drive » From I-90 or LA 83, take the exit for LA 329 towards Avery Island. The exit is essentially attached to the cute town of New Iberia, with its handsome historic center and the evocatively named plantation Shadows-on-the-Teche. The trip takes about 30 miles.

TRIP HIGHLIGHT

❸ Avery Island

The most famous hot sauce in the world, Tabasco, and all of its many variants, is produced here on Avery Island, known for its red chili peppers and natural salt deposits. A dollar gets you onto the island and into the factory for a (very) brief tour, which includes a creepily optimistic promotional video hosted by (seemingly) a Tabasco-swag-wearing Laura Bush. More interesting are the gardens: in 1890, EA McIlhenny, son of the founder of Tabasco, started a bird sanctuary now known as **Jungle Gardens** (📞337-369-6243; www.junglegardens.org; Avery Island Rd; adult/child $8/5, incl Tabasco Factory tour $12.50/9.50; ⏰9am-5pm). Here you can drive or walk through 250 acres of subtropical flora and view an amazing array of water birds (especially snowy egrets, which nest here in astounding numbers), turtles and alligators. Watch for turtles and peacocks crossing the road and an

enormous, centuries-old Buddha meditating serenely over the wetlands, a gift acquired by EA McIlhenny himself.

🛏 p253

The Drive » From I-90, take LA 1 southbound; at Larose, get off of 1 and onto LA 3235. From here it's about a 46-mile drive down to Grand Isle (you'll re-merge with LA 1 after about 16 miles), past miles of marshy lowlands and the ever-present hump of the levee.

❹ Grand Isle

The end of the road down bayou way is 70 miles southeast of **Houma**, in Grand Isle. The wind-swept barrier-island town seems to consistently take a beating from hurricanes and disasters like the BP Gulf oil spill, yet this beach village retains charm and character. In addition to seafood shacks and fishing camps, boat charters are the big business here. Watching the waves lap ashore at **Grand Isle State Park** (📞985-787-2559; http://crt.louisiana.gov/louisiana-state-parks/parks/grand-isle-state-park; Admiral Craik Dr; $3; ⏰6am-9pm Sun-Thu, to 10pm Fri & Sat; 🅿), it's easy to imagine the power of Mother Nature. Rent canoes ($20 per day) to explore the inland canals or just watch as the brown pelicans, the state bird, dive for fish offshore.

The Drive » From I-90, take exits for LA 56/Little Caillou

Rd, which will run through the not-particularly-impressive heart of Houma. From Houma it's about a 35-mile drive south to LUMCON (look for Chauvin, LA, if you have a GPS) over a patchwork quilt of water, marsh and partially flooded plains.

❺ Louisiana Universities Marine Consortium (LUMCON)

LUMCON? Sounds like something out of a science-fiction novel, right? Well, there is science here, but it's all fact, and still fascinating. **LUMCON** (📞985-851-2800; www.lumcon.

Avery Island Snowy egrets nest on the island

edu; 8124 Hwy 56, Chauvin; ⏱8am-4pm; 👣) is one of the premier research facilities dedicated to the Gulf of Mexico; if you want to dig deeper into the natural biomes and ecosystems that make up the region, you shouldn't pass this place up. There are nature trails running through hairy tufts of grassy marsh, nine small aquariums and an observation tower that gives visitors an unbeatable view (short of climbing into a helicopter) of the great swathes of flat, fuzzy wetlands that makes up the south Louisiana coast.

The Drive » Work your way back to I-90 to New Orleans, and hop I-10 to the Gulfport exit, about 160 miles east.

TRIP HIGHLIGHT

6 Gulf Islands National Seashore

A maze of wetlands, scrubby dunes and empty white-sand beaches centered on five offshore barrier islands can be accessed from the town of Gulfport, MS. **West Ship Island** is the most reachable island in the archipelago. There's a twice daily **ferry** (☎228-864-1014; www.msshipisland. com; 1040 23rd Ave, Gulfport

Ferry Pier; round-trip adult/child $29/19) from Gulfport servicing the island all summer, and ferries run Wednesday to Sunday in the spring and fall. In addition to snorkeling, body boarding, swimming and beachcombing, you can visit **Fort Massachusetts**, a brick fort built in 1868, right on the beach. Four of the wilderness islands, **Horn**, **Petit Bois**, **Sand** and **East Ship Island**, are open to camping, but you'll need to charter a boat to get there (check www.nps.gov/guis) for a list of approved charters). During the osprey nesting season some parts of the islands will be off-limits to nurture the nesting flocks.

The Drive » Hug the coastline on Beach Blvd for 17 miles through Biloxi and take the Bienville Blvd Bridge into Ocean Springs.

- - - - - - - - - - - - - - -

⑦ Ocean Springs

Ocean Springs remains charming with a romantic lineup of shrimp boats in the harbor alongside recreational sailing yachts, a historic downtown core, and a powdery fringe of white sand on the gulf. The highlight is the **Walter Anderson Museum** (☎228-872-3164; www.walterandersonmuseum. org; 510 Washington St; adult/child $10/5; ⏰9:30am-4:30pm Mon-Sat, from 12:30pm Sun; 👶). A consummate artist and lover of Gulf Coast nature, Anderson suffered from mental illness, which spurred the solitary, almost monastic, existence that fueled

his life's work. After he died, the beachside shack where he lived on **Horn Island** was discovered to be painted in mind-blowing murals, which you'll see here. You can also access the **Davis Bayou**, part of **Gulf Islands National Seashore** (☎228-875-9057; www.nps.gov/guis; 3500 Park Rd; $3; 👶).

✖ p253

The Drive » Stay off the interstate a while, and stay on Hwy 90, a causeway with alternating gulf and wetland views, through the shipbuilding port of Pascagoula, skirt the Grand Bay Wildlife Refuge, then hop on I-10 and drive 55 miles into Alabama.

- - - - - - - - - - - - - - -

TRIP HIGHLIGHT

⑧ Mobile

The city that spawned baseballer Hammerin' Hank Aaron, with its impressive industrial port, the nation's 13th biggest, and homey, historic downtown,

Mobile is a surprisingly fun and friendly place. The stroll down Dauphin St from the waterfront to its inner heart is pocked with green squares and fountains, and more than a few pubs, bars, cafes and restaurants bustling with young people, thanks to Mobile's three universities. The biggest attraction is the striking and modern **Gulf Coast Exploreum** (☎251-208-6893; www.exploreum.com; 65 Government St; adult/student/child $12/10.50/10 with IMAX $16/15/13.50; ⏰9am-4pm Tue-Thu, to 5pm Fri & Sat, noon-5pm Sun; 👶), a science center with 150 interactive exhibits and displays in three galleries, an IMAX theater and live demonstrations in its chemistry and biology labs. War geeks will want to tour the **USS Alabama** (☎251-433-2703; www.ussalabama. com; 2703 Battleship Pkwy; adult/child $15/6; ⏰8am-6pm Apr-Sep, to 5pm Oct-Mar; 🅿), a 690ft behemoth famous for escaping nine major WWII battles unscathed. Baseball historians should stop by **Hank Aaron Stadium** (☎251-479-2327; www.hankaaronstadium.com; 755 Bolling Brothers Blvd; adult/child $5/4; ⏰9am-5pm Mon-Fri; 🅿), home of the Mobile Bay Bears, where there is a museum, set in Aaron's old childhood home (moved to this location). It documents his incredible life from obscure Alabama poverty to home-run king.

✖ 🛏 p253

DISASTER ENDURANCE

In the backyard of New Orleans, the Mississippi Gulf Coast's economy, traditionally based on the seafood industry, got a shot of adrenaline in the 1990s when big Vegas-style casinos muscled in alongside the sleepy fishing villages. And then a double whammy of disasters descended. Just when the casinos in Biloxi had been rebuilt following Hurricane Katrina in 2005, the Deepwater Horizon oil spill in the Gulf in 2010 dealt the coast another unexpected blow. However, Mississippi's barrier islands helped divert much of the oil problems toward New Orleans and Alabama, and Mississippi's coastline is surprisingly serene in places. Especially on those difficult-to-access barrier islands.

Eating & Sleeping

New Orleans ❶

✖ Dante's Kitchen
Louisianan $$

(☎504-861-3121; www.danteskitchen.com; 736 Dante St; brunch $9-14, mains $23-27; ⏱6-10pm Wed-Sun, 10:30am-2pm Sat & Sun) It's hard not to feel like you've stepped into the pages of the J Crew catalog during Sunday brunch at Dante's, a country cottage on the Mississippi levee. The menu melds French, American and Louisiana traditions. Debris and poached eggs on a caramelized onion biscuit, topped with a demi-glace Hollandaise sauce is an unbelievable way to start your day, unless, of course, you decide to opt for the bread-pudding French toast. Make reservations for dinner.

🛏 Bywater Bed & Breakfast
B&B $

(☎504-944-8438; www.bywaterbnb.com; 1026 Clouet St; r without bath $100-150; ❄🤖) This is what happens when you fall through the rabbit hole and Wonderland is a B&B. This spot is popular with lesbians (it's owned by a lesbian couple), but welcomes everyone. It's about as homey and laid-back as it gets. Expect to stay in what amounts to a folk-art gallery with a bit of historical heritage and a hallucinogenic vibe.

Avery Island ❸

🛏 Estorge-Norton House
B&B $

(☎337-365-7603; www.estorge-nortonhouse. com; 446 E Main St; r $85-110; P @ 🤖) Located in a historic district, this comfortable 100-plus-year-old bungalow home with four comfortable bedrooms is decked out in frilly, if cozy, accoutrements. Two of the rooms can sleep three or more. *Pain perdu* ('lost bread,' or French toast) topped with marmalade is an excellent breakfast special.

Ocean Springs ❼

✖ Government Street Grocery
Pub Food $

(☎228-818-9410; 1210 Government St; mains $7-10; ⏱11am-11pm Tue & Wed, to 1pm Thu, to 2am Fri & Sat, to 11pm Sun) This popular spot serves an array of burgers, fried shrimp baskets and po'boys, gyro and falafel. It gets a nice bar crowd at night, especially Thursdays through Saturdays, thanks to its live-music calendar.

✖ Leo's
Pizza $$

(☎228-872-1297; 1107 Government St; mains $9-13; ⏱11am-9pm Sun-Thu, to 10pm Fri & Sat) This wood-fired pizzeria has an upmarket sensibility and – hello! – two dozen beers from the tap. Its trendy dining room spills onto the shady patio with ample bar space. As a bonus, it also makes its own pizzas, wraps, salads and sandwiches in an open kitchen.

Mobile ❽

✖ Wintzell's
Seafood $$

(☎251-432-4605; www.wintzellsoysterhouse. com; 605 Dauphin St; mains $11-26; ⏱11am-10pm Sun-Thu, to 11pm Fri & Sat) A Mobile classic since 1938, and the first of an Alabama chain. It specializes in oysters – raw, char-grilled or fried – but it also does an excellent broiled fish of the day, and serves succulent shrimp and scallops too, in brew-house, blue-jean environs.

🛏 Battle House
Hotel $$

(☎251-338-2000; www.marriott.com; 26 N Royal St; r $170-240, ste from $375; P ❄ @ 🤖 🏊 🚹) By far the best address in Mobile. Stay in the original historic wing with its ornate domed marble lobby, though the striking new tower is on the waterfront. Rooms are spacious, luxurious, four-star chic. Book ahead for discounts.

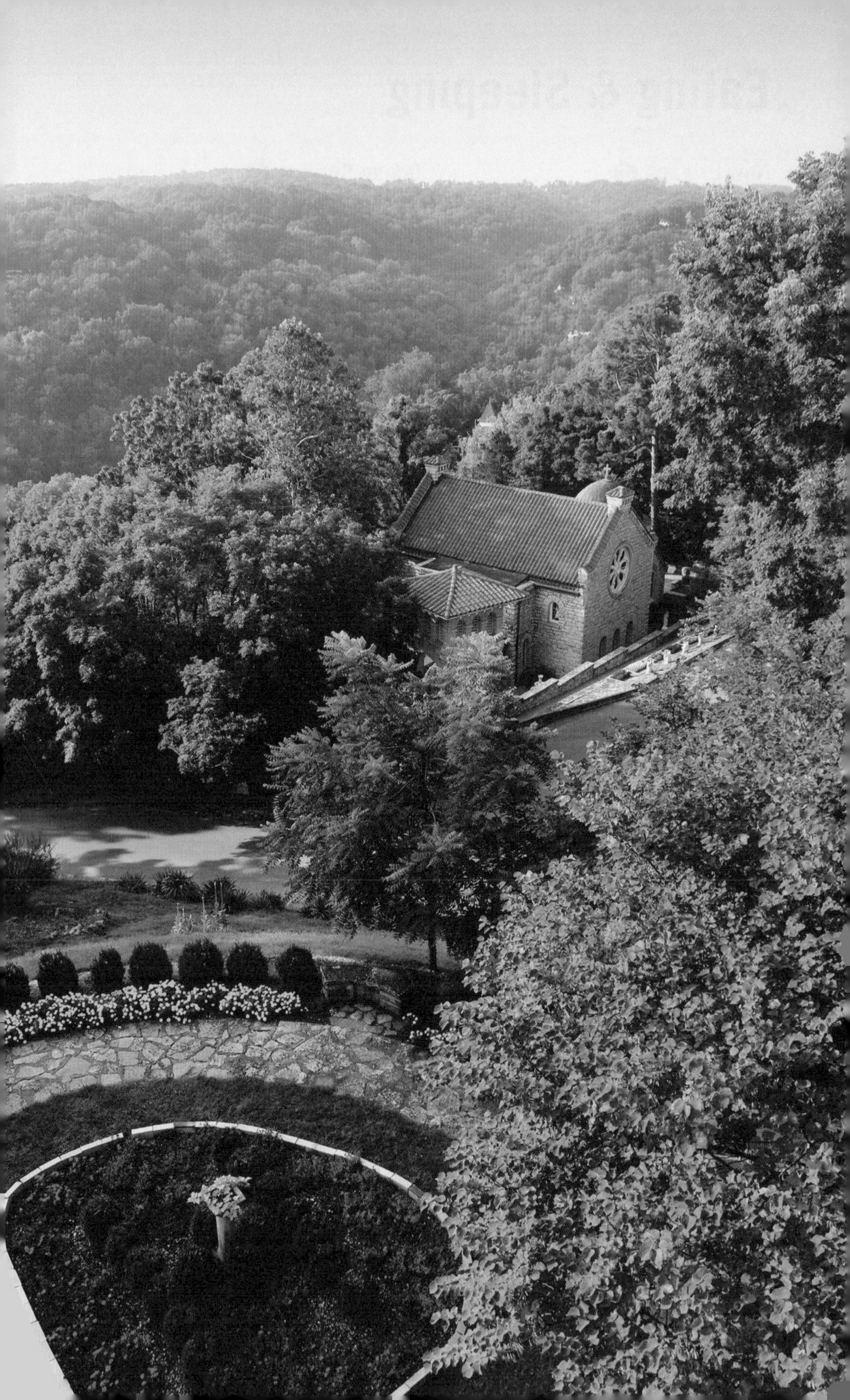

Back Roads Arkansas

22

Start on the Capitol steps, head north and veer off the interstate into layered blue mountains laced with streams and rivers, studded with quirky towns and blessed with magnificent vistas.

TRIP HIGHLIGHTS

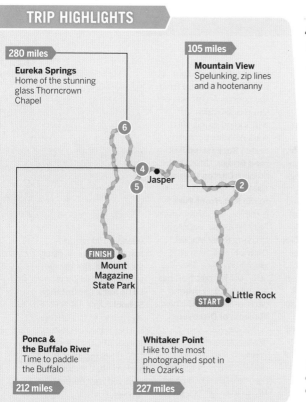

280 miles

Eureka Springs
Home of the stunning glass Thorncrown Chapel

105 miles

Mountain View
Spelunking, zip lines and a hootenanny

6

4
5
● Jasper

2

FINISH ●
Mount Magazine State Park

START ● Little Rock

Ponca & the Buffalo River
Time to paddle the Buffalo

212 miles

Whitaker Point
Hike to the most photographed spot in the Ozarks

227 miles

4 DAYS
507 MILES / 816KM

GREAT FOR...

BEST TIME TO GO
From March to May, when new leaves bud and the Buffalo River swells.

 ESSENTIAL PHOTO
Whitaker Point has black granite bluffs that jut over a beautiful riverine valley.

 BEST FOR OUTDOORS
From wooded walks to plummeting bluffs, connect with Arkansas' elements.

Eureka Springs Scenic view over St Elizabeth's Catholic Church

255

Back Roads Arkansas

Arkansas offers dry counties and left-wing history, folk music and hot springs. Its two-lane country back roads roll by tucked-away cattle ranches, magically disintegrating barns, cathedral caverns and the rushing, beautiful Buffalo River. Frequently tree shaded and generally spectacular, you will see a snapshot of Americana far off the beaten track.

❶ Little Rock

It would be easy to dismiss this leafy, attractive state capital on the Arkansas River as quiet, and maybe a little dull, certainly conservative. But you'd be wrong. Little Rock is young, up-and-coming, gay- and immigrant-friendly, and just friendly in general. Start at the **William J Clinton Presidential Center** (☎501-374-4242; www.clintonlibrary.gov; 1200 President Clinton Ave; adult/students & seniors/child $10/8/6; ⊙9am-5pm Mon-Sat, 1-5pm Sun; P ♿), where you'll learn that, at 32, Bill became the youngest governor in American history. The display commemorating his unlikely, victorious 1992 presidential campaign includes a video clip from the famous debate when Clinton defended his wife's good name. Next, walk past the perfectly rusted **Rock Island Railroad Bridge**, through the 30-acre **Clinton Presidential Park**, which connects to the **Riverfront Park** (☎501-371-4770; Ottenheimer Plaza; ⊙sunrise-sunset) and thriving **River Market District** (www.rivermarket.info; 400 President Clinton Ave; ♿) – the Market Hall has a range of tasty ethnic eateries. Nearby, the new **Museum of Discovery** (☎501-396-7050; www.museumofdiscovery.org; 500 President Clinton Ave; adult/child $10/8; ⊙9am-5pm Tue-Sat, 1-5pm Sun, plus 9am-5pm Mon summer; ♿) is a proper science- and natural-history museum perfect for families. But the most riveting attraction is **Little Rock Central High School** (☎501-374-1957; www.nps.gov/chsc; 2125 Daisy L Gatson Bates Dr; ⊙9am-4:30pm; P), the site of the 1957 desegregation crisis and eventual victory that changed the country forever.

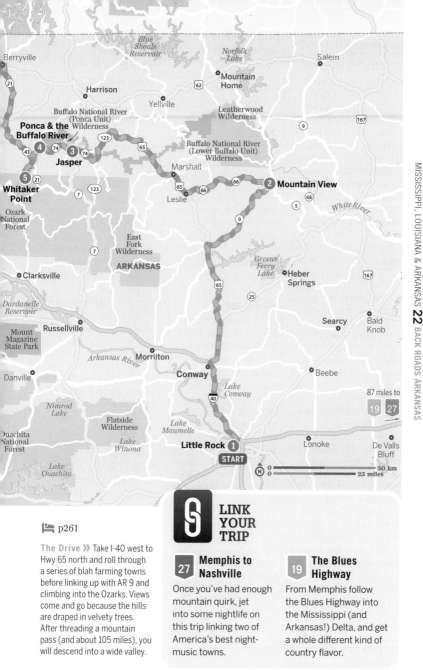

📖 p261

The Drive ⟫ Take I-40 west to Hwy 65 north and roll through a series of blah farming towns before linking up with AR 9 and climbing into the Ozarks. Views come and go because the hills are draped in velvety trees. After threading a mountain pass (and about 105 miles), you will descend into a wide valley.

🔗 LINK YOUR TRIP

27 Memphis to Nashville

Once you've had enough mountain quirk, jet into some nightlife on this trip linking two of America's best night-music towns.

19 The Blues Highway

From Memphis follow the Blues Highway into the Mississippi (and Arkansas!) Delta, and get a whole different kind of country flavor.

② Mountain View

Promoted as the 'Folk Music Capital of the World,' Mountain View hosts impromptu hill music, gospel and bluegrass jams in and around the attractive sandstone buildings of Court Square by the **Stone County Courthouse** (especially on Saturday night). The **Ozark Folk Center State Park** (☎870-269-3851; www.ozarkfolkcenter.com; 1032 Park Ave; auditorium adult/child $12/7; ☺10am-5pm Tue-Sat Apr-Nov, evening shows 6pm; 🅿), just north of town, hosts ongoing old-time craft demonstrations, as well as frequent live performances (folk, bluegrass, Shakespeare) that lure an avid, older crowd.

The park's newest concession, **LocoRopes** (☎870-269-6566; www.locoropes.com; 1025 Park Ave; per zip line $7.50; ☺10am-5pm Mar-Nov) offers a ropes course, slack lining, a free fall, a climbing wall and three zip lines.

From here take Hwy 87 north 14 miles to Mountain View's best sight, **Blanchard Springs Caverns** (☎870-757-2211; www.blanchardsprings.org; NF 54, Forest Rd, off Hwy 14; Drip Stone Tour adult/child $10/5, Wild Cave Tour $75; ☺hours vary; 👣), where you can opt for the rather staid, one-hour Drip Stone Tour, or sign up for three to four hours of genuine spelunking. Shimmy through a crawl space, and emerge into an underground cathedral. You'll return filthy, exhausted and smiling.

✖ 🛏 p261

The Drive » AR 66 winds west through gorgeous pastureland, rolling green hills and stunning pastoral villages. In quaint Leslie turn onto Hwy 65 and head north. Cross the Buffalo River and take AR 123 south past gorgeous views of granite bluffs, to AR 74 west into Jasper. The drive is about 90 miles.

③ Jasper

Here's a simple rustic town that leans heavily on Buffalo River tourism. Come here to prepare for exploration of the region's wilderness treasures. There are a couple of good eateries, affordable lodgings and adventure outfitters selling pocket knives, hammocks, quick-dry T-shirts, water bottles, camp stoves and kayaks, of course.

✖ p261

The Drive » Take AR 74 west from Jasper, wrap around the gorgeous horseshoe canyon where you can see more river bluffs, and drop into Low Gap. From here, curve around the hairpin before the Steel Creek put-in, where there are still more outrageous bluff views, meet AR 43 and buzz into Ponca, 15 miles away.

④ Ponca & the Buffalo River

Ponca is an early 20th-century mining camp turned ranch town whose current perch makes it the best launch point for a day's paddle on the Buffalo. Rent canoes or kayaks from **Lost Valley Canoe** (☎870-861-5522; www.lostvalleycanoe.com; AR 43; kayaks per day from $55, shuttle service from $20) or **Buffalo Outdoor Center** (BOC; ☎870-861-5514; www.buffaloriver.com; 4699 AR 43; kayak/canoe per day $55/62, zip-line tour $89; ☺8am-6pm Mar-Oct, to 5pm Nov-Feb; 👣🧒) in Ponca. Both will shuttle your car to your landing spot. From Ponca the river snakes between multicolored granite bluffs. Those at **Big Bluff** are a mind-boggling 550ft, the highest rock faces in mid-America. Once you pass them, the river makes a 90-degree bend to the right, where you'll find a thumb. Pull into it, and find the **Goat Trail** on the left bank. It leads to a sublime lookout 350ft above the river. A few miles downstream, three bluffs after the well-marked **Jim's Bluff**, the river makes a hard right. Stay left, and stop on the gravel bar in the center of that curve. Follow the unmarked spur trail to **Hemmed-in-Hollow**, the Ozarks'

Mount Magazine State Park Cliff overlook in the Arkansas River Valley

tallest waterfall. Paddle on to **Kyle's Landing**, a campground 10 miles downstream from Ponca, and pull out.

🛏 p261

The Drive ≫ Take AR 43 past the AR 21 turnoff and go over two small bridges. Just before the third, make a right onto a graded dirt road. In 6 miles, just past Cave Mountain Church, you'll find a trailhead. The entire drive covers about 12 miles.

TRIP HIGHLIGHT

❺ Whitaker Point

You can't leave the Buffalo River area until you've hiked this easy 1.5-mile trail (one way) to a granite table-top jutting out from streaked bluffs, draining rainwater 500ft above the lush river valley. Pristine, verdant ridges roll to the horizon in all directions. It's simply spectacular. No wonder it's the most photographed location in the Ozarks.

The Drive ≫ Double back to AR 21 and head north past still more stunning countryside until you get to the forgettable commercial sprawl of Berryville. From here follow Hwy 62 west to Eureka Springs, 53 miles from Ponca.

TRIP HIGHLIGHT

❻ Eureka Springs

Eureka Springs is a weird little Ozarks Town, half oriented towards gun-toting, Bible-thumping bikers on the one hand, and crunchy, granola-jarring hippies on the other. It's a joy to walk around the main street or embark on a **trolley tour** (📞479-253-9572; www.eurekatrolley. org; 137 W Van Buren St; day pass adult/child $6/2; ⏰10am-6pm Sun-Fri, 9am-8pm Sat May-Oct, reduced hours other times; ♿) through the historic district, which includes some fine examples of late

THE LITTLE ROCK NINE

Despite the landmark 1954 *Brown v Board of Education* ruling by the US Supreme Court, which unanimously determined segregation in public schools to be unconstitutional, until 1957 black students were still being barred from Little Rock's public schools. A handful of educators and members of the local school board, some of whom were well-meaning white Southerners, were determined to change this. They identified nine pioneering African American students to enroll at Little Rock Central High School (p256) that fall, but they were not prepared for the vitriolic backlash when more than 1000 white people – including several local students, as well as agitators from across the state – descended on the school to deny their entry. Police escorted the nine students inside, but as violence spread, they were secretly shuttled home. The next day, President Eisenhower federalized the Arkansas National Guard and ordered the 101st Airborne Battalion to escort the students into school. For the remainder of the year, the students were shadowed by soldiers who watched their back (and flirted with local girls).

The Little Rock Nine crisis was a major early milestone in the struggle to end desegregation, but in many ways, the incident foreshadowed deep rifts that have yet to be healed in American society. As schools across the country became either desegregated or admitted minority students bussed into majority white school zones, white families responded by relocating or placed their children in private schools. Today, for myriad complicated reasons, many school systems in the USA remain effectively as segregated as they were in the 1950s.

19th- and early 20th-century architecture. Or head out for a hike in the hills at **Lake Leatherwood City Park** (☎479-253-7921; www.lakeleatherwoodcitypark.com; 1303 Co Rd 204; ⏱24hr; P) – 'city' is an ambitious description, as the park gives you a good taste of Ozark wilderness. Just outside of town, **Thorncrown Chapel** (☎479-253-7401; www.thorncrown.com; 12968 Hwy 62 W; ⏱9am-5pm Apr-Nov, 11am-4pm Mar & Dec; P) is a fascinating house of worship, a church built of glass and wood that is effectively an open window unto the surrounding forests and mountains.

✕ ⌂ p261

The Drive » Take AR 23 south past wide pastures and gentle hills to Harrison, and the road snakes along jade fingerling valleys and shallow rivers, disintegrating barns and weather-beaten log cabins. Cross under I-40, to AR 309 south through the impoverished mid-century town of Paris, before climbing Mount Magazine, about 120 miles from Eureka Springs.

- - - - - - - - - - - - - - - - - - - -

❼ Mount Magazine State Park

The magnificent vistas begin immediately after entering **Mount Magazine State Park** (☎479-963-8502; www.mountmagazinestatepark.com; 577 Lodge Drive, Paris, N 35°09'52.4" W 93°38'49.7"; ⏱24hr). The lodge and visitor center is across the street from an excellent lookout over the **Arkansas River Valley**. The 2753ft **Signal Hill**, Arkansas' highest point, looms just behind. The visitor center is useful for maps, as there are 14 miles of **hiking trails** to explore. The park is also popular with rock climbers and paragliders, who ride and glide the thermals. From here it's an easy two-hour drive back to Little Rock via the I-40.

Eating & Sleeping

Little Rock ❶

🛏 Capital Hotel — Boutique Hotel $$

(📞501-374-7474; www.capitalhotel.com; 111 W Markham St; r/ste from $220/375; P ❄ @ 🖙) This 1872 former bank building with a cast-iron facade – a near-extinct architectural feature – is the top digs in Little Rock. There is a wonderful outdoor mezzanine for cocktails and a sense of suited, cigar-chomping posh throughout; if you want to feel like a wining, dining lobbyist, you've found your spot.

Mountain View ❷

✖ Tommy's Famous Pizza and BBQ — Pizza, Barbecue $

(📞870-269-3278; www.tommysfamous.com; cnr Carpenter & W Main Sts; pizza $7-26, mains $7-13; ⏰from 3pm) Tommy's Famous Pizza and BBQ is run by the friendliest bunch of backwoods hippies you could hope to meet. The BBQ pizza marries Tommy's stated specialties indulgently. The affable owner, a former rocker from Memphis, plays great music, has a fun vibe, and just two conditions: no attitude and no loud kids.

🛏 Wildflower B&B — B&B $

(📞870-269-4383; www.wildflowerbb.com; 100 Washington St; r $99-139; P ❄ 🖙) Set right on Court Square with a rocking-chair-equipped wraparound porch and cool folk art on the walls. Ask for the front room upstairs; it's flooded with afternoon light, and has a queen bed and joint sitting room with TV. Booking online is best.

Jasper ❸

✖ Arkansas House — Cafe $$$

(📞lodging 888-274-6873, restaurant 870-446-5900; www.thearkhouse.com; 215 E Court St, Jasper; mains $16-35; r/cabin from $70/$100; ⏰4-8pm Fri, from 11am Sat & Mon, 11am-5pm Sun; P 🖙 🛗) Specializes in artisanal meats, like organic beef, wild-caught razorback (pork), elk, buffalo and local trout, too. Its elk chili is popular, as is its crawfish étoufée. Also rents cozy, rustic rooms and cabins for those exploring the Buffalo National River.

Ponca & the Buffalo River ❹

🛏 RiverWind Lodge & Cabins — Cabin $$

(📞800-221-5514; www.buffaloriver.com; N 36°03'05.6" W 93°22'38.2", off Fire Tower Rd; cabins $129-359; 🛗 🐾) Choose from among 20 immaculate, well-appointed log cabins, built from local hardwoods, that sleep up to eight people comfortably (depending upon the cabin), and have outrageous mountain and valley views.

Eureka Springs ❻

✖ Mud Street Café — Cafe $$

(📞479-253-6732; www.mudstreetcafe.com; 22G S Main St; mains $9-13; ⏰8am-3pm Thu-Mon) You'll find simple, tasty options such as gourmet sandwiches, wraps and main-sized salads. The brilliant coffee drinks and breakfasts cultivate a devoted local following to this underground nook.

🛏 Treehouse Cottages — Cottage $$

(📞479-253-8667; www.treehousecottages.com; 165 W Van Buren St; cottages $149-169; P ❄ 🖙) Sprinkled amid 33 acres of pine forest, these cute, kitschy and spacious stilted wooden cottages are worth finding. There's lovely accent tile in the baths, a Jacuzzi tub overlooking the trees, a private balcony with grill at the ready, a flat-screen TV and fireplace. Two-night minimum stay.

STRETCH YOUR LEGS
NEW ORLEANS

Start/Finish St Augustine Church

Distance 2.2 miles

Duration Three hours

Few destinations have as many sensational ways to kill time as the Crescent City. Its history runs deep, the colonial architecture is exquisite, and there's mouthwatering Cajun and Creole food, historic dive bars, gorgeous countryside and lashings of great free live music.

Take this walk on Trips

St Augustine Church

We'll start in the Tremé, one of the country's oldest African American neighborhoods, at **St Augustine's Church** (☎504-525-5934; www.staugchurch.org; 1210 Governor Nicholls St; ◷ mass 10am Sun & 5pm Wed), home to one of the oldest black congregations in the US. Even if only appreciated from the outside, the church is a fascinating window into the African American experience in Louisiana, which stands out from the rest of the US due to the French-colonial connection.

The Walk » Proceed southeast along Governor Nicholls St then turn right onto Henriette Delille St.

Backstreet Cultural Museum

New Orleans is often described as both the least American city in the US and the northernmost city in the Caribbean. This is due to a unique colonial history that preserved the bonds between black New Orleanians and Africa and the greater black diaspora. Learn about this deep culture at the **Backstreet Cultural Museum** (☎504-522-4806; www.backstreetmuseum.org; 1116 Henriette Delille St; ◷10am-4pm Tue-Sat), a small but fascinating peek into the street-level music, ritual and communities that underlay the singular New Orleans experience.

The Walk » Get on Governor Nicholls St and continue walking southeast. Once you cross busy Rampart St, you've entered the French Quarter. Turn right onto Royal St, a pretty lane with cute art galleries, antique shops and wonderful architecture.

Historic New Orleans Collection

The **Historic New Orleans Collection** (THNOC; ☎504-523-4662; www.hnoc.org; 533 Royal St; admission free, tours $5; ◷9:30am-4:30pm Tue-Sat, 10:30am-4:30pm Sun, tours 10am, 11am, 2pm & 3pm Tue-Sat) is an interesting museum, spread over several exquisitely restored buildings and packed with thoughtfully curated exhibits. Rotating exhibitions are inevitably fascinating.

The Walk » Continue in the same, southerly direction on Royal St; at the 400 block, you'll pass the marbled magnificence of the Louisiana

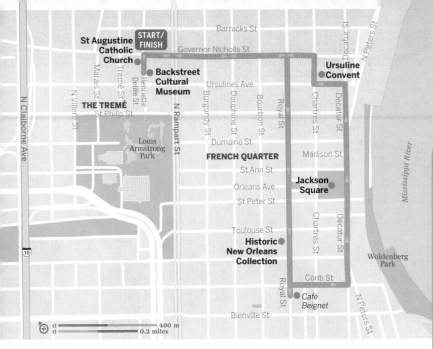

State Supreme Court. It's only about 500ft to the next stop.

Café Beignet

You've likely heard about the beignets (fried, sugar-covered donuts) at Café du Monde. They're good, but the place is horribly crowded. For the romantic experience of sipping coffee at a wrought-iron table while surrounded by lazy cats, head to **Café Beignet** (☎504-524-5530; www.cafebeignet.com; 334 Royal St; meals $6-8; ⏰7am-10pm). Watch pedestrians stroll by, and try a beignet; they're delicious.

The Walk » Turn around and turn right (east) on Conti St, follow it for two blocks, then turn left (north) on Decatur St. To your right, over the levee, is the Mississippi River. Walk north four blocks to get to Jackson Sq.

Jackson Square

Stroll over to **Jackson Square** (Decatur & St Peter Sts), the city green. Lovers lanes and trimmed hedges surround a monument to Andrew Jackson, the hero of the Battle of New Orleans and the seventh president of the USA. But the real stars are the magnificent, French-style St Louis Cathedral, flanked by the Cabildo and Presbytère. The former houses a Louisiana state-history museum; the latter a permanent exhibition on the Mardi Gras holiday.

The Walk » Continue north on Decatur St for three blocks, then turn left onto Ursulines Ave. After one block, turn right onto Chartres St (pronounced 'Charters') for the convent.

Ursuline Convent

In 1727, 12 Ursuline nuns arrived in New Orleans to care for the French garrison's 'miserable little hospital' and to educate the young girls of the colony. Between 1745 and 1752 the French colonial army built the **Ursuline Convent** (☎504-503-0361; www.stlouiscathedral.org; 1112 Chartres St; adult/student $8/6; ⏰10am-4pm Mon-Fri, 9am-3pm Sat), which is now the oldest structure in the Mississippi River Valley and the only remaining French building in the Quarter. Take in rotating exhibits and beautiful St Mary's chapel.

The Walk » Walk up Chartres St and turn left on Governor Nicholls St. From here it's a half-mile back to the Tremé and your starting point.

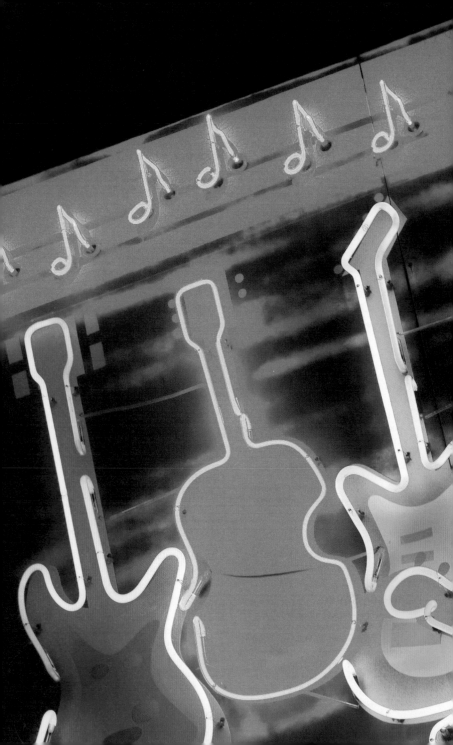

Tennessee & Kentucky

Bourbon and blues, bluegrass and honky-tonks, and some of the finest cities in America: welcome to an undercover wonderland. Tennessee has three distinct regions, represented by the three stars on the state flag. In the east you'll hike through the heather-colored Great Smokies. In the middle of the state you'll check out the glittering honky-tonks of Nashville, and in the Delta lowlands of the west, you'll dig barbecue and blues. Kentucky is stitched together with bluegrass pastures and jutting seams of limestone. Lonely two-lane roads link distilleries on the Bourbon Trail and skirt the breeding grounds of million-dollar thoroughbreds in the countryside surrounding Lexington and Louisville – homes to one of America's best parties.

Memphis Neon-lit signs line Beale St, home of blues music
TETRA IMAGES / GETTY IMAGES ©

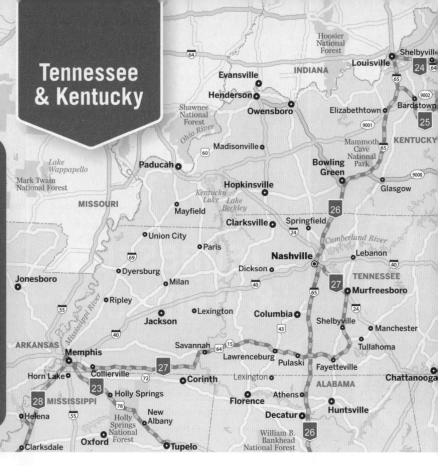

Tennessee & Kentucky

 Elvis Presley Memorial Highway 3 Days
Rejoice in the King, from humble Tupelo to glittering Graceland. (p269)

Kentucky Bluegrass & Horse Country 4 Days
Watch throroughbreds gallop at sunrise on this picturesque journey through Kentucky bluegrass. (p277)

The Bourbon Trail 3 Days
Taste and tour your way through America's finest whiskey distilleries. (p287)

 Tailgate Tour 6 Days
A wild ramble linking iconic sports venues and the parties they inspire. (p295)

Memphis to Nashville 3 Days
From Soulsville juke joints to beer-soaked honky-tonks, music reigns supreme. (p305)

Big Muddy 5 Days
Follow the mighty Mississippi River from Memphis to the river mouth. (p315)

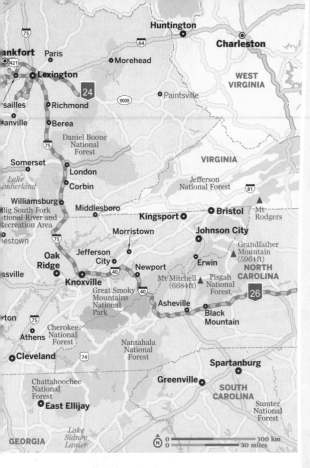

DON'T MISS

Graceland

If you make one stop in Memphis, it ought to be the sublimely kitschy, gloriously bizarre home of the king of rock and roll. Visit it on Trips 23 27

Churchill Downs

On the first Saturday in May, upper-crust America puts on its pinstripe suits and flamboyant hats for the Kentucky Derby. Join them on Trips 24 26

Woodford Reserve

A gorgeous setting, an artful distillery and some fine bourbon are waiting at this historic site. See and taste it on Trips 24 25

Stax Museum of American Soul Music

The legendary Stax recording studio is now a museum documenting the rise of 1960s soul music. Explore it on Trips 19 27

Sun Studio

Tours of this recording studio explain how Jerry Lee Lewis, Johnny Cash, Roy Orbison and Elvis became stars. Take the tour on Trips 19 23 27 28

Churchill Downs The famous Kentucky Derby horse race

Elvis Presley Memorial Highway

Trace the journey of a king from his humble Tupelo origins to his nouveau riche castle in the Memphis suburbs. Along the way drive the 109-mile Elvis Presley Memorial Hwy.

23

TRIP HIGHLIGHTS

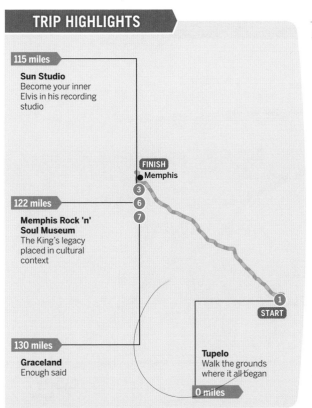

115 miles

Sun Studio
Become your inner Elvis in his recording studio

FINISH
● Memphis

122 miles

Memphis Rock 'n' Soul Museum
The King's legacy placed in cultural context

130 miles

Graceland
Enough said

Tupelo
Walk the grounds where it all began

START

0 miles

3 DAYS
130 MILES / 209KM

GREAT FOR...

BEST TIME TO GO
Thanks to its mild, hospitable climes, spring is king in Graceland.

ESSENTIAL PHOTO
There are any number of photo ops at Graceland, from the shag-carpeted Jungle living room to Elvis' hall of gold records.

BEST FOR MUSIC
We're talking about Elvis, baby!

23 Elvis Presley Memorial Highway

When Elvis wiggled his hips, women fainted, preachers raged about damnation and hellfire, and the National Guard stormed in to keep the peace. But before all that, he was just another working-class kid from Tupelo. When his family moved to Memphis, the seed of a dream blew into the fertile soil of a musical mind. And a king bloomed.

TRIP HIGHLIGHT

1 Tupelo

Two hours southeast of Memphis in Tupelo, MS, is **Elvis Presley's Birthplace** (☎662-841-1245; www.elvispresleybirthplace. com; 306 Elvis Presley Dr; adult/senior/child $17/14/8, house only adult/child $8/5; ⏱9am-5pm Mon-Sat, 1-5pm Sun; P). His 18-year-old father, Vernon, built the two-room shotgun shack just before his son was born. Elvis was actually a twin, but his brother was stillborn just a half hour before Elvis arrived

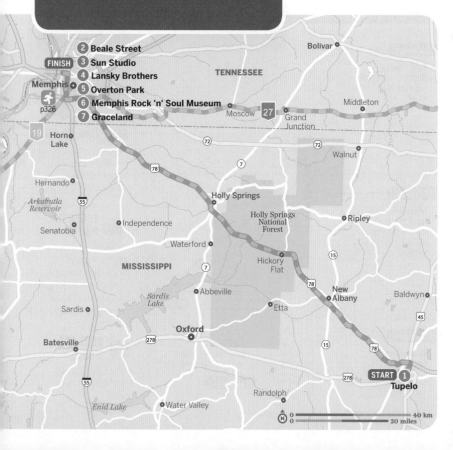

2 Beale Street
FINISH 3 Sun Studio
4 Lansky Brothers
5 Overton Park
6 Memphis Rock 'n' Soul Museum
7 Graceland

Memphis
p326

19 Horn Lake

Hernando

Arkabutla Reservoir 55

Senatobia

Independence

Sardis

Batesville

55

Enid Lake

TENNESSEE

Bolivar

Middleton

Moscow 27 Grand Junction

72

72

Walnut

7

78

Holly Springs

Holly Springs National Forest

Ripley

Waterford

7

Hickory Flat

15

Abbeville

Sardis Lake

Etta

78

New Albany

Baldwyn

45

Oxford

278

15

78

278

Water Valley

Randolph

START 1
Tupelo

MISSISSIPPI

N 0 —— 40 km
0 —— 20 miles

on January 8. The family was soon on government assistance and money was scarce. When Elvis was three, his father was jailed for eight months and the family lost their home. Elvis and his mother, Gladys – 22 when she gave birth to her son – attended the Assembly of God church in Tupelo, and Elvis often hopped off mama's lap and ran to the pulpit when the choir was rocking, letting the music flow through him. You can visit his childhood church on a tour of his birthplace site, which includes a dated section of downtown Tupelo known as the Walk of Life. It includes a mock-up of the hardware store where he got his first guitar.

LINK YOUR TRIP

27 Memphis to Nashville

Now that you're steeped in Elvis lore, and in touch with the bluesy, soulful roots that made him king, head east to Tennessee's other music mecca and feel its country twang.

19 The Blues Highway

Trace Elvis' musical roots back into the funky soil of the Mississippi Delta.

The Drive » Hwy 78, aka the Elvis Presley Memorial Hwy, bisects the Holly Springs National Forest and Wall Doxey State Park as it rambles into Memphis in just under two hours.

---

❷ Beale Street

With a gospel base rooted in the fertile ground of his mind, Elvis Aaron Presley and his family moved to Memphis, this sultry, gritty city on the banks of the Mississippi River, when he was 13 years old, and a whole new world opened. The hallelujahs of Pentecostal Holiness choirs blended with the rhythms of the blues singers in the Beale St clubs, sounds that would later inform his genre-bending rock and roll.

Beale St began to form into the walking street filled with nightclubs and good times in the 1890s. WC Handy penned 'Beale Street Blues' in 1916, and from the 1920s to the 1940s greats like Muddy Waters, Memphis Minnie and BB King honed their craft here. Elvis did the same. Today it's less hip and more kitsch, but **BB King's** (📞901-524-5464; www.bbkingclubs.com; 143 Beale St; ⏰11am-11:30pm Mon-Thu, noon-2am Fri, 11am-midnight Sat, 11am-11pm Sun), the guitar great's first-ever blues club, remains a Beale St staple. **Rum Boogie** (www.rumboogie.com; 182 Beale St; ⏰11am-1am) is

also good for live music nightly, and **WC Handy's home** (www.wchandymem phis.org; 352 Beale St; adult/child $6/4; ⏰11am-4pm Tue-Sat winter, 10am-5pm summer) is a museum.

🍴 🛏 p275, p312

The Drive » Once you've been bitten by the Beale St bug (theoretically), make like Elvis and walk for a mile down Beale to Myrtle. Make a left and you'll find Sun Studio.

TRIP HIGHLIGHT

❸ Sun Studio

Welcome to rock-and-roll ground zero. An 18-year-old Elvis reportedly walked into **Sun Studio** (📞800-441-6249; www.sunstudio.com; 706 Union Ave; adult/child $12/free; ⏰10am-6:15pm) and, when asked what famous musician he most sounded like, replied (cue warbling accent) 'I don't sound like nobody.' The best part of the fact-filled tour is the old studio itself, where you can pose for pictures on an 'X' marking the spot where Elvis stood while recording his breakout single, 'That's All Right.'

Starting in the early 1950s, Sun's Sam Phillips also recorded blues artists such as Howlin' Wolf, BB King and Ike Turner, followed by the rockabilly dynasty of Jerry Lee Lewis, Johnny Cash and Roy Orbison. Forty-minute guided tours through the tiny

studio offer a chance to hear original tapes of historic recording sessions. Guides are witty and full of anecdotes; many are musicians themselves. Don't leave without picking up a CD of the 'Million Dollar Quartet,' Sun's spontaneous 1956 jam session between Elvis, Johnny Cash, Carl Perkins and Jerry Lee Lewis.

The Drive » It's less than a mile down Union from Sun Studio to Memphis' long-running fashion depot.

- - - - - - - - - - - - - - - -

④ Lansky Brothers

The posh **Lansky Brothers** (☎901-425-3960; www. lanskybros.com; 126 Beale St; ⏱11am-7pm Sun-Wed, to 9pm Thu-Sat) department store once supplied Elvis with his hi-boy collar shirts and gold lamé suits. After years of admiring their threads from afar, Elvis began to rock them in his senior year in high school, before he could afford them. By then he had already grown out his sideburns and coated and combed his hair in Vaseline. These days, you can buy your own pink-and-black-striped 'speed-way' shirt, sequined button-up, or Humes High School (Elvis' alma mater) tee.

The Drive » From here, jog over to Poplar Ave, and take it for 3 miles through Midtown and into Memphis' signature green space.

- - - - - - - - - - - - - - - -

⑤ Overton Park

After recording with Sam Phillips, Elvis and his trio performed live for the first time at the Bon Air Club on July 17, 1954. At the end of the month he booked his first stage show at **Overton Park** on Poplar Ave in leafy Midtown. It is said that the large crowd made him so nervous that his normal rhythmic stage movements became even more exaggerated. His legs and hips quaked and the women in the audience began shrieking with delight. In recent years the band shell decayed and was narrowly saved from demolition. It reopened as **Levitt Shell** (www.levittshell.org; 1928 Poplar Ave) in 2008, with a full concert schedule.

Graceland Vintage car at Presley Motors, Elvis Presley's automobile collection

🍴 p275

The Drive » Double back to Beale St down Poplar Ave, to a museum which places Elvis' career in cultural context.

- - - - - - - - - - - - - - -

TRIP HIGHLIGHT

⑥ Memphis Rock 'n' Soul Museum

Elvis didn't just drive the ladies wild, he also helped invent youth culture as we know it. That's certainly the position of the **Memphis Rock 'n' Soul Museum** (www.memphisrocknsoul. org; 191 Beale St; adult/child $12/9; ☺10am-7pm), part of downtown's massive **FedEx Forum** (🎵box office 901-205-2640; www. fedexforum.com; 191 Beale St, Beale Street Entertainment District). It also further explains how gospel and the blues fed rock and roll and soul music. You'll hear the low lonely howls of sweet Delta blues-men, and the skit-skat of early rock and roll on the song-packed audio tour. Don't miss its new sister museum nearby, either, the **Memphis Music Hall of Fame** (www. memphismusichalloffame.com; 126 S 2nd St; adult/child 8/6; ☺10am-7pm).

THE KING IS DEAD, LONG LIVE THE KING

Elvis died at home, facedown in the bathroom, on August 16, 1977, felled by heart failure likely brought on by chronic prescription drug abuse. He was 42. He's buried behind the house, with his parents and grandmother in the Meditation Gardens, next to the kidney-bean-shaped pool.

His passing and his life are celebrated across Memphis during **Elvis Week** (☏901-332-3322; www.elvisweek.com; Elvis Presley Blvd, Graceland) in mid-August, when tens of thousands of shiny-eyed pilgrims descend for seven days of festivities. *This is Weird America.* Attend a *Viva Las Vegas* or *Aloha From Hawaii* screening and dance party, an International Elvis Tribute Artist competition, and run an Elvis 5K – sideburns not included. The signature event, held on August 15, is a spooky, solemn candlelight march to his grave.

The Drive » If you opt not to hop the free shuttle between this museum, Sun Studio and Graceland, make your way to I-69 south and exit on Elvis Presley Blvd. You're going to Graceland, Graceland in Memphis, Tennessee!

TRIP HIGHLIGHT

❼ Graceland

The white-columned Colonial-style mansion that is **Graceland** (☏901-332-3322; www.graceland.com; Elvis Presley Blvd/US 51; adult/child 7-12yr house only $38.75/17, with airplanes $43.75/22, with Elvis Presley's Memphis $57.50/27, expanded tours from $62.50/32; ☉9am-5pm Mon-Sat, to 4pm Sun, shorter hours & closed Tue Dec; ℗) is smaller than one might have imagined and sees 600,000 visitors a year. A then-22-year-old Elvis bought it for about $100,000 in 1957, the year after his self-titled debut record was released by RCA.

Press play on the free audio tour and enter a shrine to both Elvis and his ostentatious 1970s style. Highlights include a wood-panelled kitchen where housekeepers once fixed vats of banana pudding; a stairwell covered entirely – ceiling included – in pea-green shag carpet; the tiki-styled Jungle Room, with its faux waterfall and leopard-print furniture. Out back, you'll find the movie-memorabilia-filled Trophy Room, the racquetball court and Elvis' old office. After touring the mansion, you can tack on Elvis' private planes; as well as all the new museums that make up Graceland's revamped visitor experience, **Elvis Presley's Memphis** (www.graceland.com; 3765 Elvis Presley Blvd; adult/child 7-12yr $28.75/$25.90; ☉9am-5pm Mon-Sat, to 4pm Sun, shorter hours & closed Tue Dec), including Elvis' automobile collection (**Presley Motors**), a spectacular jumpsuit collection (**Elvis Fashion King Exhibit**), and all of the King's gold and platinum records (**Elvis: The Entertainer Museum**).

Despite never learning to read music Elvis made 149 top-100 records, and had 90 albums in the top 100. He sold more than a billion records overall, and produced each one himself.

🛏 p275

Eating & Sleeping

Beale Street ②

✗ Arcade — Diner $

(www.arcaderestaurant.com; 540 S Main St; mains $7-10; ⊙7am-3pm Sun-Wed, to 11pm Thu-Sat)
Step inside this ultra-retro diner, Memphis' oldest, and wander to the Elvis booth, strategically located near the rear exit. The King used to sit here and eat griddle-fried peanut butter and banana sandwiches and would bolt out the door if fan-instigated pandemonium ensued. Crowds still pack in for sublime sweet-potato pancakes – as fluffy, buttery and addictive as advertised.

✗ Cozy Corner — Barbecue $

(www.cozycornerbbq.com; 735 N Pkwy; plates $6-14; ⊙11am-9pm Tue-Sat) Slouch in a torn vinyl booth and devour an entire barbecued Cornish game hen ($11.75), the house specialty at this recently renovated cult favorite. Ribs and wings are spectacular too, and the fluffy, silken sweet-potato pie is an A-plus specimen of the classic Southern dessert.

⌆ Peabody Hotel — Hotel $$

(☎901-529-4000; www.peabodymemphis.com; 149 Union Ave; r from $229-365; ❋🗖🕸🐾) Memphis' most storied hotel has been catering to a Who's Who of Southern gentry since the 1860s. The current incarnation, a 13-story Italian Renaissance Revival–style building, dates to the 1920s and remains a social center, with a spa, shops, restaurants, an atmospheric lobby bar and 464 guestrooms in soothing turquoise tones.

⌆ Lauderdale Courts — Inn $$$

(☎901-523-8662; www.uptownsquareapts. com; 252 N Lauderdale St; Elvis ste $250, tour $10; P❋) Sleep in the Elvis Suite, part of a Depression-era public housing complex where the Presley family lived at No 328 from 1949 through 1953 (today, it's known as Uptown Square apartments).

Overton Park ⑤

✗ Bar DKDC — International $

(www.bardkdc.com; 964 S Cooper St; dishes $6-12; ⊙5pm-3am) Cheap and flavorful and – at times global – street food is the calling at this ever-evolving Cooper-Young staple. The menu includes muffalatas, Vietnamese *banh-mi* sandwiches, Thai chicken dumplings and so on. The space sports an eclectic decor, chalkboard wine and beer list, and friendly bartenders.

✗ Beauty Shop — Fusion $$

(☎901-272-7111; www.thebeautyshoprestaurant. com; 966 S Cooper St; dinner mains $24-27, brunch mains $10-17; ⊙11am-2pm & 5-10pm Mon-Thu, 11am-2pm & 5-11pm Fri & Sat, 10am-3pm Sun) All the many strands that make a contemporary restaurant appealing are here. There's a sleek design, excellent lighting and soundtrack, and a creative menu. We love the Thai steak or the grilled pear salad to start. Mains include chipotle lamb chops, and crispy Peking duck served with muddled blackberries and cinnamon star anise dust. The Sunday brunch is a madhouse: 15 or so egg variations prepared with international flair draws hip and hot Memphis in droves. Reserve ahead; it books up weeks – not days – in advance.

Graceland ⑦

⌆ Graceland RV Park & Campground — Campground $

(☎901-396-7125; www.graceland.com; 3691 Elvis Presley Blvd; tent sites/cabins from $25/47; P🗖🕸) Keep Lisa Marie in business when you camp out or sleep in the no-frills log cabins (with shared bathrooms) next to Graceland.

Kentucky Bluegrass & Horse Country

Drive the scenic byways from Louisville to Lexington and beyond, stopping to tour storybook country estates, ride horses through the poplar forests and sip the region's famous bourbon.

24

TRIP HIGHLIGHTS

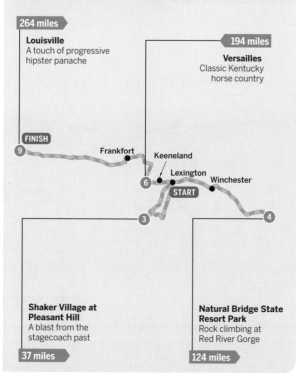

264 miles

Louisville
A touch of progressive hipster panache

FINISH
9

Frankfort

Keeneland

6

Lexington

START

Winchester

3

4

194 miles

Versailles
Classic Kentucky horse country

Shaker Village at Pleasant Hill
A blast from the stagecoach past

37 miles

Natural Bridge State Resort Park
Rock climbing at Red River Gorge

124 miles

4 DAYS
264 MILES / 425KM

GREAT FOR...

BEST TIME TO GO
Spring is when the horses run and summer is when the bluegrass pastures are lush.

ESSENTIAL PHOTO
Churchill Downs, home of the Kentucky Derby.

BEST FOR OUTDOOR ACTIVITIES
Driving country roads and backcountry trails, and the sound of horses pounding the turf.

Louisville Spectacular fall foliage

277

24

Kentucky Bluegrass & Horse Country

This trip leads from the cradle, or stud ranches, surrounding Lexington, to the ultimate winners' circle at Churchill Downs in Louisville. The secret to the state's unparalleled success in breeding and training champions is found underground, in Kentucky's rich limestone deposits.The limestone not only filters water, its natural fertilizers feed the lush meadows that in turn nourish grazing thoroughbreds.

---

① Lexington

Lexington was once known as the 'Athens of the West' for its architecture and culture, and remains a mecca for thoroughbred racing fans. The 1200-acre **Kentucky Horse Park** (www.kyhorsepark.com; 4089 Iron Works Pkwy; adult/child summer $20/10, winter $12/6, horseback riding Mar-Oct $25; ⊙9am-5pm mid-Mar–mid-Nov, 9am-5pm Wed-Sun mid-Nov–mid-Mar; 🚶), on its outskirts, has a daily Parade of Breeds; its **Museum of the Horse** has life-sized displays on horses through history, and you can saddle up on a guided trail ride here, too.

To tour a working stable and training facility, visit the **Thoroughbred Center** (📞859-293-1853; www.thethoroughbredcenter. com; 3380 Paris Pike; adult/child $15/8; ⏱tours 9am Mon-Sat Apr-Oct, Mon-Fri 9am Nov-Mar), where visitors get to see a day in the life of Derby hopefuls, from morning workouts to cool-down currying. In the evening, put your money down on an old-school harness race at the famed **Red Mile** (www. redmileky.com; 1200 Red Mile Rd; $2; ⏱races Jul 27-Oct 8). Fans have been cheering from the grandstands at this red dirt track since 1875. Live races are only held from the end of July to October, but simulcasts and off-track betting are offered year-round.

🍴 🛏 p284

LINK YOUR TRIP

26 **Tailgate Tour**
Take in some of America's most mythic speedways, football fields and basketball gyms, and the nearby bars that fuel the local face-painted fanatics.

25 **The Bourbon Trail**
Interspersed between pasture and race tracks are Kentucky's fine distilleries where America's tastiest hooch is crafted.

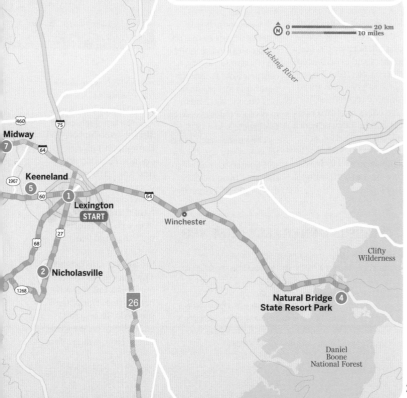

Licking River

0 — 20 km
0 — 10 miles

460 75
Midway
7 64

1967 **Keeneland**
5 60 1 64
Lexington
START Winchester
68 27

Clifty Wilderness

2 **Nicholasville**
1268

26
Natural Bridge 4
State Resort Park

Daniel Boone National Forest

The Drive » It's a straight 18 miles from Lexington on Hwy 27, past the suburban corporate bloom, south to the farming town of Nicholasville.

---

❷ Nicholasville

Strictly speaking, the area surrounding Lexington is what's known as the Inner Bluegrass (or Horse Country), and it has been a center of horse breeding for three centuries. Set on a dead-end road among wooden houses, broken-down barns and stunning pastures stitched with corral fencing, **Sunburst Horsemanship Center** (☎859-224-8480; www.sun bursthorsemanshipschool.com; 1129 Durham Lane; intro lessons $60; 🐎) isn't a stud farm, but a horse-riding school that offers clinics to beginners and experienced riders alike, from basic horse safety to advanced jumping techniques. It also offers fun intro rides to visiting tourists, which include instruction on how to brush and saddle a horse, as well as how to walk and trot, canter and lope.

The Drive » To take KY 1268 to the Hwy 68 west into Harrodsburg is to enjoy the finest scenery in the state. This narrow two-lane road bisects vast pastures, skirts sycamore trees and wraps around hairpin bends that overlook cascading streams. At times the land cleaves and the green Kentucky River snakes along great limestone bluffs known as the Palisades.

TRIP HIGHLIGHT

❸ Shaker Village at Pleasant Hill

As you close in on the **Shaker Village at Pleasant Hill** (www.shakervillage ky.org; 3501 Lexington Rd; adult/child $10/5, riverboat rides $10/5; ⏲10am-5pm Tue-Thu & Sun, to 8pm Fri & Sat) the countryside fencing begins to morph from corral to the stone pile flagstone variety, a centuries-old technique that hints at the age of this bucolic settlement, part of an old stagecoach mail route since 1839.

The village itself offers tours but you can take a self-guided tour among the dwellings. In the early 1800s these softly

EHRLIF / SHUTTERSTOCK ©

rolling hills were home to a communal society of 500 peace-loving men and women. Though the Shakers worshipped God through uninhibited ecstatic dancing, they practiced strict celibacy (probably why there aren't any left). See their remarkable artisanship in dozens of restored buildings and learn about their history at the **Shaker Life Exhibit**. The Shaker Village Inn operates a lovely 3-mile paddle-boat ride aboard the **Dixie Belle** (adult/ child $10/5) on the Kentucky River, which offers

---

GRASS IS GENERALLY GREENER

Kentucky's Bluegrass Region encompasses the north-central part of the state, including the cities of Lexington, Frankfort and Louisville, and is home to half the state's population. Yet, despite the name, the grass is not actually blue. *Poa pratensis* (Kentucky Bluegrass) gets its name from the bluish-purple buds it sprouts in early summer, which, from a distance, can give the fields a slightly sapphire cast.

Lexington Sculptures by Gwen Reardon in Thoroughbred Park

incredible views of the stunning Palisades.

🛏 p284

The Drive » The longest drive of the journey takes you back to Lexington on Hwy 68 to I-64 east. At Winchester veer onto KY 9000 east into the limestone-studded Natural Bridge State Resort Park.

TRIP HIGHLIGHT

④ Natural Bridge State Resort Park

Eastern Kentucky's Red River Gorge is abundant with jutting limestone bluffs offering some of America's best rock climbing. **Natural Bridge State Resort Park** (☎606-663-2214; www.parks. ky.gov; 2135 Natural Bridge Rd, Slade; P ♿) is the most accessible of the climbing hot spots in this region, thanks to its abundance of campsites and legendary climbing shop–pizza joint. In fact, your first stop should be Miguel's Pizza (p284), where you'll pick up climbing tips and find out which routes may be closed. The Natural Bridge region offers 20 different climbing routes ranging in difficulty from 5.9 to 5.13b. Red River Climb ing (www.redriverclimb ing.com) is the area's best online resource for trail and route information. There are also 12 hiking and biking trails in the park, though most are rather short. The second-longest option, the **Hoods Branch Trail**, runs for 3.75 miles along the base of the limestone cliffs. At 7.5 miles, the **Sand Gap Trail** is the longest, and runs along an old logging road. It takes four to six hours to complete.

🍴 🛏 p284

The Drive » Double back to Lexington, head west on Versailles Rd to Keeneland.

⑤ Keeneland

Second only to Churchill Downs in terms of race competition, **Keeneland** (☎859-254-3412; www.keeneland.com; 4201 Versailles Rd; general admission $5; ⊙races Apr & Oct) hosts two racing seasons. The first, in April, is a prelude to the Kentucky Derby, and there's another season in October, as well as at least two mega horse auctions that attract big-money buyers from around the world. The gorgeous stone grandstand, and thick bluegrass turf on the infield, steeps the place in history. Show up early on race day and you may see the horses work out from 6am to 10am for free. Every Saturday during race season, Keeneland offers a Sunrise Trackside tour that begins with a full breakfast at 7am and includes a two-hour tour of the facility.

The Drive » From Keeneland take Hwy 60/Versailles Rd then KY 1967 through the rolling pastureland and past corrals full of horses.

TRIP HIGHLIGHT

⑥ Versailles

The landscape around the quaint, historic town of Versailles (pronounced Vur-sails) is simply stunning horse country. Think: rolling pastures, stone pile and corral fencing, and gorgeous stallions and steeds basking in pre-eminent stud-ranch country. One zip through the Versailles area may be enough to make you jealous of said horses put out to stud, if not their stable mates (and there are plenty of them). Among the thoroughbred ranches you'll find here, **WinStar Farm** (☎859-297-1328; www.winstarfarm.com; 3001 Pisgah Pike; adult/child $20/11; ⊙tours 1pm Mon, Wed & Fri) is arguably the most accomplished. Family-owned since the 1700s, this 1864-acre ranch has born, broken and trained numerous champions. Free 30-minute tours of the Stallion Complex are available on Monday, Wednesday and Friday afternoons and require a reservation at least one day in advance. And if you took a beating at Keeneland or Red Mile, drown your sorrows with a taste of **Woodford Reserve** (☎859-879-1812; www.woodfordreserve.com; 7855 McCracken Pike, Versailles; tours $14-30; ⊙shop 9am-5pm Mon-Sat, noon-4pm Sun, tours 10am-3pm Mon-Sat, 1-3pm Sun, closed Jan-Feb). Its magnificent distillery can be found among these pastures and streams, and is worth visiting.

The Drive » The countryside stays verdant and luscious as you roll west on the two lane KY 1681 to Hwy 62 west to Midway.

⑦ Midway

Diminutive Midway is the state's first railroad town and home to Kentucky's only all-female college, Midway College. It's darling and historic, with railroad tracks running down the middle of a restored Main St (just one long block), freckled mostly with antique galleries. Age-old wood, brick and stone homes dot the undulating streets on both sides of a town that makes a worthy diversion, and with its surprisingly tempting and cheerful kitchens, it is a terrific place for lunch or dinner.

⌂ p284

The Drive » Take the Hwy 62 east to Leestown Rd, hang a right on KY 1685 and a left on Hwy 460, all of which are thin, two-lane strips through rolling countryside that lead to Frankfort.

⑧ Frankfort

About an hour east of Louisville is Kentucky's tiny capital, Frankfort. The **Thomas D Clark Center for Kentucky History** (Kentucky Historical Society; www.history.ky.gov; 100 W Broadway St; adult/child $8/6; ⊙10am-5pm Tue-Sat) is a museum and research facility with over 3000 artifacts on display, tracing the state's story from pre-historic settlements to the emergence of Muhammad Ali. Architecture buffs will want to tour the **Old State Capitol** (☎502-564-1792, ext 4424; www.history.ky.gov; 300 W Broadway; adult/child $8/6; ⊙tours 10:30am, noon, 1:30pm & 3pm Sat, groups

DECADENT & DEPRAVED

Muhammad Ali may be Louisville's favorite son, and for good reason, but Hunter S Thompson – while certainly an acquired taste – is no slouch. After bouncing around newspapers in the 1960s, the Good Doctor discovered his way-out voice with an essay for the obscure literary journal *Scanlan's Monthly* in June 1970, titled 'The Kentucky Derby Is Decadent & Depraved.' Widely considered his first Gonzo journalism piece, the possibly insane, certainly drunken (or worse) writer became central to the tale. The essay follows his misadventures in and around his native Louisville during Derby weekend, and in the throes of what he later confessed to be the darkest days of his life. In fact, he thought his career was over, though it would soon launch. British illustrator (his would-be long-time collaborator) Ralph Steadman was along for a ride that included the hijacking of press passes, the spraying of mace, the hoodwinking of rubes, and the discovery of a darkness lurking deep inside. It's hilarious, of course, and a must-read.

of 10 or more by appt only Tue-Fri), which looks positively quaint, though it was the seat of power from 1830 to 1910. Learn more about how America's many wars affected or involved Kentucky at the **Kentucky Military History Museum** (☎502-564-1792, ext 4424; www.history.ky.gov; 125 E Main St; adult/child $8/6; ⏱10am-5pm Tue-Sat, off-season by appt only), housed in the former State Arsenal, built in 1850. And you can visit Daniel Boone's grave in the **Frankfort Cemetery** (E Main St; ⏱7:30am-7:30pm, to 5:30pm Nov-Mar).

The Drive ≫ Take the slow road, Hwy 60, through the Arcadian countryside and the town of Shelbyville, where you'll pick up KY 1848 for your last agrarian vistas. Head south on I-264 to I-64 west into Louisville.

- - - - - - - - - - - - - - - - - -

TRIP HIGHLIGHT

9 Louisville

Louisville is Kentucky's most engaging and progressive town. The

number of incredible kitchens multiplies every year, especially in the engaging NuLu area, where there are numerous galleries and boutiques to explore. Check them out on the **First Friday Trolley Hop** (www.firstfridayhop.com; Main & Market Sts; ⏱5-11pm, 1st Fri of month). Downtown parallels the Ohio River, and is a wonderful stroll for fans of sports and culture alike. The **Muhammad Ali Center** (www.alicenter.org; 144 N 6th St; adult/senior/child $12/11/7; ⏱9:30am-5pm Tue-Sat, noon-5pm Sun) is a revelation; *Confidence* is an incisive exhibit about how Ali's swaggering bravado signified a true self-love.

Louisville is also, of course, the crown jewel of horse racing. The Run for the Roses, as the Kentucky Derby is known, is the longest-running sporting event in America, and has happened at **Churchill Downs** (☎502-636-4400;

www.churchilldowns.com; 700 Central Ave) on the first Saturday in May for the past 138 years. Though most seats are reserved years in advance, if you're around on Derby Day you can pay $50 to get into the overflowing Paddock area. Nobody gets turned away! Though don't expect to see much of the race. You will see plenty of big hats, seersucker suits and perhaps the wildest party in America. Churchill Downs is worth a visit at any time of year, whether you're interested in its history – on display at the **Kentucky Derby Museum** (www.derbymuseum.org; Gate 1, Central Ave; adult/senior/child $15/14/8; ⏱8am-5pm Mon-Sat, 11am-5pm Sun mid-Mar–Nov, from 9am Mon-Sat, 11am-5pm Sun Dec–mid-Mar) – or you wish to glimpse training rides, warm-up races and simulcasts, available from April to November.

✕ 🛏 p284, p293

Eating & Sleeping

Lexington ❶

✕ Village Idiot   Modern American $$

(📞859-252-0099; www.lexingtonvillageidiot.com; 307 West Short St; dishes $12-24; ⏱5-10pm Sun-Thu, to 11pm Fri & Sat, 10am-2pm Sat & Sun) Hip young foodies descend for dishes comfy and familiar, but with a twist. Think: duck confit and waffles, pulled pork mac 'n' cheese, or fried chicken eggs Benedict. It has a decent bourbon selection too.

🛏 Gratz Park Inn   Hotel $$

(📞859-231-1777; www.gratzparkinn.com; 120 W 2nd St; r from $179; 🅿 ❄ @ 📶) Once a spot to draw the brocade curtains and fall asleep on a 19th-century poster bed, this staple of Lexington's historic district has revamped its rooms, leaving just a few antique four-poster beds for guests. The revamped rooms maintain a classic style save the bathrooms, where modern subway-tiled showers have an edgier, industrial feel.

Shaker Village at Pleasant Hill ❸

🛏 Shaker Village Inn   Inn $$

(📞859-734-5611; www.shakervillageky.org; 3501 Lexington Rd; r $110-300; 🅿 📶) The main building is set in the village's old trustee office, with its elaborate double helix stairwell. Rooms are large, lovely and full of light and with high ceilings, wood furnishings and two rockers to read/snooze in. Rooms in 13 other buildings follow suit.

Natural Bridge State Resort Park ❹

✕ Miguel's Pizza   Pizza $

(📞606-663-1975; www.miguelspizza.com; 1890 Natural Bridge Rd, Slade; pizza from $10; ⏱7am-9:45pm, closed Dec-Feb; 📶) Nosh on great little cheap pizzas, and climbers and hikers (only) can also pay $3 to camp out for the night. There is also a nicer lodge with rooms from $39.

🛏 Hemlock Lodge   Lodge $

(📞606-663-2214; www.parks.ky.gov; Hemlock Lodge Rd, Slade; r from $85, cottages from $117) The choice sleep in the Red River Gorge area. Here are 35 simple yet comfortable rooms in a mountain lodge with private balconies overlooking the pool and surrounding beauty. Cottages are nestled in the forest and have full kitchens. Rooms offer daily maid service. Not so for cottages.

Midway ❼

✕ Holly Hill Inn   Southern US $$$

(📞859-846-4732; www.hollyhillinn.com; 426 N Winter St; 3-course brunch & lunch/dinner menu $22/45; ⏱5:30-10pm Thu-Sat, 11am-2pm Sun year-round, plus 11am-2pm Fri & Sat spring & summer; 📶) This winsome 1845 Greek Revival estate, nestled beneath the oaks, houses one of the best restaurants in Kentucky. The married chef-owners serve a simple but elegant multicourse brunch or dinner of wholesome soups, handmade pastas, locally raised meats and farmstead cheeses.

Louisville ❾

✕ Garage Bar   Pub Food $$

(www.garageonmarket.com; 700 E Market St; dishes $9-18; ⏱5-10pm Mon-Thu, 11am-10pm Fri-Sun; 📶) The best thing to do on a warm afternoon in Louisville is to make your way to this uber-hip converted NuLu service station (accented by two kissing Camaros) and order a round of basil gimlets and the ham platter (a tasting of four regionally cured hams, served with fresh bread and preserves; $26). Then move onto the menu that concentrates on the best brick-oven pizza in town.

🛏 21c Museum Hotel — Hotel $$$

(📞502-217-6300; www.21chotel.com; 700 W Main St; r from $199; P ❄ 📶) This contemporary art museum-cum-hotel features edgy design details: video screens project your distorted image and falling words on the wall as you wait for the elevator; water-blurred, see-through glass urinal walls line the men's rooms. Rooms, though not as interesting as the five contemporary art-gallery common areas, have iPod docks and mint julep kits.

🛏 Brown Hotel — Hotel $$$

(📞502-583-1234; www.brownhotel.com; 335 West Broadway; r $200-600; P ❄ 📶) Opera stars, queens and prime ministers have trod the marble floors of this storied downtown hotel, now restored to all its 1920s glamor with 294 comfy rooms and an impressive lobby bourbon bar under original English Renaissance gilded ceilings. In 1926, Louisville's signature dish, the Hot Brown (open-faced turkey sandwich with turkey, bacon, pimentos and Mornay sauce) was invented here and is still served (from $17).

The Bourbon Trail

25

Bourbons can be fiery, stern or honey droplets of heart-opening heat. They say there's a bourbon for everyone. Visit the distilleries and taverns of Bluegrass Country, and discover yours.

TRIP HIGHLIGHTS

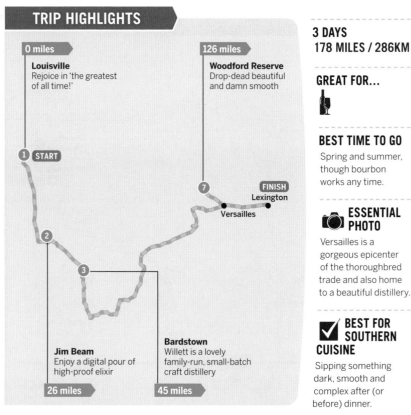

0 miles

Louisville
Rejoice in 'the greatest of all time!'

126 miles

Woodford Reserve
Drop-dead beautiful and damn smooth

1 START

7

FINISH
Lexington

Versailles

2

3

Jim Beam
Enjoy a digital pour of high-proof elixir

26 miles

Bardstown
Willett is a lovely family-run, small-batch craft distillery

45 miles

**3 DAYS
178 MILES / 286KM**

GREAT FOR...

BEST TIME TO GO

Spring and summer, though bourbon works any time.

ESSENTIAL PHOTO

Versailles is a gorgeous epicenter of the thoroughbred trade and also home to a beautiful distillery.

☑ **BEST FOR SOUTHERN CUISINE**

Sipping something dark, smooth and complex after (or before) dinner.

Woodford Reserve The distillery's bourbon is aged in wooden barrels

287

25 The Bourbon Trail

A golden inch of bourbon, silky and mellow with notes of wood and vanilla, is Southern living in a glass. Bourbon was first distilled by a Lexington preacher in 1789, and over 80% of the world's supply is still produced in state. While all bourbons are whiskey, all whiskeys are not bourbon. Bourbon must be made with at least 51% corn, and aged for at least two years.

TRIP HIGHLIGHT

1 Louisville

Best known as the home of the Kentucky Derby (p283), Louisville (or Louahvul, as the locals say) is an up-and-coming, progressive city (Kentucky's largest) with good eating kitchens, period architecture, fine museums, leafy streets and some fabulous bars where you may want to sip some bourbon. After giving downtown museums, like the fabulous Muhammad Ali Center (p283) and **Frazier History Museum**

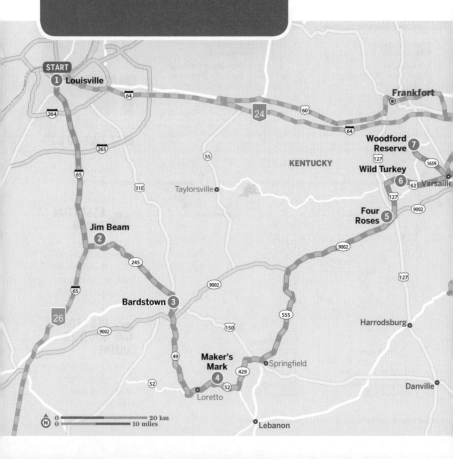

(www.fraziermuseum.org; 829 W Main St; adult/senior/child $12/10/8; ⏰9am-5pm Mon-Sat, noon-5pm Sun), a look, head to **NuLu**, the nearby arts district. You can try the good stuff at **Taste** (📞502-409-4646; www.taste finewinesandbourbons.com; 634 E Market St; tastings $5-12; ⏰noon-8pm Tue-Thu, 11am-10pm Fri & Sat, 1-5pm Sun), a high-end wine and bourbon shop on Market St. It pours craft stuff that's hard to find, and you can taste it before you buy it, from $5 a hit. If you'd like a deeper pour and a longer linger, head back downtown to 21c Museum

Hotel (p285), where you can peruse edgy modern art and head into upscale Proof (p293) to sample superb cocktails and sip from a fine bourbon list, which may include special editions of Van Winkle.

🍴🛏️ p284, p293

The Drive » From Louisville head south on I-65 for 24 miles, head left on KY 245 and make another left on Happy Hollow Rd.

- - - - - - - - - - - - - - - - - -

2 Jim Beam

Jim Beam (📞502-543-9877; www.jimbeam.com; 526 Happy Hollow Rd, Clermont; tours per person $12; ⏰gift shop 9am-5:30pm Mon-Sat, noon-4pm Sun, tours 9am-3:30pm Mon-Sat, 12:30-3pm Sun) is the world's largest and best-known bourbon distiller. Though its namesake hooch won't wow whiskey snobs, you'll soon learn that the Beam family has a history of small-batch bourbons. Jim Beam ages all its bourbon for at least four years, twice the legal minimum. Longer aging produces a deeper, smoother charac-

ter. Absorb the whole operation on the 80-minute tour, or do a self-guided walk along the grounds then head to its fabulous, digitized, automated tasting room. You'll get a half-shot of two bourbons. Beam makes Knob Creek (good), Knob Creek Single Barrel (better), Basil Hayden's (velvety) and the fabulous Booker's (high-proof enlightenment), which is best described as damn smooth with rocket boosters.

The Drive » Double back to KY 245 and head south for 15 miles, and head right on Hwy 31E into Bardstown.

- - - - - - - - - - - - - - - - - -

3 Bardstown

There are seven major distilleries within a 50-mile radius of Bardstown, while the town itself, with its weathered red-brick Georgian churches and fairy-tale stone cottages, belongs to a different era. For an overview of bourbon history, head to **Oscar Getz Museum of Whiskey History** (www.

Midway 26
75
64
60 FINISH Lexington
24
68
27

🔗 LINK YOUR TRIP

24 Kentucky Bluegrass & Horse Country

Bourbon and horses go together like mint juleps and the Kentucky Derby. Visit legendary race tracks and watch the horses fly.

26 Tailgate Tour

Now that you have your bottle of bourbon, follow sports fans to the nearest stadium, and do sip before the game begins.

KENTUCKY BOURBON FESTIVAL

This week-long annual Bardstown **festival** (www.kybourbonfestival.com; ☼Sep) draws whiskey aficionados from all over the world for taste tests from local distilleries, bourbon barrel relay races, liquor-infused cooking demos, and bourbon and cigar dinners. Kids will dig the historic train rides and night-time ghost tours of old Bardstown. And everyone can get into a competitive round of Kentucky's state game, cornhole (a sort of beanbag toss).

The Drive » The ride from Bardstown south on KY 49 offers the most beautiful countryside at this end of the bourbon trail. Narrow roads wind through classic wooded rolling horse country braided with corral fencing. Follow it south for 8 miles, then head east on KY 52 for nearly 5 miles.

whiskeymuseum.com; 114 N 5th St; ☼10am-4pm Tue-Sat, noon-4pm Sun), housed in a former Civil War hospital.

Heaven Hill (☎502-337-9593; www.bourbonheritagecenter.com; 1311 Gilkey Run Rd; tours $10-20; ☼10am-5:30pm Mon-Fri, noon-4pm Sun Mar-Dec, 10am-5pm Tue-Sat Jan-Feb), one of Kentucky's largest distilleries, is best known for its Evan Williams label. But its higher end – and higher proof – offering, Elijah Craig, is what gets whiskey converts salivating. Heaven Hill caters to visitors with its Bourbon Heritage Center displays on bourbon history, an educational film and a tasting bar inside a huge barrel. Elsewhere on campus, seventh-generation master distiller Craig Beam holds the keys to 16% of the world's bourbon supply – you can smell it in the air.

Willet (☎502-348-0899; www.kentuckybourbonwhiskey.com; Loretto Rd; tours $12; ☼shop 9:30am-5:30pm Mon-Fri, noon-4:30pm Sun Mar-Dec, tours 10am-4pm Mon-Sat, Sun 12:30-3:30pm), launched in 1936 and still family-owned, acted as a sub-

contractor for larger labels for decades, bottling its family recipe for another brand. Then, in January 2012, the grandson of the label's founder and the new 31-year-old master distiller quit law school and began bottling Willett under the family name yet again. You'll enjoy the hour-long tour through the 120-acre property, which includes a prolonged look into the refurbished chalet-like distillery, where big stainless-steel corn-mash cookers, and 10,000-gallon stainless steel fermenters, are open-topped – their aroma dizzying and tempting. An expanded visitor center with a bar and restaurant hosting pop-up chefs is set to open.

The owners at **Chapeze House** (☎502-507-8338; www.chapezehouse.com; 107 E Stephen Foster Ave; bourbon tastings $25-99; ☼by arrangement) will lead you through a tasting from a collection of more than 100 premium and vintage bourbons inside their lavish Federal-style mansion, where you can also overnight.

🛏 p293

➍ Maker's Mark

South of the Bardstown distilleries, **Maker's Mark** (☎270-865-2099; www.makersmark.com; 3350 Burks Spring Rd, Loretto; tours $12; ☼9:30am-3:30pm Mon-Sat, 11:30am-3:30pm Sun) has been operating at the same site, near the town of Loretto, since 1805. Makes sense, since the distillery sits on a 10-acre limestone-filtered, spring-fed lake, providing the pure water used in the distilling process. In fact, Kentucky's natural limestone filtration – you will see karsts jutting here and there in the countryside – is precisely why distillers can craft such a fine product here. Touring Maker's Mark is like visiting a small, historic theme park, but in the best way. You'll see the old grist mill, the 1840s master distiller's house, and the old-fashioned wooden firehouse with an antique fire truck. Watch oatmeal-esque sour mash ferment in huge cypress vats, see whiskey being double-distilled in copper pots and peek at bourbon barrels aging in old wooden warehouses. At the gift shop you can even stamp your own bottle with the iconic red-wax seal.

The Drive » From Maker's Mark, head northeast on KY 429 to KY 152 to KY 555, and finally KY 9002 toward the town of Lawrenceburg. It's about an hour's drive, and what a pleasant drive it is, with dogwoods sprouting in the springtime and outrageous fall color when the weather turns cold.

- - - - - - - - - - - - - - - - - -

5 Four Roses

In Lawrenceburg, **Four Roses** (502-839-3436; www.fourrosesbourbon.com; 1224 Bonds Mills Rd, Lawrenceburg; tours $5; ⊙ shop 9am-4pm Mon-Sat, noon-4pm Sun, tours 9am-3pm Mon-Sat, noon-3pm Sun) sits on the banks of the Salt River. Check out the unique architecture – red-roofed Spanish Mission–style buildings like these are rarely seen in this neck of the woods. For years, Four Roses was only sold overseas and some labels, like its Platinum, are still only available in Japan. But the company made a triumphant US comeback in 2002, when for the first time since the 1960s you could actually have a Four Roses Manhattan in Manhattan. Take a walking tour of the distillery and have some free sips afterwards in the tasting room. Note that the distillery shuts down in summer, but the gift shop and visitor center remain open. You can also call to arrange a free private tour of the aging warehouse, about an hour away in Cox's Creek.

THOMAS CARR / SHUTTERSTOCK ©

Maker's Mark Distilling bourbon since 1805

The Drive » No need to leave Lawrenceburg for your next tipple. Just follow Hwy 127 north for 9 miles.

- - - - - - - - - - - - - - - - - -

6 Wild Turkey

Wild Turkey (502-839-2182; www.wildturkey bourbon.com; 1417 Versailles Rd, Lawrenceburg; ⊙ shop 9am-5pm Mon-Sat, 11am-4pm Sun Mar-Dec, tours 9am-4pm Mon-Sat, 11am-3pm Sun Mar-Dec) distillery sits on Wild Turkey Hill overlooking the Kentucky River. More industrial and less self-consciously old-fashioned than some other distiller-ies, it offers a frills-free tour of the facilities. If you're lucky, you'll get to meet master distiller Jimmy Russell, who's worked here since 1954. Wild Turkey is made a bit differently to most bourbons, aged in a heavily charred barrel for extra-deep amber color, with very little water added at the end of the process.

The Drive » Backtrack on Hwy 127 then get ready for more deep beauty, because Versailles – a thoroughbred epicenter – is laced with streams and swathed in Kentucky bluegrass, which

WHISKEY TEA

Whiskey tea is a staple of church picnics and family reunions in the Bluegrass State. Ask one of the distilleries if you may buy a freshly dumped oak aging barrel. Take it home and fill it with 10 to 15 gallons of hot tea, then allow it to sit in the sun. At least a quart of whiskey will leach out of the wood, giving the tea flavor and kick.

BETTER WITH AGE

As we get older our character deepens, becomes more complex and interesting. The same is true of bourbon. In fact, you can't actually call it 'bourbon' until the whiskey has aged. Before then it's called 'green whiskey.' Most widely available bourbons are aged no longer than eight years, but some ultra-premium labels are aged 14, 16 or even 21 years. With each turn of the calendar, the bourbon gets a little bit darker and a lot smoother.

Kentucky has the perfect climate for aging bourbon. Hot summers cause the whiskey to expand into the wood of the barrel, where it sucks up toasty, caramelized flavors, to be released when the liquid contracts during the cold winters. The barrels sit, stacked several stories high, in wood and metal 'rackhouses' that dot the central Kentucky landscape like massive barns; you'll see them at all the distilleries.

you'll glimpse, point and shoot as you roll east on Hwy 62, which intersects with the stunning KY 1659 in historic Versailles. Head north on KY 1659 to Woodford Reserve.

TRIP HIGHLIGHT

7 Woodford Reserve

Set just outside Versailles (pronounced locally as 'vur-sails' despite the spelling and the area's Louisiana Purchase history), Woodford Reserve (p282) is one of the most beautiful distilleries in Kentucky. You're smack in the middle of thoroughbred stud country, on a 700-acre ranch originally settled in 1812. That's when the owners, who were cattle ranchers, started distilling for themselves and made their first 10 barrels. Two decades later there were nearly 2000 distilleries operating in the Kentucky hills, with a still for every 200 citizens. The Woodford Reserve label was launched much more recently, in 1996. It's

known for its 72% corn mash concentration, and triple copper pot distilling method, which it claims removes three times as many sulfates as single distilled products. Critics might counter that it hurts its flavor. We enjoy it. And its new **Double Oaked** label, which hit shelves in 2011, is aged an extra six to 12 months for a smooth and smoky finish that's pretty special.

The Drive » Go slow and take the Old Frankfort Pike – a national scenic byway – from Versailles to Lexington. Head south on KY 1659 to Hwy 60 east to the Hwy 62 to the Old Frankfort Pike.

------

8 Lexington

Lexington is home to million-dollar houses and multimillion-dollar horses. Once the wealthiest and most cultured city west of the Allegheny Mountains, it was tagged 'the Athens of the West,' and is home to the University of Kentucky. The small downtown has some pretty Victorians and intriguing restaurants. It's

also home to an up-and-coming bourbon label, **Barrel House Distilling Company** (www.barrelhouse distillery.com; 1200 Manchester St; tours $5; ☺11am-4pm Wed-Sun), a micro-distiller set in the barrel house of the now defunct Pepper Distillery. It bottles two moonshines (one aged in bourbon barrels), vodka and oak rum, and has a cozy lodge-bar to taste a tipple. Before leaving town, stop by the quirky **Headley-Whitney Museum** (www.headley-whitney.org; 4435 Old Frankfort Pike; adult/ student $10/7; ☺10am-5pm Tue-Fri, noon-5pm Sat & Sun Mar-Dec), a jewelry designer with a remarkable collection of stones, trinkets, doll houses and seashells. History buffs will want to visit the childhood home of **Mary Todd-Lincoln** (www.mtlhouse.org; 578 W Main St; adult/child $12/5; ☺10am-3pm Mon-Sat mid-Mar–Nov). You know, Abe's wife. And if it's basketball season, catch a UK game at Rupp Arena (p301).

✗ ⊫ 293

Eating & Sleeping

Louisville ❶

✖ Proof   Modern American $$$

(📞502-217-6360; www.proofonmain.com; 702 W Main St; mains $13-38; ⏰7-10am, 11am-2pm & 5:30-10pm Mon-Thu, to 11pm Fri, 7am-3pm & 5:30-11pm Sat, to 1pm Sun; 🛜) Arguably Louisville's best restaurant. The cocktails ($10 to $12) are incredible, the wine and bourbon 'library' (they're known to pour from exclusive and rare barrels of Woodford Reserve and Van Winkle) is long and satisfying, and startling dishes range from gourmet grilled cheese to a deliciously messy bison burger or a high-minded take on 'hot' fried chicken. Save room for the caramel-drizzled cardamom coffee cake with espresso gelato!

🛏 Brown Hotel   Hotel $$$

(📞502-583-1234; www.brownhotel.com; 335 West Broadway; r $200-600; P ❄ 🛜) Opera stars, queens and prime ministers have trod the marble floors of this storied downtown Louisville hotel, now restored to all its 1920s glamor with 294 comfy rooms and an impressive lobby bourbon bar under original English Renaissance gilded ceilings. In 1926, Louisville's signature dish, the Hot Brown (open-faced turkey sandwich with bacon, pimentos and Mornay sauce) was invented here and is still served (from $17).

Bardstown ❸

🛏 Old Talbott Tavern   Inn $

(📞502-348-3494; www.talbotts.com; 107 W Stephen Foster Ave; r $76-131; P ❄) Have a meal (mains $9 to $19), a bourbon, and a good night's sleep in the dim limestone environs of this inn, which has been welcoming guests like Abraham Lincoln and Daniel Boone since the late 1700s. Its restaurant is open daily from 11am and the atmospheric bourbon bar serves up 163 labels.

🛏 Jailer's Inn   Inn $$

(📞502-308-5551; www.jailersinn.com; 111 W Stephen Foster Ave; r $110-245; P ❄ 🛜) Sleep in a former cell in the Old Nelson County Jail, now outfitted with floral wallpaper and antique furniture. The seven rooms in the original 1819 building feature epic wooden ceilings and impenetrable stone walls.

Lexington ❽

✖ Village Idiot   Modern American $$

(📞859-252-0099; www.lexingtonvillageidiot. com; 307 West Short St; dishes $12-24; ⏰5-10pm Sun-Thu, to 11pm Fri & Sat, 10am-2pm Sat & Sun) Hip young foodies descend for dishes comfy and familiar, but with a twist. Think: duck confit and waffles, pulled pork mac 'n' cheese, or fried chicken eggs Benedict. It has a decent bourbon selection too.

🛏 Gratz Park Inn   Hotel $$

(📞859-231-1777; www.gratzparkinn.com; 120 W 2nd St; r from $179; P ❄ @ 🛜) Once a spot to draw the brocade curtains and fall asleep on a 19th-century poster bed, this staple of Lexington's historic district has revamped its rooms, leaving just a few antique four-poster beds for guests. The revamped rooms maintain a classic style save the bathrooms, where modern subway-tiled showers have an edgier, industrial feel.

Tailgate Tour

Visit the holy temples of Southern sport, where fanatics converge to visualize, embrace and celebrate victory...before the game even begins.

26

TRIP HIGHLIGHTS

697 miles

Louisville
Ali, basketball and the greatest party of them all

1239 miles

Cameron Indoor Stadium
Love Duke or hate 'em, this is a college basketball institution

Lexington

Knoxville

Chapel Hill

Athens

Tuscaloosa
The best football party, and the best football team in the SEC

Talladega Superspeedway
Impresses even the non-race fans

276 miles

173 miles

6 DAYS
1250 MILES / 2010KM

GREAT FOR...

BEST TIME TO GO

Tailgate Tours are held when school is in session. Basketball heats up in February, and football kicks off in September.

📷 ESSENTIAL PHOTO

Talladega Super-speedway: one of the iconic sports venues.

☑ BEST FOR HISTORY

Feeling the gravity of US sports history.

Talladega Action in the pit at the Talladega Superspeedway

295

Classic Trip

26 | Tailgate Tour

In the American South, football is king, car racing is a constitutional right and basketball is a religion. The most legendary venues have become pilgrimage sights to devoted fans who, before the lights shine, the whistle blows and the flag falls, gather in college quads, nearby sports bars and parking areas to make questionable dietary choices, and rejoice in the teams they love. Join them, won't you?

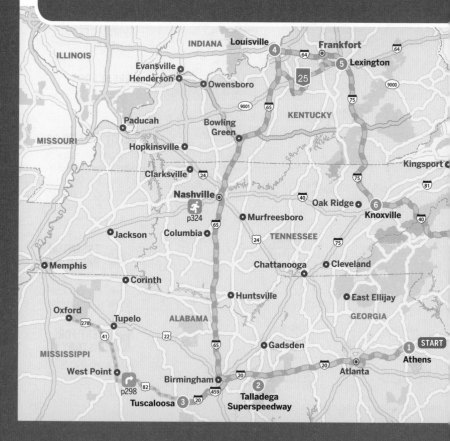

1 Athens

Beery, artsy, laid-back and roughly 70 miles east of Atlanta, Athens is a prototypical American college town. The **University of Georgia** (UGA visitors center 706-542-0842; www.uga.edu; 405 College Station Rd) drives the culture of Athens and ensures an ever-replenishing supply of young bar-hoppers, concert-goers and sports fans. And the University of Georgia – part of the fabled Southeastern Conference (SEC), college football's most competitive league – has a devoted following. The games happen on fall Saturdays at **Sanford Stadium** (706-542-9036; www.georgiadogs.com; 100 Sanford Dr), in the middle of the lovely, leafy campus that rambles over rolling hills east of a pleasant downtown. If you can't get a ticket, make your way to **Cutter's** (706-353-9800; 120 E Clayton St; 2:30pm-2am Mon-Fri, noon-2am Sat), a popular sports bar with gargantuan flat screens. Before the game it's buzzing, and if victory is grasped, the interior becomes a sloshed dance hall of depravity. But in a good way. The hipster vortex of **Normal Bar** (706-548-6186; www.facebook.com/normal.bar.7; 1365 Prince Ave; 4pm-2am Mon-Fri, 11:30am-2am Sat;) is a much more sophisticated place to watch the game. Any game.

✕ 🛏 p303

The Drive ≫ There's nothing especially pretty about the 173-mile high-speed run from Athens into Alabama on I-20, but then again, this next stop is all about speed.

TRIP HIGHLIGHT

2 Talladega Superspeedway

Nestled in the East Alabama hills, the **Talladega Superspeedway** (877-462-3342; www.talladegasuperspeedway.com; 3366 Speedway Blvd; tickets $50-205) is the

LINK YOUR TRIP

25 The Bourbon Trail
Since you're in Kentucky, stay and sip awhile. Visit America's best distilleries and drive away with some good hooch for your next pre- or post-game party.

8 North Carolina's Outer Banks
From Tobacco Rd in the triangle, head to the wild windswept beaches of North Carolina's Outer Banks.

fastest in the NASCAR circuit thanks to a 2.6-mile oval and high bank turns (30 degrees and over five stories high). The grandstand is a mile long and seats 130,000. You can visit the track on a guided 30-minute bus tour that leaves from the **International Motor Sports Hall Of Fame** (☎256-362-5002; www.motorsportshalloffame.com; 3366 Speedway Blvd, Talladega; adult/child museum $12/5, track tour $8/5, combo tickets $16/8; ☺9am-4pm; [P]). The best time to visit is when the cars are running in May and October. True tailgaters will opt for the motorhome camping

area called the **Infield**. It's an RV camp in the middle of the track with views of the race. In fact, that's where the drivers live during race week. Of course, they fly in on private planes and live in rock-star tour buses. The most indulgent deal for the rest of us may be the seats overlooking pit row. The ticket price ($400) includes a buffet and unlimited beer and wine – a high-end tailgate picnic.

The Drive » One hundred and three miles away, via I-20 and I-459, is yet another leafy college campus, and Alabama's top sports mecca.

- - - - - - - - - - - - - - - -

TRIP HIGHLIGHT

❸ Tuscaloosa

'Roll Tide!' is the call you'll hear, well, pretty much everywhere in Tuscaloosa, but especially on

Saturdays in the fall when students and alumni gather in the **University of Alabama** (☎205-348-6010; www.ua.edu; 711 Capstone Dr) quad, hours before the game even starts, for a pre-game party like none other. White tents, wired with satellite TV, fill the expansive lawn. Barbecue is smoked and devoured, cornhole (drunken bean bag toss) is played, 'Roll Tide' is shouted and shrieked. At game time all migrate to **Bryant-Denny Stadium** (☎205-348-3680; www.rolltide.com; 920 Paul W Bryant Dr; ☺tours 11am Mon-Fri), a 102,000-capacity football stadium that looks out onto the rolling hills and is always packed with rabid fans. With good reason: the Alabama Crimson Tide have won 16 national championships. Get a full dose of Crimson Tide football history at the **Paul W Bryant Museum** (☎205-348-4668; www.bryantmuseum.com; 300 Paul W Bryant Dr; adult/senior & child $2/1; ☺9am-4pm). Downtown Tuscaloosa unfurls along University Ave, with a student hood a half-mile closer to campus. That's where you'll find **Houndstooth** (☎205-752-8444; www.facebook.com/pages/Houndstooth-Sports-Bar/118838634902120; 1300 University Blvd; ☺4pm-2am, to 3am Fri), a quintessential sports bar, generally mobbed before and after the game.

🍴🛏 p303

DETOUR:
OXFORD

Start: ❸ Tuscaloosa

It's a pretty drive down a series of two- and four-lane highways through the countryside from Tuscaloosa to Oxford, MS, and while Ole Miss football has rarely struck fear into the heart of its opponents like the Crimson Tide, even with two-time Superbowl MVP Eli Manning lined up behind center, it can be fun to party with lovable losers. One of the school's great traditions happens on game-day mornings when the **Grove** – a woodland in the heart of the **University of Mississippi** (www.olemiss.edu) campus – is packed with students and fans who merge with the marching band and stomp to the stadium en masse to cheer for the Rebels! Tiny by SEC standards, the **Vaught-Hemmingway Stadium** seats about 62,000.

THE BEST OF THE REST

Although the destinations in this trip may be the crown jewels of Southern sport, we'd be remiss without pointing out a few additional options for getting your tailgate (and face paint) on.

University of Florida (www.floridagators.com) Set in Gainesville, this perennial football and basketball powerhouse is no stranger to the spotlight. Recent stars Al Horford and Joaquim Noah (basketball) and Tim Tebow (football) prove their pedigree.

Louisiana State University (www.lsusports.net) Set in Baton Rouge, and arguably third in line behind University of Alabama and University of Florida in terms of football supremacy in the SEC. It's also the alma mater of Shaquille O'Neal.

University of South Carolina (www.gamecocksonline.com) Steve Spurrier, the former University of Florida coach, keeps the Columbia-based Gamecocks in contention on the gridiron.

Durham Bulls (www.milb.com) The AAA affiliate of the Tampa Bay Rays, a fictional take on this Durham, North Carolina–based team and stadium, was featured in the iconic Kevin Costner, Susan Sarandon and Tim Robbins baseball flick *Bull Durham*.

Spring Training The Sunshine State has long hosted Major League Baseball teams during spring training in February and March, when there are games nearly every day. The New York Yankees (www.steinbrennerfield.com) and Philadelphia Phillies (http://mlb.com/phi/spring-training/ballpark) are two of the big league clubs with training complexes in the Tampa–St Petersburg area.

The Drive » From Tuscaloosa find I-65 north and hammer the gas for 421 miles all the way to Louisville.

TRIP HIGHLIGHT

4 Louisville

Boxing, basketball, baseball and horse racing, Louisville, KY, may be one of the South's most progressive and intellectual towns, but they love their sport. How could they not, with a favorite son like Muhammad Ali? You can learn all about the iconic Louisville-born heavyweight at the wonderful Muhammad Ali Center (p283). Baseball fans should wander down to that 10-story-tall baseball bat and the **Louisville Slugger Museum** (www. sluggermuseum.org; 800 W Main St; adult/senior/child $14/13/8; ☺9am-5pm Mon-Sat, 11am-5pm Sun, to 6pm Jul;). Also downtown is the charming and antiquated **Louisville Slugger Field** (✆855-228-8497; www. batsbaseball.com; 401 E Main St; tickets $10-25). The outpouring of love directed at the University of Louisville Cardinals men's basketball team, however, is pure and all encompassing. The defending national champion at research time, it plays its home games in a pro-grade downtown arena, the **KFC Yum! Center** (✆502-690-9000; www. gocards.com; 1 Arena Plaza). But when it comes to the tailgate party, no venue, event and or sport can match that of the Kentucky Derby at Churchill Downs (p283). A **festival** (www.kdf.org; kickoff event tickets from $30) kicks the party off two weeks ahead of time, and on race day everyone with $60 is welcome.

✕ ⫞ p284, p293, p303

The Drive » It's less than a 90-minute drive from here on I-64 to yet another basketball hot bed in the state of Kentucky.

299

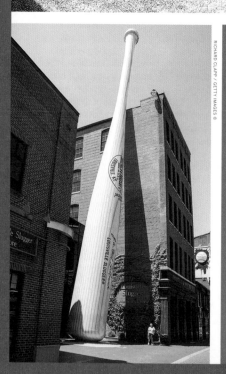

Classic Trip

WHY THIS IS A CLASSIC TRIP
KEVIN RAUB, WRITER

Battle born on Indiana basketball and educated on University of Georgia football, I understand what it's like to attend an all-in at an American collegiate sport powerhouse. We know allegiances of this nature carry way more significance in our lives than they should, but college sports, NASCAR and the Kentucky Derby are reasons we didn't need to make America great again. They're already part of what makes America great.

RICHARD CLAPP / GETTY IMAGES ©

Top: Alabama Crimson Tide mascot Big Al at Tuscaloosa's Bryant-Denny Stadium
Left: Louisville Slugger Museum
Right: Duke University's Blue Devils on court at Cameron Indoor Stadium

⑤ Lexington

Lexington may be the heart of thoroughbred country, but the people of Kentucky consider basketball their first and deepest love, and in Lexington it's all about the **University of Kentucky** (www.uky.edu). The Wildcats have the all-time best record in the history of men's college basketball and are second only to UCLA in national titles. They're a juggernaut, famous for their title teams – the most recent of which was crowned champion in 2012. And their Goliath-like fall in 1966 (when their Pat Riley–led all-white starting five lost the title game to Texas Western's all-black squad) is legendary. UK plays its home games in the town center at **Rupp Arena** (www.rupparena.com; 430 W Vine St; ⊙ box office 10am-6pm Mon-Fri), and when it runs, hotels sell out, downtown bars and restaurants are full, and the party spills into the streets. If you do love the horses, don't miss nearby Keeneland (p282), perhaps the best track in the US not named Churchill Downs. The pre-Derby races are especially high class.

✕ ⊨ p284, p303

The Drive 》 From a men's basketball mecca it's less than three hours down I-75 south to the epicenter of the women's game.

⑥ Knoxville

Knoxville is home to the University of Tennessee, the alma mater of Peyton Manning and long-time residency of the greatest women's basketball coach ever. During her career Pat Summitt won more games than any coach had in the history of NCAA basketball (including the boys). She coached for 40 seasons, and her Lady Volunteers won eight national titles, before retiring in 2012 after being diagnosed with Alzheimer's. The best place to get an appreciation for Summitt and her basketball teams is at the **Women's Basketball Hall of Fame** (www.wbhof.com; 700 Hall of Fame Dr; adult/child $8/6; ⊙10am-5pm Mon-Sat summer, 11am-5pm Tue-Fri, 10am-5pm Sat winter; 🚼), easily identified by the the Baden Ball – a 30ft-high 10-ton basketball that sits atop the building. Exhibits date all the way back to a time when women played in full-length dresses. Naturally, Pat Summitt headlined the first class ever inducted in 1999, along with Cheryl Miller – one of the greatest to ever play the woman's game. Peyton Manning first made his name at **Neyland Stadium** (www.utsports.com/facilities/neyland; 1600 Stadium Dr; tours $8), on the otherwise forgettable University of Tennessee campus.

⊨ p303

STACY REVERE / GETTY IMAGES ©

DAVID FRIE / ALAMY ©

Classic Trip

The Drive » It's a 336-mile drive east on I-40 to the ultimate rivalry in American college basketball.

TRIP HIGHLIGHT

7 Durham

In North Carolina, 11 miles separate two college basketball power-houses. **Duke University** (www.duke.edu; Campus Dr) in Durham is home to the great Mike Krzyzewski's Blue Devils. Duke fans worship inside **Cameron Indoor Stadium** (box office 919-681-2583; www. goduke.com; 115 Whitford Dr), which opened in 1940. As of the 2016–17 season, the men's home record was 965 wins, 193 losses, for a winning percentage of more than 80%. If there's not a scheduled event, you can step inside the stadium during business hours and occasionally sit in on practice. Off court, check out old photos and the **Duke Hall of Fame**. How to score tickets? Sell your first born, get accepted to Duke and camp out with students, or follow @duke_tickets on Twitter. You can also call the ticket office in early October to find out when tickets will go on sale. Best bet is a noncon-ference game or a game played over Christmas break.

The Drive » Drive 11 miles south down Hwy 501, otherwise known as Tobacco Rd.

8 Chapel Hill

Chapel Hill, known as Blue Heaven to basket-ball fans, is a cute, pro-gressive town where the culture revolves around North Carolina Universi-ty's 30,000-odd students. The Tar Heels play at the **Smith Center** (www. goheels.com; 300 Skipper Bowles Dr; box office 8am-5pm Mon-Fri). Less historic than Cameron Indoor, the center is named for legendary coach Dean Smith, who retired in 1997 with 879 career wins and two national titles. His record has since been eclipsed by Duke's Mike Krzyzewski, who begins the 2018 season with a staggering 1071 wins in a 42-year career, including five national titles – argu-ably he's the second-best coach ever, behind John Wooden. Of course, Tar Heels fans would counter that their current coach, Roy Williams is no slouch either, having notched up three titles and still going strong. And so the argu-ment goes on. Perhaps the politest way to de-scribe college basketball fans in North Carolina would be...fanatical.

p303

LEGENDS OF TOBACCO ROAD

These days the Raleigh-Durham area is referred to as the Research Triangle, or simply the Triangle, thanks to the abundance of top-shelf universities and researchers, but to sports fans it will always be Tobacco Rd. The moniker originally referred to the state's cash crop, but when it comes to basketball riches North Carolina stands alone. Legendary coaches? How about Dean Smith (UNC) and Mike Krzyzewski (Duke), two of the winningest ever. The greatest player of all time, some guy named Michael Jordan, was born and raised in North Carolina and played at UNC. Two of the NCAA Men's Basketball Tournament's iconic moments involved these teams. Jordan sank a last-second game winner to win the 1982 title over Georgetown, and Grant Hill made a spectacular three-quarter court pass to Christian Laettner who sank a turn-around shot to pull out a miracle victory that propelled Duke to the Final Four, and its second straight title in 1992.

Eating & Sleeping

Athens ❶

✕ Ike & Jane — Cafe $

(📞706-850-1580; www.ikeandjane.com; 1307 Prince Ave; mains $3.50-8; ⏰6:30am-5pm Mon-Fri, 8am-2pm Sat & Sun; 🖉🖰) This sunny little shingle in Normal Town serves decadent doughnuts bedazzled with crazy creative ingredients like red velvet, Cap'n Crunch cereal and peanut butter, banana and bacon. If that's all a bit much for you, the pimento cheese biscuit or roasted jalapeño and egg sandwich are both divine.

🛏 Hotel Indigo — Boutique Hotel $$

(📞706-546-0430; www.indigoathens. com; 500 College Ave; r/ste from $160/265; 🅿@🛜🖰🐾) Rooms are spacious, loft-like pods of cool at this eco-chic boutique hotel. Part of the Indigo chain, it's a Leadership in Energy and Environmental Design (LEED) gold-certified sustainable standout. Green elements include regenerative elevators and priority parking for hybrid vehicles; 30% of the building was constructed from recycled content.

Tuscaloosa ❸

✕ Nick's Original Filet House — Steak $

(📞205-758-9316; 4018 Culver Rd; mains $8-17; ⏰5-9pm Mon-Thu, to 10pm Fri & Sat; 🅿) Also known as Nick's in the Sticks, this is a rickety back-road joint if ever there was one, and it's a Tuscaloosa classic. Nestled in the trees about 5 miles out of town, with a flock of signed dollar bills stapled to the ceiling, it does tender filet mignon on the cheap as well as ribeye, and they fry all parts of the chicken (think livers and gizzards). Oh, and about that Nicodemus. Um, it's a drink. Beware the Nicodemus.

🛏 Hotel Capstone — Hotel $$

(📞205-752-3200; www.hotelcapstone.com; 320 Paul Bryant Rd; r from $145; 🅿❄🛜) A decent three-star room, walking distance from the quad and stadium. Digs are spacious with flat-screen TVs, wide desks and a slight corporate vibe. But it's on campus and has room service plus a lobby bar. Reserve well in advance on game day. During the off-season, rates drop by around $50.

Louisville ❹

✕ Garage Bar — Pub Food $$

(www.garageonmarket.com; 700 E Market St; dishes $9-18; ⏰5-10pm Mon-Thu, 11am-10pm Fri-Sun; 🛜) The best thing to do on a warm afternoon in Louisville is to make your way to this uber-hip converted NuLu service station and order a round of basil gimlets and the ham platter (a tasting of four regionally cured hams, served with fresh bread and preserves; $26). Also has the best brick-oven pizza in town.

Lexington ❺

✕ Village Idiot — Modern American $$

(📞859-252-0099; www.lexingtonvillageidiot. com; 307 West Short St; dishes $12-24; ⏰5-10pm Sun-Thu, to 11pm Fri & Sat, 10am-2pm Sat & Sun) Hip young foodies descend for dishes comfy and familiar, but with a twist. Think: duck confit and waffles, pulled pork mac 'n' cheese, or fried chicken eggs Benedict.

Knoxville ❻

🛏 Oliver Hotel — Boutique Hotel $$

(📞865-521-0050; www.theoliverhotel.com; 407 Union Ave; r $160-360; 🅿❄@🛜) Knoxville's only boutique hotel boasts 28 modern, stylish rooms with fun subway-tiled showers (with rain showerheads), luxe linens, plush throwback furniture and carpets, and gorgeous hand-crafted coffee tables. The bar draws craft cocktail enthusiasts by night and the restaurant, Oliver Royale, is highly recommended.

Chapel Hill ❽

✕ Neal's Deli — Breakfast, Deli $

(www.nealsdeli.com; 100 E Main St, Carrboro; breakfast $3.50-7, lunch $5.50-8.50; ⏰7:30am-4pm Tue-Fri, 8am-4pm Sat & Sun; 🛜) Dig into a delicious buttermilk breakfast biscuit at this tiny deli. The egg, cheese and bacon is some kind of good. For lunch, Neal's serves sandwiches and subs, from chicken salad to pastrami to a three-cheese pimiento with a splash of bourbon. Chapel Hill's best coffee is next door.

Memphis to Nashville

When two of America's legendary musical towns are within three hours of one another, they must be linked. Your journey will last longer, and include a shot of history – and whiskey – along the way.

27

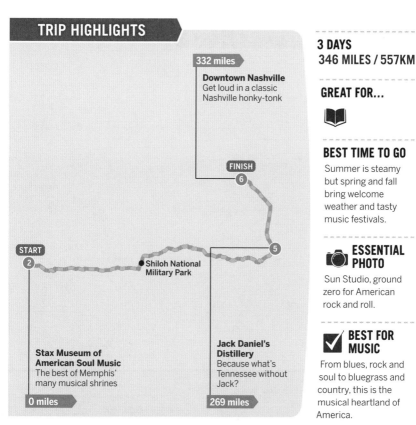

TRIP HIGHLIGHTS

332 miles

Downtown Nashville
Get loud in a classic Nashville honky-tonk

FINISH
6

5

START
2

● Shiloh National Military Park

Stax Museum of American Soul Music
The best of Memphis' many musical shrines

0 miles

Jack Daniel's Distillery
Because what's Tennessee without Jack?

269 miles

3 DAYS
346 MILES / 557KM

GREAT FOR...

BEST TIME TO GO
Summer is steamy but spring and fall bring welcome weather and tasty music festivals.

ESSENTIAL PHOTO
Sun Studio, ground zero for American rock and roll.

BEST FOR MUSIC
From blues, rock and soul to bluegrass and country, this is the musical heartland of America.

Stax Museum of American Soul Music The birthplace of soul music

27 Memphis to Nashville

Memphis is a warm summer night on the riverside. Nashville is a springtime picnic in the sun. Memphis is a smoky blues club: sweaty and cramped, it offers grit with a smile, a twisted history and sweet memories. Nashville is a glamour girl, a fine Southern town with cowboy crass, platinum-blonde diamond beauty and beer-soaked stages. Nashville is bluegrass. Memphis is blues. But why choose sides? Enjoy their differences.

① Beale Street & Around

By the early 1900s Beale St was the hub of African American social and civic activity, becoming an early center for what was to be known as blues music. In the 1950s and '60s, local recording companies cut tracks for blues, soul, R&B and rockabilly artists such as Al Green, Johnny Cash and Elvis, cementing Memphis' place in the American music firmament. Sprinkled on Memphis' most famous block are BB

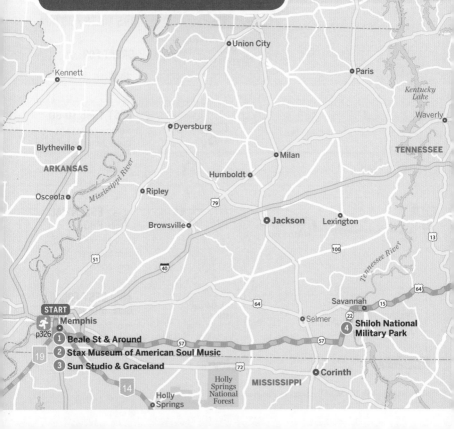

King's (p271), the original nightclub from the Mississippi kid who came to Memphis and became a star; the **New Daisy Theater** (📞901-525-8981; www.newdaisy.com; 330 Beale St; 🕙box office noon-4pm day of show), which hosts indie rock acts on the regular; and **A Schwab** (www.a-schwab.com; 163 Beale St; 🕙noon-5pm Mon-Wed, to 7pm Thu, 10am-9pm Fri & Sat, 11am-5pm Sun), with three floors of quirk – don't miss the cool antique gallery upstairs.

Gibson Beale Street Showcase (www.gibson.com; 145 Lt George W Lee Ave; $10; 🕙hourly tours 11am-4pm Mon-Sat, noon-4pm Sun) offers a fascinating 45-minute tour where you can see master craftspeople transform solid blocks of wood into legendary Gibson guitars. Journey back into the roots of the American popular music at Memphis Rock 'n' Soul Museum (p273). Its audio tour has over 100 songs, and explains how gospel, country and blues mingled in the Mississippi Delta to create modern sound. The blues are palpable once again when you visit the **National Civil Rights Museum** (www.civilrightsmuseum.org; 450 Mulberry St; adult $15, student & senior $14, child $12; 🕙9am-5pm Mon & Wed-Sat, 1-5pm Sun), which chronicles the ongoing struggles for African American freedom and equality in the US. Visit Beale St on our walking tour, p326.

 p275, 312

The Drive » Make your way over to 3rd St then head south to E McLemore Ave, where the ragged edge of Memphis begins to show.

TRIP HIGHLIGHT

② Stax Museum of American Soul Music

There are few (or no) funkier places on earth than the birthplace of soul music. The **Stax** (📞901-942-7685; www.stax

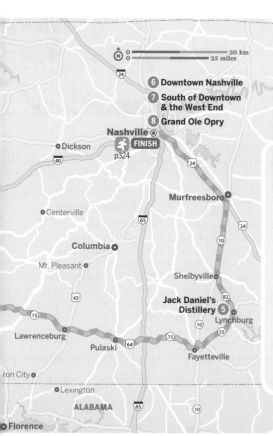

LINK YOUR TRIP

19 **The Blues Highway**
Follow the blues trail south from Memphis, and into the Mississippi Delta, where American popular music all began.

14 **Civil Rights Tour**
Martin Luther King Jr met his end in Memphis, but you can follow him back to the beginning on this inspirational and historic road trip.

museum.com; 926 E McLemore Ave; adult/child $13/10; ⏱10am-5pm Tue-Sat, 1-5pm Sun) experience begins with a moving 20-minute introductory film and the exhibits build on that. This is the label which used an integrated house band to back legends like Sam Cooke, Booker T Jones and the amazing Otis Redding. Ike Turner is given reverence as the visionary he was. His guitar and Tina's dress are on display (his domestic violence history conspicuously absent). Named for brother-sister founders Jim Stewart and Estelle Axton, there was always was a record shop in front of the studio (now it's a gift shop that sells CDs). It was originally a country label, but neighborhood demographics changed and African American musicians began drifting in. The unique combination of gospel, country and blues formed what became soul music. You can walk through the guts of the recording studio, and enjoy splashy displays for Albert King, the Staple Singers and the great Isaac Hayes, the headliner of the 1972 Wattstax festival, the label's high-water mark. Eventually the label went under, but it is now on a campus of the **Soulsville Foundation** that includes the **Stax Music Academy**, a public charter school.

The Drive » Head back across town on the I 240N, take the Union Ave exit and head west.

❸ Sun Studio & Graceland

Sun Studio (p271) is where the rockabilly dynasty of Jerry Lee Lewis, Johnny Cash, Roy Orbison and, of course, the King himself (who started here in 1953), was born. Today, packed 40-minute guided tours through the tiny studio offer a chance to hear original tapes of historic recording sessions. Guides spin yarns while you pose for photos in the old recording studio on the 'X' where Elvis once stood. Afterwards, hop on the free shuttle to Graceland (p274). Though born in Mississippi, Elvis Presley was a true son of Memphis: raised in the Lauderdale Courts public housing projects, and inspired by the blues in the Beale St clubs, in the spring of 1957, the already-famous 22-year-old spent $100,000 on a Colonial-style mansion, named Graceland by its previous owners. Priscilla Presley (who divorced Elvis in 1973) opened Graceland to tours in 1982, and now millions come here to pay homage to the King and gawk at the infamous decor.

The Drive » Take the I 240 east to the Bill Morris Pkwy, which will take you out of town. Take TN 57 east from there for

about 52 miles, paralleling the Mississippi border. Head north on TN 22 to the park.

❹ Shiloh National Military Park

Located north of the Mississippi border near the town of Crump, TN, **Shiloh National Military Park** (📞731-689-5275; www. nps.gov/shil; 1055 Pittsburg Landing Rd, Shiloh; ⏱park dawn-dusk, visitor center 8am-5pm) reveals the drama behind one of the early major battles of the Civil War. Ulysses S Grant,

Sun Studio Recording studio of the King, Elvis Presley

then a major general, led the Army of Tennessee. After a vicious Confederate assault on the first day that took Grant by surprise, his creative maneuver on the second day held Pittsburgh Landing, and turned the Confederates back. A relative unknown at the beginning of the war, Grant went on to lead the Union to victory and eventually became the 18th president of the United States. The vast park can only be seen by car. Sights along the route include the Shiloh National Cemetery, the final resting place of 4000 soldiers, an overlook of the Cumberland River where Union reinforcement troops arrived by ship, and various markers and monuments. The visitor center gives out maps, shows a video about the battle, and sells an audio driving tour.

The Drive » Continue down the Tennessee backroads, and make your way north on TN 22 to TN 15 east. The road jogs so be conscious of signage. After about 45 miles, turn left on TN 50 east which leads into TN 55 east toward Lynchburg.

TRIP HIGHLIGHT

⑤ Jack Daniel's Distillery

Set in tiny Moore County – the smallest in all of Tennessee – is the state's most famous product, **Jack Daniel's Tennessee Whiskey** (www.jackdaniels. com; 182 Lynchburg Hwy, Lynchburg; tours $13-75; ⊙9am-4:30pm). And strange gets stranger when you consider that it's also a dry county and has been since the soulless scourge of prohibition. Yes, 90 years later dry counties still exist in the South. But don't fret – while at least one of its five tours are dry (as if!), the serious excursions, ranging from the 90-minute Flight of Jack Daniel's to the three-hour Taste of Lynchburg, include a bit more than an angel's share of whiskey. It's best to book ahead. Free tours without a tasting are offered daily on the hour and are available on a first-come, first-served basis. The distillery itself sells no memorabilia, so if you want some Old No 7 trinkets, visit the **Lynchburg Hardware & General Store** (www.jackdaniels.com; 51 Mechanic St; ⏰9am-6pm Mon-Fri, from 10am Sat, from 1pm Sun) in town – which is actually owned by the distillery.

🍴 p312

The Drive » It's an easy 1½-hour drive, mostly off the major interstate, to Nashville. Take TN 55 east to TN 82 north to TN 10 south until you merge with I 24 north for the final 32 miles.

6 Downtown Nashville

For country-music fans and wannabe songwriters all over the world, a trip to Nashville is the ultimate pilgrimage. Think of any song involving a pickup truck, a bottle of booze (Jack Daniel's, perhaps?), a no-good woman or a late, lamented hound dog and chances are it came from Nashville. Downtown is where you'll find the lion's share of the honky-tonks, as well as the excellent **Country Music Hall of Fame** (www.countrymusichalloffame.com; 222 5th Ave S; adult/child $25/15, with audio tour $30/20, with Studio B 1hr tour $40/30; ⏰9am-5pm). Here you can gawk at Patsy Cline's cocktail gown, Johnny Cash's guitar, Elvis' gold Cadillac and Conway Twitty's yearbook picture (back when he was Harold Jenkins). Over on Broadway – the heart and

soul of the downtown strip – be sure to duck into **Hatch Show Print** (www.hatchshowprint.com; 224 5th Ave S; tours $18; ⏰9.30am-6pm). For 130 years this classic Nashville printer has been block printing publicity posters. It gets orders from all over the world, and you can buy reprints of original Louis Armstrong, Hank Williams and Bill Monroe shows past. For music in the present make your way to **Robert's Western World** (www.robertswesternworld.com; 416 Broadway; ⏰11am-2am Mon-Sat, noon-2am Sun). Name another dive where you can buy boots, have a burger, a beer or something stronger and listen to a rockabilly band for free all day every day. **Tootsie's Orchid Lounge** (☎615-726-7937; www.tootsies.net; 422 Broadway; ⏰10am-2:30am) is equally appealing: a torn-up linoleum-floor dive bar drenched with boot-stomping, hillbilly, beer-soaked grace. Visit

THIRD MAN

Jack White's move to Nashville and away from his downbeat, Detroit White Stripes roots has been well publicized. You can and should visit his excellent new operation, **Third Man Records** (www.thirdmanrecords.com; 623 7th Ave S; ⏰10am-5pm), in a still-industrial slice of downtown Nashville two blocks from active train tracks. There's a tiny record shop selling only Third Man recordings on vinyl and CD, as well as White Stripes and Raconteurs (his current band) albums. The T-shirts, stickers and headphones are cool too. They do live shows in the studio's Blue Room once a month, which are typically open to the public but are only announced a few days in advance, so keep your ear to the asphalt. Often these shows (Jerry Lee Lewis' recent performance comes to mind) become available on limited-edition vinyl sold in the store. The shows are $10.

these and more on our walking tour, p324.

🍴 🛏 p208, p312

The Drive » Nashville is sprawled out, so you will want to drive between downtown and areas south and west. The gridlike streets make it relatively easy to get around.

---

❼ South of Downtown & the West End

Nashville sprawls a bit, and within the shadow of the downtown skyline are a number of can't-miss clubs and sights for music lovers. Our favorite club in town is **Station Inn** (☎615-255-3307; www.stationinn.com; 402 12th Ave S; ☺ open mike 7pm, live bands 9pm). Sit at one of the small cocktail tables, all squeezed together on the worn wood floor, in this beer-only dive. There is no haunt more momentarily famous than **Bluebird Cafe** (☎615-383-1461; www.bluebirdcafe.com; 4104 Hillsboro Rd; cover free-$30). Set in a strip mall in suburban South Nashville, some of the best original singer-songwriters in country music have graced this tiny stage, Steve Earle, Emmylou Harris and the Cowboy Junkies included, which is how it became the central location in the popular TV series, *Nashville*. Also in a strip mall, yet still a legit cultural force, is renowned author Anne Patchett's **Parnassus Books** (www.parnassus

books.net; 3900 Hillsboro Pike; ☺10am-8pm Mon-Sat, noon-5pm Sun; 🚻), arguably one of America's most famous indie booksellers. The bright space hosts special events, readings and signings, promotes local authors and even sells e-books. Little nuggets of independence like this may just save our literary souls. The most famous sight on this end of town is **Music Row** (Music Sq West & Music Sq East), a stretch of 16th and 17th Aves, home to the production companies, agents, managers and promoters who run Nashville's country-music industry. There's not much to see, but you can pay to cut your own record at some of the smaller studios.

The Drive » Take I 40 east to the TN 155 north and watch for the signs. You really can't miss it.

---

❽ Grand Ole Opry

Starting as a radio hour in 1925, country music's signature star-making

broadcast operated out of the legendary **Ryman Auditorium** (☎615-889-3060; www.ryman.com; 116 5th Ave N) from 1943 to 1974 before moving out here to the suburbs. After a brief run as a doomed theme park, today Opryland is a splashy, labyrinthian resort and shopping mall (complete with IMAX theater), but the signature sight remains the **Grand Ole Opry House** (☎615-871-6779; www.opry.com; 2804 Opryland Dr; tours adult/child $26/21, with Ryman Auditorium $36/35; ☺tours 9am-4pm), a modern brick building that seats 4400 on Friday and Saturday from March to November. Guided backstage tours are offered daily by reservation – book online up to two weeks ahead.

Across the plaza, a small, free museum tells the story of the Opry with wax characters, colorful costumes and dioramas.

Eating & Sleeping

Memphis ❶

✖ Alcenia's   Southern US $

(www.alcenias.com; 317 N Main St; mains
$9.50-13; ◷9am-5pm Tue-Fri, to 3pm Sat) The
lunch menu at this funky little gold- and purple-
painted cafe rotates daily – look for killer fried
chicken and catfish, melt-in-the-mouth spiced
cabbage and an exquisite eggy custard pie.

✖ Dyer's   Burgers $

(www.dyersonbeale.com; 205 Beale St; burgers
$4.50-7.50; ◷11am-3am, to 5am Fri & Sat)
Purportedly sells one of America's best burgers
– anointed so by both *Esquire* and *Playboy*.
Spatula-flattened meat is submerged in
bubbling grease, which is continuously filtered
like it is life-giving elixir when, well, it's probably
the opposite. But no matter. Dyer's has been
doing it this way since 1912, and it makes a late-
night snack of the gods.

✖ Charlie Vergos'
Rendezvous   Barbecue $$

(☏901-523-2746; www.hogsfly.com; 52 S 2nd
St; mains $8-20; ◷4:30-10:30pm Tue-Thu,
11am-11pm Fri, from 11:30am Sat) Tucked in its
own namesake alleyway off Monroe Ave, this
subterranean institution sells an astonishing
5 tons of its exquisite dry-rubbed ribs weekly.
The ribs don't come with any sauce, but the
pork shoulder does, so try a combo and you'll
have plenty of sauce to enjoy. The beef brisket is
also tremendous. Expect a wait.

▙ Pilgrim House Hostel   Hostel $

(☏901-273-8341; www.pilgrimhouse.org; 1000
S Cooper St; dm/r $25/55; P ❄ @ ⸙) Yes, it's
in a church. No, no one will try to convert you.
Dorms and private rooms are clean and spare.
An international crowd plays cards and chats
(no alcohol) in open common areas flush with
secondhand furniture, and all guests must do a
brief daily chore.

▙ Talbot Heirs   Guesthouse $$

(☏901-527-9772; www.talbothouse.com; 99 S
2nd St; ste $160-200; ❄ @ ⸙) Inconspicuously
located on the 2nd floor of a busy downtown
street, this cheerful guesthouse is one of

Memphis' best kept and most unique secrets.
Spacious suites, all with recently modernized
bathrooms, are more like hip studio apartments
than hotel rooms, with Asian rugs, funky local
artwork and kitchens stocked with (included!)
snacks. Big stars like Harvey Keitel, Matt Damon
and John Grisham have nested here, as well as
Bobby Whitlock of Derek and the Dominos fame,
who signed a piano.

▙ Madison Hotel   Boutique Hotel $$$

(☏901-333-1200; www.madisonhotelmemphis.
com; 79 Madison Ave; r from $279;
P ❄ @ ⸙ ✲ ⸙) If you're looking for a sleek
treat, check into these swanky, music-themed
boutique sleeps. The rooftop Sky Terrace ($10
for non-guests) is one of the best places in town
to watch a sunset, and stylish rooms have nice
touches like hardwood entryways, high ceilings
and Italian linens. Parking is $29.

Lynchburg ❺

✖ Miss Mary Bobo's
Boarding House   Southern US $

(☏931-759-7394; 295 Main St; per person $23;
◷11am-2pm Mon-Sat) Now that it has expanded
to seven seatings per day between 11am and
2pm (by reservation only), more folks can
indulge in the massive and delicious Southern
meals that have been served family-style at this
classic boarding house since 1908. The menu
rotates, but includes at least two meats, six
veggies and biscuits and corn bread, along with
dessert, sweet tea and coffee.

Nashville ❻

✖ Provence   Bakery, Cafe $

(www.provencebreads.com; 1705 21st Ave S;
mains $4-13; ◷7am-7pm Mon-Fri, 8am-7pm Sat,
to 6pm Sun; ⸙) A popular spot in the Hillsboro
District, where lovers of bread will want to stop
for a loaf or a ready-made turkey, chicken salad
or tuna sandwich. It also does frittatas, salads,
tasty pastries, and a French toast made with a
peach compote. Grab a table in the bright dining
area, which is popular at lunch.

✕ City House   Southern US $$

(☎615-736-5838; www.cityhousenashville.com;
1222 4th Ave N; mains $15-29; ⏲5-10pm Mon &
Wed-Sat, to 9pm Sun) This signless brick building
in Nashville's smart Germantown district hides
one of the city's best restaurants. The food,
cooked in an open kitchen in the warehouse-like
space, is a crackling bang-up of Italy meets New
South. On offer are tangy kale salads, a tasty
smoked lamb with chard, lemon and pecorino,
pastas featuring twists like octopus ragu, or
baked grits in cauliflower ragu. The folk at City
House cure their own sausage and salamis, and
take pride in their cocktail and wine list. Save
room for dessert. Sunday supper features a
stripped-down menu. The bar, pizza counter and
screened-in porch are saved for walk-ins.

🛏 Nashville Downtown Hostel   Hostel $

(☎615-497-1208; www.nashvillehostel.com;
177 1st Ave N; dm $32-45, r $100-165; ℗) Well
located and up-to-the-minute in style and

function. The common space in the basement,
with its rather regal exposed stone walls and
beamed rafters, is your all-hours mingle den.
Dorm rooms are on the 3rd and 4th floors,
and have lovely wood floors, exposed timber
columns, silver-beamed ceilings and four, six
or eight bunks to a room. Several new private
rooms with kitchenettes will sometimes serve as
en-suite dorms for $10 extra. In and out parking
for $20 per day is a good deal for Nashville.

🛏 Hotel Indigo   Boutique Hotel $$

(☎615-891-6000; www.hotelindigo.com; 301
Union St; r from $189; ℗ ❄ @ 🛜) Part of a
boutique international chain, the Indigo has a
fun, pop-art look, with 161 rooms (30 of which
are brand new). Avoid the original (but tacky)
Terrazo floor rooms in favor of those spacious
King Rooms, with brand new hardwood floors,
high ceilings, flat-screens, leather headboards
and office chairs.

Big Muddy

It gave us Huck Finn and the blues. Plantation owners depended on it for commerce. Slaves used it to escape. The Civil War streaked it with blood. The Mississippi River is America.

28

TRIP HIGHLIGHTS

99 miles

Clarksdale
Delve into the Mississippi Deltas blues tradition

Helena

0 miles

Memphis
One of the USA's great cities, full of music, history and soul

Vicksburg

313 miles

Natchez
Antebellum panache, Huck Finn soul

Baton Rouge

528 miles

Venice

New Orleans
The Mississippi's most glorious city

5 DAYS
598 MILES / 962KM

GREAT FOR...

BEST TIME TO GO

In spring and fall the sun is warm yet forgiving.

ESSENTIAL PHOTO

Mud Island is connected by monorail to Memphis, but feels like another world.

BEST FOR HISTORY

To follow the Mississippi is to track the story of America and its people.

New Orleans A paddlesteamer cruises the Mississippi River

28 Big Muddy

The Mississippi bubbles up in Minnesota where the river is still narrow enough to swim across, but in the South it is a commercial artery that ferries fuel, goods and people from the Gulf of Mexico to the Midwest, and back again, as it has for centuries. It twists for 2320 miles, and at nearly every bend there's a story.

TRIP HIGHLIGHT

1 Memphis

Memphis is one of the river's most soulful cities, and the Memphis Rock 'n' Soul Museum (p273) delves into the social and cultural history that produced the blues in the Mississippi Delta. That sound eventually morphed into rock and roll when Elvis sang 'Hound Dog,' an old blues tune, in Sun Studio (p271); attaching the song to Elvis made the music marketable to white teenagers. But long before Elvis and local heroes like Otis Redding, this section of the river was used to shepherd slaves to freedom. Learn more at the **Slave Haven Underground Railroad Museum** (www.slavehaven undergroundrailroadmuseum. org; 826 N 2nd St; adult/child $10/8; ☺10am-4pm Mon-Sat, to 5pm Jun-Aug), in a modest clapboard house laced with tunnels fed by trapdoors.

The **Mississippi River Museum** (www.mudisland. com; 125 N Front St; adult/child $10/free; ☺10am-5pm Tue-Sun mid-Apr–Oct) is the place to learn more about the river's cultural and natural history. Check out the scaled model of the lower Mississippi, including a 40,000-gallon Gulf of Mexico–aquarium school-ing with sharks and rays. It's part of **Mud Island** (www.mudisland.com; 125 N Front St; ☺10am-5pm Tue-Sun mid-Apr-Oct; 🚶) river park. Linked to Memphis by a monorail, you can rent kayaks, canoes and bikes and explore.

See more of the city on our walking tour, p326.

✕ 🛏 p181, p237, p275, p312, p322

The Drive » Pick up the Blues Highway (Hwy 61), in Memphis and drive through the city's rough edge into the wide open spaces of the Mississippi Delta, where the blues were born.

----

2 Tunica

The gateway to Delta blues country is the juke-joint mock-up that is the Tunica **Visitor Center** (📞888-488-6422; www. tunicatravel.com; 13625 US 61, Robinsonville; ☺8am-5:30pm Mon-Fri, from 10am Sat, 1-5pm Sun), where interac-tive digital guides offer background checks on famed blues musicians and can't-miss destina-tions on the **Blues Trail** itself. You will learn, for instance, that Robert Johnson, the original blues star, was born in Tunica, MS, yet this small riverside town has morphed into a maze of casinos, which aren't worth your time. Best to check out the visitor center and keep moving.

The Drive » Blitz through the flat, green, big-sky delta on Hwy 61, before heading west on Hwy 49, across the river and into Arkansas, a distance of 31 miles.

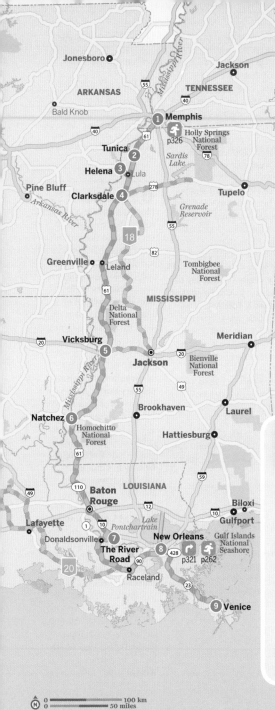

----

❸ Helena

A depressed mill town
still hoping for a second
wind, Helena was once
home to the late Sonny
Boy Williamson, a regu-
lar on *King Biscuit Time,*
America's first blues
radio show. BB King
listened religiously as a
child, and it was Sonny
who introduced King to
his first audience on that
radio show. The show,
which begins weekdays
at 12:15pm, is still run-
ning, and broadcasts
out of the **Delta Cultural
Center** (☎870-338-4350;
www.deltaculturalcenter.com;
141 Cherry St; ⏰9am-5pm
Tue-Sat; **P**)), which is also
a terrific blues museum.
You're welcome to watch
the broadcast live, and
you may even get on the
air. Down the street is
Bubba's Blues Corner

🔗 LINK YOUR TRIP

20 **Cajun Country**
Head west from New
Orleans and delve into the
black-water bayous and
spiced cultural gumbo
that is Louisiana's Cajun
Country.

18 **Historical Mississippi**
Detour from the water in
Mississippi to absorb the
heartbreaking and soul-
stirring history of the river's
namesake state.

(☎870-338-3501; 105 Cherry St; ◷9am-5pm Tue-Sat), the type of record store – owned by an old-school blues vinyl savant – that is a dying breed. If you time it right you can join the three-day **King Biscuit Blues Festival** (☎870-572-5223; www.king biscuitfestival.com; tickets $45; ◷Oct).

The Drive » Double back across the river on Hwy 49, skirt Moon Lake and head south in a straight shot for 16 miles on Hwy 61.

- - - - - - - - - - - - - - - - - -

TRIP HIGHLIGHT

④ Clarksdale

Clarksdale is the hub of Delta blues country. This is where you'll find the **Crossroads** (Hwy 61 & Hwy 49), where Robert Johnson made his famous deal with the devil and became America's first guitar hero. And it's here where live music and blues history are most accessible. The **Delta Blues Museum** (☎662-627-6820;

www.deltabluesmuseum.org; 1 Blues Alley; adult/senior & student $10/5; ◷9am-5pm Mon-Sat Mar-Oct, from 10am Nov-Feb; ⓟ), downtown, has the best collection of blues memorabilia in the delta, including Muddy Waters' reconstructed Mississippi cabin. Creative, multimedia exhibits also honor BB King, John Lee Hooker, Big Mama Thornton and WC Handy, whose original 1912 composition popularized the 12-bar blues. There's live music in Clarksdale at least four nights a week (typically Wednesday to Saturday). **Cat Head Delta Blues & Folk Art** (☎662-624-5992; www.cathead.biz; 252 Delta Ave; ◷10am-5pm Mon-Sat) is the best place to inquire about local shows, but if you land here on a weekend head to directly to **Red's** (☎662-627-3166; 395 Sunflower Ave; cover $7-10; ◷live music 9pm Fri & Sat), a ragged downtown juke joint run with in-your-face charm

by its namesake. Sometimes Red has moonshine behind the bar.

✕ 🛏 p227, p237, p322

The Drive » Hwy 61 parallels the Mississippi all the way to the Louisiana border, but Helena will be your last glimpse of it, until you reach Vicksburg, 144 miles south.

- - - - - - - - - - - - - - - - - -

⑤ Vicksburg

Most famous for a pivotal battle that turned the Civil War to the Union's favor, this charming, if struggling, town offers sublime Mississippi River vistas from its bluffs. And it was control of that river that drove General Ulysses S Grant to besiege the city for 47 days, until its surrender on July 4, 1863. Inland at **Vicksburg National Military Park** (☎601-636-0583; www.nps.gov/vick; 3201 Clay St; per bicycle/car $5/15; ◷8am-5pm; ♿), you can drive, or pedal, along the 16-mile **Battlefield Dr** which winds past 1330 monuments and markers – including statues, battle trenches, a restored Union gunboat and a National Cemetery. It makes for a fascinating afternoon. The **Lower Mississippi River Museum** (☎601-638-9900; www.lmrm.org; 910 Washington St; ◷9am-4pm Mon-Sat, 1-4pm Sun; ♿), downtown, delves into such topics as the famed 1927 flood, and a background of the Army Corps of Engineers

---

OIL!

Think land traffic is hazardous? On July 24, 2008, a cargo barge collided with an oil tanker on the Mississippi in New Orleans, causing a 500,000-gallon oil slick. Within minutes 100 miles of the river were closed to boat traffic, costing the Port of New Orleans up to $250,000 per day. Downriver waterfowl were covered in the thick, black sludge, and there were concerns about contamination of urban tap-water supplies and the estuaries along the Gulf Coast. Thankfully cleanup was swift, but the spill served as a reminder that this great and powerful river is not indestructible.

Clarksdale The legendary Crossroads at the junction of Hwys 49 and 61

who have managed the river – for better and worse – since the 18th century. Kids will dig its aquarium and rambling around the dry-docked research vessel, the MV *Mississippi IV*. Art buffs shouldn't miss the wonderful **Attic Gallery** (☎601-638-9221; 1101 Washington St; ⊙10am-5pm Mon-Sat), as there are some fabulous finds here.

✕ ⫞ p227, 322

The Drive » From Vicksburg, Hwy 61 once again drifts inland, rolling over mogul-like foothills before bending back to the riverside in Natchez, about 72 miles south.

TRIP HIGHLIGHT

6 Natchez

Historic antebellum mansions will greet you in Natchez, MS. In the 1840s there were more millionaires per capita here than anywhere in the world. When Union soldiers marched through with orders to torch the place during the Civil War, there weren't any men in town. Legend has it the women greeted the soldiers at their doors, and Southern hospitality saved the city. Those mansions are open to visitors during the twice annual 'Pilgrimage seasons' held in the spring and fall. The **Visitor and Welcome Center** (☎800-647-6724; www. visitnatchez.org; 640 S Canal St; ⊙8:30am-5pm Mon-Sat, 9am-4pm Sun) is your best pilgrimage resource. You may visit the **Auburn Mansion** (☎601-446-6631; www.auburnmuseum.org; 400 Duncan Ave; adult/child $15/10; ⊙11am-3pm Tue-Sat, last tour departs 2:30pm; ♿) year-round.

When Mark Twain passed through, during his riverboat captain days, he crashed in a room above the local saloon. The **Under the Hill Saloon**

(☎601-446-8023; 25 Silver St; ⊙10am-late) remains the best bar in town, with terrific free live music on weekends. The name works, because the saloon is built into a hillside and overlooks a captivating bend of the Mississippi.

✗ 🛏 p209, p322

The Drive » Cross the Louisiana state line and Hwy 61 bleeds into the I 110 south, which merges with I 10 in Baton Rouge. Take Hwy 44 south to LA 70 west to LA 18 toward Donaldsonville, just off of Louisiana's River Road (actually a series of highways that skirt both sides of the Mississippi). The entire drive takes about 150 miles.

➐ The River Road

Elaborate plantation homes dot the east and west banks of the Mississippi River between New Orleans and Baton Rouge. First indigo, then cotton and sugarcane – and the slavery that produced these goods – brought great wealth to these plantations, many of which are open to the public.

Laura Plantation

(☎225-265-7690; www.lauraplantation.com; 2247 Hwy 18, Vacherie; adult/child $20/6; ⊙10am-4pm; P), in Vacherie on the west bank, offers the most dynamic

and informative tour. It teases out the distinctions between Creole, Anglo and African American antebellum life via meticulous research and the written records of the Creole women who ran the place for generations.

Next, step into the **Whitney Plantation** (☎225-265-3300; www.whitneyplantation.com; 5099 Highway 18, Wallace; adult/student/child under 6yr $22/10/free; ⊙museum 9:30am-4:30pm Wed-Mon), which maintains the only plantation museum dedicated to the slave experience. Where other plantations center

BOOKS ON THE BIG MUDDY

The greatest river in North America has inspired a slate of books – fiction and nonfiction – on its waters, floods, geography and characters. Here are some of our favorite books on the Father of Waters.

» *Life on the Mississippi* (1883) Mark Twain's iconic memoir of working as a boat pilot on the river.

» *High Water* (1954) Former river pilot Richard Pike Bissell tells a tense tale of steering barges through a Mississippi flood.

» *Rising Tide* (1997) Ostensibly a nonfiction account of the Mississippi Flood of 1927, this incredible book by historian John Barry is also a meditation on politics, culture and the social divisions that define America.

» *The River Queen: A Memoir* (2007) Travel writer Mary Morris, a rat terrier – and some actual rats – pilot a houseboat down the river.

» *The Adventures of Huckleberry Finn* (1884) Another Mark Twain work – in this case, a novel that both challenged slavery and helped launch the buddy-road-trip genre.

» *Shantyboat* (1953) Harlan Hubbard tells the tale of piloting a houseboat with his wife down the river to New Orleans.

» *Mississippi Solo: A River Quest* (1988) Eddy Harris' wonderful travelogue on canoeing from Minnesota to New Orleans.

» *Old Man River: The Mississippi River in North American History* (2013) Paul Schneider tackles the river's past all the way to prehistory.

» *One Woman's River: A Solo Source-to-Sea Paddle on the Mighty Mississippi* (2016) Artist and educator Ellen Kolbo McDonah paddles from Minnesota to the mouth of the Mississippi.

DETOUR:
WEST BANK NEW ORLEANS

Start: ❽ New Orleans

We're sending you to Algiers! No, not northern Africa – just to the West Bank of the Mississippi River, which lays…east of New Orleans? We know, it's confusing – it has to do with the way the river curves around the Crescent City – but in any case, the West Bank is worth a visit from anyone stopping in NO. You can get here via car or the **Algiers Ferry** ($2; 🕑6am-9:45pm Mon-Thu, to midnight Fri, 10:30am-midnight Sat, to 10pm Sun), which departs from the foot of Canal St. The ferry drops you off in **Algiers**, a cute residential neighborhood filled with colorful New Orleans houses. If you're in need of some grub, consider heading to the excellent Vietnamese eatery **Tan Dinh** (📞504-361-8008; 1705 Lafayette St, Gretna; mains $8-18; 🕑9:30am-9pm Mon, Wed-Fri, 9am-9pm Sat, to 8pm Sun, closed Tue; 🅿🍴). Or just wander along the levee and appreciate the lights of New Orleans while standing across the river.

the story on the masters in the 'Big House,' this museum focuses on the slaves who were sold, bought, and worked to death by said masters. It's a powerful, vital location.

The Drive » From Donaldsonville take I 10 east for 65 miles, skirt Lake Pontchartrain and follow it all the way into the Crescent City.

TRIP HIGHLIGHT

❽ New Orleans

No city is better associated with the Mississippi River than New Orleans – for better and for worse. This city, packed with life, passion, music and angst, has been formed, nourished and flooded by it for centuries. **Jackson Sq** (Decatur & St Peter Sts) is a clear choice for just soaking up the local street scene; visit on our walking tour, p262.

Don't miss the **French Market** (📞504-636-6400; www.frenchmarket.org; 1100 N

Peters St; 🕑10am-6pm): New Orleanians have been trading goods for over 200 years from this spot on the Mississippi River-banks. The river is nearby, up the levee, and you get nice views over the sweet, brown, polluted, sloshing water from there.

When the moon rises over the Mississippi, it's time to seek night music. For live music that's on the river, you can't really go wrong with the **Rivershack Tavern** (📞504-834-4938; 3449 River Rd; 🕑11am-midnight Mon-Thu, to 2am Fri & Sat). **Chickie Wah Wah** (📞504-304-4714; www.chickiewahwah.com; 2828 Canal St; 🕑5pm-midnight Mon-Fri, 7pm-midnight Sat & Sun) – not on the river, but it's close enough (as is all of Frenchman St) – is a dependable jazz venue. Local legends like the Sweet Olive String band and vocalist Meschiya Lake make their way

across that small stage regularly.

✕ 🛏 p219, p253, p323

The Drive » From New Orleans take the 428E through Algiers and head south on LA 23, a continuation of the Great River Road, which follows the river's west bank until it ends 70 miles south of New Orleans amid the stilted vacation homes, oil infrastructure and sport fishing marina of Venice.

----

❾ Venice

This is the mouth of the Mississippi and you'll see the river spread into rivulets that flood a vast estuary protected by the Fish and Wildlife Service as the **Delta National Wildlife Refuge**. There are redfish and speckled trout in the wetlands, and tarpon, snapper and grouper in the Gulf. Charter a boat for a day, or you may wish to cast off a defunct offshore oil platform.

Eating & Sleeping

Memphis ❶

✕ Cozy Corner   Barbecue $

(www.cozycornerbbq.com; 735 N Pkwy; plates $7-14; ⏰11am-9pm Tue-Sat) Slouch in a torn vinyl booth and devour an entire barbecued Cornish game hen ($11.75), the house specialty at this recently renovated cult favorite. Ribs and wings are spectacular too, and the fluffy, silken sweet-potato pie is an A-plus specimen of the classic Southern dessert.

✕ Alchemy   Tapas $$

(📞901-726-4444; www.alchemymemphis.com; 940 S Cooper St; tapas $9-18, mains $17-24; ⏰4pm-1am Mon, to 11pm Tue-Thu, 4:30pm-1:30am Fri & Sat, 10:30am-3pm & 4-10pm Sun) A flash spot in the Cooper-Young district, serving tasty Southern tapas like truffle deviled eggs with blue crab remoulade and caviar, shrimp and grits with smoked Gouda and chorizo pan gravy, and scallop bruschetta with gremolata and ponzu vinaigrette. The kitchen stays open until midnight on weekends.

✕ Sweet Grass   Southern US $$$

(📞901-278-0278; www.sweetgrassmemphis.com; 937 S Cooper St; mains $19-34; ⏰5pm-late Tue-Sat, 11am-2pm & 5pm-late Sun; 🛜) Contemporary Lowcountry cuisine (the seafood-heavy cooking of the South Carolina and Georgia coasts) wins raves at this casual Midtown restaurant, split between a more rambunctious bar side called Next Door (go for the fried egg sandwich!) and a more refined bistro side with a more sophisticated menu, a new raw bar and some unforgettable shrimp and grits. Oysters go for 50¢ each during the 5pm to 7pm Tuesday to Friday happy hour. Save room for that deep-dish sour-cream apple pie, which ain't a bit like your granmomma's!

🛏 Sleep Inn at Court Square   Hotel $$

(📞901-522-9700; www.sleepinn.com; 400 N Front St; r from $129; 🅿 ❄ 🛜) Our pick of the cheaper downtown digs, this stubby stucco box, part of a jumble of corporate sleeps, has pleasant, airy rooms with flat-screen TVs. Parking is $12.

Clarksdale ❹

✕ Bluesberry Cafe   Southern US $

(📞662-627-7008; 235 Yazoo Ave; ⏰7:30am-1pm Sat & Sun, noon-6pm Mon) This isn't just a greasy spoon – there's grease on the forks, knives and napkins too. But who cares? The food – eggs, bacon, homemade sausages and big sandwiches – is cooked to order and delicious, and on many a morning, some legend of the blues will stop in and play an impromptu set. Pass the hot sauce.

🛏 Shack Up Inn   Inn $$

(📞662-624-8329; www.shackupinn.com; 001 Commisary Circle, off Hwy 49; d $75-165; 🅿 ❄ 🛜) At the Hopson Plantation, this self-titled 'bed and beer' allows you to stay in refurbished sharecropper cabins or the creatively renovated cotton gin. The cabins have covered porches and are filled with old furniture and musical instruments.

Vicksburg ❺

✕ Rusty's Riverfront Grill   Southern US $$

(www.rustysriverfront.com; 901 Washington St; mains $17-34; ⏰11am-2pm & 5-10pm Tue-Fri, 11am-10pm Sat; 👶) Set at the north end of downtown, this down-home grill is known for the terrific rib eye, but it has a nice selection of Southern-style seafood too, including crab cakes, blackened redfish and a nice New Orleans–style gumbo.

Natchez ❻

🛏 Mark Twain Guesthouse   Guesthouse $

(📞601-446-8023; www.underthehillsaloon.com; 33 Silver St; r without bath $65-85; ❄ 🛜) Mark Twain used to crash in room 1, above the bar at the current Under the Hill Saloon (p319), when he was a riverboat pilot passing through town. There are three rooms in all, sharing one bath and laundry facilities.

New Orleans ⑧

✕ Elizabeth's
Cajun, Creole $$

(📞504-944-9272; www.elizabethsrestaurant
nola.com; 601 Gallier St; mains $15-26; ⏱8am-
2.30pm & 6-10pm Mon-Sat, 8am-2.30pm Sun)
Elizabeth's is deceptively divey, but the food's
as good as the best New Orleans chefs can
offer. This is a quintessential New Orleans
experience: all friendliness, smiling sass, weird
artistic edges and overindulgence on the food
front. Brunch and breakfast are top draws – the
praline bacon is no doubt sinful, but consider us
happily banished from the Garden.

✕ Gautreau's
Modern American $$$

(📞504-899-7397; www.gautreausrestaurant.
com; 1728 Soniat St; mains $30-45; ⏱6-10pm
Mon-Sat) There's no sign outside Gautreau's,
just the number 1728 discreetly marking a
nondescript house in a residential neighborhood.
Cross the threshold to find a refined but
welcoming dining room where savvy diners,
many of them New Orleanian food aficionados,
dine on fresh, modern American fare. Chef Sue
Zemanick has won every award a rising young
star can garner in American culinary circles.

🛏 Columns Hotel
Historic Hotel $$

(📞504-899-9308; www.thecolumns.com;
3811 St Charles Ave; r $145-180; ❄🛜) This
white-porched Southern manse, built in 1883, is
a snapshot from the past. Fortunately, that past
doesn't take itself too seriously. A magnificent
mahogany staircase climbs past a stained-glass
window to the rooms, ranging from smallish
doubles to the two-room Pretty Baby Suite
(named for the 1970s Louis Malle film shot here).
The environs aren't exactly posh, but they're
well loved. Elaborate marble fireplaces, richly
carved armoires and claw-foot tubs are among
the highlights. To absorb the late-night revelry,
take a front room on the 2nd floor. A lavish hot
breakfast is included. Guests enter through the
columned front verandah and continue past two
wood-paneled parlors that double as a bar-cafe.

STRETCH YOUR LEGS
NASHVILLE

Start/Finish Country Music Hall of Fame & Museum

Distance 2.7 miles

Duration Three hours

Nashville will spin you around and leave your ears ringing with the sound of steel guitar. But it has a brainy side too, with great museums and grand old government buildings not far from those addictive honky-tonks.

Take this walk on Trips

Country Music Hall of Fame & Museum

Head directly to downtown's **Country Music Hall of Fame** (www.countrymusichall offame.com; 222 5th Ave S; adult/child $25/15, with audio tour $30/20, with Studio B 1hr tour $40/30; ⏰9am-5pm), where Elvis' gold Cadillac and Johnny Cash's guitar are enshrined like religious relics. Exhibits trace country's roots from the original banjo-pickin' hillbillies of the early 20th century through to today's tattooed and pierced stars, while listening booths give you access to the vast archives of sound.

The Walk » Head north for one block on 5th Ave and make a right on Broadway.

The District

Lower Broadway between 2nd and 4th Aves is famous for its neon-lit honky-tonks, the crowds of tourists in painfully new cowboy boots, and the kid on the corner singing his heart out on a battered guitar. For rockabilly tunes, we love **Robert's Western World** (www.robertswest ernworld.com; 416 Broadway; ⏰11am-2am Mon-Sat, noon-2am Sun). **Tootsie's Orchid Lounge** (☎615-726-7937; www.tootsies.net; 422 Broadway; ⏰10am-2:30am) is a classic beer-drenched joint too. Both have free live music from 11am. And don't miss **Hatch Show Print** (www.hatchshowprint. com; 224 5th Ave S; tours $18; ⏰9.30am-6pm), a long-running block print company with a tremendous archive.

The Walk » Continue down Broadway until it dead-ends at 1st Ave and the Cumberland River. Head upriver to Church St, make a left and a right on 3rd Ave. Between Church and Union Sts you'll find Printer's Alley.

Printer's Alley

Cobblestone-paved Printer's Alley, now lined with bars and restaurants, used to be home to the city's thriving printing industry. Beginning in the early 1800s, horse carts carried paper and ink to the alley's mostly religious publishing houses. The printing of Christian hymnals gave way to secular music

publishing, which helped attract the large record labels in the 1940s and '50s.

The Walk » Take Church to 5th Ave. Make a left and walk two long blocks to Nashville's most historic venue.

Ryman Auditorium

Ryman Auditorium (www.ryman.com; 116 5th Ave N; tours adult/child self-guided $20/15, backstage $30/25; 9am-4pm) is a soaring Gothic Revival building commissioned in the late 1800s by crusty old riverboat captain Thomas Ryman, after his soul was saved by a popular Christian evangelist. These days, the 2000-seat Ryman hosts distinctly secular acts, such as alt-rock giants the National.

The Walk » Take 5th Ave to Broadway, and make a right.

Frist Center for the Visual Arts

This massive **art museum** (www.frist center.org; 919 Broadway; adult/senior/child $12/9/free; 10am-5:30pm Mon-Wed & Sat,

to 9pm Thu & Fri, 1-5.30pm Sun; P ⩗) is on par with those you'll find in the world's great cities. It has a collection that spans from indigenous American pottery to Picasso to mind-melting modernist sculpture; contemporary works are installed on the 1st-floor gallery.

The Walk » Continue on Broadway to 12th Ave and make a left. In four blocks you'll find our favorite place in town for night music.

Station Inn

Station Inn (615-255-3307; www.station inn.com; 402 12th Ave S; open mike 7pm, live bands 9pm), an unassuming stone building and beer-only dive, is the best place in town for serious bluegrass. The room is lit only by stage lights, neon signs and the lightning fingers of bluegrass savants. We are talking stand-up bass, banjo, mandolin, fiddle and a modicum of honey-throated yodeling.

The Walk » Walk two blocks to Demonbreun St, which leads you back to the Hall of Fame.

STRETCH YOUR LEGS
MEMPHIS

Start/Finish Beale St

Distance 2.5 miles

Duration Three to four hours

Memphis is alive with blues, soul and rock and roll, pulsating out of bars, concert halls and...museums? Indeed, a gritty city of warm smiles, smoky barbecue and deep history, its best sights are huddled close and demand a stroll.

Take this walk on Trips

Beale Street

This is where the blues bloomed from a wild Mississippi Delta seed into American popular music. From **WC Handy's home** (www.wchandymemphis.org; 352 Beale St; adult/child $6/4; ⏰11am-4pm Tue-Sat winter, 10am-5pm summer), a homage to the Father of the Blues, to the original **BB King's** (☎901-524-5464; www.bbkingclubs.com; 143 Beale St; ⏰11am-11:30pm Mon-Thu, noon-2am Fri, 11am-midnight Sat, 11am-11pm Sun) to the **Elvis statue**, Memphis royalty is honored here. And this pedestrian street remains a giant street carnival, with free live music nightly.

The Walk » Walk a block over from the pedestrian rave, to the FedEx Forum campus on 3rd St.

FedEx Forum & Around

The FedEx Forum, home of the Memphis Grizzlies, hosts two special attractions on its sprawling plaza. The **Gibson Beale Street Showcase** (www.gibson.com/Gibson/Gibson-Tours.aspx; 145 Lt George W Lee Ave; $10; ⏰hourly tours 11am-4pm Mon-Sat, noon-4pm Sun) offers a 45-minute tour of the factory where the iconic guitars are crafted. Around the corner, the Smithsonian-affiliated **Memphis Rock 'n' Soul Museum** (www.memphisrocknsoul.org; 191 Beale St; adult/child $12/9; ⏰10am-7pm) shows Memphis' many influences and how this cross-cultural stew revolutionized American music.

The Walk » Continue down 3rd St, turn right on Vance Ave and head left onto Mulberry St until you see the preserved Lorraine Motel.

National Civil Rights Museum

Housed across the street from the 1950s-era Lorraine Motel, where the Reverend Dr Martin Luther King Jr was fatally shot on April 4, 1968, is the gut-wrenching **National Civil Rights Museum** (www.civilrightsmuseum.org; 450 Mulberry St; adult $15, student & senior $14, child $12; ⏰9am-5pm Mon & Wed-Sat, 1-5pm Sun). Extensive exhibits include a detailed timeline and insights into the incred-

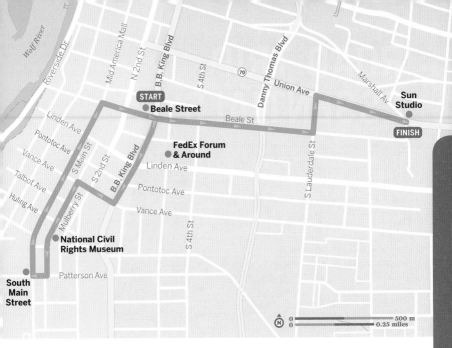

ible efforts of the movement for African American freedom and equality.

The Walk » Continue on Mulberry to Patterson Ave, and hang a right to South Main St.

South Main Street

Head to this up-and-coming arts district and make like Elvis, and pop into **Arcade** (www.arcaderestaurant.com; 540 S Main St; mains $7-10; ⏲7am-3pm Sun-Wed, to 11pm Thu-Sat) for breakfast. Crowds still descend for sublime sweet-potato pancakes. If it's late find **Earnestine & Hazel's** (www.earnestineandhazelsjukejoint. com; 531 S Main St; ⏲5pm-3am Mon-Fri, from 11am Sat & Sun), a spooky brothel turned dive bar, named after its late madams.

The Walk » If you have it in you, double back to Beale, and walk south to Union Ave for more Elvis lore.

Sun Studio

Sun Studio (☎800-441-6249; www. sunstudio.com; 706 Union Ave; adult/child $12/ free; ⏲10am-6:15pm) is where founder Sam Phillips took a chance on a series of scrawny nobodies barely out of their teens (ever heard of Elvis, Johnny Cash or Roy Orbison?). Tours are led by enthusiastic guides, many of them country singers themselves. Descriptions of the studio's history are interspersed with loudspeaker clips, like Elvis' first recording. Pose with the old-school mike in the recording studio then hop the free shuttle back to Beale St.

ROAD TRIP ESSENTIALS

Florida & the South Driving Guide

Thrumming big-city boulevards, high-speed causeways, coastal highways and winding backcountry roads connect every corner of Florida and the Deep South.

DRIVER'S LICENSE & DOCUMENTS

Foreign visitors can legally drive in the USA for up to 12 months with their home driver's license. However, getting an International Driving Permit (IDP) is recommended; this will have more credibility with US traffic police, especially if your home license doesn't have a photo or is in a foreign language. Your automobile association at home can issue an IDP, valid for one year, for a small fee. You must carry your home license together with the IDP. To drive a motorcycle, you need either a valid US state motorcycle license or an IDP specially endorsed for motorcycles.

INSURANCE

Don't put the key into the ignition if you don't have insurance, which is legally required, or you'll risk financial ruin if there's an accident. If you already have auto insurance (even overseas), or if you buy travel insurance, make sure that the policy has adequate liability coverage for a rental car; it probably does, but check.

Rental-car companies will provide liability insurance, but most charge extra. Always ask. Rental companies almost never include collision-damage insurance for the vehicle. Instead, they offer an optional Collision Damage Waiver (CDW) or Loss Damage Waiver (LDW), usually with an initial

Road Trip Websites

AUTOMOBILE ASSOCIATIONS

American Automobile Association (www.aaa.com) Offers roadside assistance 24 hours per day.

Better World Club (www.betterworldclub.com) Offers the same services, and donates 1% of its profits to environmental nonprofit organizations.

ROAD RULES
Department of Motor Vehicles (www.dmv.org)

CONDITIONS & TRAFFIC
Federal Highway Administration (www.fhwa.dot.gov)

MAPS

Google Maps (www.maps.google.com)

Rand McNally (www.randmcnally.com)

DRIVING FAST FACTS

Right or left? Drive on the right.

Legal driving age? 16

Top speed limit? 75 mph (on interstate)

Best bumper sticker? Remember Who You Wanted To Be

deductible of $100 to $500. For an extra premium, you can usually get this deductible covered as well. However, most credit cards now offer collision-damage coverage for rental cars if you rent for 15 days or less and charge the total rental to your card. This is a good way to avoid paying extra fees to the rental company, but note that if there's an accident, you sometimes must pay the rental-car company first and then seek reimbursement from the credit-card company. Check your credit-card policy. Paying extra for some or all of this insurance increases the cost of a rental car by as much as $15 to $30 a day.

RENTING A CAR

Car rental is a very competitive business. Most rental companies require that you have a major credit card, that you be at least 25 years old and that you have a valid driver's license (your home license will do).

Some national companies may rent to drivers between the ages of 21 and 24 for an additional charge. Those under 21 are usually not permitted to rent at all. **Car Rental Express** (www.carrentalexpress.com) rates and compares independent car-rental agencies in US cities; it's particularly useful for searching out cheaper long-term rentals.

National car-rental companies:

Alamo (www.alamo.com)

Avis (www.avis.com)

Budget (www.budget.com)

Dollar (www.dollar.com)

Enterprise (www.enterprise.com)

Hertz (www.hertz.com)

National (www.nationalcar.com)

Rent-a-Wreck (www.rentawreck.com)

Thrifty (www.thrifty.com)

Rental cars are readily available at all airport locations and many downtown city locations. With advance reservations for a small car, the daily rate with unlimited mileage is about $35 to $55, while typical weekly rates are $200 to $400, plus myriad taxes and fees. If you rent from a non-airport location, you save the exorbitant airport fees, but may pay a fee for a drop-off out of state.

An alternative in Miami and Atlanta is **Zipcar** (www.zipcar.com), a car-sharing service that charges hourly/daily rental fees with free gas, insurance and limited mileage included; pre-payment is required.

Driving Problem-Buster

What should I do if my car breaks down? Call the service number of your car-hire company and they will call out a tow truck. If you're bringing your own car, it's a good idea to join AAA (American Automobile Association), a 24-hour roadside assistance service which can be called out to breakdowns at any time. You can join, on call, at the time of your breakdown.

What if I have an accident? For minor accidents you can simply exchange insurance information with the other party and then call your insurance (and/or rental-car company) immediately to report it. If you distrust the other party, call the police, who will fill out an objective report.

What should I do if I get stopped by the police? Show your license, passport (if necessary) and proof of insurance (mandatory). And whatever you do, act natural.

What if I can't find anywhere to stay? This is likely only a problem in big cities during a major event or festival. If you head out of town (not too far) on the interstate, you are likely to find a cheap corporate motel that will have a room.

Road Distances (Miles)

	Asheville, NC	Atlanta, GA	Charleston, SC	Chattanooga, TN	Clarksdale, MS	Durham-Chapel Hill, NC	Fort Lauderdale, FL	Jackson, MS	Laffayette, LA	Lexington, KY	Little Rock, AR	Louisville, KY	Memphis, TN	Miami, FL	Nashville, TN	New Orleans, LA	Orlando, FL	Oxford, MS	Savannah, GA
Atlanta, GA	210																		
Charleston, SC	270	320																	
Chattanooga, TN	225	120	435																
Clarksdale, MS	580	390	710	380															
Durham-Chapel Hill, NC	220	380	310	445	775														
Fort Lauderdale, FL	770	640	560	755	1000	810													
Jackson, MS	590	380	700	385	155	760	890												
Laffayette, LA	790	580	540	600	365	960	950	230											
Lexington, KY	285	380	855	280	495	470	1020	625	855										
Little Rock, AR	640	515	835	475	150	860	1130	265	355	555									
Louisville, KY	360	420	615	305	460	530	1065	590	815	80	520								
Memphis, TN	505	385	700	340	80	725	965	210	440	425	135	385							
Miami, FL	790	660	585	780	1025	830	30	910	975	1045	1150	1080	1015						
Nashville, TN	295	250	550	135	285	510	890	415	645	210	350	175	210	910					
New Orleans, LA	680	470	740	490	335	850	840	185	135	745	425	710	395	865	535				
Orlando, FL	585	440	380	555	800	625	215	690	750	820	925	860	765	235	690	640			
Oxford, MS	530	330	650	295	65	710	915	160	390	445	215	410	80	940	235	345	735		
Savannah, GA	310	250	110	365	640	350	465	580	750	585	765	670	630	485	495	640	280	580	
Tampa, FL	640	455	435	575	790	680	265	705	770	835	940	880	810	280	705	660	85	745	335

BORDER CROSSINGS

Rental cars from Canada and Mexico are eligible to cross the border and operate in the US. Leased cars are also eligible, though you must have a letter of permission from the leasing company. If you own your car, you will more than likely be allowed to cross the border without filling out a customs bond, but the border officer does reserve the right to ask for the bond to be completed.

MAPS

Rand McNally (www.randmcnally.com) is a long-time publisher of high-quality road maps. But they won't show you any more than Google or Map Quest. **National Geographic Road Atlas** (www.national-geographic.com) is the best ink-and-paper map going, with special attention paid to national parks and forests.

ROAD CONDITIONS

The vast majority of all roads you'll encounter will be free, and paved. Though gravel roads, otherwise known as fire roads, do exist, as does the rare tollway, which requires a fee of 50¢ or more. Interstates are eight lane (at least), high-speed freeways. Highways can be two to six lanes in width and are the most common long-distance strip of asphalt in America. In the cities, traffic can back up between 7am and 9am and between 4pm and 7pm for rush hour. In the country, traffic is virtually nonexistent.

ROAD RULES

If you're new to US roads, here are some basics:

➡ The maximum speed limit on interstates is 75mph, but that drops to 65mph and 55mph in

Florida & the South Playlist

Got My Mojo Workin' Muddy Waters

Shake Your Moneymaker Elmore James

Can't You Hear Me Callin' Bill Monroe

Ring of Fire Johnny Cash

A Big Hunk O'Love Elvis Presley

Home Grown Booker T & the MG's

Just One More Day Otis Redding

Soul Power Derek Martin

I'll Take You There The Staple Singers

Everyday I Have the Blues BB King

Smokestack Lightning Howlin' Wolf

When My Train Pulls In Gary Clark Jr

PARKING

In the countryside parking is generally free. In cities you will have to pay at a parking meter (the cheapest) in a designated lot or structure, or you can look for free neighborhood street parking. There is usually a time limit, and occasionally permit-only parking, so read the signs, or you may get an expensive ticket.

FUEL

Gas stations are extremely common, except in national parks and high in the mountains, though you will never be more than 50 miles (at the very most) from one. The vast majority sell unleaded, unleaded plus and premium gas, as well as diesel. Unleaded is cheapest and will be fine for your rental car.

SAFETY

Country roads generally lack road lights, and unless you are used to dark highways it can be intimidating. Generally, these are also the highways where cows or deer may try to cross the road. Be very careful. Cows kill. Seriously.

Cities such as Atlanta, Memphis, Miami and New Orleans certainly have their rougher areas, though driving through any neighborhood in daylight is rarely a problem. Be sure to keep all valuables out of sight and doors locked while parked to avoid theft.

RADIO

90.7 FM (WWOZ) New Orleans' best jazz station, and one of the best in the country. Featured in the HBO series *Treme*.

960 AM (WABG) Broadcasting blues from the Mississippi Delta.

89.9 FM (WEVL) Memphis' only listener-supported, independent radio station, broadcasting blues, rock, world and bluegrass music.

100.1 FM (WRLT) Lightning 100, Nashville's independent radio station brings a number of local and well-known artists into the studio.

107.9 FM Atlanta's premier hip-hop station deluxe.

urban areas. Pay attention to the posted signs. City street speed limits vary between 15mph and 45mph.

➡ Police officers are generally strict with speed-limit enforcement, and speeding tickets are expensive. If caught going over the speed limit by 10mph, the fine is upwards of $150.

➡ All passengers in a car must wear seat belts or you may be cited and fined. All children under three must be in a child safety seat.

➡ As in the rest of the US, drive on the right-hand side of the road. On highways, pass in the left-hand lane (but anxious drivers often pass wherever space allows).

➡ Right turns on a red light are permitted after a full stop, unless signs dictate otherwise. At four-way stop signs, the car that reaches the intersection first has right of way. In a tie, the car on the right has right of way.

Florida & the South Travel Guide

GETTING THERE & AWAY

AIR

Florida

Whether you're coming from within the US or from abroad, the entire state is well served by air, with a number of domestic and international airlines operating services into Florida. Major airports include:

Orlando International Airport (MCO; ☑407-825-8463; www.orlandoairports.net; 1 Jeff Fuqua Blvd) Handles more passengers than any other airport in Florida. Serves Walt Disney World® Resort, the Space Coast and the Orlando area.

Miami International Airport (MIA; ☑305-876-7000; www.miami-airport.com; 2100 NW 42nd Ave) One of Florida's busiest international airports. It serves metro Miami, the Everglades and the Keys, and is a hub for American, Delta and US Airways.

Fort Lauderdale-Hollywood International Airport (FLL; ☑866-435-9355; www.broward.org/airport; 320 Terminal Dr) Serves metro Fort Lauderdale and Broward County. It's about 30 miles north of Miami: be sure to check flights into Fort Lauderdale as they are often cheaper or have availability when flights into Miami are full.

Tampa International Airport (TPA; ☑813-870-8700; www.tampaairport.com; 4100 George J Bean Pkwy) Florida's third-busiest airport is located 6 miles southwest of downtown Tampa and serves the Tampa Bay and St Petersburg metro area.

Other airports with international traffic:
Daytona Beach (☑386-248-8030; www.

flydaytonafirst.com; 700 Catalina Dr) and **Jacksonville** (JAX; ☑904-741-4902; www.flyjax.com; 2400 Yankee Clipper Dr; 🛜).

Most cities have airports and offer services to other US cities; these airports include the following:

Palm Beach (PBI; ☑561-471-7420; www.pbia.org; 1000 James L Turnage Blvd) Actually in West Palm Beach.

Sarasota (SRQ; ☑941-359-2770; www.srq-airport.com; 6000 Airport Circle)

Tallahassee (☑850-891-7802; www.talgov.com/airport; 3300 Capital Circle SW)

Gainesville (☑352-373-0249; www.gra-gnv.com; 3880 NE 39th Ave)

Fort Myers (RSW; ☑239-590-4800; www.flylcpa.com; 11000 Terminal Access Rd)

Pensacola (☑850-436-5000; www.flypensacola.com; 2430 Airport Blvd)

Key West (EYW; ☑305-809-5200; www.eyw.com; 3491 S Roosevelt Blvd).

The South

Atlanta has the busiest airport in the world by passenger traffic, and hosts carriers from across the globe. The other airports listed here host most major domestic carriers, and some international airlines – New Orleans, for example, now receives direct flights from London via British Airways. In addition, Atlanta is a hub for Delta, and Charlotte is a hub for US Airways.

Major airports in the South:

Hartsfield–Jackson Atlanta International Airport (ATL, Atlanta; ☑800-897-1910; www.atl.com)

Nashville International Airport (BNA; ☑615-275-1675; www.flynashville.com; One Terminal Dr)

Charlotte Douglas International Airport (CLT; ☑704-359-4013; www.cltairport.com; 5501 Josh Birmingham Pkwy)

Louis Armstrong New Orleans International Airport (MSY; ☑504-303-7500; www.flymsy.com; 900 Airline Hwy; ☎)

Memphis International Airport (MEM; ☑901-922-8000; www.flymemphis.com; 2491 Winchester Rd)

Charleston International Airport (CHS; ☑843-767-7000; www.chs-airport.com; 5500 International Blvd)

Birmingham-Shuttlesworth International Airport (BHM; ☑205-599-0500; www.flybirmingham.com)

Louisville International Airport (SDF; ☑502-367-4636; www.flylouisville.com; 600 Terminal Dr)

Bill & Hillary Clinton National Airport (Little Rock) (LIT; Little Rock National Airport; ☑501-372-3439; www.fly-lit.com; 1 Airport Dr)

CAR & MOTORCYCLE

Florida

Driving to Florida is easy; there are no international borders or entry issues. Incorporating Florida into a larger USA road trip is very common, and having a car while in Florida is often a necessity: there's lots of ground to cover and some of the most interesting places and state parks are only accessible by car.

The South

The American South is served by an extensive highway network. Major roads include I-95, which runs down the length of the East Coast; I-75 crosses Georgia, Tennessee and Kentucky; I-65 crosses Alabama, Tennessee and Kentucky; I-10 cuts across the Gulf Coast through Louisiana, Mississippi and Alabama.

BUS

Major cities in Florida and the South – and many second-tier towns – are served by **Greyhound** (www.greyhound.com). While you'll save money by booking tickets in advance, it's not difficult to purchase tickets on the day of travel. Important regional Greyhound stations:

Miami (☑305-871-1810; 3801 NW 21st)

Orlando (☑407-292-3424; 555 N John Young Pkwy)

New Orleans (☑504-299-1880; 1001 Loyola Ave)

Atlanta (☑404-584-1728; 232 Forsyth St)

Charleston (☑843-744-4247; 3610 Dorchester Rd)

Nashville (☑615-255-3556; 709 5th Ave S)

Birmingham (☑205-252-7190; 618 19th St N)

Louisville (☑800-231-2222; 720 W Muhammad Ali Blvd).

BOAT

Florida

Florida is nearly completely surrounded by the ocean, and it's a major cruise-ship port. Fort Lauderdale is the largest transatlantic harbor in the US. Adventurous types can always sign up as crew members for a chance to travel the high seas.

The South

Some cruise ships service the Southern USA by docking in New Orleans.

TRAIN

Florida

From the East Coast, **Amtrak** (www.amtrak.com) makes a comfortable, affordable option for getting to Florida. Amtrak's Silver Service (which includes Silver Meteor and Silver Star trains) runs between New York and Miami, with services that include Jacksonville, Orlando, Tampa, West Palm Beach and Fort Lauderdale, plus smaller Florida towns in between.

There is no direct service to Florida from Los Angeles, New Orleans, Chicago or the Midwest. Trains from these destinations connect to the Silver Service route, but the transfer adds a day or so to your travel time.

Amtrak's Auto Train takes you and your car from the Washington, DC, area to the Orlando area; this saves you gas, the drive and having to pay for a rental car. The fare for your vehicle isn't cheap, though, depending on its size and weight. The Auto Train leaves daily from Lorton, VA, and goes only to Sanford, FL. It takes about 18 hours, leaving in the afternoon and arriving the next morning. On the Auto Train, you pay for your passage, cabin and car separately. Book tickets in advance. Children, seniors and military personnel receive discounts.

Amtrak lines are subject to federal funding and regulation. Check for the latest fares and routes before you leave for your trip.

The South
There are major Amtrak stations in towns across the South, but bear in mind, these facilities are in thrall to the infrastructure bills passed by the US Congress. Train connections here can connect you to the larger Amtrak network: **Atlanta** (1688 Peachtree St NW), **Memphis** (545 S Main St), **New Orleans** (☑504-299-1880; 1001 Loyola Ave), **Charleston** (4565 Gaynor Ave), **Raleigh** (320 West Cabarrus St) and **Birmingham** (☑205-324-3033; 1 19th St North).

DIRECTORY A–Z

ACCOMMODATIONS

In Florida, seasonal/holiday fluctuations can see rates rise and fall dramatically, especially in Orlando and tourist beach towns. Booking in advance for high-season tourist hot spots can be essential to ensure the room you want. Note that air-conditioning is standard in all Florida accommodations (barring camping).

You'll find the full range of accommodations in the South, from luxury resorts to cheap hostels. In general, nicer hotels often flaunt a sort of historic chic style, especially in cities with preserved historical neighborhoods like New Orleans, Charleston and Savannah. Larger cities also boast contemporary design hotels. In smaller

towns, you'll often find a mix of chain highway hotels and frilly bed-and-breakfasts that invariably occupy older homes.

ELECTRICITY

Type A
120V/60Hz

Type B
120V/60Hz

Sleeping Price Ranges
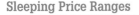
Price ranges refer to a standard double room in high season with private bathroom. Prices in the South include breakfast unless otherwise indicated.

$	less than $120
$$	$120–200
$$$	more than $200

Book Your Stay Online

For more accommodations reviews by Lonely Planet authors, check out http://hotels.lonelyplanet.com. You'll find independent reviews, as well as recommendations on the best places to stay. Best of all, you can book online.

FOOD

The treasures of the ocean, the citrus-scented whiff of farmland and an immigrant population give Florida serious culinary cred. On the flip side, strip malls, an all-too-American emphasis on reliability over adventure and a bad habit of cloning rather than creating trends are all marks against Florida's gastronomic reputation. Where does the truth lie? In the middle. In the meantime, gourmets can genuflect before celebrity chefs, while gourmands hunt Florida's delicacies, like boiled peanuts, frogs legs and gator.

Southerners will brag, and not without cause, that they eat better than anyone else in America. The concepts of eating locally and seasonally are baked into Southern culture, which is often only a generation or so removed from the farm. A history of making do under duress has yielded a cuisine that revels in rich sauces and flavors.

INTERNET ACCESS

➡ The USA and Florida are wired. Nearly every hotel and many restaurants and businesses offer high-speed internet access. With few exceptions, most hotels and motels offer in-room

Eating Price Ranges

Price ranges refer to a typical dinner main course. The Florida state sales and use tax is 6%, which will be added to the total of your bill. Prices are slightly higher in Miami and Orlando.

$	less than $15
$$	$15–25
$$$	more than $25

wi-fi; it's generally free of charge, but do check for connection rates.

➡ Many cafes and all McDonald's offer free wi-fi and most transport hubs are wi-fi hot spots. Public libraries provide free internet terminals, though sometimes you must get a temporary nonresident library card ($10).

➡ For a list of wi-fi hot spots, check Wi-Fi Free Spot (www.wififreespot.com) or Open Wi-Fi spots (www.openwifispots.com).

LGBT TRAVELERS

Major tourist destinations, beaches and cities have high levels of tolerance, but this does not always extend into the more rural parts of the region.

In Florida, Miami and South Beach are as 'out' as it's possible to be, with some massive gay festivals. Fort Lauderdale, West Palm Beach and Key West have long supported vibrant gay communities and are now regarded as some of the 'gayest' destinations in the world. Despite the tragedy of the 2016 Pulse nightclub shooting, Orlando retains a vibrant, active and strong gay community. Notable gay scenes and communities also exist in Jacksonville, Pensacola and, to far lesser degrees, Tampa and Sarasota.

In the South, major cities – particularly New Orleans, Atlanta and Charleston – boast active, vibrant LGBT scenes and are major centers for gay tourism. Events like Southern Decadence (New Orleans) and Atlanta Pride are some of the largest LGBT celebrations in the country.

Good resources for gay and lesbian travelers:

Damron (www.damron.com) An expert in LGBT travel offering a searchable database of LGBT-friendly and specific travel listings. Publishes popular national guidebooks, including *Women's Traveller, Men's Travel Guide* and *Damron Accommodations.*

Gay Cities (www.gaycities.com) Info for every major city in the US and beyond.

Gay Yellow Network (www.glyp.com) City-based yellow-page listings include six Florida cities.

Out Traveler (www.outtraveler.com) Travel magazine specializing in gay travel.

Purple Roofs (www.purpleroofs.com) Lists queer accommodations, travel agencies and tours worldwide.

MONEY

➡ ATMs are widely available everywhere.

➡ Personal checks not drawn on US banks are generally not accepted.

➡ Exchange foreign currency at international airports and most large banks in major cities.

➡ Major credit cards are widely accepted, and they are required for car rentals. Most ATM withdrawals using out-of-state cards incur surcharges of $3 or so.

Tipping

Tipping is standard practice across the US.

➡ In restaurants, for satisfactory to excellent service, tipping 15% to 25% of the bill is expected.

➡ Bartenders expect $1 per drink; cafe baristas, put a little change in the jar.

➡ Taxi drivers and hairdressers expect 10% to 15%.

➡ Skycaps (airport porters) and porters at nice hotels expect $1 a bag or so. If you spend several nights in a hotel, it's polite to leave a few dollars for the cleaning staff.

OPENING HOURS

Standard business hours are as follows:

Banks 8:30am to 4:30pm Monday to Thursday, to 5:30pm Friday; sometimes 9am to 12:30pm Saturday.

Bars Most bars 5pm to midnight; to 2am Friday and Saturday.

Businesses 9am to 5pm Monday to Friday.

Post offices 9am to 5pm Monday to Friday; sometimes 9am to noon Saturday.

Restaurants Breakfast 7am to 10:30am Monday to Friday; brunch 9am to 2pm Saturday and Sunday; lunch 11:30am to 2:30pm Monday to Friday; dinner 5pm to 9:30pm, later Friday and Saturday.

Shops 10am to 6pm Monday to Saturday, noon to 5pm Sunday; malls keep longer hours..

PUBLIC HOLIDAYS

On the following national public holidays, banks, schools and government offices (including post offices) are closed, and transportation, museums and other services operate on a Sunday schedule. Many stores, however, maintain regular business hours. Holidays falling on a weekend are usually observed the following Monday.

New Year's Day January 1

Martin Luther King, Jr Day Third Monday in January

Presidents Day Third Monday in February

Easter March or April

Memorial Day Last Monday in May

Independence Day July 4

Labor Day First Monday in September

Columbus Day Second Monday in October

Veterans Day November 11

Thanksgiving Fourth Thursday in November

Christmas Day December 25

SAFE TRAVEL

Cities like New Orleans, Miami, Memphis and Atlanta suffer the same urban problems facing other major US cities such as New York and Los Angeles. Don't walk alone into unfamiliar neighborhoods at night. In Florida and the South, gun ownership is relatively common, and there is often substantial leeway given to the concept of self-defense. As a general rule, you should avoid altercations while traveling, but it may pay to be extra vigilant in this regard in this region. In any interaction with the police, *keep your hands visible at all times.*

If you need any kind of emergency assistance, such as police, ambulance or firefighters, call ☑911. This is a free call from any phone.

Hurricanes

The Atlantic hurricane season extends from June through November, but the peak is September. Relatively speaking, very few Atlantic Ocean and Gulf of Mexico storms become hurricanes, but the devastation they wreak when they do can be enormous. Travelers should take all hurricane alerts, warnings and evacuation orders seriously.

Hurricanes are generally sighted well in advance, allowing time to prepare. When a hurricane threatens, listen to radio and TV news reports. For more information on storms and preparedness, check in with the **National Weather Service** (www.weather.gov).

In September 2017 Florida was devastated by Hurricane Irma, a category 4 storm; see the boxed text, p338, for information on the impact of the hurricane.

Hurricane Irma

On September 10, 2017, one of the largest hurricanes ever recorded barrelled over the state of Florida, leaving flooding and destruction in its wake. Hurricane Irma made landfall in the Florida Keys as a category 4 storm the width of Texas, with wind speeds in excess of 130 mph. Nearly 7 million people across the state evacuated; there were widespread power outages; and storm surges were seen as far north as Jacksonville. But the Florida Keys and the Everglades bore the brunt of the storm. Homes and businesses in the tiny town of Everglades City were left battered and mud-soaked after an 8ft storm surge receded. Meanwhile, in the Keys, an FEMA survey reported that 25% of buildings had been destroyed, with another 65% damaged.

The research for this book was conducted before the storm hit and the content was sent to print soon afterwards, when Irma's long-term effects were still unknown. In a state so heavily reliant on tourism, most cities were already announcing intentions to be ready for visitors soon. Still, those planning travel to Florida, especially the Florida Keys (www.fla-keys.com) or the Everglades region (www.nps.gov/ever), should check official websites for the latest information.

TELEPHONE

➡ Always dial 🖋1 before toll-free (🖋800, 🖋888 etc) and domestic long-distance numbers. Some toll-free numbers only work within the US. For local directory assistance, dial 🖋411.

➡ To make international calls from the US, dial 🖋011 + country code + area code + number. For international operator assistance, dial 🖋0. To call the US from abroad, the international country code for the USA is 🖋1.

➡ Pay phones are readily found in major cities, but are becoming rarer. Local calls cost 50¢. Private prepaid phonecards are available from convenience stores, supermarkets and drugstores.

➡ Most of the USA's cell-phone systems are incompatible with the GSM 900/1800 standard used throughout Europe and Asia. Check with your service provider about using your phone in the US. Cellular coverage is generally excellent, except in the Everglades and parts of rural northern Florida.

TRAVELERS WITH DISABILITIES

Because of the high number of senior residents in Florida, most public buildings are wheelchair accessible and have appropriate restroom facilities. In the rest of the South, the experience varies by city;

New Orleans, for example, with her root-damaged sidewalks, narrow streets and stairs-only historical buildings, can be a nightmare for disabled travelers. Transportation services are generally accessible to all, and telephone companies provide relay operators for the hearing impaired. Many banks provide ATM instructions in braille, curb ramps are common and many busy intersections have audible crossing signals.

A number of organizations specialize in the needs of travelers with disabilities:

Flying Wheels Travel (www.flyingwheels travel.com) A full-service travel agency specializing in travel for people with disabilities.

Mobility International USA (www.miusa. org) Advises on mobility issues and runs an educational exchange program.

Wheelchair Travel (www.wheelchairtravel. org) An excellent website with many links.

VISAS

All visitors should confirm entry requirements and visa guidelines before arriving.

➡ A passport is required for all foreign citizens. Nationals qualifying for the Visa Waiver Program are allowed a 90-day stay without a visa; all others need a visa.

➡ Travelers entering under the Visa Waiver Program must register with the US government's program, ESTA (https://esta.cbp.dhs.

gov), at least three days before arriving; earlier is better, since if denied, travelers must get a visa.

➡ Upon arriving in the US, foreign visitors must register with the Office of Biometric Identity Management, also known as the US-Visit program. This entails having two index fingers scanned and a digital photo taken. For information see www.dhs.gov/obim. Canadian citizens are often exempted.

➡ The US State Dept (www.travel.state.gov) maintains the most comprehensive visa information, with lists of consulates and downloadable application forms.

➡ As of 2017, the USA has embarked on a policy of pursuing more stringent border controls. Be warned that the above information is perishable; keep an eye on the news and www.travel.state.gov.

WOMEN TRAVELERS

The community resource Journeywoman (www.journeywoman.com) facilitates women exchanging travel tips, with links to resources.

In terms of safety issues, single women need to exhibit the same street smarts as any solo traveler, but they are sometimes more often the target of unwanted attention or harassment. Some women like to carry a whistle, mace or cayenne-pepper spray in case of assault. Federal law prohibits these items being carried on planes.

If you are assaulted, it may be better to call a rape-crisis hotline before calling the police (☎911); telephone books have listings of local organizations, or contact the 24-hour National Sexual Assault Hotline (☎800-656-4673), or go straight to a hospital. Police can sometimes be insensitive with assault victims, while a rape-crisis center or hospital will advocate on behalf of victims and act as a link to other services, including the police.

BEHIND THE SCENES

SEND US YOUR FEEDBACK

We love to hear from travelers – your comments help make our books better. We read every word, and we guarantee that your feedback goes straight to the authors. Visit **lonelyplanet. com/contact** to submit your updates and suggestions.

Note: We may edit, reproduce and incorporate your comments in Lonely Planet products such as guidebooks, websites and digital products, so let us know if you don't want your comments reproduced or your name acknowledged. For a copy of our privacy policy visit lonelyplanet.com/privacy.

WRITER THANKS

ADAM KARLIN

Thanks y'all: to Lauren Keith and Trisha Ping, editors extraordinaire; to my brother in arms on Southern road trips, Kevin Raub; to the parks workers and bartenders and baristas and service-industry folks who showed me how much there is to discover in my own backyard; to Mom and Dad, for their constant support; to Karen Shacham and Michelle Putnam (and Lior!), the best hosts Atlanta could provide; and Rachel and Sanda, both for joining me on the road and tolerating my absences.

KATE ARMSTRONG

La'Vell Brown: thank you for your magic wand, plus your passion, knowledge and insights into Disney World, and for transforming me from the Beastess into Cinderella herself. Thanks to Cory O'Born, Visit Orlando; Nathalia Romano and Ashlynn Webb, Universal Orlando; Jessica Savage, Greater Fort Lauderdale Convention & Visitors Bureau; and to Chris, for your flexibility, patience and everything (except holding my hand on the Hogwarts Express). Finally, thank you to Lauren Keith and Trisha Ping for their understanding and helping to put out a few nothing-but-Disney fireworks.

ASHLEY HARRELL

Thanks to: editors Lauren and Trisha, and my co-authors for your support. Josie, Nora and Ashley Guttuso for having me at the fort. Tiffany Grandstaff for the upgrade.

Alex Pickett for existing. Trevor, Malissa and Soraya Aaronson for being my surrogate family. Tom Francis for finally coming. Alanna Bjork for dog-sitting and the cozy shack. Beanie Guez for destroying me in shuffleboard and Elodie Guez for bringing wine (and glasses). Andy Lavender for showing up in Sarasota, and in general.

KEVIN RAUB

Thanks to my wife, Adriana Schmidt Raub, who shockingly sticks around despite my travels! Lauren Keith, Trisha Ping, MaSovaida Morgan and all my partners in crime at Lonely Planet. On the road: Jana Clauser, Kristi Amburgey, Susan Dallas, Dawn Przystal, Niki Heichelbech-Goldey, Erin Hilton, Courtney McKinney, Brian Mansfield, Alison Duke, Erin Donovan, Liz Beck, Eleanor

THIS BOOK

This 3rd edition of Lonely Planet's *Florida & the South's Best Trips* guidebook was curated by Adam Karlin and researched and written by Adam Karlin, Kate Armstrong, Ashley Harrell, Kevin Raub and Regis St Louis. The previous edition was written by Amy Balfour, Adam Karlin, Mariella Krause and Adam Skolnick. This guidebook was produced by the following:

Destination Editors Lauren Keith, Trisha Ping

Product Editors Susan Paterson, Anne Mason

Senior Cartographer Alison Lyall

Cartographer Julie Dodkins

Book Designers Lauren Egan, Jessica Rose

Assisting Editors Judith Bamber, Imogen Bannister, Melanie Dankel, Gabrielle Innes, Anita Isalska, Kellie Langdon, Jodie Martire, Rosie Nicholson,

Kristin Odijk, Gabrielle Stefanos, Saralinda Turner, Simon Williamson

Cover Researcher Brendan Dempsey-Spencer

Thanks to Nichole Cancellare, Hannah Cartmel, Joel Cotterell, Sasha Drew, Liz Heynes, Indra Kilfoyle, Cat Naghten, Claire Naylor, Karyn Noble, Lauren O'Connell, Kirsten Rawlings, Alexander Roberson, Ellie Simpson, David Vence, Tony Wheeler

Talley, Dodie Stephens, Sarah Lowery, Anne Fitten Glenn, Kaitlin Sheppard, Heather Darnell, Scott Peacock, Doug Warner, Halsey Perrin, Charlie Clark, Kim Jamieson and Jeff Hulett.

REGIS ST LOUIS

Countless people helped along the way, and I'm grateful to national park guides, lodging hosts, restaurant servers, barkeeps and baristas who shared tips and insight throughout South Florida. Big thanks to Adam Karlin who did such an outstanding job on previous editions. I'd also like to thank Cassandra and our daughters, Magdalena and Genevieve, who made the Miami trip all the more worthwhile.

ACKNOWLEDGE-MENTS

Climate map data adapted from Peel MC, Finlayson BL & McMahon TA (2007) 'Updated World Map of the Köppen-Geiger Climate Classification', Hydrology and Earth System Sciences, 11, 163344.

Front cover photographs: (top) Bald cypress trees, Apalachicola Forest, Florida, Danita Delimont Stock/AWL ©; (bottom left) Vintage car, Miami Beach, Benny Marty/Alamy ©; (bottom right) Live-music venues on Broadway, Nashville, Richard Taylor/4Corners ©

Back cover photograph: Boat to Fort Sumter with Arthur Ravenel Jr Bridge in the background, Charleston, Danita Delimont Stock/AWL ©

INDEX

ASHLEY HARRELL

After a brief stint selling day spa coupons door-to-door in South Florida, Ashley decided she'd rather be a writer. She went to journalism grad school, convinced a newspaper to hire her, and started covering wildlife, crime and tourism, sometimes all in the same story. Fueling her zest for storytelling and the unknown, she traveled widely and moved often, from a tiny NYC apartment to a vast California ranch to a jungle cabin in Costa Rica, where she started writing for Lonely Planet. From there her travels became more exotic and farther flung, and she still laughs when paychecks arrive.

KEVIN RAUB

Atlanta native Kevin started his career as a music journalist in New York, working for *Men's Journal* and *Rolling Stone* magazines. He ditched the rock 'n' roll lifestyle for travel writing and has written nearly 50 Lonely Planet guides, focused mainly on Brazil, Chile, Colombia, USA, India, the Caribbean and Portugal. Raub also contributes to a variety of travel magazines in both the USA and UK. Along the way, the self-confessed hop-head is in constant search of wildly high IBUs in local beers.

https://auth.lonelyplanet.com/profiles/Kraub

REGIS ST LOUIS

Regis grew up in a small town in the American Midwest – the kind of place that fuels big dreams of travel – and he developed an early fascination with foreign dialects and world cultures. He spent his formative years learning Russian and a handful of Romance languages, which served him well on journeys across much of the globe. Regis has contributed to more than 50 Lonely Planet titles, covering destinations across six continents. His travels have taken him from the mountains of Kamchatka to remote island villages in Melanesia, and to many grand urban landscapes. When not on the road, he lives in New Orleans. Follow him on www.instagram.com/regisstlouis.

https://auth.lonelyplanet.com/profiles/regisstlouis

OUR WRITERS

OUR STORY

A beat-up old car, a few dollars in the pocket and a sense of adventure. In 1972 that's all Tony and Maureen Wheeler needed for the trip of a lifetime – across Europe and Asia overland to Australia. It took several months, and at the end – broke but inspired – they sat at their kitchen table writing and stapling together their first travel guide, *Across Asia on the Cheap*. Within a week they'd sold 1500 copies. Lonely Planet was born.

Today, Lonely Planet has offices in Franklin, London, Melbourne, Oakland, Dublin, Beijing, and Delhi, with more than 600 staff and writers. We share Tony's belief that 'a great guidebook should do three things: inform, educate and amuse'.

ADAM KARLIN

Adam is a Lonely Planet author based out of wherever he happens to be. Born in Washington, DC and raised in the rural Maryland tidewater, he's been exploring the world and writing about it since he was 17. For him, it's a blessedly interesting way to live life. Also, it's good fun. He just read two good quotes, so with thanks to Italy, ancient and modern: 'Tutto il mondo e paese' and 'Ambulare pro deus'. If you ever meet Adam on the road, be sure to share a drink and a story.

https://auth.lonelyplanet.com/profiles/adamkarlin

KATE ARMSTRONG

Kate has spent much of her adult life traveling and living around the world. A full-time freelance travel journalist, she has contributed to around 40 Lonely Planet guides and trade publications and is regularly published in Australian and worldwide publications. She is the author of several books and children's educational titles. You can read more about her on www.katearmstrongtravelwriter.com and @nomaditis.

https://auth.lonelyplanet.com/profiles/kate_armstrong

◀ MORE WRITERS

Published by Lonely Planet Global Limited
CRN 554153
3rd edition – February 2018
ISBN 978 1 78657 346 9
© Lonely Planet 2018   Photographs © as indicated 2018
10 9 8 7 6 5 4 3 2 1
Printed in China

FSC MIX
Paper from responsible sources
FSC™ C021741
www.fsc.org

Paper in this book is certified against the Forest Stewardship Council™ standards. FSC™ promotes environmentally responsible, socially beneficial and economically viable management of the world's forests.